CliffsTestPrep®

PCAT®: 5 Practice Tests

An American BookWorks Corporation Project

Contributing Authors/Consultants

Elaine Bender, MA

Richard Bleil, PhD

Tracy Halward, PhD

Barbara Laurain, MS

Mark Weinfeld, MA

WILEY

Wiley Publishing, Inc.

D1314745

About the Author

Since 1976, American BookWorks Corporation has been producing and publishing a wide variety of educational books for many of the major publishing houses. The company specializes in test preparation books, as well as K–12 review books and study guides. In its role as a book producer, it functions as a "co-publisher," providing publishers with strong editorial, marketing, and technological expertise, based on more than 30 years of experience.

Publisher's Acknowledgments

Editorial

Project Editor: Suzanne Snyder

Acquisitions Editor: Greg Tubach

Copy Editor: Elizabeth Kuball

Technical Editors: Tom Page (Quantitative), Max Rechtman (Biology), Charles Henrickson (Chemistry)

Production

Proofreader: Cindy Ballew

Wiley Publishing, Inc. Composition Services

CliffsTestPrep® PCAT®: 5 Practice Tests

Published by:
Wiley Publishing, Inc.
111 River Street
Hoboken, NJ 07030-5774
www.wiley.com

Copyright © 2006 Wiley, Hoboken, NJ

Published by Wiley, Hoboken, NJ
Published simultaneously in Canada

Library of Congress Cataloging-in-Publication data is available from the publisher upon request.

ISBN-13 978-0-7645-9586-8

ISBN-10 0-7645-9586-5

Printed in the United States of America

10 9 8 7

1B/QW/QT/QW/IN

For general information on our other products and services or to obtain technical support, please contact our Customer Care Department within the U.S. at 800-762-2974, outside the U.S. at 317-572-3993, or fax 317-572-4002.

Wiley also publishes its books in a variety of electronic formats. Some content that appears in print may not be available in electronic books. For more information about Wiley products, please visit our web site at www.wiley.com.

WILEY

Table of Contents

PART I: INTRODUCTION

PART II: PRACTICE TESTS

PART III: APPENDIX

INTRODUCTION

Introduction

Congratulations! Because you bought this book, you are obviously interested in pursuing a career in pharmacology. It is a field with growth opportunities for you once you have completed your schooling.

The first step, of course, is getting admitted into a pharmacy college, and this book has been written to help you prepare for the admission test. We have presented the material you should know, in a unique way—actual sample tests. This book contains five simulated tests, and through diligent practice, you should be entirely familiar with the type of material you will encounter on the actual exam, as well as be comfortable with the style and format of the exam. It is a well-known fact that the more you practice on sample tests, the better you will do on the actual test.

We suggest that you read through this introductory section to learn something about the test itself, including the subjects covered. In addition, we have also provided some insight into the art of answering multiple-choice questions. Once you have learned the techniques we provide, any multiple-choice test will be easy for you.

Finally, in this section, we have given you an overview of the writing section of the exam: the "Critical Thinking Essay." If writing is not your strong point, read the "Basics of Good Writing" section. It will help you organize your thoughts and give you some ideas on how to put these thoughts into words.

About the Test

The Pharmacy College Admission Test (PCAT) is a multi-section test for applicants to pharmacy college. The American Association of Colleges of Pharmacy (AACP) is the major organization that represents the interests of pharmacy education. The AACP endorses this test and, thus, it is the preferred entrance exam.

The test consists of five subject areas plus an essay. The following is a general breakdown of the test by subject and number of questions.

Subject	Approximate Number of Questions	Time
Verbal Ability	58	35 minutes
Biology	58	35 minutes
Reading Comprehension	48	50 minutes
Quantitative Ability	58	50 minutes
Chemistry	58	35 minutes
Critical Thinking Essay	1 Topic	30 minutes
	280 Questions	

Verbal Ability

This section consists of approximately 58 questions. These are nonscientific questions and the questions are broken into two categories:

- Analogies (60%)
- Sentence completions (40%)

Biology

This section measures your basic knowledge of the principles and concepts of biology. The questions cover three areas of knowledge:

- General biology (60%)
- Microbiology (20%)
- Anatomy and physiology (20%)

Reading Comprehension

This section tests your ability to understand, analyze, and evaluate science-related reading passages. These skills are broken down as follows:

- Comprehension (30%)
- Analysis (40%)
- Evaluation (30%)

Quantitative Ability

This is a mathematics section that measures your ability to understand the process of math. It also tests your understanding of quantitative concepts. You will be tested on the following areas:

- Geometry (20%)
- Algebra (20%)
- Probability and statistics (10%)
- Precalculus (20%)
- Calculus (30%)

Chemistry

Chemistry is divided into two major areas: general and organic. You will be asked to demonstrate your basic knowledge of the principles and concepts of both, as follows:

- General chemistry (65%)
- Organic chemistry (35%)

Critical Thinking Essay

This section measures the basic conventions of language and composition skills. You will be given two topics from which to choose either an argument or problem-solving essay. We cover this in greater detail later in this section.

How to Answer Multiple-Choice Questions

All the questions in the five subject areas on the PCAT are multiple choice. Including the essay, you will have about four and a half hours to complete the exam; you will receive a short break about halfway through the test. It is, therefore, important for you to work quickly but carefully.

It is also necessary to answer as many questions as you can. Since there is no penalty for incorrect answers, you should attempt to answer every question. The key to success in this type of test is in knowing how to answer these types of questions, and the following section should help you develop that knowledge and skill.

In many cases, it is a decided advantage to take a test with multiple-choice questions; the better your skill at answering them, the better your chances of doing well. Of course, besides the skill, you must also have a basic knowledge of the material.

There are three basic steps to follow.

1. The first approach is to read the question. If you read the question and immediately know the answer, look at the choices given, select the correct one and mark it on your answer page. This is the easiest way to answer the question—you know the answer.

2. The second method is to read the question and if the answer does not immediately come to mind, read the answer choices. If you know the material fairly well, the correct answer will be clear to you at once. If it is not immediately clear, a little thought will root out the right answer.

3. The third step is to use the process of elimination. Very simply, it involves eliminating the wrong answer choices so that you are left with the correct one, or at least have narrowed down the choices. When test developers create questions for multiple-choice tests, there is a process that is often followed. In questions with four choices, like those you will find in this book, there is always one answer choice that will be undeniably correct. The other choices are called "distracters." Of the distracters, there is usually one choice that is completely incorrect and can be quickly eliminated. The other two choices may be similar to the correct answer, but there may be clues in the answers that make them incorrect. The question setup may be something like this:

1. Question

   A. Totally incorrect choice
   B. Almost correct, but not quite correct
   C. Correct choice
   D. Almost correct, but not quite correct.

In mathematics, there may be things like decimals in different places in the answer choices. For instance, there is a big difference between .106, 1.06, 10.6, and 106. Keep these things in mind as you solve math problems. They should also all be labeled correctly and consistently.

Look for "giveaway words" like *always, never,* or *not.* Most things in the world are not *always* or *never,* and you should be careful if a question asks, "Which of the following is NOT. . . ."

By using the process of elimination you increase your chances of getting the right answer. Remember that you are not penalized for incorrect answers on the exam, so taking a chance is worthwhile. What this means is that if you just guess, you have a one-in-four chance of guessing correctly—25%.

But what if you are able to eliminate one of the choices because it just seems wrong to you? You now have a one-in-three chance of selecting the correct answer—33%, which is surely better than 25%.

If you are able to narrow it down to only two choices, your chances will then improve to one out of two, or 50%. You just want to improve your odds of increasing your score, and you can see that it does not take much. It is definitely to your advantage that you do not lose points for incorrect answers. And of course, the more correct answers you receive, the better your score will be.

Basics of Good Writing: The Critical Thinking Essay

The PCAT exam has a new section that is counted as part of your score: the Critical Thinking Essay. This writing section is designed to test your ability to write a clear and cogent essay. On the exam, you will be given either an argumentative or a problem-solving topic—you have no choice in the matter—and you will have to write an essay. Because this essay is an integral part of your score, the following section reviews some of the basics of good writing techniques. We suggest that you read through this section carefully and refer back to it when writing some of the suggested essays presented in this chapter, as well as in the accompanying exams.

At the end of this section are a number of sample topics that you can use to practice your writing skills. They will also give you an idea of the types of topics that you might find on the actual exam. When you have finished this section, you should be able to adopt the skills you have learned to help you write an appropriate essay.

I. Prewriting: How to Begin a Writing Assignment

Because you are preparing to take the PCAT, writing is not a new task for you. You have written papers throughout your school years and you may have had other writing tasks related to work and personal concerns. Even though in the PCAT exam you will be given a specific topic on which to write, having an understanding of the process is still important.

This section presents a review of the writing process that may seem familiar to you; it reviews the process as it is usually taught in a college composition class. Some writers find these methods helpful. Other writers, through experience, may depart from them.

The best way to become a skillful writer is to write. By reviewing these chapters and practicing writing, your skills will be enhanced and developed. Even though the PCAT is a timed writing assignment that does not permit you to prepare, draft, revise, and edit as you would for a writing task for which you have more time, using these guidelines to practice writing with the essay subjects suggested will help you with the timed writing assignment. The more essays you write, the easier each one becomes.

The Writing Process

Writing is a process. The formula some writers follow consists of prewriting, writing, and rewriting, or revising and editing.

Your purpose in writing can be to inform, persuade, or entertain. Defining your purpose is the first step. When writing an essay, select a topic that is narrow enough to be explained within your page limitations. A thesis, unlike a topic, is a single statement that makes an assertion about a topic. It is usually placed somewhere near the beginning of an essay. Often, a thesis sentence will give the reader a clear overview of the essay by stating the essay's main ideas. In the case of the PCAT, your topic is already defined.

The Steps in Writing

Although it is a process, writing does not progress as neatly from one step to the next as does, for example, baking a cake or changing a tire. Roughly speaking, when you write you

1. Decide on a topic (or have a topic assigned to you).
2. Explore ideas about the topic through thinking, reading, listening, and so on.
3. Formulate a thesis or main idea and decide what points you want to make to support it.
4. Select details and examples (from reading, research, and personal experience).
5. Decide on the order in which you will present your ideas and examples.
6. Write a first draft; edit and revise for content, style, and writing mechanics; then write a final draft.

At any time during this process, you may need to stop and go back several steps. For example, when you are selecting details and examples, you may realize that your topic is too broad or that your thesis statement is weak. Or when you are organizing your points, you may see that the thesis you thought you were developing is not the one that you are developing. Often the act of writing itself generates new ideas that you may want to pursue. Even as late as your final draft, you may decide that the organization is not working, or you may spot a flaw in your argument that causes you to throw out much of what you have written and rework the rest. The most realistic way to view writing is not as a straight line but as a back-and-forth movement.

Types of Writing

The writing you have done varies—for example, timed writings and essay questions on exams; autobiographical essays for college applications; high-school and college papers on a variety of subjects; and business letters, proposals, and reports related to your work. In most of your writing you will be doing one of the following:

- Describing a person, place, or thing
- Telling a story or recounting an incident
- Reporting information
- Providing instructions or explaining a process
- Arguing a position or proving a point
- Analyzing something—a text, a theory, an attitude, or an event

The techniques you use will overlap. For example, if you are writing a descriptive essay about your Aunt Gladys, you might narrate an incident that reveals her personality. If you are arguing that taxes need to be raised, you will need to report information about costs of services and revenues.

Understanding Your Assignment

If you are given a writing assignment, fulfilling it is your main purpose. Understand what you are asked to do. In an examination question, for example, if you are asked to analyze how an author's techniques contribute to his theme, and if you describe the theme thoroughly but do not discuss the techniques, then you have failed to fulfill the assignment. For a psychological study, if you are asked to compare and contrast two recent theories about selective amnesia, and you write five pages on one of the theories and only half a page on the other, you probably have not done what is required. On the PCAT, you may be asked to defend a position or merely expound upon a specific statement.

Understanding Your Audience

For whom are you writing? Before you begin, think about your **audience.** A reader is at the other end of your writing, and you should keep that reader in mind. Ask yourself some specific questions about your audience before you begin. Among some things to consider are the following

- **Are you writing for people in a particular field, such as psychology, English literature, or genetics?** Can you assume knowledge of the terminology and concepts you will be using, or do you need to define them in the paper? Will you need to provide extensive background information on the subject you plan to discuss, or will a brief summary be enough?

- **What expectations does your audience have?** An audience of marine biologists will have different expectations from an article on marine biology than will a general audience, for example.

- **What is the reading level of your audience?** Instructions and explanations written for elementary students should not include college-level vocabulary. Readers of your writing for the PCAT will expect a mature style and vocabulary.

- **Are you writing for an audience that is likely to agree or disagree with your point of view?** Consider this question if you are writing an argumentative essay. It can make a difference in the language you select, the amount of proof you offer, and the tone you use.

Choosing a Topic

Obviously on the PCAT exam, you will not be able to choose a topic. It will be assigned to you. However, in any other situation, where you are either asked to choose a topic yourself to write about or asked to choose among several, keep the following in mind.

- **Choose a topic appropriate to the length of your paper.** Sometimes, writers choose topics that are too broad to be adequately covered. Narrow topics lead to close observation, while broad topics lead to generalizations and sketchy development.

- **Avoid a topic that will tempt you to summarize rather than to discuss or analyze.** Do not choose the plot of *Macbeth;* instead, choose to write about how the final scene of *Macbeth* illustrates the play's theme. The second topic is narrower and less likely to lead to summary. When considering a topic, ask yourself if it can lead to a reasonable thesis.

- **Choose a topic that interests you.** If you do not care about First Amendment freedom-of-speech issues, do not select it as a topic for a persuasive essay. You will have more to say and write better on something you care about.

- **If your assignment requires research, choose a topic on which you can find material.** Even when you are not writing a research paper, make sure that you have picked a subject that you can develop with sufficient details.

- **After you have picked a topic, do not be afraid to change it if it is not working out.** Readers would rather you write a good essay than that you grind out pages on something you realize was a bad choice.

Topic Versus Thesis

Do not confuse a topic with a main idea or thesis. The topic provides the subject; the thesis makes an assertion about that subject. Here are a few examples of topics:

> Discuss the following statement: "No matter how much we may deplore human rights violations in China, the United States should not impose sanctions on the Chinese government." Do you agree or disagree? Support your opinion.

> Analyze Shakespeare's use of clothing imagery in *King Lear.*

> Describe an incident in your life that caused you to change an opinion or attitude.

> "The Civil War had much more to do with economics than with morality." Do you agree or disagree with this statement? Support your opinion.

Two of these topics (the first and the fourth) ask the writer to argue a position. A sentence expressing that position is a **thesis statement.** A thesis statement for the first topic might be, "Imposing sanctions on China would be a mistake because it would hurt the American economy, because sanctions are notoriously unsuccessful as a way to force change, and because the United States should not interfere in the internal policies of other countries."

While the remaining second and third topics do not ask the writer to take a position, for a good essay on any of these topics, the writer should formulate a thesis. A thesis statement for the third might be, "When at age twenty-five, I had to assist with my grandmother's care because she had Alzheimer's disease, I became a more compassionate person." With this thesis statement, the writer makes a point about the topic and sets up a direction for the essay.

Writing a Thesis Statement

Whenever you write a paper analyzing, discussing, comparing, identifying causes or effects, or arguing a position, you should be able to write a thesis statement. You can refine and improve it as you go along, but try to begin with a one-sentence statement. A thesis statement can help you unify your writing, avoiding the danger of digression.

A thesis statement is a general statement; a thesis is never a fact. It should limit the scope of the paper. It should not be too broad. It should not be a vague, unsupportable generalization. Make your thesis statement say something. Do not be satisfied with weak generalities. The following are examples of pseudo thesis statements:

> People hold different opinions as to whether it is wise to impose sanctions on China because of their human rights violations.

> Shakespeare uses quite a bit of clothing imagery in *King Lear.*

Neither of these statements provides a clear direction for an essay because the assertions they make are so vague that they are useless. A better thesis statement for the second example might be, "Clothing images in *King Lear* reflect the development of Lear from a man blinded by appearances to a man able to face the naked truth." Remember that the creation of a thesis statement is important to the way you approach your topic, helping you direct your thinking as well as your writing.

II. Prewriting: Generating Content for Your Writing

Some writers think that they have to determine a thesis before beginning to write. This is a mistake. A thesis must be based on the content of the piece of writing. Once you have narrowed your topic, you need to consider what you know about it and what you need to find out about it in order to develop a working thesis.

Finding Examples and Evidence

The content of your writing may come from personal experience, direct observation, reading and research, or interviews and questionnaires. Writers and rhetoricians have developed several techniques that help to generate content for writing.

One way to begin is to list or brainstorm whatever ideas occur to you about your topic. This list need not be organized; after it is written, noticing the connections between the items on the list may provide you with a working thesis.

Freewriting is another alternative. In freewriting, one writes, for a limited period of time, consecutive sentences that are not necessarily related to each other or even to the specific topic. Theoretically, something emerges from the freewrite that will be useful in the finished piece.

Writers who prefer to work in a more organized fashion ask themselves questions about their topic. The classical journalist's questions—who, what, why, where, when, and how—provide responses that can help focus a topic into a thesis.

When you are writing a timed piece—such as the writing assignment on the PCAT—and you do not know what topic will be assigned, it is still possible to be prepared with useful information. It is likely some significant personal experience in your life may support a thesis. Knowledge of contemporary events and issues that you have learned by reading newspapers and magazines helps to generate content.

If your writing will be based on research, make notes as you read. If you want to use quotations, write them down accurately. Remember that you will need to cite facts, ideas, or quotations you borrow from other sources, so be sure to include bibliographical information in your notes. Some of what you write down will probably never appear in your essay. Your notes might even include questions that occur to you as you read, possibilities you want to explore, warnings to yourself, or reminders to check further on certain points. This stage of preparing a paper is not only to ensure that you have examples and evidence but also to help you think in more detail about your topic and thesis.

The Importance of Specific Details

A frequent mistake in writing is failing to provide specific examples, evidence, or details to support an idea or thesis. In an essay about a poem, for example, it is not enough to say that the author's language creates a dark, gloomy atmosphere; you must cite particular words and images that demonstrate this effect. If you are arguing that magnet schools in cities improve education for minority students, you must provide some evidence—statistics, anecdotes, examples. In a timed writing on the statement "We learn more from our failures than our successes," you should not merely reflect on the statement; you should cite examples from your life, from the news, or from history. Writing that is filled with general unsupported statements is not only unconvincing, but also uninteresting.

Quoting and Paraphrasing

When should you use quotations in a paper, and when should you paraphrase information instead? If an author's words are particularly effective and strongly stated, use a quotation. In the analysis of a literary work, to make a point about the author's language or style, use quotations.

But do not quote lengthy passages if you are going to comment on only two words. Do not give up your responsibility to analyze the content of your source materials simply by quoting. Quotations and paraphrases from sources should begin with a lead-in linking them to the idea that you are developing, and they should be followed by a comment or analysis explaining the relevance of the material to your text.

If your interest is in the information that a source conveys rather than in the author's expression, consider paraphrasing (putting the information in your own words) rather than quoting, particularly if the relevant passage is long and includes material you do not need. The question to ask is, "Why am I choosing to include this quotation?" If you have a good reason—an author's language or tone, for example, or a particularly apt expression—go ahead. But often you are after only the information or part of the information.

The Writing Assignment

After finding and generating ideas for the content of your writing, formulate a preliminary or working thesis for the piece. The material you have found will provide the support for your thesis.

All assignments are not identical, and you can use different strategies as you approach each writing task. The main purpose of your project may be research, argument, analysis, or narrative. In each of these areas, you can learn some basic skills that will make the work easier.

Argument or Problem-Solving Essays

If your assignment is to take a position on an issue, determine the strongest and weakest arguments. Decide what evidence you will use to support your position on the issue. If you are asked to agree or disagree with a particular issue or respond to a specific problem, read it more than once. When you write your paper, you should provide a brief, fair summary of the author's position, whether you agree with it or not. In an argumentative essay, you must support your own viewpoint *and* answer the opposition.

III. Organizing and Drafting

On the actual PCAT exam, you will not have time to write a draft, but it is important to understand the basic concepts of writing a draft and use it as your starting point for the final essay. A common misconception about writing is that the first draft will need only small changes. If the writer is prepared and organized, there will be fewer revisions, but most writers create multiple drafts before they are content with their writing.

Working from a Thesis Statement

One way to begin when you are ready to organize your paper is with your main idea or thesis statement. Putting yourself in a reader's place, imagine how you would expect to see the main idea developed. Then look at the notes you have taken. If you used your thesis statement as a guide in gathering information, you should see a pattern.

Look at the following thesis statement:

> Imposing sanctions on China would be a mistake because it would hurt the American economy, because sanctions are notoriously unsuccessful as a way to force change, and because the United States should not interfere in the internal policies of other countries.

This statement suggests that the paper will be divided into three main parts; it even indicates an order for those sections. When you go through your notes, decide where each note most logically fits. For example, a note about U.S. clothing manufacturers' increasing use of Chinese labor would fit into the first section, and a note about the failure of sanctions in the Middle East in the second section.

Of course, things are not always this neat. Your thesis statement might not be this precise, or the kind of essay you are writing might not lend itself to such an easy division. But starting from the moment you look at your topic and decide on your main idea, you should be thinking about ways to develop it. This thinking leads you to your organizing principle.

A review of some common methods of organization will help you. Remember, however, to avoid an overly rigid approach. After you begin to write, you may realize that your plan needs to be changed. Writing itself often generates new ideas or suggests a different direction.

Spatial or Chronological Organization

Some topics lend themselves to organization based on space or time. A descriptive essay might work well if you begin with a distant view and move closer—first describe how a barn looks from the road, for example; then describe the view you see when you stand directly in front of the barn; then describe the view (and smell and sounds) when standing inside the barn door; and complete your description with what you see when you climb the ladder into the loft.

In the narration of an event and in some kinds of technical writing describing a process, you write about events in the order they occur. Dividing your material into stages avoids the "and then . . . and then . . . and then" effect. If you were writing about making a ceramic vase, you could divide the process into three main stages: selecting and preparing the clay, forming and refining the shape of the vase on the potter's wheel, and glazing the piece and firing it in a kiln. The detailed steps in making the vase could then be organized sequentially under these sections.

Dividing a Subject into Categories

Just as you can divide a process into stages, you can divide a subject into categories. When you look over your notes, and using your thesis statement as a guide, see if logical groupings emerge. Look at the following topic and thesis statement, written by a fictional writer.

TOPIC   Write an essay addressing an environmental concern and suggesting ideas for a solution.

THESIS   The United States is losing its forests, and the solution is everyone's responsibility.

Note that the second half of this thesis statement is weak: ". . . the solution is everyone's responsibility" is a vague assertion.

In looking over notes, the student quickly identifies those that relate to the first part of the thesis statement ("Less than 1 percent of U.S. old-growth forests remain," "U.S. consumption of wood is up 3 percent since 1930," and so on). However, when he looks at the rest of his notes, he finds he has everything from "Logging bans have been effective in many areas" to "Do not use disposable diapers," to "Agricultural waste can be effectively processed to make building materials that provide excellent insulation."

At this point, he decides to create categories. He finds that many notes are related to simple, everyday actions that can help reduce wood and paper consumption (no disposable diapers, e-mail instead of memos, cloth bags instead of paper bags, recycling newspapers, and so on). Still others cover alternatives for wood, such as agricultural waste, engineered wood manufactured by the forest products industry, the use of steel studs in construction rather than wooden ones, a method of wall forming called "rammed earth construction," and so on. Then he notices that several notes relate to government actions—logging bans, wilderness designations, Forest Service reforms, and so on. He decides to use three general classifications as a principle of organization for the second part of the paper.

  I. Problem

 II. Solutions

    A. Consumer actions

    B. Alternatives to wood

    C. Government regulations

He may decide to change the order of the classifications when he writes his paper, but for now he has a principle of organization.

If some notes do not fit into these classifications, he may want to add another category, or add some subsections. For example, if several notes deal with actions by major conservation groups, he may want to add a division under "Solutions" called "Conservation group activities." Or, if he finds some notes relating to disadvantages of wood alternatives, he may add some subtopics under B—for example, "price stability," "public perception."

Dividing material into categories is one of the most basic forms of organization. Make sure the categories are appropriate to the purpose of your paper and that you have sufficient information under each one.

Organizing Essays of Comparison and Contrast

Sometimes students have problems with topics that ask them to compare and contrast two things. After gathering information on each thing, they fail to focus on the similarities and dissimilarities between them. There are two simple patterns of organization that help to solve this problem.

When you compare and contrast, you have two (or more) subjects, and a basis on which to compare and contrast them. For example, in an often reprinted essay on General Robert E. Lee and General Ulysses S. Grant by Bruce Catton, the subjects are Lee and Grant, and the basis for comparison and contrast is their personal history, ideology, and character.

One method for writing this essay would be to write about Lee's history, ideology, and character and then to write about the same areas for Grant. This is the subject-by-subject method of organization. The second half of the essay, about Grant, could include both similarities to and differences from Lee.

While the subject-by-subject method provides organization, it is often too simple and mechanical for effective writing. In the point-by-point method, the basis for comparison and contrast organizes the essay. Writing about Lee's and Grant's personal histories, then explaining their ideologies, and finally discussing their characters makes their similarities and differences clearer to the reader.

Inductive or Deductive Patterns of Organization

In a logical argument, the pattern in which you present evidence and then draw a general conclusion is called *inductive*. This term can also be used to describe a method of approaching your material, particularly in an essay presenting an argument. You are using this method in an essay even when you state the general conclusion first and present the supporting evidence in successive paragraphs.

EVIDENCE   The student action committee failed to achieve a quorum in all six of its last meetings.

       During the past year, the student action committee has proposed four plans for changing the grievance procedure and has been unable to adopt any of them.

       According to last month's poll in the student newspaper, 85% of the respondents had not heard of the student action committee. Two openings on the committee have remained unfilled for eight months because no one has applied for membership.

CONCLUSION The student action committee is an ineffective voice for students at this university.

       (*Note:* In an essay, this would be a thesis statement.)

Another type of organization borrowed from logical argument is called *deductive*. With this pattern, you begin with a generalization and then apply it to specific instances. In a timed writing, you might be given a statement such as "It is better to be safe than sorry" or "Beauty is in the eye of the beholder" and then asked to agree or disagree, providing examples that support your view. With such essays, you are not proving or disproving the truth of a statement, but offering an opinion and then supporting it with examples. For example, if you begin with a generalization such as "Beauty is in the eye of the beholder," you could cite instances such as different standards for human beauty in different cultures, or different views of beauty in architecture from era to era. You could also use examples from your own experience, such as your brother's appreciation of desert landscapes contrasted with your boredom with them.

Outlining

Creating an outline—either a formal or an informal one—helps you stay with your organizational plan. Sometimes an outline helps you see problems in your original plan, and you can eliminate them before you have spent time writing.

If you prefer writing papers without an outline, try an experiment. Create an outline *after* a paper is finished to see if your organization is clear and logical. If your paper cannot be outlined logically, your organization may be weak, and you will need to revise.

Informal Outlines

An *informal outline* can be little more than a list of your main points. You can refine it by following each main point with notations of the evidence or examples that support it. You are, in effect, grouping your notes. A simple outline like this is often all you need. It is especially valuable for timed writings. Thinking through your approach before you begin—and jotting down your thoughts—will help you avoid rambling and moving away from the assignment. Given that you have only 30 minutes to write your essay on the PCAT, you might want to spend only a brief amount of time on outlining— but do not overlook the process. It is especially helpful when working on a timed test.

Formal Outlines

You may want to prepare a more **formal outline.** Sometimes you may even be asked to submit an outline with a writing assignment. Following are a few guidelines:

Use Roman numerals for main topics. Use alternate letters and Arabic numerals for subtopics. Indent subtopics.

    I.
      A.
      B.
        1.
        2.
            a.
            b.

Each topic and subtopic must have at least two divisions; there can be no I without a II, no A without a B, and so on. Remember that topics and subtopics are divisions of your subject, and you cannot divide something into one part. If your outline shows solitary topics or subtopics, reevaluate to see whether you are misplacing or poorly stating your headings. The information should perhaps be worked into an existing larger category or divided into two topics or subtopics.

Make outline topics parallel in form. Make subtopics parallel in form also. For example, if you use a sentence for the first topic, use sentences for all subsequent topics, but if you use a noun for the first subtopic, use a noun for the following ones.

Watch the logic of your outline. The main topics generally indicate the basic structure of your essay. The second level of your outline (A, B, C) covers the major ideas that contribute to the larger units. The next level of subtopics is for narrower points related to these ideas. Do not stick irrelevant ideas in your outline under the guise of subtopics. Make sure each element logically fits under its heading, or else you are defeating the purpose of an outline.

Sentence Outlines and Topic Outlines

In a **sentence outline,** all elements are stated in complete sentences. In a **topic outline,** the elements may be presented as single words or as phrases.

Drafting

First drafts are usually preliminary attempts to put content on paper. (Remember: This section presents you with the basics of writing skills. *You will not have time to actually write drafts on the PCAT examination.*) Few writers expect first drafts to resemble a finished product. Your first draft may well be a mixture of planning and improvising—letting yourself move in a direction you had not originally intended. Remember that writing is not a straightforward process, and even when you begin a first draft you may make changes in your thesis statement or in your organizational plan. These changes may occur in your second draft; in this draft, you may need to move paragraphs around, add or eliminate content, rewrite the thesis, and tighten the focus of the paper by ensuring that your paragraphs are unified and coherent.

Computers and word processors have made the drafting process physically easier. Some writers do all their editing and revision on the screen, printing out only final versions. Others find it useful to print out drafts and save sections that have been removed in case they will be returned to the text. Other writers may print out a draft and write in the revisions until each sentence is perfect, but this kind of labor is relatively uncommon. Whichever method a writer uses, that does not eliminate the difficult and thoughtful part of drafting—deciding what changes to make.

Experienced writers often find that after the shape and content of the paper have been determined in a second draft, in the third draft they reword phrases and sentences.

The exception to the rule about first drafts is in timed writing assignments like the PCAT, for which you may have time for only one draft. Spend a few moments planning your answer, noting examples you intend to use, and then move ahead. Graders of these assignments are looking for substance, support for the thesis, and clear organization.

The Paragraph

A **paragraph** develops one idea with a series of logically connected sentences. Most paragraphs function as small essays themselves, each with a main topic (stated or implied) and several related sentences that support it.

How many paragraphs do you need in your paper? That depends on your content and thesis and the assignment. That an essay consists of five paragraphs, an introduction, three paragraphs of examples, and a conclusion is a formula only used by beginners. You will probably read no texts that follow this pattern. You may well have more than three examples or points to make, and you may have an example or point that requires several paragraphs of development in itself. Do not limit yourself. Let your particular topic and supporting points guide you in creating your paragraphs.

Paragraph Length

Paragraphs vary in length. For example, short paragraphs (one to three sentences) are used in newspaper stories where the emphasis is on reporting information without discussion, or in technical writing where the emphasis is on presenting facts such as statistics and measurements without analysis. Written dialogue also consists of short paragraphs, with a new paragraph for each change of speaker. In an essay, a short paragraph can also be effectively used for dramatic effect or transition. Generally, however, avoid a series of very short paragraphs in your essays. They suggest poor development of an idea.

On the other hand, paragraphs a page or more in length are difficult for most readers, who like to see a subject divided into shorter segments. Look carefully at long paragraphs to see whether you have gone beyond covering one idea or are guilty of repetition, wordiness, or rambling. Do not arbitrarily split a long paragraph in half by indenting a particular sentence, however. Make sure that each paragraph meets the requirement of a single main idea with sentences that support it.

Paragraph Unity

A **unified paragraph** is one that focuses on one idea and one idea only. Look at the following example of a paragraph that *lacks* unity.

Identification of particular genes can lead to better medicine. For example, recently, scientists identified a defective gene that appears to cause hemochromatosis, or iron overload. Iron overload is fairly easily cured if it is recognized and treated early, but currently it is often misdiagnosed because it mimics more familiar conditions. The problem is that when not treated in time, iron overload leads to a variety of diseases, from diabetes to liver cancer. The identification of the faulty gene can prevent misdiagnosis by allowing physicians, through a screening test, to identify patients who carry it and treat them before the condition becomes too advanced. *It is interesting that most people do not realize the exact role of iron in the body.* They know that it is important for their health, but few are aware that only about 10 percent of the iron in food is normally absorbed by the small intestine. Most of the rest is tied up in hemoglobin, which carries oxygen from the lungs.

The first sentence of the paragraph presents the main idea that identification of genes leads to improved medical care. This idea is developed by the example of how the identification of a gene causing iron overload can lead to better diagnosis and early treatment. In the italicized sentence, the paragraph begins to wander. It is a topic sentence for a different paragraph, one about the role of iron in the body and not about a benefit of genetic research.

To test the unity of your paragraphs, locate your topic sentence (if you have left it unstated, be clear on your paragraph's main idea) and then test the other sentences to see if they are developing that particular idea or if they are wandering off in another direction.

Paragraph Coherence

Along with developing a single idea, a paragraph should be well organized. You can use many of the same principles—chronology, inductive and deductive patterns, and so on—that you use to organize complete essays.

Once you have decided on the order of your details, make sure the connections between sentences in the paragraph are clear. The smooth, logical flow of a paragraph is called **paragraph coherence.** Write each sentence with the previous one in mind.

Connecting Sentences through Ideas

Connect your sentences through their content, by using an idea from one sentence and carrying it into the next.

Follow a sentence that makes a general point with an illustration of that point. Look at the following example:

> Changes in table manners have been studied for western Europe, and they reflect social attitudes. Medieval nobles thought their manners distinguished them from peasants, although by modern standards, they were not very refined.

You can also use one sentence to reflect or comment on the previous sentence, as in the following example:

> The classic example of unprotected speech, shouting "Fire!" in a crowded theater, stems from a Supreme Court opinion written by Justice Oliver Wendell Holmes. It has achieved the status of a folk argument. However, in was a weak analogy in its original context and its applicability is limited. [The paragraph would go on to explain the problems with the analogy.]

You can also connect sentences by asking a question and following it with an answer or making a statement and following it with a question:

> Why should the government invest in research? Research leads to technological advances that create employment, as has resulted from efforts like the space program and the Internet.

> Polls indicate that many Americans favor regulation of the Internet. Are they willing to pay both with their tax dollars and their freedoms?

The sentences in these two examples are linked by words as well as by ideas. In the first example, the word *research* has been picked up from the question and repeated in the answer. In the second example, the pronoun *they* in the question has its antecedent, *Americans,* in the previous statement.

Connecting with Words and Phrases

Achieving paragraph coherence by connecting ideas is your first step. But as indicated in the last two examples, words and phrases can help strengthen the connection between sentences.

- Use a pronoun whose antecedent appears in the previous sentence.

  Gabriel Garcia Marquez suspends the laws of reality in his novels. *He* creates bizarre and even magical situations that reveal character in surprising ways.

- Repeat a key word or phrase.

  The idea of a perfect society, though never realized, continues to intrigue political *philosophers.* None of *these philosophers* seems to agree on where perfection lies.

- Use a synonym.

  According to research, *physical beauty* is still considered a more important asset for women than for men. *Looks* are everything, according to women interviewed, while men felt that social status was at least as important as their appearance.

- Use word patterns, such as *first, second, third,* and so on.

  The reasons for the dean's announcing a decision today are clear. *First,* students will recognize that they have been heard. *Second,* faculty will applaud the end of a disruptive period of indecision. *Third,* though not particularly pleased by all the details of the plan, they will be overjoyed that the controversy will be off the front page of the paper.

- Use transitional words and phrases. Many words and phrases signal connections between sentences in a paragraph or between paragraphs in a paper. Look at the italicized words in the following sentences:

  The main character worships her. *Later,* his adoration turns to hatred.

  The manor house stood at the top of the hill. *Below* stretched miles of orchards.

  Modern literary critical theory can be confusing. *For example,* deconstruction theory seems to say the text means the opposite of what it says.

  The product promised he would grow new hair. *But* all he grew was a rash.

In the preceding examples, the italicized words or phrases explicitly connect the second sentence to the first by creating a particular relationship. Vary the transitional words you use.

Following is a list of words classified according to the relationships they suggest:

Time or place: above, across from, adjacent to, afterward, before, behind, below, beyond, earlier, elsewhere, farther on, here, in the distance, near by, next to, opposite to, to the left, to the right

Example: for example, for instance, specifically, to be specific

Contrast: but, however, nevertheless, on the other hand, to the contrary

Similarity: similarly, in the same way, equally important

Consequence: accordingly, as a result, consequently, therefore

Emphasis: indeed, in fact, of course

Amplification: and, again, also, further, furthermore, in addition, moreover, too

Restatement: in other words, more simply stated, that is, to clarify

Summary and conclusion: altogether, finally, in conclusion, in short, to summarize

Connecting Paragraphs in an Essay

Your essay should move from paragraph to paragraph smoothly, each point growing out of the preceding one. If you are shifting direction or moving to a different point, prepare your reader with a transition. Achieving continuity in your essay is similar to achieving continuity in a paragraph.

Beginnings and Introductions

The beginning of a paper should lead naturally into the rest of the paper and be appropriate to its subject and tone. In some professional and academic papers, it is acceptable to begin with a statement of what the paper intends, but these are special situations. A good beginning engages the reader's attention. Ways to do this include giving a vivid example or relating an anecdote, providing a description, using a quotation or a bit of dialogue, asking a question, or setting up an analogy.

The beginning may provide background or context for your thesis. Barbara Ehrenreich argues "Workfare, as programs to force welfare recipients to work are known, was once abhorred by liberals as a step back towards the 17th century workhouse—or worse, slavery. *(context)* But today no politician dares step outdoors without some plan for curing welfare dependency by putting its hapless victims to work. *(thesis)*

Your topic may suggest any number of creative beginnings.

Endings and Conclusions

How should you end your paper? Writing a **conclusion** is the last thing you do, but it also gives your final effort a finishing touch. If your ending works, your reader will feel satisfied.

Suggestions for Conclusions

The two most important things a conclusion should do is give your readers a sense of completion and leave them with a strong impression. You can do this with a single statement or with a paragraph. If you do write a concluding paragraph, consider these possibilities.

- Echo your main idea without repeating it by using a detail, example, or quotation related to the thesis or that echoes the beginning of the paper.
- Without directly repeating your thesis, come full circle by relating the final paragraph to a point you made in your introduction.

    Preserving old-growth forests and finding substitutes for wood should concern everyone who cares about the environment. The days when Americans could view this country as an unlimited provider of resources are as gone as roaming herds of buffalo and pioneers in covered wagons.

- End with a story related to your thesis.
- Use a humorous, witty, or ironic comment.
- Summarize your points. Because summaries are not particularly interesting conclusions, consider one only if your paper is fairly long and if a summary would be helpful to your reader. Keep summaries brief and avoid wishy-washy final sentences, such as, "For all these reasons, the Internet should not be regulated."

IV: Revising and Editing

Since titles are important, choose one that is interesting and informative. Consider the formality of the writing assignment and the audience when selecting a title for your work. Try reading your draft aloud during your practice sessions with this book and, if possible, ask someone you trust to review your essay.

After the review is completed, edit and revise the essay. **Editing,** which can be done with most computers and word processors, involves looking at the grammatical and mechanical content of your work. **Revising** means looking not only at grammar, but also at the overall effect of the essay. Editing and revising ensure that the final draft is appropriate for the assignment and audience, grammatically and mechanically correct, well organized and supported, and well crafted.

Titles

While you are writing an essay, if you have a good idea for a title, write it down. Sometimes the best time to choose a title is when you have completed a first draft and read it over, but because the draft may change in later stages, it may be a good idea to wait to choose a title. You will have a more complete picture of your essay. Be creative, but do not overdo it. For example, if you are writing a paper about deforestation, "Knock on Wood" might seem clever, but it does not accurately fit the topic.

Use good judgment when you choose a title. Consider the tone of your essay and your audience. "No More Mr. Nice Guy" might be a good title for a personal essay on the loss of your gullibility, but think twice before using it as the title of your analytical paper on Shakespeare's character Macbeth. (It is true, however, that one instructor who had received dozens of papers with unimaginative titles reacted well to the student who called hers "Dial M for Murder: The Character of Macbeth.")

The best advice is to take a middle road. Avoid both dullness and strained cleverness. Consider a good quotation from a work you are writing about, an effective phrase from your own essay, or an appropriate figure of speech:

"Gaining Safety or Losing Freedom: The Debate over Airport Security Measures"

RATHER THAN "Airport Security Measures"

"The Beauty Myth"

RATHER THAN "The Importance of Beauty to Today's Woman"

"Fit to Be Tried: An Examination of the McNaughton Rule"

RATHER THAN "Judging Legal Sanity"

Reviewing the First Draft

When you read your first draft, you will probably make your most extensive revisions. Here are a few suggestions that can help you in reviewing your first draft.

- If possible, leave some time between writing the first draft and reviewing it. Your objectivity will improve.
- Try reading your paper aloud to yourself; sometimes your ear catches problems your eye misses.
- Ask someone to read your draft and offer suggestions. Choose a reader you can trust to be honest and fair. You are looking for an objective opinion, not simply reassurance. Judge your reader's suggestions carefully, and decide for yourself their value and whether to act on them.
- Remember that nothing is unchangeable. Until preparation of your final draft, you can change your thesis, your organization, your emphasis, your tone, and so on. A review of your first draft should *not* be limited to minor mechanical errors.
- Use a revision checklist to make sure you have reviewed your draft thoroughly.

Preparing the Final Draft

You may be able to move directly from your revised first draft to a final draft, but careful writers often prepare several drafts before they are ready to call a piece finished. Within your time constraints, follow their example. As you rewrite, you may continue to discover wordy constructions, poor connections, awkward sentences, and so on. Only when you are satisfied that you have done your best should you prepare the final draft.

Writing and Editing a Draft

The computer allows you to produce a legible first draft that is easy to change by using a few basic functions, such as Delete, Insert, Merge, Block, and Move. When you try making changes to a handwritten draft, on the other hand, you can end up with something so messy that it is indecipherable. If you want to change a word-processed draft but you are not certain whether you will want to keep the changes, save both your original and your revised drafts under different file names and decide later which you want to use or import parts of one into the other. You can also reorder the paragraphs in a paper with a few keystrokes.

You can do much of your editing directly on the screen. If you think of a better way to say what you have just said, make the change immediately and move on. For more global editing, however, many writers like to print out sections or complete drafts, mark them up by hand, and then go back to the computer to input the changes. This method has advantages. Working on the screen limits you to a small section of text; scrolling back and forth in the document can be confusing, and it is difficult to get a beginning-to-end picture of what you have written. Another advantage of printing out your document is that it forces you to slow down and read carefully. Sometimes, because you can write so quickly on a computer, your fingers may get ahead of your thoughts. Remember that good writing requires deliberation and judgment and that you should always review a computer draft closely.

Spell-Checking, Grammar-Checking, and Search-and-Replace Functions

A spell-check function is useful for catching misspelled words, typos, and accidental repetitions ("the the," for example). But be careful. The checker will not signal a word that is actually a word, even if it is not the one you intended—for example, when you inadvertently type *form* instead of *from.* Spell-checking also does not distinguish between homonyms, so if you have trouble with *its* and *it's,* it will not help you. Consider the spell-checker as an aid, not a replacement for your own careful proofreading. Of course, on the PCAT, you will not have the luxury of the spell-check, but it is important that you double-check your spelling.

Grammar- or style-checkers require even more caution because grammar and style are less clear-cut than spelling. Many writers do not use these functions at all, and unless you already have a good grasp of grammar, they can be confusing or misleading. For example, the checkers will catch pronoun agreement and reference errors but not dangling participles or faulty parallelism. Some checkers flag possible homonym confusions, usage problems (*literal* used incorrectly, for example), and passive constructions, but they also signal every sentence beginning with *but* and every sentence ending with a preposition (which are not errors but are common in contemporary writing style). If you use a checking function, do so critically. Do not automatically change a passive construction or restructure a sentence ending with a preposition, for example, simply because the checker flags it.

A search-and-replace feature in word-processing programs lets you correct a particular error throughout your paper automatically. If you find you have misspelled a person's name, you can spell it correctly and ask the program to locate every instance of the name in your 25-page document and replace it with the correct version. Just be sure that the error is one that you want replaced in the same way every time.

Final Checklist

Good writing often comes after revision and rewriting. If you can view your work critically, you will be able to improve it. Use the following checklist before you write a final draft.

Purpose, Audience, and Tone

These three elements deal with the overall effect of your essay and should guide you throughout your writing.

- If I am writing in response to an assignment, does my essay fulfill all parts of the assignment?
- Is my topic too broad?
- Do I state my thesis or main idea early in the paper? If I do not state a thesis or main idea, is it clearly implied so that there can be no mistake about my purpose?
- Is my thesis or main idea interesting? If this is an essay of argument, is my thesis statement fair? Do I take into account opposing viewpoints?
- Have I thought about my audience? Does my audience have any special requirements? Is my tone appropriate to my audience and purpose?
- Is my tone consistent throughout the essay?

Examples, Evidence, and Details

These are specific details in the writing process. When you read your essay, you can determine whether you have used these elements well.

- Have I adequately developed my thesis or main idea? Do I use specific details rather than generalities?
- Are my examples and evidence accurate, relevant, and convincing?
- Do I use quotations appropriately? Is too much of my paper quotations? Do I paraphrase carefully?
- Do I cite sources for the words and ideas of others?

Structure

Use an outline to determine the structure of your paper, but be aware that you may need to alter it as you write. Keep in mind the following:

- Do I have a principle of organization? Do I avoid repetition and digressions?
- Is my organization appropriate to my topic and thesis?
- Do I adequately introduce and conclude my paper?
- Are my paragraphs well-developed, unified, and coherent?

- Does one paragraph grow out of another? Do I use transitions?
- Are my examples, evidence, and details in the best order? Do I save the strongest point for last?

Language and Style

Rely on a dictionary and your word-processing tools to help you with language and style. Ask yourself some questions.

- Have I chosen my words carefully? Am I sure of meanings?
- Is my language appropriate to my purpose, tone, and audience?
- Have I avoided wordy expressions? euphemisms? clichés?
- Have I avoided pretentious language?
- Have I used idioms correctly?
- Have I followed the guidelines of current written usage?
- Have I avoided sexism in the use of nouns and pronouns?
- Have I preferred the active to the passive voice of the verb?

Sentence Construction

Use your editing and revision skills to make sure your sentences are well constructed. Keep the following in mind:

- Are my sentences correct? Have I avoided both fragments and run-ons?
- Are my modifiers in the right place? Do I have any dangling modifiers?
- Do my subjects and predicates agree in number?
- Do I keep parallel constructions parallel?
- Have I avoided short, choppy sentences?
- Do I combine sentences effectively?
- Are my sentences varied in length and structure? Do I avoid monotony?

Grammar

Keep in mind the principles of grammar and usage.

- Have I checked spelling (including correct plural forms), hyphenation, capitalization, correct use and consistency of verb tense agreement (nouns, verbs, pronouns), pronoun cases, pronoun antecedents, use of adjectives with linking verbs, and comparative degrees of adjectives and adverbs?
- Does my punctuation make my meaning clear? Have I followed punctuation rules?

    Commas with nonrestrictive elements; no commas with restrictive elements

    Commas with interrupting elements, with introductory phrases and clauses when necessary, between series items, and between independent clauses
- Have I checked the following?

    Correct use of periods and question marks

    Correct use (and not overuse) of exclamation points

    Correct use of semicolons and colons

    Correct use (and not overuse) of dashes and parentheses

    Correct use (and not overuse) of quotation marks

    Correct use of other punctuation with quotation marks

V: Sample Topics

As we said earlier, the Critical Thinking Essay portion of the test presents a topic that requires you to write either an argumentative or problem-solving essay. We've discussed some of the basics of good writing techniques throughout this section. Now is the time to practice your writing skills.

However, if time is limited for you, go through each of these sample topics and create outlines for them. Make sure you can identify a thesis statement, organize your thoughts, and, in outline form, put together a cogent argument or a logical solution to the problems presented.

Argumentative Essay Topics

1. Large public corporations support our economy, and, therefore, the compensation of its officers should not come under public scrutiny.

2. Drug companies stress their need for animal testing, which is at odds with those who feel that this testing represents a cruel punishment for these animals.

3. America has become the policeman of the world, but is in conflict with those countries that do not want to accept the American concept of democracy and may represent a threat to our country.

4. The government has mandated standardized testing on a state-by-state basis, but many of the individual states do not want to be responsible for funding these tests.

5. Prior to memorization of facts in school, students should first study concepts and trends. One who has learned only facts has learned very little.

Problem-Solving Topics

1. Discuss a solution to the problem of America's support of certain political regimes that are at odds with our own system of democracy but represent economic benefits to our country.

2. Offer a solution to the situation of selecting federal judges based on their personal beliefs rather than their judicial abilities.

3. Discuss a solution to the problem of teaching to the "lowest common denominator" in the school classroom.

4. Discuss a solution to the problem of our dependence upon computer systems and the possibilities of intrusion into these systems by outside individuals.

5. Offer a solution to the problem of the growing number of obese Americans.

Once you have completed writing, or at least outlining, any of these topics, make a copy of the Final Checklist that precedes this section and use it to evaluate your writing skills and, more importantly, your ability to organize your thinking.

Practice!

The next step in the process of test preparation for the PCAT is to practice on the tests. Take each test in a simulated situation. Set up a quiet place in which you can work undisturbed for a couple of hours. Use a watch to time yourself. We suggest that you "warm up" to the tests, beginning with the first test. What this means is that in Test 1, start with the Verbal Ability section, time yourself for 35 minutes, and then take a break. Then take the Biology section for 35 minutes and take another break. In this way, you will develop your pacing slowly, but when you have finished Test 1, you will understand the questions and the directions, and get an idea as to how fast and accurately you can work.

When you have completed the entire five subject areas, take a break for a day, and then come back to check your answers. Spend time reviewing those answers that you got wrong. Do you know why? Did you not understand the material? Did you try the process of elimination? You can always go back to a textbook to refresh your memory about specific topics.

Once you have completed Test 1 and checked your answers, it is time to take Test 2. From that test through Test 5, take the first three sections of the test, take a break, and then complete the test. This is more like the actual exam, in which you get a break about halfway through.

A final word about directions, before you begin your review: Make sure you understand them clearly *before* you take the test. Since this is a timed test, you want to make sure you have as much time as possible to answer the questions, and it is a waste of time to have to go over the directions several times to make sure you understand them during the actual test. You should be able to skim them to make sure nothing has changed, and then dig into the first set of questions.

Now you can start your review. Good luck on the final examination.

PART II

PRACTICE TESTS

Verb____ ____ty: Analogies

Verb____ ____ty: Analogies

Direc____ ____ ____ word that best completes the analogy.

____ ____US : DISCORDANT :: DULCET:

  ____strous
  ____ongruous
  harmonic
  D. duet

2. CONVICT : ERRANT :: SAINT:

  A. convincing
  B. upright
  C. sinful
  D. happy

3. SIMPLE : AUSTERE :: DECORATED:

  A. beautiful
  B. expensive
  C. garish
  D. strict

4. RACONTEUR : NARRATIVE :: LYRICIST:

  A. poem
  B. short story
  C. editorial
  D. operetta

5. REITERATE : REPEAT :: RECAPITULATE:

  A. redo
  B. restate
  C. resign
  D. remorse

6. PLUMB : STRAIGHTNESS :: PROTRACTOR:

  A. circles
  B. squares
  C. angles
  D. waves

7. PANACEA : REMEDY :: PLACEBO

  A. substitute
  B. antidote
  C. aspirin
  D. vaccination

8. MINIATURE : PALATIAL :: LILLIPUTIAN

  A. people
  B. flowers
  C. colossal
  D. lackadaisical

9. APEX : NADIR :: PINNACLE:

  A. zenith
  B. mountaintop
  C. base
  D. point

10. MISER : FRUGAL :: MISCREANT:

  A. money
  B. evil
  C. creation
  D. stinginess

11. DISTASTEFUL : REPUGNANT :: TALKATIVE:

  A. noisome
  B. friendly
  C. quiet
  D. loquacious

12. LEXICON : DEFINITION :: ALMANAC:

  A. facts
  B. farmers
  C. weather
  D. fun

GO ON TO THE NEXT PAGE

13. TRICKLE : INUNDATE :: FLICKER:

    A. blaze
    B. fail
    C. flood
    D. fumes

14. MOLLIFY : ALLAY :: APPEASE:

    A. allow
    B. mitigate
    C. circumvent
    D. appeal

15. IOTA : MYRIAD :: PAUCITY:

    A. ions
    B. fluidity
    C. profusion
    D. poverty

16. PEDESTRIAN : FOOT :: EQUESTRIAN:

    A. bridle
    B. horse
    C. hand
    D. dog

17. PARIAH : PARAGON :: OUTCAST:

    A. exemplar
    B. paramour
    C. bigot
    D. pedestrian

18. MALEFACTOR : EVIL :: AUTOCRAT:

    A. omnipotence
    B. country
    C. insecurity
    D. laws

19. OAK : ARBOREAL :: PINE:

    A. needle
    B. whine
    C. cones
    D. coniferous

20. ASCETIC : HEDONISTIC :: PURITANICAL:

    A. religious
    B. heathen
    C. indulgent
    D. pensive

21. APPARITION : ETHEREAL :: SPIRIT:

    A. corporeal
    B. scary
    C. diaphanous
    D. substantial

22. CACOPHONY : HARSH :: HARMONY:

    A. orchestra
    B. notes
    C. happy
    D. mellifluous

23. AMALGAMATE : DISSEMINATE :: FUSE:

    A. explode
    B. box
    C. split
    D. spit

24. BANAL : TRITE :: HACKNEYED:

    A. fluent
    B. weak
    C. colloquial
    D. lackluster

25. COMESTIBLE : SAVORY :: EDIBLE:

    A. fragrant
    B. odorous
    C. pungent
    D. tasty

26. ERRATIC : IRREGULAR :: FICKLE:

    A. stern
    B. stalwart
    C. capricious
    D. careful

27. ENGRAVE : CUT :: EMBROIDER:

    A. knit
    B. sew
    C. crochet
    D. create

28. ELEGY : SORROW :: EULOGY:

    A. laudation
    B. recrimination
    C. death
    D. ecstasy

29. ADHESIVE : BOND :: DECORATIONS:

    A. beautiful
    B. expensive
    C. embellish
    D. superfluous

GO ON TO THE NEXT PAGE

Verbal Ability: Sentence Completions

Directions: Select the word or words that best complete the sentence.

30. When soaking a turkey in brine, be sure to _____ the entire bird in the solution.

   A. convert
   B. immerse
   C. converge
   D. emerge

31. Because the size of their rural habitat has _____, coyote sighting in _____ areas have become more frequent.

   A. divided . . . . . country
   B. solidified . . . . . tropical
   C. rusted . . . . . flooded
   D. decreased . . . . . suburban

32. Although advertisements in magazines rely heavily on _____ elements, their texts also play a part in their _____ power.

   A. sensational . . . . . pictorial
   B. visual . . . . . persuasive
   C. contrasting . . . . .demanding
   D. productive . . . . . human

33. The casserole of potatoes, made without salt, pepper, or spices, tasted _____.

   A. savory
   B. complex
   C. necrotic
   D. insipid

34. Aspirin, often used to _____ pain, can cause side effects that, unfortunately, most people _____.

   A. contradict . . . . . choose
   B. recuperate . . . . . restrain
   C. alleviate . . . . . ignore
   D. restore . . . . . consider

35. The voters showed their _____ by staying away from the polls.

   A. affluence
   B. apathy
   C. interest
   D. registration

36. A lunar _____ occurs during a full moon when the Earth is directly between the sun and the moon.

   A. lull
   B. volcano
   C. collapse
   D. eclipse

37. One of the requirements for employment as a translator is _____ in speaking more than one _____.

   A. adaptation . . . . . English
   B. customs . . . . . country
   C. courtesy . . . . . jargon
   D. proficiency . . . . . language

38. Sodium chloride is the _____ name for table salt.

   A. everyday
   B. chemical
   C. luxurious
   D. polite

39. Because she was a _____ vegetarian, she glared at anyone eating a hamburger.

   A. militant
   B. violent
   C. pacified
   D. vociferous

40. A career as an independent contractor rather than as an employee may provide _____, but without a steady source of income, it can create financial _____.

   A. autonomy . . . . . insecurity
   B. difficulties . . . . . satisfaction
   C. dependence . . . . . wealth
   D. chaos . . . . . contradictions

41. When the employee was late for the fourth time, the manager began to _____ about tardiness as a sign of _____.

   A. gesture . . . . . wealth
   B. orate . . . . . illness
   C. demonstrate . . . . . forensics
   D. rant . . . . . irresponsibility

42. Her lively and smiling face mirrored her _____ personality.

   A. talkative
   B. somber
   C. vivacious
   D. irate

43. The _____ wind blowing off the lake and the freezing temperatures made it seem as if winter would never end.

   A. relentless
   B. temperate
   C. calming
   D. relevant

44. Stalactites descend from the _____ of a cave, but stalagmites grow _____ when water containing dissolved minerals drips to the cave's floor.

   A. bottom . . . . . horizontally
   B. hole . . . . . sideways
   C. ceiling . . . . . vertically
   D. acme . . . . . inward

45. On the one-hundredth anniversary of Mapleton's founding, the city held a _____ celebration to _____ the occasion.

   A. binary . . . . . recreate
   B. memorial . . . . . bless
   C. centennial . . . . . commemorate
   D. consecration . . . . . eulogize

46. The king planned an elaborate wedding for the princess, but his _____ vision was _____ by a shortage of funds in the royal treasury.

   A. grandiose . . . . . constrained
   B. fantastic . . . . . implemented
   C. imaginary . . . . . omitted
   D. beautiful . . . . . built

47. Lye is a _____ and _____ cleaning agent that can cause burns on contact with the skin.

   A. weak . . . . . acid
   B. fearful . . . . . convenient
   C. reactionary . . . . . profligate
   D. potent . . . . . caustic

48. As people age, the spaces between the bones of the spinal column begin to _____, causing their height to decrease by _____.

   A. swell . . . . . feet
   B. narrow . . . . . inches
   C. open . . . . . pounds
   D. create . . . . . grams

49. Seemingly appearing on every utility pole in town, the _____ posters for yard sales contribute to visual _____.

   A. helpful . . . . . integrity
   B. unusual . . . . . contraries
   C. proximate . . . . . color
   D. ubiquitous . . . . . pollution

50. The alleged criminal's alibi was so peculiar that jurors thought it was _____.

   A. incredulous
   B. inedible
   C. inordinate
   D. incredible

51. Many in the audience left after the first act of the play; their _____ opinion of it was clear.

   A. verbal
   B. tacit
   C. dramatic
   D. admiring

52. The saying "look before you leap" implies one shouldn't make _____ decisions.

   A. itchy
   B. lucky
   C. wrong
   D. rash

53. A _____ plan for improving elementary education must consider not only the standards pupils should meet, but also the _____ available to the schools.

   A. revolting . . . . . mediocrity
   B. willful . . . . . education
   C. practical . . . . . resources
   D. noble . . . . . playgrounds

GO ON TO THE NEXT PAGE

54. In Victorian England, the wealthy ate _____ dinners consisting of many courses of rich heavy food.

   A. sumptuous

   B. nutritious

   C. spartan

   D. polite

55. One of the tasks of the Red Cross is to provide material _____ to victims of disasters.

   A. laughter

   B. misery

   C. solace

   D. alms

56. Adolescents who differ from their peers may suffer from _____ and _____.

   A. alienation . . . . . discomfort

   B. hostility . . . . . enjoyment

   C. euphoria . . . . . disenchantment

   D. enlightenment . . . . . tranquility

57. In the Middle Ages, bubonic plague was so _____ that it killed almost all of its victims.

   A. hostile

   B. transitory

   C. virulent

   D. temporary

58. Because the bystanders did not react to the beating of the innocent victim, their _____ made them _____ in the crime.

   A. inaction . . . . . guiltless

   B. shouts . . . . . helpful

   C. ferocity . . . . . useful

   D. acquiescence . . . . . complicit

Biology

59. Which of the following processes must occur in order for an individual to express a particular characteristic (for example, blue eye color)?

- **A.** Genes must be transcribed directly into proteins.
- **B.** Genes must be transcribed onto tRNA and then translated into proteins.
- **C.** Genes must be transcribed onto mRNA and then translated into proteins.
- **D.** Genes must be translated directly into proteins.

60. A DNA molecule that is composed of 30% adenine molecules will also contain

- **A.** 30% thymine molecules.
- **B.** 70% thymine molecules.
- **C.** 30% guanine molecules.
- **D.** 30% cytosine molecules.

61. An organism that contains a segment of DNA from a different organism inserted into its own DNA is referred to as a

- **A.** transgenic organism.
- **B.** vector.
- **C.** plasmid.
- **D.** hybrid.

62. If a small amount of DNA (for example, a drop of blood) is found at a crime scene, large quantities of identical DNA can be produced for analysis through the use of

- **A.** DNA fingerprinting techniques.
- **B.** restriction fragment length polymorphism (RFLP) techniques.
- **C.** DNA hybridization techniques.
- **D.** polymerase chain reaction (PCR) techniques.

63. Which of the following statements best describes the process of evolution?

- **A.** changes in the genetic composition of a population over time
- **B.** natural selection
- **C.** genetic drift
- **D.** failure of a population to change in genetic composition over time

64. Which of the following is NOT a characteristic of all living cells?

- **A.** All cells are self-contained (surrounded by a plasma membrane).
- **B.** All cells contain DNA.
- **C.** All cells contain a nucleus.
- **D.** All cells contain cytoplasm.

65. Which of the following statements regarding cell structure is FALSE?

- **A.** Plant cells have chloroplasts, while animal cells do not.
- **B.** Animal cells have mitochondria, while plant cells do not.
- **C.** Animal cells lack cell walls surrounding their plasma membranes.
- **D.** Plant cells typically have a large central vacuole, while animal cells typically have one or more small vacuoles.

66. Which of the following cellular organelles serves as the primary site of protein synthesis?

- **A.** nucleus
- **B.** mitochondria
- **C.** ribosome
- **D.** peroxisome

67. In humans, dermal tissue serves which of the following functions?

- **A.** provides the outer covering of the body
- **B.** provides a defense mechanism against invading microorganisms
- **C.** serves as a sensory organ
- **D.** all of the above

GO ON TO THE NEXT PAGE

68. Most cellular membranes are selectively permeable. This means that they

    A. do not allow any substances to pass through them.

    B. control which substances pass through them, but not the rate at which those substances pass through.

    C. allow all substances to pass through them, but control the rate at which those substances pass through.

    D. control which substances pass through them, as well as the rate at which those substances pass through.

69. Diffusion involves

    A. the passive movement of substances from a region of lower concentration to a region of higher concentration.

    B. the passive movement of substances from a region of higher concentration to a region of lower concentration.

    C. the input of energy to move substances from a region of higher concentration to a region of lower concentration.

    D. the input of energy to move substances from a region of lower concentration to a region of higher concentration.

70. During growth, new cells are produced through the process of

    A. mitosis.

    B. meiosis.

    C. both mitosis and meiosis.

    D. budding.

71. During mitosis, a cell containing 24 chromosomes would produce which of the following?

    A. 2 cells, each containing 24 chromosomes

    B. 2 cells, each containing 12 chromosomes

    C. 4 cells, each containing 24 chromosomes

    D. 4 cells, each containing 12 chromosomes

72. During meiosis, a single cell gives rise to

    A. two identical daughter cells.

    B. four identical daughter cells.

    C. two genetically unique daughter cells.

    D. four genetically unique daughter cells.

73. The process of cellular respiration involves

    A. inhaling carbon dioxide and exhaling oxygen through the lungs.

    B. inhaling oxygen and exhaling carbon dioxide through the lungs.

    C. the breakdown of glucose molecules to produce energy in the form of ATP.

    D. the formation of glucose molecules through the breakdown of ATP.

74. Which of the following statements is incorrect?

    A. Plants are capable of producing their own food supply through the process of photosynthesis.

    B. Plants are capable of producing their own energy through the process of cellular respiration.

    C. Plants and animals are both capable of producing their own food supply through the process of photosynthesis.

    D. Plants and animals are both capable of producing their own energy through the process of cellular respiration.

75. A group of related individuals that can interbreed and produce fertile offspring is referred to as a

    A. species.

    B. population.

    C. community.

    D. gene pool.

76. All of the organisms living in a defined area, along with all of the abiotic factors with which they interact, can be defined as a(n)

    A. community.

    B. population.

    C. gene pool.

    D. ecosystem.

77. The base of every food chain consists of

    A. herbivores.

    B. carnivores.

    C. producers.

    D. decomposers.

78. The increase in the concentration of toxins at successive levels in a given food chain is referred to as

    A. toxicity.
    B. biological magnification.
    C. trophic enhancement.
    D. pollution.

79. An organism that lives on or within a host organism is referred to as a

    A. predator.
    B. microbe.
    C. disease.
    D. parasite.

80. Which of the following factors affecting population density would be considered density-independent?

    A. availability of food
    B. availability of water
    C. accumulation of toxins in the ecosystem
    D. prolonged period of drought

81. Which of the following statements regarding the function of ecosystems is incorrect?

    A. Energy cycles through an ecosystem.
    B. Energy moves in one direction through an ecosystem.
    C. Water and nutrients are cycled through an ecosystem.
    D. Carbon is cycled through an ecosystem.

82. Which of the following requires a host cell because they can not make their own proteins?

    A. protists
    B. prokaryotes
    C. bacteria
    D. viruses

83. Which of the following cellular features separates bacteria from all other groups of organisms?

    A. Bacterial cells are prokaryotic.
    B. Bacterial cells are eukaryotic.
    C. Bacterial cells contain mitochondria.
    D. Bacterial cells have a nucleus.

84. Many hospitals will not allow patients with respiratory problems to have plants in their rooms. The primary reason is because

    A. Plants release too much oxygen into the room.
    B. Plants take too much carbon dioxide out of the room.
    C. Plants release too much carbon dioxide into the room.
    D. Plants may harbor mold spores that will aggravate respiratory problems.

85. While steak tartare (chopped raw beef mixed with a raw egg) is still a popular dish, there is a real danger of illness because

    A. Uncooked beef may be infected with bacteria.
    B. Uncooked beef may be infected with tapeworm cysts.
    C. Uncooked eggs may be infected with bacteria.
    D. all of the above

86. Which type of cells is most commonly infected by the HIV virus?

    A. red blood cells
    B. helper T cells
    C. phagocytes
    D. monocytes

87. Rod-shaped bacteria are referred to as

    A. bacilli.
    B. cocci.
    C. spirilla.
    D. protozoa.

88. Which of the following is considered an infectious disease?

    A. tonsilitis
    B. asthma
    C. mumps
    D. diabetes

89. Between 3 and 3.5 billion years ago, simple prokaryotic organisms evolved that were able to capture energy from the sun and create their own food. These organisms are known as

    A. plants.
    B. green algae.
    C. cyanobacteria.
    D. eukaryotes.

GO ON TO THE NEXT PAGE

90. Which of the following organisms is NOT considered a protist?

  A. paramecium
  B. amoeba
  C. slime mold
  D. *Escherichia coli*

91. Bacteria are considered to be prokaryotic because they

  A. lack a nuclear membrane, but contain other membrane-bound organelles.
  B. lack both a nuclear membrane and other membrane-bound organelles.
  C. have a well-defined nucleus but do not have any other membrane-bound organelles.
  D. have both a well-defined nucleus and several other membrane-bound organelles.

92. The normal body temperature of a person is

  A. 37 degrees Fahrenheit.
  B. 37 degrees centigrade.
  C. 98.6 degrees centigrade.
  D. 98.6 degrees Celsius.

93. Bacteria reproduce by

  A. both sexual and asexual reproduction.
  B. sexual reproduction only.
  C. asexual reproduction only.
  D. taking over a host cell and reproducing along with the host cell.

94. *Homo sapiens* is believed to have descended from

  A. *Homo erectus.*
  B. *Homo habilis.*
  C. *Homo africanus.*
  D. *Australopithecus africanus.*

95. Which of the following hormones is NOT produced by the pituitary gland?

  A. epinephrine
  B. human growth hormone
  C. lactogenic hormone
  D. follicle-stimulating hormone

96. The function of the human circulatory system is to

  A. transport blood throughout the body.
  B. transport gasses throughout the body.
  C. transport nutrients and waste products throughout the body.
  D. all of the above.

97. The amount of force blood exerts against the walls of the blood vessels is referred to as

  A. heart rate.
  B. blood pressure.
  C. pulse.
  D. diastole.

98. Which of the following represents the correct flow of air in the human respiratory system?

  A. nose → trachea → pharynx → alveoli → bronchi
  B. nose → trachea → pharynx → bronchi → alveoli
  C. nose → pharynx → trachea → bronchi → alveoli
  D. nose → pharynx → trachea → alveoli → bronchi

99. In humans, organic molecules taken in as food must be transformed into a usable form through the process of

  A. eating.
  B. nutrition.
  C. metabolism.
  D. digestion.

100. Which of the following macromolecules represents the most basic, direct form of energy in humans?

  A. carbohydrates
  B. lipids
  C. proteins
  D. vitamins

101. During digestion, proteins are broken down into

  A. protons.
  B. nucleic acids.
  C. amino acids.
  D. sugars.

102. In the human digestive system, the primary site of digestion and absorption is the

    A.   stomach.
    B.   small intestine.
    C.   large intestine.
    D.   liver.

103. The primary functional unit of the human excretory system is the

    A.   colon.
    B.   rectum.
    C.   bladder.
    D.   kidney.

104. Chemical coordination of the systems in the human body is controlled by hormones produced in a series of glands that make up the

    A.   hormonal system.
    B.   nervous system.
    C.   endocrine system.
    D.   circulatory system.

105. In humans, the hormone responsible for regulating glucose metabolism is

    A.   insulin.
    B.   thyroxine.
    C.   adrenaline.
    D.   androgen.

106. In the human reproductive system, fertilization takes place in the

    A.   vagina.
    B.   cervix.
    C.   uterus.
    D.   fallopian tube.

107. The central nervous system in humans consists of

    A.   the brain and spinal cord.
    B.   the forebrain and hindbrain.
    C.   the spinal cord and the nerves extending from the spinal cord.
    D.   the brain and peripheral nerves.

108. The part of the human brain involved in the coordination of vision, hearing, speech, and smell is the

    A.   cerebellum.
    B.   cerebrum.
    C.   medulla.
    D.   hypothalamus.

109. The number of kilocalories needed by the human body to carry out normal metabolic activity (breathing, heartbeat, temperature regulation) is referred to as the

    A.   resting heart rate.
    B.   resting pulse rate.
    C.   sedentary blood pressure.
    D.   basal metabolic rate.

110. Fat is a necessary component of the human diet because it serves to

    A.   aid in the metabolism of vitamins A, D, and E.
    B.   protect the internal organs from injury.
    C.   insulate the body from cold temperatures.
    D.   all of the above.

111. When a person's diet is lacking certain nutrients, resulting in one or more deficiencies, that person in considered to be

    A.   starving.
    B.   undernourished.
    C.   malnourished.
    D.   impoverished

112. Part of the human body's defense system against pathogens and infectious agents is the production of macrophages which function by

    A.   producing specific antibodies to invading organisms.
    B.   phagocytizing (engulfing and destroying) pathogens and infectious agents.
    C.   attacking microorganisms and inhibiting their reproduction.
    D.   producing chemicals that kill invading microorganisms.

GO ON TO THE NEXT PAGE

113. Vaccines are usually quite effective because they

   A.   act as antigens.
   B.   stimulate the primary immune response.
   C.   stimulate the secondary immune response.
   D.   all of the above.

114. Which of the following statements regarding antibiotics is incorrect?

   A.   Antibiotics interfere with the growth and development of bacteria.
   B.   Antibiotics are only effective against bacteria.
   C.   Antibiotics are effective against bacteria, viruses, and other infectious agents.
   D.   Many bacterial strains have developed resistance to commonly used antibiotics.

115. Symptoms such as anemia, vision problems, and bone deformities can be caused by deficiencies of

   A.   specific fats.
   B.   specific proteins.
   C.   specific carbohydrates.
   D.   specific vitamins.

116. The organ in the human body that is composed primarily of lymph node tissue and is the site where red blood cells are destroyed is the

   A.   liver.
   B.   pancreas.
   C.   gall bladder.
   D.   spleen.

Reading Comprehension

Directions: Read each of the following passages and answer the questions that follow.

Passage 1

(1)   With the cloning of Dolly, the sheep, in 1997, speculators believed that such scientific breakthroughs would soon apply to cells in the human body. Soon afterwards, investigators reported isolating for the first time, human embryonic cells that have the potential to develop into muscle, blood, nerves or any other tissue cell in the human body. In fact, these types of cells are called totipotent because of their multiple possibilities. With these mother cells, scientists may someday create many sorts of tissues to treat conditions such as spinal cord injuries, diabetes, leukemia, and even the neurodegenerative disorders like Parkinson's disease.

(2)   To understand the development of human embryos and to generate tissue for transplantation, several research teams had searched for human embryonic stem cells with no success. They initially tried to separate human blastocysts, clusters of 100 or so cells that constitute a stage of embryonic development. When this didn't work, the scientists collected primordial germ cells, the cells that give rise to sperm and eggs. Grown under certain conditions, these cells come to resemble stem cells derived from blastocysts. These cells were kept alive for more than seven months. These cells are shaped like embryonic stem cells, carry several of the same surface proteins and make telomerase, an enzyme thought to keep stem cells virtually immortal. They can spontaneously form embryoid bodies, clusters of differentiated cells also formed by embryonic stem cells.

(3)   Debate continues over whether primordial germ cells are the equivalent of blastocyst-derived stem cells. As germ cells develop into sperm or eggs, some genes receive a sex-specific chemical imprint that governs their activity during development. This imprinting may compromise the use of such cells as stem cells. However, if efforts prove successful with human embryonic stem cells that generate blood stem cells, they could eliminate the use of bone marrow tissues or umbilical cord blood to treat blood disorders such as leukemia.

117. The reason for calling the cells "totipotent" is

A.   They come from all parts of the body such as muscles, blood, and nerves.

B.   They are very powerful in regenerating diseased tissue.

C.   They can be used directly to treat many conditions and injuries.

D.   They become the mother cells, which can create tissues that have many possibilities.

GO ON TO THE NEXT PAGE

118. Blastocysts are

A. cells that were kept alive for over seven months.
B. another name for primordial germ cells.
C. cells at a certain beginning stage of development.
D. any group of more than 100 cells.

119. Scientists became interested in primordial germ cells because

A. They give rise to sperm and eggs.
B. They can resemble blastocysts.
C. They will live for a long time.
D. It is easy to cultivate them.

120. The most important aspect of the germ cells is

A. their shape.
B. their size.
C. the fact that they have proteins.
D. the fact that they have enzymes.

121. Germ cells and stem cells both

A. form embryoid bodies.
B. form clusters of differentiated cells.
C. form spontaneously.
D. all of the above.

122. The use of the word "compromise" in the last paragraph best means

A. restrict.
B. enhance.
C. differentiate.
D. compliment.

123. The author's attitude about cloning can best be described as

A. optimistic about future discoveries.
B. skeptical about the application of this discovery.
C. curious about the ethics of the discovery.
D. cynical about testing on human cells.

Passage 2

(1)   The old adage "Early to bed, early to rise, makes a man healthy, wealthy, and wise" may be more true than people think. Recent interest in the power and importance of sleep has revealed that a good night's sleep "wakes up" your mind and increases your brain power. Scientists have discovered that sleep deprivation causes changes in the brain that are almost identical to those that occur naturally in people in their seventies and eighties. These changes, which are in the hardworking frontal part of the brain's cortex, affect decision-making and the ability to absorb and adapt to new information. People who are affected tend to talk more in clichés and become more rigid in their thinking. A young intern in a hospital, after a long shift, could easily make a mistake if a patient comes in with unexpected symptoms that stretch and challenge his deductive powers.

(2)   Thus, it is important for employers to ensure that their staff does not work exhaustively long hours. Even a power nap in a workplace sleep zone could help in a crisis.

(3)   However, there is good news with this research for those worrying about the decline of brainpower. You don't have to spend time reading extremely weighty books or doing crossword puzzles in order

to keep your mental acumen. It is more important to bombard your mind with information that is interesting to you—whether it be sightseeing, going to art galleries, surfing the Net, or window-shopping. The latest studies show that other parts of the brain take over from the declining frontal cortex during sleep to reorganize the fresh information gathered during the day. New neural connections are forged during the first hours of sleep.

(4)   Thus, for most people, a good night's sleep will restore their brains to full power.

124. It can be inferred from this passage, that as one grows older, one's brain

A. has more power to connect to ideas that have accumulated over time.
B. takes more time to hear the information that is being given.
C. places new information into very specific categories.
D. allows one to think creatively.

125. A sleep-deprived intern might misdiagnose a patient's condition because the intern

A. has fallen asleep.
B. can't remember details of the symptoms.
C. can't recognize and apply similar symptoms to ones in the medical textbook.
D. is irritable and doesn't want to take extra time to figure out challenging solutions.

126. The best reason for employers to have places for employees to rest on break is that

A. even short naps can rejuvenate people.
B. their snoring won't annoy those who are working.
C. the brain can only rest if the person is lying down.
D. quiet places help lower a person's heart rate.

127. In the second paragraph, the term "mental acumen" most closely means

A. memory.
B. sharpness of intellect.
C. good vocabulary.
D. ability to do math problems.

128. According to this passage, if you were a sports enthusiast, an effective way to maintain your mental acumen would be to

A. read *Sports Illustrated*.
B. read the *Wall Street Journal*.
C. read *TV Guide*.
D. do crossword puzzles.

129. Which of the following statements is NOT supported by the text?

A. Other parts of the brain can take over the role of the front of the brain.
B. The best sleep that you get is at the beginning of your cycle.
C. Your frontal cortex is important to your daytime thinking.
D. Once your brain is fatigued, those cells are never rejuvenated.

130. The main idea of this passage is

A. Healthy brain function is dependent on your frontal cortex.
B. Active people have higher intelligence levels.
C. Rest is a medicinal activity.
D. Certain activities are better for your mental health than others.

Passage 3

(1)   The Greeks believed that everything should be done in moderation. Thus, even exercise can be bad for your health. There is a pattern that is repeated every year after the holiday months of November and December. Overeating and excessive drinking during this period is followed by a nationwide

GO ON TO THE NEXT PAGE

fitness drive. Just examine the newspaper sales ads for all the diet and exercise aids. Slim-Fast and Atkins products are splashed across magazine pages with interim advertisements for those ab toners and treadmills. However, health experts are warning people to avoid the trap of "binge exercising," which can lead to injury and disillusionment.

(2)   Over-exercising can damage muscles and bones that may heal in a matter of weeks, but the damaged self-confidence may last for years. One of the most common injuries is stress fractures, which are extremely painful hairline breaks. Bones need to be strengthened gradually over time. Ones that are too weak to take the strain of new, repetitive exercise can split in as little as two or three weeks of a new exercise regimen. Furthermore, sporadic exercise of any type might increase levels of bad cholesterol. Studies have shown that although regular exercise protects the body by increasing the number of cholesterol-fighting molecules, short bursts of activity either had no effect or made it rise.

(3)   The recommendation for introducing a new exercise program suggests moderate exercise for 30 consecutive minutes five times a week. Moderate exercise, which leaves you slightly breathless but not in discomfort, includes brisk walking, cycling, and even gardening. Although gym membership is expensive, it can be a good investment because it offers

exercise in a controlled way. You cannot change the effects of overindulgence in a day. The secrets of success are patience and realistic expectations.

131. The reference to "moderation" in the first sentence implies

    A. that it is not good to be the champion of anything.

    B. that people waste their talents by trying to succeed and then fail.

    C. that too much of even a good thing can be bad.

    D. that it is healthy to drink only a little at a time.

132. The purpose of mentioning Slim-Fast and Atkins is

    A. to compare effective weight loss plans.

    B. to advertise for the companies.

    C. to suggest ways to loss weight in moderation.

    D. to give examples of the yearly cycle.

133. "Binge exercising" means

    A. only exercising in random bursts of energy.

    B. eating and then exercising immediately afterward.

    C. exercising during the month of January.

    D. exercising once a week.

134. A "stress fracture" is

    A. a very small, hardly noticeable break in a bone.

    B. an emotional breakdown.

    C. a cut near your scalp.

    D. a laceration to your skin.

135. The study that shows that exercise can release cholesterol-fighting molecules

    A. does not fully support binge exercising.

    B. is an important factor in weighing the results of binge exercising.

    C. is irrelevant to this article.

    D. supports the idea that any type of exercise is healthy.

136. Gym membership is advocated because

A. It helps the economy.

B. It gives you more choices of types of exercises.

C. It encourages a controlled approach to exercise.

D. It provides you with company while you exercise.

137. The author's attitude about exercise in this article can best be described as

A. guarded because not all exercise is good.

B. enthusiastic because exercise makes you fit and healthy.

C. objective because the type of exercise that is best is up to the individual.

D. cautionary because people need to diet along with exercise.

Passage 4

(1)   The discovery in the 1990s that other stars have planets orbiting around them raised the assumptions that the processes that led to the formation of these planets in our solar system would naturally operate in other locales. What is also fascinating is that other solar systems could exhibit many exotic architectures. Searches turned up planets that went around pulsars and super-Jupiters orbiting their stars at Mercury-like distances. In our own solar system, we know that the sun is about halfway through its 12-billion-year "main sequence" phase. This phase will end when the sun exhausts its supply of useable hydrogen fuel. Then, it will expand about 100 times its present diameter, entering a stage of evolution called a red giant. The effect that this will have on its surrounding environment will be intense heat, strong enough to consume neighboring planets. Through the observation of the evolution of stars in different stages, scientists are predicting what will happen to the solar system when the sun goes red. These stellar calculations involve knowledge about nuclear fusion rates that control the rate of energy generation in the sun's core and the response of the sun's outer layers to those internal processes. Furthermore, by using the luminosity projections of the red giant sun and the reflectivity of the planet, the approximate surface temperature of the planet around the sun can be determined. It's important to know this reflectivity, or albedo, because it tells how much energy the planet can absorb and what its approximate temperature will be.

(2)   There are other factors that can affect the planet's temperature. Scientists question the degree of internal activity in the planet along with the degree to which its atmosphere produces the greenhouse effect. Mars's atmosphere has minuscule effects, but Venus's is most severe. Furthermore, during this red giant phase, the star loses much of its mass that then causes planets to be bound less tightly to their starts. They continue to move greater distances as the star loses mass. The cozy, warm

GO ON TO THE NEXT PAGE

kind of "habitable zone" around each star will move outward as the star gets older, moving from the inner to the outer solar system. This means that the possibility of a habitable planetary abode in any given system depends on what phase of evolution the system's star is in.

(3)   The kinds of celestial worlds that were discovered in the 1990s differ from those in our own home system. Therefore, the possibilities of other galaxies sporting life are definitely plausible as long as scientists realize that the type of life might be different.

138. The first sentence of this passage implies

   A.   that the fact that other planets have stars might indicate that there might be life on other planets.
   B.   that all planets are formed the same way.
   C.   that all planets have stars.
   D.   that stars are an important influence on a planet's development.

139. The reference to "exotic architecture" in the second sentence mostly closely means

   A.   that other planets might have very strange buildings on them.
   B.   that other planets can contain rock formations or accumulations of mass that are unfamiliar to earthlings.
   C.   that tropical rainforests can be found on them.
   D.   that their atmosphere will not tolerate the same types of houses that we, on Earth, have.

140. It is important to understand nuclear fusion rates because

   A.   It tells us when the star becomes a red giant.
   B.   It will reveal the luminosity of the sun.
   C.   It will indicate how much the star will expand.
   D.   It determines energy rates within the core of the sun.

141. Albedo is

   A.   the measurement of reflectivity of the sun to the planet.
   B.   the luminosity of the sun to the planet.
   C.   the heat reflectivity of the planet to the sun.
   D.   the measurement of the heat and reflectivity of both the sun and the planet to other planets in the solar system.

142. Planets that are in the red giant phase

   A.   are becoming larger so they spread out more in the solar system.
   B.   are becoming smaller so they compact together and become smaller in the solar system.
   C.   Lose mass and therefore become further apart from their stars
   D.   become very bright and are seen more clearly than their stars.

143. Knowing the "habitable zone" means

   A.   identifying the phase of evolution of the star.
   B.   selecting the type of life on a planet.
   C.   indicating the size of the planet in relation to its star.
   D.   categorizing the type of nuclear fusion that is happening.

144. Which of the following conclusions are supported by the passage:

   I.   Knowing the albedo and habitable zone can help scientists determine the type of life form on other planets.
   II.   The greenhouse effect along with nuclear fusion rates will help determine the distance a star is from its plant.
   III.   The kind of life supported on other planets is determined by the phase of evolution of the red giant.
   IV.   Because of the greenhouse effect, Mars is more likely to have life than Venus is.

   A.   only I
   B.   only II
   C.   only II and IV
   D.   only I, II and III

Passage 5

(1) The movie *Jurassic Park* is science-fiction. DNA from animals over 50,000 years ago cannot be reliably recovered. However through the power of the computer and virtual reality, researchers have demonstrated that computers can reconstruct with 98% accuracy the DNA of a creature that was a contemporary of the dinosaurs—a small, furry, nocturnal animal. Knowing the mammal's complete genome—the sequence of As, Cs, Ts, and Gs in the DNA that made up its chromosomes—does not mean that scientists can bring the creature to life. It does mean, however, that this information can help scientists explore the evolution of human and other mammals at the molecular level. It can be called a kind of DNA-based archaeology of comparative genomics. Scientists believe that much more can be learned from this type of research than from the comparative studies of living species such as the mouse, the rat, or the chimpanzee. For instance, if a DNA sequence in the human genome is missing in the corresponding place in the mouse genome, it is uncertain whether that DNA was inserted in the evolution of humans from the mammalian ancestor or deleted in the evolution of mice. If an ancestral genome is available, the ambiguity disappears.

(2) Based on a huge amount of data from research analysis of genomic sequences from any different vertebrate species, an artificial evolutionary tree was created with a massive software program. The software program was able to simulate mammalian evolution on the molecular level. This resulted in simulated modern DNA sequences for 20 different species. Then, the reconstruction procedure was used to create an ancestral sequence. This used no information from the simulated process. When the two were compared, there was a 98% accuracy. To do a complete reconstruction of the ancestral mammalian genome, there would have to be additional genome sequencing. However, if this were accomplished, there would be not only new insights into the core biology that all mammals share but also the unique traits that define each species.

145. The reference to *Jurassic Park* sets the tone

A. that information about that period is highly speculative.

B. that movies take liberties about scientific discoveries.

C. that information about dinosaurs is very unreliable.

D. that it is an important document about DNA retrieval.

GO ON TO THE NEXT PAGE

146. Understanding and identifying an animal's complete genome

- **A.** does not mean that the creature can be replicated under similar circumstances.
- **B.** means that you have the effective blueprints for re-creation of that creature.
- **C.** is the basis of determining nocturnal animals of prehistoric times.
- **D.** does not mean that you have the sequence of the chromosomes.

147. The basic reason why scientists believe that computer-generated DNA archeology is better than comparative live species study is

- **A.** because computers can overcome human error.
- **B.** because missing elements could be contingent on an insertion of DNA in one species or the deletion of DNA in the other species along the evolutionary line.
- **C.** because even though there are similarities among rats, chimpanzees, and humans, they are not exactly alike.
- **D.** because computers are faster and more objective in their findings.

148. The most important data in creating an artificial evolutionary tree is

- **A.** the genome sequences.
- **B.** understanding of mammalian ancestry.
- **C.** blood samples from ancient mammals.
- **D.** chromosome mapping.

149. Statistics were used in this passage to

- **A.** present the effectiveness of a computer-generated study.
- **B.** show the averages of human error.
- **C.** explain how DNA typing works.
- **D.** convince you that *Jurassic Park* was a movie based on inaccuracy.

150. The end of this passage implies

- **A.** that this type of study can only be taken to a certain level before it no longer works.
- **B.** that this type of study can lead to changes in existing understandings of species.
- **C.** that it would take too long to bring this type of study up to date.
- **D.** that this type of study would be beneficial in supporting existing hypotheses.

151. The tone of this passage is

- **A.** critical of movies that misrepresent scientific facts.
- **B.** supportive of research done by computers.
- **C.** amazed at the extent to which genome sequencing has led to discoveries.
- **D.** relieved that a reliable source of study is available through DNA archeology.

Passage 6

(1)   On December 26, 2004, at 7:58 A.M., an earthquake in the middle of the ocean set off a devastating tsunami that wreaked death and havoc in over seven countries. The hardest hit was the island of Sri Lanka where over 30,000 people were killed. India and Thailand were the next worst hit. A total of over 125,000 people were killed in this disaster. Like no other natural disaster in living memory, the Asian tsunami induced a planetary torrent of sorrow along with a torrent of questions and concerns: Could people have been forewarned, and could it happen again?

(2)   Geologists describe the tectonics, the almost imperceptibility slow movement of the massive plates, of the southern floor of the Indian Ocean as the Indian plate moving north at around 2.5 inches per year. This is about twice the rate that your fingernails grow. As it moves, it is forced under the Burma plate to its east. Eighteen miles below the surface of the ocean, stresses that had been gradually accumulating forced the Burma plate to snap

upward. This earthquake measured 9.0 on the Richter scale, happened over a length of 745 miles, and within three days had set off 68 aftershocks.

(3)   The movement of these plates sent shock waves through the water. Although the tsunamis are often called tidal waves, they have nothing to do with tides. They are, instead, very long waves, some-times with hundreds of miles between their crests that race along the ocean at speeds that exceed 500 miles an hour. In open water, the height of the waves is not very noticeable, no more than a few inches. But when the water's depth decreases, the wavelengths shorten and the height of the wave in-creases. Then it crashes into the shore with the power to wreck buildings and throw trucks as if they were toys. Furthermore, there is a trick to this natural horror. If the trough of the wave hits the shore before a crest, the first thing that anyone on shore notices is not water rushing onto the land but the opposite. The sea rushes out so the beach be-comes magically gorgeous with the colorful, stranded fish. What happens next is the onslaught of the next wave, which will hit with deadly force. There is no estimate of how many lives could have been saved if there had been previous warning. However, the United Nations plans to link all the countries in South and Southeast Asia with the Pacific Ocean network that alerts countries like

Japan, Australia, and the United States when tsunamis pose risks to their territories.

152. A tsunami is

- **A.** an earthquake.
- **B.** a devastating high tide.
- **C.** a torrential rainstorm.
- **D.** a series of tremendous waves.

153. Tectonics in the second paragraph is best described as

- **A.** underground rumblings of a volcano.
- **B.** shifts in the ocean currents.
- **C.** the movement of plates on the Earth's surface.
- **D.** the irregular movement of tides.

154. Tidal waves is an erroneous term for tsunamis because

- **A.** They don't affect the tides.
- **B.** Tides don't happen at the same time.
- **C.** They aren't controlled by the tides.
- **D.** They have nothing to do with the tides.

155. In the open water, tsunamis

- **A.** travel less than 500 miles an hour.
- **B.** travel in very close groups of undulating waves.
- **C.** have an unnoticeable height.
- **D.** increase in length and height as the depth of the water decreases.

156. Which of the following statements is true?

- **A.** The trough can be more deadly than the crest.
- **B.** When you see colorful fish on the sand, you know that you are safe.
- **C.** The trough indicates that the danger has passed.
- **D.** Tsunamis hit the coasts in the same pattern each time.

GO ON TO THE NEXT PAGE

157. The last sentence of this passage indicates

   A. that the danger of the tsunamis is their unpredictability.

   B. that all lives can be saved with adequate warning.

   C. that cooperation among countries will increase the viability of an early warning system.

   D. that the United Nations should not get involved in this type of scientific problem.

158. The purpose of this article was

   A. to encourage people to be more aware of global problems.

   B. to raise questions about the prevention of further disasters.

   C. to praise the concern of the world for the victims of the tsunamis.

   D. to educate tourists about tsunamis.

Passage 7

(1) In December 2002, in Fort Myers, Florida, over 3,000 people met in the convention center to protest federal restrictions on waterfront development. These people felt that there basic rights were being violated. They did not have the freedom to use land as they wished. Since land in Florida is at a premium, especially on the intercoastal waterway, which is a superhighway for boats, these people wanted their voices to be heard. On the other hand, the government's concern is to safeguard the chubby marine mammal known as the manatee. These sea cows inhabit the many bays, canals, and rivers of Florida. The primary cause of death of these slow-moving creatures is accidents with boats. They were placed on the endangered species list in 1967.

Boaters and developers argue that these mammals have rebounded in numbers, but their protectors maintain that they are just holding their own.

(2) These creatures are certainly not beautiful, yet they endear themselves to many. Their body looks like a dumpling with a paddlelike tail and a squint like Mr. Magoo's. An average adult is about 10 feet long and weighs 1,000 pounds. The animals tend to be solitary, except when mating or when cold weather prompts them to huddle near the warm springs or power plant discharge pipes. Like seals and walruses, manatees breathe through their snouts. They surface to take breaths every three or four minutes. Manatees eat mostly aquatic vegetation and have even been seen hauling themselves onto lawns to munch the grass. Because of this grazing, they have been given the bovine nickname. They usually swim no faster then 5 miles an hour, although they can sprint nearly three times as fast.

(3) Although manatees once ranged from the Carolinas to the west coast of Africa, now they stay in the warmer waters. People once killed the manatees for their succulent meat, but even as early as the 1700s, there was recognition of their decreasing numbers. One of Florida's founding fathers, Frederick Morse, put a ban on the hunting of these mammals in 1893. Then, the major threat to their lives was the increase of boating accidents. Boat

hulls and keels crack manatees' skulls and ribs. The many scars on the animal's hide are nearly as distinctive as a fingerprint and constitute a way of identifying each individual creature. Even though these creatures are not vicious, because of man's encroachment on the waterways, their existence is constantly in peril. Proponents of expansion feel that these animals are no longer in danger and are, in fact, encroaching upon man's territory. Thus, the solution to the problem would be the development of a symbiotic relationship between man and mammal.

159. The purpose of the 3,000 people at the convention center was

   A. to protest the endangerment of the manatees.
   B. to voice their concern about the inability to develop land.
   C. to complain about the intrusion of government on local politics.
   D. to encourage people to get out and vote.

160. The biggest threat to manatees is

   A. dwindling food supplies.
   B. polluted waterways.
   C. accidents from boats.
   D. human diseases carried in the water.

161. Manatees are most like

   A. whales because of their enormous size.
   B. seals because they are cute.
   C. walruses because they breathe air.
   D. sharks because they swim slowly.

162. They are nicknamed sea cows because of

   A. how they look.
   B. how they eat.
   C. how they swim.
   D. how they reproduce.

163. The scars on their backs indicate

   A. how old they are.
   B. how aggressive they have been.
   C. what diseases they have had.
   D. how many injuries from boats have happened.

164. Scientists can best label individual manatees through

   A. their feeding habits.
   B. their scar patterns.
   C. their dorsal fins.
   D. their swimming style.

165. The author's purpose of this passage was to

   A. present a compelling reason for outlawing boats on the waterway.
   B. criticize developers for their avarice.
   C. propose solutions to the dilemma.
   D. explain the information behind a heated issue.

GO ON TO THE NEXT PAGE

Quantitative Ability

Directions: Read each of the questions and select the choice that answers the question.

166. A bread recipe calls for $3\frac{1}{4}$ cups of flour. If you only have $2\frac{1}{8}$ cups, how much more flour is needed?

    A. $1\frac{1}{8}$

    B. $1\frac{1}{4}$

    C. $1\frac{3}{8}$

    D. $1\frac{3}{4}$

167. There are 72 freshmen in the band. If freshmen make up $\frac{1}{3}$ of the entire band, the total number of students in the band is

    A. 24

    B. 72

    C. 144

    D. 216

168. Rae earns $8.40 an hour plus an overtime rate equal to $1\frac{1}{2}$ times her regular pay for each hour worked beyond 40 hours. What are her total earnings for a 45-hour workweek?

    A. $336

    B. $370

    C. $399

    D. $567

169. Davis donates $\frac{4}{13}$ of his paycheck to his favorite charity. If he donates $26.80, what is the amount of his paycheck?

    A. $8.25

    B. $82.50

    C. $87.10

    D. $348.40

170. One phone plan charges a $20 monthly fee and $0.08 per minute on every phone call made. Another phone plan charges a $12 monthly fee and $0.12 per minute for each call. After how many minutes would the charge be the same for both plans?

    A. 60 minutes

    B. 90 minutes

    C. 120 minutes

    D. 200 minutes

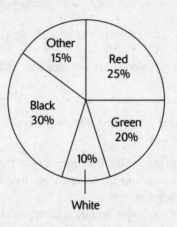

171. Heidi tallied the different car colors in the parking lot and summarized her results in a pie chart. There are 260 cars in the lot. How many cars are either red or black?

    A. 65

    B. 78

    C. 130

    D. 143

172. A cylinder whose height is 8 inches has a volume of $128\pi\,\text{cm}^3$. If the radius is doubled and its height is cut in half, the volume of the resulting cylinder is

    A. $64\pi\,\text{cm}^3$

    B. $128\pi\,\text{cm}^3$

    C. $256\pi\,\text{cm}^3$

    D. $512\pi\,\text{cm}^3$

173. What is the value of $\log_2 16$?

   A. 2
   B. 4
   C. 8
   D. 32

174. The scale on a map shows 500 feet for every $\frac{1}{4}$ inch. If two cities are 6 inches apart on the map, what is the actual distance they are apart?

   A. 125 feet
   B. 750 feet
   C. 2,000 feet
   D. 12,000 feet

175. One gallon of paint covers 400 square feet. How many gallons are needed to cover 2,225 square feet?

   A. 5 gallons
   B. 6 gallons
   C. 7 gallons
   D. 8 gallons

176. Max weighs 209 pounds. If he loses 2 pounds per week, how much will he weigh in 7 weeks?

   A. 191 pounds
   B. 195 pounds
   C. 202 pounds
   D. 207 pounds

177. Kyle ran 3 miles in $17\frac{1}{2}$ minutes on Saturday, $4\frac{1}{2}$ miles in 22 minutes on Sunday, and 2 miles in 9 minutes on Monday. What was Kyle's average rate of speed while running?

   A. 1.6 minutes per mile
   B. 5.1 minutes per mile
   C. 16.2 minutes per mile
   D. 17.8 minutes per mile

178. If $f(x) = 9^x$, then $f\left(\frac{1}{2}\right) =$.

   A. 1
   B. 3
   C. $4\frac{1}{2}$
   D. 18

179. If $a = \frac{5}{2}$ then $\frac{1}{a} =$

   A. 2
   B. 5
   C. $\frac{2}{5}$
   D. $\frac{5}{2}$

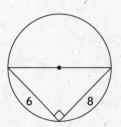

180. Find the length of the radius in the above figure.

   A. 3
   B. 4
   C. 5
   D. 10

181. If $\sin a > 0$ and $\cos a < 0$, then $\angle a$ must lie in which quadrant?

   A. I
   B. II
   C. III
   D. IV

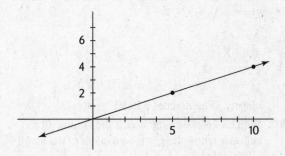

182. The slope of the line shown in the above figure is

   A. $-\frac{2}{5}$
   B. $-\frac{5}{2}$
   C. $\frac{2}{5}$
   D. $\frac{5}{2}$

GO ON TO THE NEXT PAGE

183. What is the value of $\left(\dfrac{9}{4}\right)^{-\frac{1}{2}}$?

    A. $-\dfrac{2}{3}$

    B. $\dfrac{16}{81}$

    C. $\dfrac{2}{3}$

    D. $\dfrac{3}{2}$

184. If $\log_5 x = 0$, then $x =$

    A. 0
    B. 1
    C. 5
    D. 10

185. If $2^{b+3} = \dfrac{1}{8}$, $b =$

    A. −6
    B. −3
    C. 0
    D. 2

186. If $y = 3x - 7$, then $\dfrac{dy}{dx} =$

    A. −7
    B. −4
    C. 3
    D. $3x$

187. What is the x-coordinate of the minimum value of $y = x^2 - 4x + 3$?

    A. −2
    B. 0
    C. 2
    D. 3

188. Which expression represents the volume of a cylinder whose height is equivalent to the length of the radius?

    A. πr^2
    B. πr^3
    C. $(\pi r)^2$
    D. $(\pi r)^3$

189. Jack lives $6\dfrac{1}{2}$ miles from the library. If he walks $\dfrac{1}{3}$ of the way and takes a break, what is the remaining distance to the library?

    A. $5\dfrac{5}{6}$ miles

    B. 4 miles

    C. $4\dfrac{1}{3}$ miles

    D. $2\dfrac{1}{6}$ miles

190. A square garden is to be built inside a circular area. Each corner of the square touches the circle. If the radius of the circle is 2, how much greater is the area of the circle than the square?

    A. $4 - 4\pi$
    B. $4 - 8\pi$
    C. $4\pi - 4$
    D. $4\pi - 8$

191. Which of the following values of x is a solution of the equation $\cos x = -1$?

    A. $x = 0°$
    B. $x = 90°$
    C. $x = 180°$
    D. $x = 270°$

192. There are 800 employees at a company. If 60% drive to work and 30% take the train, how many employees arrive to work by car?

    A. 240
    B. 480
    C. 540
    D. 600

193. If $c^{\frac{3}{2}} = 8$, what is the value of c?

    A. 2
    B. 4
    C. 16
    D. 64

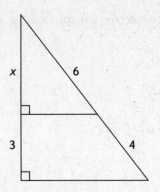

194. Find the value of *x* in the above figure:

A. 4.5
B. 4.8
C. 5
D. 5.2

195. Yan can read two pages in three minutes. At this rate, how long will it take him to read a 360-page book?

A. 30 minutes
B. 2 hours
C. 6 hours
D. 9 hours

196. $y(x) = \frac{1}{x}$, then $y'(x) =$

A. 1
B. $\frac{1}{x^2}$
C. $-\frac{1}{x^2}$
D. $-x^2$

197. The sum of $\sqrt{50} + 3\sqrt{72}$ is

A. $4 + \sqrt{122}$
B. $4\sqrt{122}$
C. $7\sqrt{2}$
D. $23\sqrt{2}$

198. Evaluate $3r^3 - 2s^2 + t$ if $r = -1$, $s = -2$, and $t = -3$.

A. 2
B. 4
C. -8
D. -14

199. If $\log C = 10$ and $\log D = 5$, then $\log\frac{C}{D} =$

A. $\frac{1}{2}$
B. 2
C. 5
D. 15

200. What is the value of $\left(\sqrt{7}^{\pi}\right)^{-\frac{2}{\pi}}$?

A. $\frac{1}{7}$
B. 7
C. 7π
D. 49π

201. The product of the square of *x* and three less than *x* is

A. $\sqrt{x}(x-3)$
B. $\sqrt{x}(3-x)$
C. $x^2(x-3)$
D. $x^2(3-x)$

202. The expression $\tan\theta\cos\theta\csc\theta$ is equivalent to

A. 1
B. $\sin\theta$
C. $\tan\theta$
D. $\sec\theta$

203. Factor $2a^2 - 4ab + ab - 2b^2$

A. $(a + 2b)(2a - b)$
B. $(a - 2b)(2a + b)$
C. $(2a - b)(a + 2b)$
D. $(2a + b)(a - b)$

204. $-3(-4 - 5) - 2(-6) =$

A. 0
B. -5
C. 15
D. 39

205. If $6m - 2$ is divided by 2, the result is -4. What is the value of *m?*

A. -1
B. 0
C. 1
D. 2

GO ON TO THE NEXT PAGE

206. What is the period of the function $g(x) = 6\sin 2x$?

    A. 2
    B. π
    C. 4
    D. 2π

207. If $x = -3$ and $y = 2$, evaluate x^{2y}.

    A. -64
    B. -81
    C. 64
    D. 81

208. What is the second derivative of $y = 3x^2 + 5x + 2$?

    A. 2
    B. 5
    C. 6
    D. $6x + 5$

209. One-fourth of the cars purchased at a dealership are luxury models. If 360 luxury models were purchased last year, how many total cars were purchased?

    A. 90
    B. 250
    C. 1,440
    D. 3,600

210. The least common multiple of 8, 12, and 20 is

    A. 4
    B. 24
    C. 60
    D. 120

211. If $0.08z = 6.4$, then $z =$

    A. 0.8
    B. 8
    C. 80
    D. 800

212. What is the slope of the line $2x + y = 7$?

    A. -2
    B. 1
    C. 2
    D. 7

213. Which of the following functions is a solution to the equation $\frac{dy}{dx} = \sin x$?

    A. $y = -\cos x$
    B. $y = \cos x$
    C. $y = -\sin x$
    D. $y = 5\sin x$

PCAT Chemistry

Directions: Read each of the questions and select the choice that answers the question. To consult the Periodic Table of the Elements, please go to the Appendix.

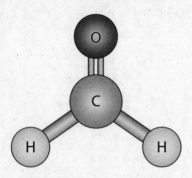

214. For the molecule shown in the above figure, what will the predominant intermolecular forces be?

    A. dipole-dipole forces
    B. coordinate covalent bonding forces
    C. hydrogen bond forces
    D. London forces

215. A solution has a pH of 6.0. What is the hydroxide ion concentration of this solution?

    A. 1×10^{-5}
    B. 1×10^{-6}
    C. 1×10^{-7}
    D. 1×10^{-8}

216. A reaction results in lower enthalpy and higher entropy. Which of the following four statements can be said of this reaction?

    A. The reaction will be spontaneous at sufficiently low temperatures.
    B. The reaction will be non-spontaneous.
    C. The reaction will be spontaneous at sufficiently high temperatures.
    D. The reaction will be spontaneous.

217. For the reaction $2\,H_3PO_4$ (aq) $+ 3\,Ba(OH)_2$ (aq) $\rightarrow$ $Ba_3(PO_4)_2$ (aq) $+ 6\,H_2O$ (l), what volume of 0.2 M phosphoric acid will be required to completely neutralize 100 mL of 0.6 M barium hydroxide?

    A. 450 mL
    B. 100 mL
    C. 300 mL
    D. 200 mL

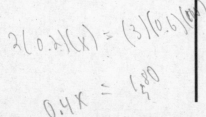

218. Of the following functional groups, which is alkaline?

    A. amines
    B. esters
    C. amides
    D. phenols

219. Keeping volume and the number of moles of gas constant, what will be the effect of doubling the absolute temperature on a container of gas?

    A. The pressure will decrease by a factor of 2.
    B. The pressure will increase by an unknown amount.
    C. The pressure will increase by a factor of 2.
    D. The pressure will decrease by an unknown amount.

$$\text{HEME} - \text{CO} + \text{O}_2 \rightleftharpoons \text{HEME} - \text{O}_2 + \text{CO}$$

220. Although carbon monoxide is usually thought to bond permanently to red blood cells, it actually is an equilibrium which, unfortunately, greatly favors the HEME-CO side. This equilibrium can be represented as in the above figure. What conditions will favor replacing the carbon monoxide with oxygen?

    A. high pressure and high oxygen content
    B. low pressure and high oxygen content
    C. high oxygen concentration
    D. high pressure

221. A saline solution (solution of sodium chloride dissolved in water) will have what property?

    A. The solution will be either acidic or basic (more information is needed).
    B. The solution will be acidic.
    C. The solution will be neutral.
    D. The solution will be basic.

GO ON TO THE NEXT PAGE

222. In the redox equation $PbSO_4(aq)+Cl_2(g)+2H_2O(l) \rightarrow$ $Pb(s)+H_2SO_4(aq)+2HClO(aq)$, what is the role being played by lead in the lead (II) sulfate?

A. the catalyst
B. the reducing agent
C. the spectator ion
D. the oxidizing agent

223. Of the gases provided, which will diffuse the slowest under identical conditions of T & P?

A. CO_2
B. O_2
C. H_2O
D. CO

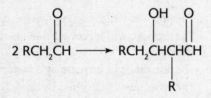

224. The aldol condensation is important for understanding the behavior of sugars. What aldol will be produced from propanal?

A. 3,4-dimethl-2-pentanol-al
B. 3-methyl-2-hexanol-al
C. 2-methyl-3-hexanol-al
D. 2,4-dimethyl-3-pentanol-al

225. What is the molecular shape of sulfur dioxide?

A. trigonal planar
B. linear
C. tetrahedral
D. bent

226. What is the correct formula for ferrous phosphate?

A. Fe_2PO_4
B. $Fe_3(PO_4)_2$
C. $FePO_4$
D. $Fe_2(PO_4)_2$

227. What is the molecular mass of aluminum carbonate?

A. 60 g/mol
B. 234 g/mol
C. 210 g/mol
D. 114 g/mol

228. What is the bond order for the MO diagram shown in the above figure?

A. 1
B. 1.5
C. 2
D. 3

229. What kind of electronic state is represented by the electronic configuration $1s^2 2s^2 2p^4 3s^1$?

A. forbidden state
B. atomic state
C. excited state
D. ground state

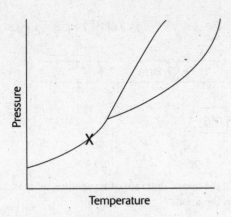

230. On the phase diagram shown in the above figure, what condition is denoted by the *x*?

- **A.** equilibrium of solid and liquid
- **B.** equilibrium of solid and gas
- **C.** equilibrium of liquid and gas
- **D.** triple point

231. What type of amine is found as an organic salt?

- **A.** quaternary
- **B.** tertiary
- **C.** secondary
- **D.** primary

232. What is the correct IUPAC name for the compound shown in the above figure?

- **A.** 4-ethyl-3-methyloctane
- **B.** 3-butyl-4-methylhexane
- **C.** 3-isobutylheptane
- **D.** 2,3-diethylheptane

233. How would you classify a compound that rotates plane polarized light?

- **A.** diastereomer
- **B.** racemic
- **C.** enantiomer
- **D.** chiral

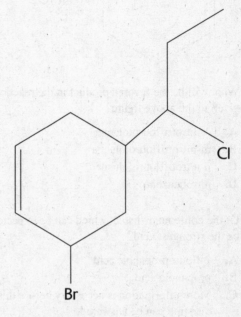

234. The compound shown in the above figure can be formed from what two reactants?

- **A.** trans-1-bromo-4-chloro-3-ethene-1-hexene and ethene
- **B.** cis-1-bromo-4-chloro-3-ethene-1-hexene and ethene
- **C.** trans-1-bromo-1,3-butadiene and 3-chloro 1-pentene
- **D.** cis-1-bromo-1,3-butadiene and 1-chloro propene

235. What is the ground state electronic configuration of Lu?

- **A.** [Xe] $6s^2 4f^{14} 5d^1$
- **B.** [Xe] $6s^2 6f^{14} 6d^1$
- **C.** [Xe] $6s^2 6d^1 6f^{14}$
- **D.** [Xe] $6s^2 5d^1 4f^{14}$

GO ON TO THE NEXT PAGE

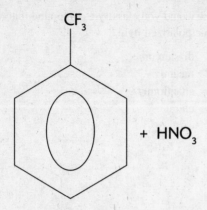

+ HNO₃

236. What will be the favored product in the reaction given in the above figure?

   A.   o-nitrotriflourotoluene

   B.   m-nitrotriflourotoluene

   C.   p-nitrotriflourotoluene

   D.   nitrobenzene

237. Of the compounds listed, which can be expected to be the strongest acid?

   A.   2-flouropropanoic acid

   B.   propanoic acid

   C.   More information is necessary before this question can be answered.

   D.   1-flouropropanoic acid

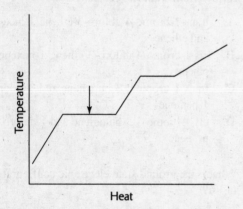

238. In the heating curve shown in the above figure, what state or change is designated by the arrow as heat is added to the sample?

   A.   gas state

   B.   melting transition

   C.   boiling transition

   D.   solid state

239. In the above diagram of a pipeline, what is acting as the anode?

   A.   the wire connecting the block of magnesium

   B.   the iron pipe

   C.   the water and magnesium

   D.   the block of magnesium

240. Which of the following is NOT a colligative property?

   A.   osmotic pressure

   B.   freezing point elevation

   C.   vapor pressure depression

   D.   boiling point elevation

241. According to the Lewis-Dot structure, how many lone pairs (or non-bonding pairs) of electrons are around the central element in the polyatomic ion IF_4^{-1}?

   A.   4

   B.   3

   C.   2

   D.   1

242. Which of the following groups is most highly oxidized?

   A.   ketone

   B.   carboxylic acid

   C.   alcohol

   D.   aldehyde

243. EDTA acts by forming coordination complexes with copper, so the copper is not available to bacteria. Which of the following terms does NOT apply to EDTA?

   A.   ligand

   B.   Lewis acid

   C.   chelate

   D.   polydentate

244. What type of chemical reaction is characterized by having more than one reactant, but only one product?

   A. decomposition
   B. addition or combination synthesis
   C. double replacement
   D. single replacement

245. Which of the following will NEVER influence solubility?

   A. the polarities of the solvent and solute
   B. changing temperature
   C. stirring
   D. pressure

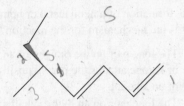

246. What is the correct IUPAC name for the compound in the above figure?

   A. trans R-5-methyl-1,3-heptadiene
   B. trans S-5-methyl-1,3-heptadiene
   C. cis R-5-methyl-1,3-heptadiene
   D. cis S-5-methyl-1,3-heptadiene

247. Which carbocation would be most stable?

   A. methyl
   B. secondary
   C. primary
   D. tertiary

248. What type of amine is NOT alkaline?

   A. tertiary
   B. primary
   C. quaternary
   D. secondary

249. What type of organic reaction is denoted in the above figure?

   A. addition
   B. condensation
   C. elimination
   D. rearrangement

250. As a general trend, how does electronegativity increase through the periodic chart?

   A. from bottom to top and left to right
   B. from bottom to top and right to left
   C. from top to bottom and right to left
   D. from top to bottom and left to right

251. Which of the following functional groups CANNOT be formed from carboxylic acids?

   A. esters
   B. amides
   C. ethers
   D. anhydrides

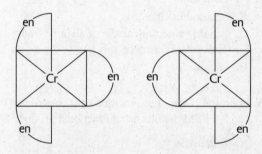

252. What best describes the two compounds shown in the above figure?

   A. hydrate isomers
   B. linkage isomers
   C. optical isomers
   D. ionization isomers

GO ON TO THE NEXT PAGE

$$\overline{\sigma^*_{2p}}$$

$$\overline{\pi^*_{2p}} \quad \overline{}$$

$$\overline{\pi_{2p}} \quad \overline{}$$

$$\overline{\sigma_{2p}}$$

$$\overline{\sigma^*_{2s}}$$

$$\overline{\sigma_{2s}}$$

$$\overline{\sigma^*_{1s}}$$

$$\overline{\sigma_{1s}}$$

253. Using the diagram in the above figure, what can you tell about diatomic oxygen?

A. It is paramagnetic with a bond order of 3.
B. It is diamagnetic with a bond order of 3.
C. It is paramagnetic with a bond order of 2.
D. It is diamagnetic with a bond order of 2.

254. A solution made from pure water and the salt sodium acetate should be what?

A. alkaline
B. neutral/unchanged
C. could be neutral, acidic or alkaline (more information is necessary)
D. acidic

255. In proton NMR, a peak with a shift between 6.0 and 9.5 PPM denotes what functional group?

A. aldehyde
B. aromatic
C. ketone
D. ether

256. In a mixture of the following cations in equal concentration, which will precipitate from the solution first?

A. Hg_2^{+2} ($K_{sp} = 6.8 \times 10^{-7}$)
B. Ba^{+2} ($K_{sp} = 1.1 \times 10^{-10}$)
C. Pb^{+2} ($K_{sp} = 1.8 \times 10^{-8}$)
D. Sr^{+2} ($K_{sp} = 2.8 \times 10^{-7}$)

257. How many grams of sodium hydroxide are required to completely neutralize 200 mL of 0.50 M sulfuric acid?

A. 2.0 g
B. 8.0 g
C. 4.0 g
D. 16.0 g

258. What is the most probable product to be formed from the fluorination of benzene?

A. fluorobenzene
B. p-difluorobenzene
C. m-difluorobenzene
D. o-diflourobenzene

259. In the formation of a hemiacetal or hemiketal, what is the mechanism for the reaction?

A. The lone pair on the oxygen of an aldehyde or ketone attacks the partial positive carbon of an alcohol.
B. The lone pair on an hydroxyl attacks the partial positive carbon of a ketone or aldehyde.
C. The lone pair on the oxygen of a ketone or aldehyde attacks the hydrogen on an alcohol to form a hydrogen bond.
D. A rearrangement occurs in which the hydrogen shifts changing the position of the aldehyde or ketone with the hydroxyl.

260. If the pK$_a$ of acetic acid is 4.74, what will be the pH of a buffer solution made from 0.1 moles sodium acetate and 0.01 moles acetic acid?

A. 3.74
B. 4.74
C. 5.74
D. 6.74

261. The subshell after f would be the g subshell. How many orbitals would this subshell have?

A. 8
B. 9
C. 12
D. 14

262. If Po undergoes β decay, what element will be formed?

    A. Rn

    B. At

    C. Bi

    D. Pb

263. In an aqueous environment, what would make the worst leaving group?

    A. halogen

    B. hydroxide

    C. hydrosulfide

    D. carbon dioxide

264. Which of the following laws specifically concerns the mixtures of gases?

    A. Charles's

    B. Dalton's

    C. Boyles's

    D. combined

265. Following is an unbalanced chemical equations.

$$Cr(NO_3)_3 \text{ (aq)} + H_2SO_4 \text{ (aq)} \rightarrow Cr_2(SO_4)_3 \text{ (s)} + HNO_3 \text{ (aq)}$$

When it is balanced, what is the Stoichiometric coefficient for the chromium(III) nitrate?

    A. 2

    B. 4

    C. 1

    D. 3

266. What type of base is categorized as a hydronium ion (H^+) acceptor?

    A. Coordination

    B. Bronsted-Lowry

    C. Lewis

    D. Arrhenius

267. What kind of compound should carbon dioxide be?

    A. non-polar covalent

    B. polar covalent

    C. slightly polar covalent

    D. ionic

268. In the following reaction, what is the reducing agent?

$$Hg \text{ (l)} + H_2S \text{ (g)} + PbSO_4 \text{ (aq)} + 2 OH^- \text{ (aq)} \rightarrow HgS \text{ (s)} + 2 H_2O \text{ (l)} + Pb \text{ (s)} + SO_4^{-2} \text{ (aq)}$$

    A. hydroxide

    B. lead (II) sulfate

    C. mercury

    D. hydrogen sulfide

269. What is the hybridization for a carbon with a linear molecular structure?

    A. sp

    B. sp^2

    C. sp^3

    D. sp^3d

270. A decomposition reaction is found to produce the experimental data in the following table. What is the order of this decomposition reaction?

$[A]_o$	Initial Rate
2.3 M	6.3 M/s
1.1 M	6.3 M/s
4.6 M	6.3 M/s

    A. zero

    B. first

    C. second

    D. third

GO ON TO THE NEXT PAGE

Critical Thinking Essay

Directions: You will have 30 minutes in which to write an essay in response to the following statement. This essay will either require you to express an opinion or will present a problem that needs a solution.

"When we study history, we tend to focus on the contributions of individuals. Most of the major events that have taken place throughout history were made possible by those various groups of people who are no longer remembered—not by those celebrated individuals."

Answer Key for Practice Test 1

Verbal Ability: Analogies

1. B	11. D	21. C
2. B	12. A	22. D
3. C	13. A	23. C
4. A	14. B	24. D
5. B	15. C	25. D
6. C	16. B	26. C
7. A	17. A	27. B
8. C	18. A	28. A
9. C	19. D	29. C
10. B	20. C	

Verbal Ability: Sentence Completions

30. B	40. A	50. D
31. D	41. D	51. B
32. B	42. C	52. D
33. D	43. C	53. C
34. C	44. C	54. A
35. B	45. C	55. C
36. D	46. A	56. A
37. D	47. D	57. C
38. B	48. B	58. D
39. A	49. D	

Biology

59. C	**79.** D	**99.** D
60. A	**80.** D	**100.** A
61. A	**81.** A	**101.** C
62. D	**82.** D	**102.** B
63. A	**83.** A	**103.** D
64. C	**84.** D	**104.** C
65. B	**85.** D	**105.** A
66. C	**86.** B	**106.** D
67. D	**87.** A	**107.** A
68. D	**88.** C	**108.** B
69. B	**89.** C	**109.** D
70. A	**90.** D	**110.** D
71. A	**91.** B	**111.** C
72. D	**92.** B	**112.** B
73. C	**93.** C	**113.** D
74. C	**94.** A	**114.** C
75. A	**95.** A	**115.** D
76. D	**96.** D	**116.** D
77. C	**97.** B	
78. B	**98.** C	

Reading Comprehension

117. D	**134.** A	**151.** B
118. C	**135.** A	**152.** D
119. B	**136.** C	**153.** C
120. D	**137.** A	**154.** D
121. D	**138.** B	**155.** C
122. A	**139.** B	**156.** A
123. A	**140.** D	**157.** C
124. C	**141.** C	**158.** B
125. C	**142.** C	**159.** B
126. A	**143.** A	**160.** C
127. B	**144.** D	**161.** C
128. A	**145.** A	**162.** B
129. D	**146.** A	**163.** D
130. C	**147.** B	**164.** B
131. C	**148.** A	**165.** D
132. D	**149.** A	
133. A	**150.** B	

Quantitative

166. A	**182.** C	**198.** A
167. D	**183.** C	**199.** C
168. C	**184.** B	**200.** A
169. C	**185.** A	**201.** C
170. D	**186.** C	**202.** A
171. D	**187.** C	**203.** B
172. C	**188.** B	**204.** D
173. B	**189.** C	**205.** A
174. D	**190.** D	**206.** B
175. B	**191.** C	**207.** D
176. B	**192.** B	**208.** C
177. B	**193.** B	**209.** C
178. B	**194.** A	**210.** D
179. C	**195.** D	**211.** C
180. C	**196.** C	**212.** A
181. B	**197.** D	**213.** A

Chemistry

214. A	**233.** D	**252.** C
215. D	**234.** C	**253.** C
216. D	**235.** A	**254.** A
217. D	**236.** B	**255.** B
218. A	**237.** D	**256.** B
219. C	**238.** B	**257.** B
220. C	**239.** D	**258.** A
221. C	**240.** B	**259.** B
222. D	**241.** C	**260.** C
223. A	**242.** B	**261.** B
224. C	**243.** B	**262.** B
225. D	**244.** B	**263.** C
226. B	**245.** C	**264.** B
227. B	**246.** D	**265.** A
228. C	**247.** D	**266.** B
229. C	**248.** C	**267.** A
230. B	**249.** B	**268.** C
231. A	**250.** A	**269.** A
232. A	**251.** C	**270.** A

Complete Answers and Explanations for Practice Test 1

Verbal Ability: Analogies

1. **B.** Mellifluous means smooth sounding which is the opposite of discordant. Dulcet is also sweet sounding and incongruous means not in harmony.

2. **B.** A characteristic of a convict is straying from the law or errant. Therefore, a saint would follow the law and be upright.

3. **C.** An extreme version of simple is austere. An extreme version of decorated is garish.

4. **A.** The person who tells a story is called a raconteur. Another name for a poet is a lyricist, someone who writes poetry.

5. **B.** To reiterate is to restate; they mean the same thing. To recapitulate means to say again, or restate.

6. **C.** A person uses a plumb to measure the straightness of something. A person uses a protractor to measure angles.

7. **A.** A panacea is a "fake" remedy. A placebo is a "fake" substitute for a drug.

8. **C.** The opposite of something palatial or like a palace is something very small or miniature. Lilliputian comes from the small people in *Gulliver's Travels* and means extremely small, so the opposite is colossal.

9. **C.** The top of something is the apex; the bottom is the nadir so the words are antonyms. Pinnacle means top and the opposite is base.

10. **B.** A characteristic of a miser is being frugal or very stingy. A miscreant is a criminal and, therefore, a characteristic would be evil.

11. **D.** Something that is distasteful is repugnant and causes people to turn away. Someone who is talkative is also loquacious.

12. **A.** An individual would use a lexicon to look up definitions and an almanac to find out facts.

13. **A.** A small drip of water would be said to trickle; a large amount would be said to inundate, so the relationship is degree. To flicker is a small flame; to blaze is a large one.

14. **B.** To mollify and to allay both mean to lessen the intensity of something. To appease and to mitigate also mean to lessen the intensity of something, so all the words are synonyms.

15. **C.** One small particle is an iota. Millions of something would be a myriad. Paucity means a small amount of something, so paucity would be the extreme.

16. **B.** A pedestrian goes on foot; an equestrian goes on a horse.

17. **A.** A pariah is a social outcast, which is the opposite of a model or paragon. Thus, the opposite of an outcast would be an exemplar.

18. **A.** A malefactor is an evil person. An autocrat is a person with unlimited power. Omnipotence means all-powerful.

19. **D.** An oak is a type of tree and the adjective is arboreal. A pine is a special type of tree with cones, so it is called coniferous.

20. **C.** An ascetic is someone who denies himself any pleasure. A hedonist only seeks his own pleasure. A puritanical person is very strict, while an indulgent person is one who gives into whims.

21. **C.** An apparition is a ghost whose quality is ethereal or unearthly. A spirit is also a ghost, and diaphanous means without substance or unearthly.

22. **D.** Cacophony is a series of harsh sounds. Harmony is a series of mellifluous or pleasant sounds.

23. C. To amalgamate is to gather things together; to disseminate is to throw things apart, so the words are opposite. To fuse means to put together and to split means to separate.

24. D. Banal and trite both mean to be very worn out and ordinary. Hackneyed and lackluster also mean worn out and trite, so all four words are synonyms.

25. D. Comestible means something that is able to be eaten, and savory means tasting very good. Edible means being able to be eaten and tasty means tasting good.

26. C. Erratic means happening at different times, and irregular means the same. Fickle means changing one's mind frequently, so a synonym is capricious, which means changing one's mind frequently.

27. B. To engrave something is to cut into something. To embroider means to sew.

28. A. An elegy is a formal way to display sorrow. A eulogy is a formal way to show praise or laudation.

29. C. An individual would use an adhesive to bond to attach something together. An individual would use decorations to embellish or decorate something.

Verbal Ability: Sentence Completions

30. B. Immerse means to cover completely in a liquid.

31. D. The word *rural* in the item suggests that the second blank should mean something that is not rural. If the rural area has decreased, the coyotes must go elsewhere.

32. B. The purpose of advertising is to persuade. The word text suggests the first blank should mean an element other than the text—a visual element.

33. D. Insipid means dull or lacking strength.

34. C. Alleviate, meaning relieve, is the only word that fits the meaning of the beginning of the sentence.

35. B. Apathy means indifference.

36. D. The sentence defines an eclipse, and none of the other choices would make sense.

37. D. Proficiency means having advanced ability or competence.

38. B. The words *sodium* and *chloride* are names of chemical elements.

39. A. Militant means having an aggressive nature on behalf of a cause. Violent is not as good a choice because glaring is not a violent action.

40. A. Autonomy means self-directed or not controlled by others. That there is no steady source of income implies that a lack of financial stability would result.

41. D. Rant means speak angrily and violently.

42. C. Vivacious means lively.

43. C. Relentless means with great force that will not stop.

44. C. The word *descend* means ceiling is the only logical answer for the first blank in the sentence, and the word *but* indicates the second blank requires a contrast with something that grows from top to bottom.

45. C. A centennial is the celebration of a one-hundredth anniversary.

46. A. Grandiose means having great scope or intent. Constrained means compelled by a force. The lack of money prevented the king from fulfilling his plan for an elaborate wedding.

47. D. Because the sentence says lye causes burns, potent, meaning powerful, and caustic, meaning capable of burning or eating away, is the best answer.

48. B. The word *decrease* suggests the best answer uses a word that means something is becoming smaller in the first blank. Narrow is the only possible choice.

49. D. Ubiquitous means seeming to be everywhere at once. The best word for the second blank is *pollution,* because of its negative connotations.

50. D. The jurors may have been incredulous; they did not believe what they heard, but the alibi was incredible—not believable.

51. B. Tacit means unspoken.

52. D. Rash, as an adjective, means hasty and unconsidered. (Rash as a noun is an itchy eruption on the skin.)

53. C. Choices **B** and **A** provide words with negative connotations for the first blank, which would contradict the word *improving.* Choice **D** provides a word with a positive connotation, but playgrounds would not be a logical means of providing improved education.

54. A. Sumptuous means of great size or splendor.

55. C. Solace means comfort.

56. A. The sentence's meaning requires two words that have negative connotations.

57. C. Virulent means poisonous.

58. D. Acquiescence means acceptance or agreement; to be complicit is to be an accomplice or to share guilt.

Biology

59. C. For a given trait to be expressed, genes on DNA in the nucleus of the cell must be transcribed onto a molecule of mRNA (messenger RNA) and carried out of the nucleus into the cytoplasm. The mRNA attaches to a ribosome in the cytoplasm, while tRNA (transfer RNA) molecules add appropriate amino acids to the growing polypeptide chain, according to the message encoded on the mRNA, translating the DNA message into protein.

60. A. A DNA molecule that is composed of 30% adenine molecules, will also contain 30% thymine molecules, 20% guanine molecules, and 20% cytosine molecules.

61. A. An organism that contains a segment of DNA from a different organism inserted into its own DNA is referred to as being transgenic. A vector (Choice **B**) is used to transfer segments of DNA from one organism to another. A plasmid (Choice **C**) is one type of vector. A hybrid (Choice **D**) is an organism produced by conventional breeding methods.

62. D. Large quantities of identical DNA can be obtained from a very small sample by using PCR (polymerase chain reaction) techniques. DNA fingerprinting (Choice **A**), RFLP analysis (Choice **B**), and DNA hybridization (Choice **C**) can all be used to analyze DNA samples once sufficient quantities are available for study.

63. A. Evolution can be described as changes in the genetic composition of a population over time. Natural selection (Choice **B**) and genetic drift (Choice **C**) are forces that influence evolution.

64. C. Only eukaryotic cells contain a nucleus. Bacterial cells are prokaryotic and lack a nucleus.

65. B. Both plant and animal cells have mitochondria.

66. C. Ribosomes are the primary sites of protein synthesis in cells. The nucleus (Choice **A**) houses the cell's genetic material, mitochondria (Choice **B**) are responsible for cellular respiration, and peroxisomes (Choice **D**) aid in getting rid of toxins within the cell.

67. D. Human dermal tissue serves as the outer covering of the body, as a line of defense against invading organisms, and as a sensory organ.

68. D. Differentially permeable membranes control which substances may pass through them, as well as the rate at which those substances pass through.

69. B. Diffusion involves the passive movement of substances from a region of higher concentration to a region of lower concentration. For substances to move from a region of lower concentration to a region of higher concentration usually requires an input of energy and is referred to as active transport.

70. A. Mitosis results in the formation of two identical daughter cells from each parent cell. It occurs within most cells of the body and is essential for normal growth to occur. Meiosis takes place only in germ cells that give rise to gametes; each parent cell produces four unique daughter cells during the process of meiosis.

71. A. Mitosis results in the formation of two identical daughter cells from each parent cell; therefore, a cell containing 24 chromosomes that underwent mitosis would produce two new cells, each containing 24 chromosomes.

72. D. Crossing over and independent assortment result in the production of four unique daughter cells from each parent cell during meiosis.

73. C. The process of cellular respiration takes place in the mitochondria of cells and results in the production of energy (ATP) through the breakdown of glucose molecules.

74. C. While plants can produce their own food supply through the process of photosynthesis, animals cannot. Both plants and animals are capable of producing their own energy through cellular respiration.

75. A. A group of individuals that can interbreed and produce fertile offspring is referred to as a species. A population (Choice **B**) is a group of organisms of the same species that occupy a given area at the same time. A community (Choice **C**) includes all organisms occupying a given area at the same time. A gene pool (Choice **D**) is the genetic makeup of a given population.

76. D. A group of organisms living in a defined area, along with all the abiotic factors with which they interact, can be defined as an ecosystem. See answer to #75 for an explanation of a community (Choice **A**), a population (Choice **B**), and a gene pool (Choice **C**).

77. C. Producers, organisms that can make their own food through the process of photosynthesis, form the base of all food chains. Herbivores (Choice **A**) feed on the producers (typically plants or algae), carnivores (Choice **B**) feed on the herbivores, and decomposers (Choice **D**) work at each level of the food chain breaking down and recycling organic matter.

78. B. The increase in concentration of toxins at successive levels of a food chain is referred to as biological magnification.

79. D. An organism that lives on or within a host is referred to as a parasite.

80. D. A prolonged period of drought would cause a decrease in population size, regardless of the initial density of the population and, thus, would be considered a density-independent factor affecting population size. The availability of food or water, and the level of toxins present in the ecosystem would affect denser populations to a greater degree than less dense populations, and would thus be considered density-dependent factors affecting population size.

81. A. While carbon, water, and nutrients all cycle through an ecosystem, energy moves through an ecosystem in one direction.

82. D. Viruses cannot make their own proteins and, therefore, are dependent on a host cell for survival and reproduction. Protists and prokaryotes (bacteria) are capable of making their own proteins and are not dependent on a host cell for survival and reproduction.

83. A. Bacterial cells are prokaryotic, meaning they lack a nucleus and well-defined organelles. All other organisms are eukaryotic.

84. D. While plants remove carbon dioxide from the atmosphere and release oxygen during the day (while carrying out photosynthesis) and release some carbon dioxide at night (as a result of cellular respiration), unless the room is filled with plants, the levels of carbon dioxide and oxygen involved are negligible. Plants and the soil they are planted in may contain mold or bacterial spores; therefore, many hospitals prohibit plants in the rooms of respiratory patients.

85. **D.** Bacteria may be found in both uncooked beef *(Escherichia coli)* and uncooked eggs *(Salmonella).* Uncooked beef also may contain tapeworm cysts.

86. **B.** The HIV virus typically infects Helper T-cells, which function to initiate many specific immune responses. Phagocytes (Choice **C**) and monocytes (Choice **D**) function to engulf and destroy invading organisms and are generally not infected by the HIV virus. As HIV is an immunodeficiency disorder, red blood cells (Choice **A**) are generally not infected by the HIV virus.

87. **A.** Rod-shaped bacteria are referred to as bacilli. Spherical or oval-shaped bacteria are referred to as cocci (Choice **B**), while spirilla (Choice **C**) bacteria are spirally twisted or coiled. Protozoa (Choice **D**) are not classified as bacteria.

88. **C.** Mumps are caused by a virus and, therefore, considered infectious. Tonsillitis (Choice **A**) is an inflammation of the tonsils; asthma (Choice **B**) is often an allergic reaction to an antigen and can be induced by anxiety, stress, exercise, and cold air; diabetes (Choice **D**) results from an inability to produce or manage proper insulin levels in the body, and is usually under genetic or environmental control.

89. **C.** Cyanobacteria (photosynthesizing prokaryotic organisms) are thought to be the first organisms that evolved the ability to capture light energy from the sun and use it to make their own food.

90. **D.** Paramecia, amoebae, and slime molds are all eukaryotic organisms that are grouped into the category referred to informally as "protists." *Escherichia coli* is a prokaryotic bacterium.

91. **B.** Bacteria lack both a nuclear membrane and other membrane-bound organelles and, thus, are classified as prokaryotic organisms.

92. **B.** The normal body temperature of a person is 37 degrees centigrade (98.6 degrees Fahrenheit). Celsius and centigrade are equivalent measures of temperature.

93. **C.** Bacteria only reproduce through asexual mechanisms.

94. **A.** *Homo sapiens* (the species to which modern humans belong) descended from *Homo erectus. Homo habilis* (Choice **B**) predated *Homo erectus,* while *Australopithecus africanus* (Choice **D**) predated *Homo habilis.* There was no such species as *Homo africanus* (Choice **C**).

95. **A.** Epinephrine is produced by the adrenal glands.

96. **D.** The human circulatory system functions to transport blood, gasses, nutrients, and waste products throughout the body.

97. **B.** Blood pressure is a measure of the amount of force exerted by the blood against the walls of the blood vessels.

98. **C.** The path of air through the human respiratory system proceeds as follows: nose → pharynx → trachea → bronchi → alveoli.

99. **D.** Digestion is the process through which humans transform organic molecules taken in as food into a form that is readily usable by the body.

100. **A.** Carbohydrates, primarily glucose, provide the most basic, direct source of energy for use by the human body.

101. **C.** During digestion, proteins are broken down into amino acids, their component building blocks.

102. **B.** In humans, the small intestine serves as the primary site for digestion and absorption.

103. **D.** The kidney serves as the primary functional unit of the human excretory system.

104. **C.** The human endocrine system is comprised of a series of glands that produce the hormones responsible for chemical coordination of the body's systems.

105. **A.** In humans, insulin is the hormone responsible for glucose metabolism. Thyroxine (Choice **B**) is responsible for regulating the rate of metabolism. Adrenaline (Choice **C**) helps prepare the body for the fight-or-flight response by increasing heart rate, blood pressure, and so on. Androgen (Choice **D**) promotes the development of secondary male characteristics.

106. **D.** In human reproduction, fertilization takes place in the fallopian tube. The vagina (Choice **A**) receives the penis and sperm. The cervix (Choice **B**) is the constricted region at the base of the uterus. The uterus (Choice **C**) is a muscular organ within which the fetus develops.

107. **A.** The brain and spinal cord make up the human central nervous system. The nerves leading from the spinal cord to other regions of the body comprise the peripheral nervous system.

108. **B.** The cerebrum serves as the site in the brain for coordinating vision, hearing, speech, and smell. The cerebellum (Choice **B**) serves as the coordinating center for motor activity. The medulla (Choice **C**) serves as a passageway for nerves extending to and from the brain and controls automatic functions such as breathing, heart rate and digestion. The hypothalamus serves as a control center for hunger, thirst, body temperature, and blood pressure, as well as the synthesis of hormones that will be stored in the pituitary gland.

109. **D.** The number of kilocalories needed by the body to carry out normal functions is referred to as the basal metabolic rate.

110. **D.** A certain amount of fat is a necessary component of the human diet, as fat aids in the metabolism of vitamins A, D, and E; helps protect the internal organs from injury; and helps to insulate the body from cold temperatures.

111. **C.** When a person's diet is lacking in certain nutrients, leading to one or more deficiencies, that person is considered to be malnourished. If a person's diet is lacking in sufficient total calories, that person is said to be undernourished (Choice **B**) or starving (Choice **A**). If a person is classified as being impoverished (Choice **D**), that is an indication of an economic classification rather than a nutritional classification.

112. **B.** Macrophages are part of the human immune system that function by engulfing and destroying (phagocytizing) invading organisms and infectious agents.

113. **D.** Vaccines are usually quite effective because they act as antigens, while stimulating both the primary and secondary immune responses.

114. **C.** Antibiotics are only effective against bacteria; they are not effective against viruses or other infectious agents.

115. **D.** Anemia, vision problems, and bone deformities are caused by deficiencies in vitamins B, A, and D, respectively.

116. **D.** The spleen is composed primarily of lymph nodes and is responsible for destroying old red blood cells. The liver (Choice **A**) helps to sequester and remove toxins from the body. The pancreas (Choice **B**) and gall bladder (Choice **C**) produce enzymes that aid in digestion.

Reading Comprehension

117. **D.** They do not come from different parts of the body (Choice **A**), and although they can help regenerate tissue (Choice **B**), that is not the reason for this name. These cells are not directly used to treat anything (Choice **C**).

118. **C.** The length of time being kept alive (Choice **A**) does not categorize these cells nor does the number (Choice **D**). Primordial germ cells (Choice **B**) are a different type. The blactocysts are in an "embryonic" stage of development; hence, they are the "beginning" stage of development.

119. **B.** It is irrelevant that they give rise to eggs and sperm (Choice **A**); there is no textual evidence that they are easy to cultivate (Choice **D**). There is no evidence that their living for seven months was the reason for interest (Choice **B**).

120. **D.** Although their shape and proteins are interesting in connection with the other cells (**A, C**), it is the production of the enzyme telomerase that is significant. There is nothing said about their size (Choice **B**).

121. **D.** The last two sentences of the second paragraph contain all those facts.

122. **A.** To compromise something means to give up a little to get something. Hence, (Choice **A**) *enhance* and (Choice **D**) *compliment* are positive words. To differentiate (Choice **C**) means to be able to see the differences in something. The imprinting of the chemical would limit the use of the cells.

123. **A.** The last sentence indicates a positive feeling about this research. Therefore (Choice **B**) and (Choice **D**) are not appropriate. There is nothing mentioned about ethical concerns (Choice **C**).

124. **C.** When they talk about the elderly speaking in clichés and being rigid in their thinking, this eliminates creativity (Choice **D**). There is nothing mentioned about the ability to hear (Choice **B**) or the relationship of new ideas to previous ones (Choice **A**).

125. **C.** The passage indicates that deductive reasoning powers are affected. It doesn't talk about irritability (Choice **D**) or actually sleeping on the job (Choice **A**), nor does it mention that the memory is affected (Choice **B**).

126. **A.** The last sentence of the first paragraph states the fact. Choices **B, C,** and **D** are not even mentioned.

127. **B.** Acumen means mental sharpness and is not restricted to only math (Choice **D**), vocabulary (Choice **C**), or memory (Choice **A**).

128. **A.** The passage directly states that acquiring knowledge about things that interest you is the best way to keep mentally sharp. Thus, a sports person would enjoy reading about sports in a magazine devoted to such.

129. **D.** Choices **A, B,** and **C** are all found in the last paragraph. The last sentence of the passage is directly opposite of this statement (Choice **D**).

130. **C.** The word *medicinal* means acting like a remedy. The last sentence says that rest will restore people to full brain power much like a type of medicine. Choices **A, B,** and **D** are not supported by the passage.

131. **C.** The next sentence supports the idea that even good things in excess can be bad. The text does not talk about competition (Choice **A**), talents (Choice **B**), or the idea of drinking and its solutions (Choice **D**).

132. **D.** The author uses the information to help support the idea that the sudden concern for exercise is cyclical. There is no attempt to fully examine any type of dieting (choices **A** and **C**), and it is obviously not selling a product (Choice **B**).

133. **A.** There are no textual examples of exercising immediately after eating (Choice **B**). A certain month for exercise is not advocated (Choice **C**), and evidence of exercising on a regular basis is not bad (Choice **D**).

134. **A.** The definition directly follows the word.

135. **A.** The factors combine physical and emotional effects (Choice **B**), and there are problems with binge exercising (Choice **D**). It is stated that short bursts of activity could even raise cholesterol levels.

136. **C.** The third to the last sentence in the last paragraph states this fact.

137. **A.** The main idea of the passage is that not all exercise is good. Thus, there is skepticism. Guarded means having doubts.

138. **B.** There is no statement about life on other planets (Choice **A**) or that they all have stars (Choice **C**). Although there is a relationship between stars and planets, it is not stated in the first sentence (Choice **D**).

139. **B.** The word *architecture* is used as a metaphor. It does not literally mean building. It is referring to formations on other planets.

140. **D.** Nuclear fusion deals with energy outside and within the core of the planet. It does not measure the brightness (Choice **B**) or mention the expansion (Choice **C**) because the planet actually loses mass. The entire study of all the elements will reveal the stage of being a red giant (Choice **A**).

141. **C.** The term is defined immediately before the word.

142. **C.** The second to the last paragraph states this fact. Choices **A, B,** and **D** are factually incorrect.

143. **A.** The last sentence in the second to the last paragraph states "the abode in any system depends on what phase of the evolution of the star it is in."

144. **D.** Statements I, II, and III are all found directly in the text. Although the text does compare Venus and Mars, there is no conclusion about types of life on these planets (IV).

145. A. The phrase "highly unreliable" indicates that speculation is involved in determining information about dinosaurs. The passage is not focused on the quality of movies (Choice **B**). The statement in the text says that the retrieval of DNA is unreliable (choices **C** and **D**).

146. A. Although the knowledge of the genome provides a kind of pattern for the recreation, it isn't necessarily possible to actually re-create it (Choice **B**). The focus is not on only how to re-create nocturnal creatures (Choice **C**). Chromosome are what make up the DNA (Choice **D**).

147. B. The focus is not trying to convince you of the speed of the computer (Choice **D**) or the ability of people making mistakes (Choice **B**). The relationships between mammals is not relevant here (Choice **C**).

148. A. The first sentence of the second paragraph states this.

149. A. This is not a persuasive essay on film (Choice **D**), nor does it give examples of how they type DNA (Choice **C**). The purpose is not to evaluate human error, as it is to show the advantages to using computers.

150. B. The last sentence says "there would be new insights into the core biology," which indicates that new information might challenge the existing ones.

151. B. This is a basic expounding of information that demonstrates the worth of computer research. Hence, it is not critical (Choice **A**) nor amazed (Choice **C**) at anything. There is not anxiety in the tone, so there is no need to be relieved (Choice **D**).

152. D. Description and definition is found in the third paragraph.

153. C. The definition follows the word in the first sentence of the second paragraph.

154. D. The third paragraph states this fact.

155. C. Choices **A**, **B**, and **D** are all incorrect facts as evidenced in the third paragraph.

156. A. The trough is the "calm" before the hit of the wave so that you aren't safe (choices **B** and **C**), and there is no prediction as to whether the crest or the trough will hit a coastline first (Choice **D**).

157. C. Mentioning all the different countries indicates that cooperation is needed to create an effective future warning system.

158. B. The ending of the first paragraph and the last sentence of the passage support this idea.

159. B. The purpose of the people was to "protest federal restrictions" so they would not be supporting the manatees (Choice **A**), and it didn't have anything to do with voting (Choice **D**). There was no mention of a clash between federal and local politics (Choice **C**).

160. C. Disease, pollution, and feeding grounds were never included in the passage.

161. C. Both creatures need to surface in order to breathe.

162. B. It states that sea cows graze on vegetation and can be seen munching on people's lawns.

163. D. The passage never talks about age (Choice **A**), temperament (Choice **B**), or disease (Choice **C**) in the animals.

164. B. The unique scar patterns are like fingerprints.

165. D. The purpose is not to outlaw boats (Choice **A**) or to put value judgments on the developers (Choice **B**). There is no concrete solution (Choice **C**). It purely talks about the different perspectives on the problem.

Quantitative

166. A. $3\frac{1}{4} - 2\frac{1}{8} = \frac{13}{4} - \frac{17}{8} = \frac{26}{8} - \frac{17}{8} = \frac{9}{8} = 1\frac{1}{8}$ more cups of flour.

167. D. Let n represent the number of students in the band. Then $\frac{1}{3}n = 72$, so $n = 72 \times 3 = 216$.

168. C. The overtime rate is $8.40 \times 1.5 = 12.60. Five hours of overtime were completed, so the total earnings are (8.40×40) + (12.60×5) = $336 + $63 = $399.

169. C. Let p represent the amount of the paycheck. $\frac{4}{13}p = 26.80 so $p = $26.80 \times \frac{13}{4} = 87.10.

170. D. Let m represent the minutes of the phone calls. The monthly charge for the first plan is $20 + 0.08m$. The monthly charge for the second plan is $12 + 0.12m$. When the monthly charges are the same, $20 + 0.08m = 12 + 0.12m$. Solve for m to find the number of minutes both plans have at the same rate.

$$20 + 0.08m - 0.08m = 12 + 0.12m - 0.08m$$
$$20 = 12 + 0.04m$$
$$20 - 12 = 12 + 0.04m - 12$$
$$8 = 0.04m, \text{ so } m = \frac{8}{0.04} = \frac{800}{4} = 200 \text{ minutes.}$$

171. D. The percent of cars that are either red or black are $25\% + 30\% = 55\%$. The total cars that are either red or black is $260 \times 55\% = 143$.

172. C. The volume of a cylinder is $\pi r^2 h$. In the original cylinder, $\pi r^2 8 = 128\pi$, so $r^2 = \frac{128\pi}{8\pi} = 16$ and the radius, r, equals $\sqrt{16} = 4$. In the new cylinder, the radius is doubled to 8 and the height is cut in half to 4. The resulting volume is $\pi \cdot 8^2 \cdot 4 = 256\pi$ cm^3.

173. B. Let $\log_2 16 = x$. Then, by the definition of logarithm, $16 = 2^x$, so that $x = 4$.

174. D. The proportion $\frac{500 \text{ ft}}{\frac{1}{4} \text{ in}} = \frac{x \text{ ft}}{6 \text{ in}}$ can be used to find the number of actual distance. Cross-multiply.

$$500 \times 6 = \frac{1}{4}x, \text{ so } 3,000 = \frac{1}{4}x \text{ and } x = 3,000 \times 4 = 12,000 \text{ ft.}$$

175. B. If 1 gallon covers 400 square feet, then $\frac{2,225}{400} = 5.5625$ or 6 whole gallons are needed to cover 2,225 square feet.

176. B. If 2 pounds are lost each week, then after 7 weeks, $7 \times 2 = 14$ pounds are lost. The weight after 7 weeks is $209 - 14 = 195$ pounds.

177. B. Average is the total time divided by the total miles run. The total time is $17.5 + 22 + 9 = 48.5$ minutes. The total number of miles run is $3 + 4.5 + 2 = 9.5$. The average is $\frac{48.5}{9.5} = 5.1$ minutes per mile.

178. B. Since $f(x) = 9^x$, then $f\left(\frac{1}{2}\right) = 9^{\frac{1}{2}} = \sqrt{9} = 3$.

179. C. Substitute $\frac{5}{2}$ for a. $\frac{1}{a} = \frac{1}{\frac{5}{2}} = 1 \div \frac{5}{2} = 1 \cdot \frac{2}{5} = \frac{2}{5}$.

180. C. The hypotenuse of the triangle is the diameter of the circle. By the Pythagorean theorem, $d^2 = 6^2 + 8^2 = 36 + 64 = 100$. So $d = \sqrt{100} = 10$ and the radius is $\frac{10}{2} = 5$.

181. B. The sine function is positive in the first and second quadrants. The cosine function is negative in the second and third quadrants. Overall, then, $\angle a$ must lie in the second quadrant.

182. C. Slope is found by identifying two points on the line and finding the $\frac{\text{change in } y}{\text{change in } x}$. The points (0,0) and (5,2) form the slope $\frac{2-0}{5-0} = \frac{2}{5}$.

183. C. $\left(\frac{9}{4}\right)^{-\frac{1}{2}} = \left(\frac{4}{9}\right)^{\frac{1}{2}} = \sqrt{\frac{4}{9}} = \frac{2}{3}$.

184. B. We are told that $\log_5 x = 0$. By the definition of logarithms, this is equivalent to $x = 5^0$, which is equal to 1.

185. A. $\frac{1}{8} = \frac{1}{2^3} = 2^{-3}$ so $2^{b+3} = 2^{-3}$ and $b + 3 = -3$. Therefore, $b + 3 - 3 = -3 - 3 = -6$.

186. C. The derivative of $3x$ is 3, and the derivative of a constant is 0, so the derivative of $3x - 7$ is 3.

187. C. The x-coordinate of the minimum value can be found by taking the first derivative of the function and setting it equal to 0. Note that $y' = 2x - 4$ and that this expression is equal to 0 when $x = 2$. Note that, since the function is a parabola that "opens up," there is only one extreme point, and it is a minimum.

188. B. The volume of a cylinder is given by the formula $V = \pi r^2 h$, where r is the radius of the circular base and h is the height. Since $h = r$, $V = \pi r^2 r = \pi r^3$.

189. C. $\frac{1}{3}$ of $6\frac{1}{2}$ miles is $\frac{1}{3} \times 6\frac{1}{2} = \frac{1}{3} \times \frac{13}{2} = \frac{13}{6}$ miles walked. The remaining distance is

$6\frac{1}{2} - \frac{13}{6} = \frac{13}{2} - \frac{13}{6} = \frac{39}{6} - \frac{13}{6} = \frac{26}{6} = 4\frac{1}{3}$ miles.

190. D.

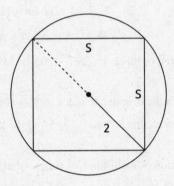

Find the difference between the area of the circle and the area of the square. The area of the circle is $\pi r^2 = \pi \cdot 2^2 = 4\pi$. The area of the square is s^2, where s represents the length of the square. The radius is half the length of the square's diagonal, so the diagonal is 4. By the Pythagorean theorem, $s^2 + s^2 = 4^2$. The equation $2s^2 = 16$ so $s^2 = 8$. The difference in area is $4\pi - 8$.

191. C. The only one of the three given angles for which $\cos x = -1$ is $x = 180°$.

192. B. 60% arrive to work by car, so $800 \times 60\% = 480$.

193. B. In order to solve the equation $c^{\frac{3}{2}} = 8$ for c, raise both sides of the equation to the $\frac{2}{3}$ power. The equation becomes $\left(c^{\frac{3}{2}}\right)^{\frac{2}{3}} = 8^{\frac{2}{3}}$, or $c = 8^{\frac{2}{3}} = \left(\sqrt[3]{8}\right)^2 = 2^2 = 4$.

194. A. The proportion $\frac{x}{6} = \frac{x+3}{10}$ can be used to find x. Cross-multiply. $10x = 6(x + 3)$ and $10x = 6x + 18$. Bring all x terms to one side by subtracting $6x$ from each side. Then $4x = 18$ and $x = \frac{18}{4} = 4.5$.

195. D. Using the ratio $\frac{\text{pages}}{\text{minutes}}$, the proportion $\frac{2}{3} = \frac{360}{x}$ can be used to find the time. Cross-multiply. $2x = 3 \times 360$ so $2x = 1,080$ and $x = \frac{1080}{2} = 540$ minutes. Convert minutes to hours. There are 60 minutes in 1 hour so $\frac{540}{60} = 9$ hours.

196. C. Rewrite $\frac{1}{x}$ as x^{-1}, and use the power rule for derivatives. We obtain $y'(x) = (-1)x^{-2} = -\frac{1}{x^2}$.

197. D. Simplifying $\sqrt{50} + 3\sqrt{72}$ yields $\sqrt{25 \cdot 2} + 3\sqrt{36 \cdot 2} = 5\sqrt{2} + 18\sqrt{2} = 23\sqrt{2}$.

198. A. Substituting the given values for r, s, and t into $3r^3 - 2s^2 + t$ gives $3(-1)^3 - 2(-2)^2 + (-3) = 3(-1) - 2(4) - 3 = -3 + 8 - 3 = 2$.

199. C. By the properties of logarithms, $\log\frac{C}{D} = \log C - \log D = 10 - 5 = 5$.

200. A. $\left(\sqrt{7}^{\pi}\right)^{-\frac{2}{\pi}} = \left(\sqrt{7}\right)^{\pi \times \left(-\frac{2}{\pi}\right)} = \left(\sqrt{7}\right)^{-2} = \frac{1}{\left(\sqrt{7}\right)^2} = \frac{1}{7}$.

201. C. The square of x is x^2. Three less than x is $x - 3$. Their product is $x^2(x - 3)$.

202. A. $\tan\theta\cos\theta\csc\theta = \frac{\sin\theta}{\cos\theta} \times \cos\theta \times \frac{1}{\sin\theta} = 1$.

203. B. Group the first two terms and the last two terms together. $(2a^3 - 4ab) + (ab - 2b^2)$. Factoring out common terms from each group gives $2a(a - 2b) + b(a - 2b)$. Common to both terms is $(a - 2b)$. Factoring this out results in $(a - 2b)(2a + b)$.

204. D. Using the correct order of operations, $-3(-4 - 5) - 2(-6) = -3(-9) - 2(-6) = 27 - (-12) = 27 + 12 = 39$

205. A. $\dfrac{6m - 2}{2} = -4$. So $3m - 1 = -4$. Solve for m by adding 1 to both sides. $3m - 1 + 1 = -4 + 1$ and $3m = -3$. Dividing both sides by 3 gives $m = -1$.

206. B. To find the period, set $2x$ equal to 2π, and solve for x. It is easy to see that $x = \pi$ is the period.

207. D. If $x = -3$ and $y = 2$, then $x^{2y} = (-3)^{2(2)} = (-3)^4 = 81$.

208. C. The first derivative of $y = 3x^2 + 5x + 2$ is $y'(x) = 6x + 5$. Thus, the second derivative is $y''(x) = 6$.

209. C. $\dfrac{1}{4}$ of the total cars, t, sold are luxury. Luxury cars sold = 360, so $\dfrac{1}{4}t = 360$ and $t = 360 \times 4 = 1{,}440$ total cars sold.

210. D. Factors of 8 are $2 \times 2 \times 2$; factors of 12 are $2 \times 2 \times 3$; factors of 20 are $2 \times 2 \times 5$. The least common multiple of 8, 12, and 20 is $2 \times 2 \times 2 \times 3 \times 5$ or 120.

211. C. If $0.08z = 6.4$ then $\dfrac{0.08z}{0.08} = \dfrac{6.4}{0.08}$. Moving the decimal two places to the right in both the numerator and denominator gives $z = \dfrac{640}{8} = 80$.

212. A. Rewrite the equation in slope-intercept form as $y = -2x + 7$. The slope is the coefficient of the x, which is -2.

213. A. We are asked to find the function whose first derivative is equal to $\sin x$. The function with this property is $y = -\cos x$.

Chemistry

214. A. This molecule (formaldehyde) has a permanent dipole between the carbon and the oxygen. It is not hydrogen bonding because, although it does have both oxygen and hydrogen, the hydrogen is not directly bonded to the oxygen.

215. D. There are two ways to go about solving this. The easiest is this; for any aqueous solution, pH+pOH = 14, so if pH = 6.0, then pOH = 8.0. Then, $[OH^-] = 10^{-pOH}$. Alternatively, $[H^+] = 10^{-pH}$, and then use $[H^+][OH^-] = 1 \times 10^{-14}$ (again, for any aqueous solution).

216. D. Natural processes want to decrease enthalpy (internal energy) and increase entropy (disorder). Any process that does both will be spontaneous at any temperature. If a process both increases enthalpy and decreases entropy, it will not be spontaneous. Using Gibb's free energy equation, $\triangle G = \triangle H - T\triangle S$, one can see that processes that increase both will be spontaneous at low temperatures, while processes that decrease both will be spontaneous at high temperatures.

217. D. Molarity is moles per liter, or millimoles per milliliter. Since we have 100 mL of 0.6 M Barium hydroxide, we have 60 mmol of barium hydroxide. From the reaction stoichiometry, we see that every 3 mmol of barium hydroxide are neutralized by 2 mmol of phosphoric acid. Therefore, we need 40 mmol of phosphoric acid. Since the solution strength of phosphoric acid is 0.2 mmol/mL, we need 200 mL of phosphoric acid.

218. A. Amides are actually acidic through resonance with the adjacent oxygen. Amines are the only alkaline groups in the list, provided, of course, they are not quaternary amines. Phenols are acidic, and esters are neutral.

219. C. This is not a law that has a name attached to it, but looking at the ideal gas law, PV = nRT, we can see that increasing temperature will increase pressure if n and V are constant.

220. C. We can shift the equilibrium to the right by increasing the concentration of oxygen. Pressure will have no effect on the equilibrium, however, since both oxygen and carbon monoxide are gases and at equivalent molar ratios on both sides of the equation.

221. C. Sodium chloride is a salt that is created from a strong acid (HCl) and a strong base (NaOH). Thus, the conjugate base (Cl^-) and the conjugate acid (Na^+) will both be weak, and therefore will not significantly change the pH of the water.

222. D. Here, lead (II) ion is picking up two electrons, taking its oxidation state from +2 to 0. Because it is gaining electrons, it is being reduced, making it the oxidizing agent. Chlorine is the reducing agent, and sulfate is a spectator ion.

223. A. The higher the molecular mass, the slower the gas will diffuse. In this list, CO_2 has the greatest molecular mass—all else being equal.

224. C. The general form of the reaction is shown in Figure 3. Notice that the alcohol ends up on the β carbon relative to the aldehyde functional group.

225. D. To figure out the Lewis Dot Structure (shown in Figure 4) you must use the extended octet rule. With a bond to two atoms, and one lone pair on sulfur, the parent shape of the 3 electron domain is trigonal planar, but the molecular shape is bent.

226. B. This is the older convention for nomenclature, but it's still commonly used for certain compounds. The *–ous* ending indicates that iron has the lesser of its common oxidation states, or +2 (if the oxidation state were +3, it would be ferric phosphate). The charge of the phosphate polyatomic ion is –3.

227. B. Aluminum has a +3 charge, while carbonate is –2. Therefore, the correct formula for aluminum carbonate is $Al_2(CO_3)_3$. This means that, in the compound, there are 2 Al with an atomic mass of 27 g/mol, 3 C with an atomic mass of 12 g/mol, and 9 O with an atomic mass of 16 g/mol.

228. C. From the bonding configuration, we see that there are 8 electrons in bonding orbitals, and 4 electrons in antibonding orbitals. Thus, the bond order is $(8–4) \div 2 = 2$.

229. C. The p subshell can hold up to six electrons, so the ground state would be $1s^2 2s^2 2p^5$.

230. B. Solids occur at higher pressure and lower temperature, liquids occur at high pressure and higher temperatures, and gases occur at any temperature if the pressure is low enough.

231. A. Standard covalent bonds are used in the formation of primary through tertiary amines, but the only way to form a quaternary amine is by having the amine behave as a Lewis base. By donating the lone pair electrons on the nitrogen to form another bond, the formal charge of the nitrogen becomes +1, making quaternary amines ionic compounds.

232. A. The parent chain has 8 carbon atoms, starting from the right and turning down at the fourth carbon.

233. D. Chiral compounds are particularly important in medicine, since enzymes are all chiral as well. Diastereomers do not rotate light because they have more than one chiral center that cancels out the rotation, and enantiomers are more correctly thought of as the specific forms of stereoisomers. A racemic mixture is a 50/50 mixture of enantiomers, so it will not rotate plane polarized light either.

234. C. This reaction is the Diels-Alder reaction, a very important reaction for ring closure. It might help to remember in these reactions that in the final ring, the pi bond ends up between where the two pi bonds were in the original diene.

235. A. There are a couple of things to remember here: The Aufbau process tells us that the 4f subshell fills *before* the 5d subshell; La is placed in the main body of the periodic chart as a "placeholder" for the lanthanide series. In addition, when you start filling f subshells, you have to drop back 2 shells from the first, and when filling d, you drop back 1 shell. Thus, starting with 6s, we next go to 4f (dropping back two shells from 6) then 5d (dropping back one shell from 6).

236. B. The fluorines are highly electron withdrawing (high electronegativities), making CF_3 group a "meta-director," or sometimes referred to as a "deactivating group."

237. D. Flourine is a strong electron withdrawing group, so its presence will increase the acidic nature of an acid by helping to stabilize the resulting anion. The closer flourine is to the carbon, the stronger the inductive effect will be.

238. B. Remember, as we add heat, the temperature remains constant for any phase change (melting, boiling, sublimation). Since this transition (flat part) occurs at a lower temperature than the other transition, it must be melting.

239. D. The magnesium is added to provide electrons, because it gives up electrons more easily than iron. This is called a "sacrificial anode," because it is cheaper to periodically replace the magnesium than it is to repair a rusting section of the pipe.

240. B. Solutions always freeze at a lower temperature than pure solvents; the correct colligative property should be freezing point depression.

241. C. To work out the Lewis-Dot structure, you need to remember two things: First, you will have to use the extended octet rule for this compound, and second, add one electron for the negative charge.

242. B. While it is true that you cannot further oxidize a ketone (without forming carbon dioxide), it is still less oxidized than carboxylic acid. The order of oxidation is alcohol < ketone, aldehyde < carboxylic acid.

243. B. Since EDTA is donating electrons to copper ions, it is a Lewis base. A ligand is a generic term for a Lewis base in a coordinate covalent compound, and a chelate is a ligand with more than one binding region. Polydentate means "multiple bonding regions" (EDTA forms six coordinate covalent bonds with copper).

244. B. In decomposition, you have a single reactant but two or more products, while replacement reactions always have at least two reactants and at least two products.

245. C. Stirring most definitely increases the *rate* of dissolution, but will not influence solubility, which is a measure of the maximum amount of solute that can be dissolved in a given solvent. Pressure will not influence *all* solubilities but will influence the solubility of a gas in a solid or liquid solvent.

246. D. The hydrogen atoms on atoms 3 and 4 are on opposite sides, making this a cis isomer. Hydrogen has the lowest priority, and the way the compound is drawn, it is already in the back. Looking from highest to lowest priorities, the rotation is counterclockwise, making this the S enantiomer.

247. D. The more carbons surrounding the carbocation, the more help there is in stabilizing that carbocation. Thus, a tertiary carbocation would be the most stable.

248. C. The only way an amine can become quaternary is by donating its lone pair electrons to act as a Lewis base, leaving the nitrogen with a formal charge of +1. Quaternary amines are less volatile than any other amine, which is why many drugs are listed as "HCl," which means the amine has been neutralized and converted into a quaternary amine to increase shelf life.

249. B. Condensation reactions (which involve the loss of water or other species to link two molecules together) is incredibly important in biochemical applications, since this is the basis for the formation of DNA, RNA, proteins, fats, and so on. The opposite reaction (hydrolosis—breaking down these compounds by addition of water) is equally important because of metabolic breakdown of these compounds from foodstuffs.

250. A. Flourine is the most electronegative element on the periodic chart; keeping this in mind will help you to remember this very important trend.

251. C. Esters, amides, and anhydrides are all formed by dehydration condensations with carboxylic acids (esters from alcohols, amides from amines, and anhydrides from another carboxylic acid).

252. C. Hydrate isomers exchange anions on the inner complex with water, linkage isomers change which atom is bound to the acceptor, while ionization isomers changes the ions inside the coordination sphere with those outside. These two compounds are not superimposable. The shorthand "en" stands for "ethylenediamine."

253. C. With 16 electrons, you should have come up with the bonding configuration $\sigma_{1s}^2 \sigma*_{1s}^2 \sigma_{2s}^2 \sigma*_{2s}^2 \sigma_{2p}^2 \pi_{2p}^4 \pi*_{2p}^2$. With 10 bonding and 6 antibonding, the bond order is $(10 - 6) \div 2 = 2$. With two unpaired electrons, this is paramagnetic.

254. A. Sodium comes from sodium hydroxide, which is a strong base; therefore, sodium is a weak conjugate acid. Acetate comes from acetic acid, a weak acid, making the acetate ion a strong conjugate acid. Because this salt is formed from a strong conjugate base and a weak conjugate acid, it will create an alkaline solution.

255. B. Aldehydes have shifts 9.5–10.5, ketones 2.1–2.6, and ethers 3.3–3.9.

256. B. The smaller the K_{sp}, the lower the solubility. This one was easy because all of them had the same Stoichiometric coefficients; beware if these ratios are *not* 1:1!

257. B. The reaction is 2 NaOH (s) + H_2SO_4 (aq) → Na_2SO_4 (aq) + 2 H_2O (l), so we can set up the problem as shown.

$$(200 \text{ mL acid})\left(\frac{1 \text{ L acid}}{1000 \text{ mL acid}}\right)\left(\frac{0.5 \text{ mol } H_2SO_4}{\text{L acid}}\right)\left(\frac{2 \text{ mol NaOH}}{1 \text{ mol } H_2SO_4}\right)\left(\frac{40 \text{ g NaOH}}{\text{mol NaOH}}\right) = 8.0 \text{ g NaOH}$$

258. A. The halogenation of benzene is an important reaction, because it demonstrates the unusual stability of aromatic compounds. Fluorination of a standard alkene would form a difluorocompound, but benzene will not.

259. B. This is a very important reaction to understand the cyclic form of sugars. The lone pair on the oxygen of the alcohol is attracted to the partial positive carbon of an aldehyde or ketone, forming a bond by kicking the pi bond off of the carbon. This is followed by a transfer (of sorts) of the hydrogen from the oxygen on the original alcohol, to the oxygen on the original aldehyde or ketone.

260. C. According to the Henderson-Hasselbalch equation, pH = pK_a+log([conj. base] ÷ [acid]). Since these are in the same solution, we can replace moles for concentration in this equation; thus, [conj. base] ÷ [acid] = 0.1 ÷ 0.01 = 10, and log10 = 1.

261. B. The number of orbitals increases by 2 as you go from one subshell to the next. Thus, there is 1 s orbital, (2 + 1 =) 3 p orbitals, (3 + 2 =) 5 d orbitals, (5 + 2 =) 7 f orbitals; thus, there would be 7 + 2 = 9 g orbitals.

262. B. β decay is the loss of an electron from a neutron in the nucleus. This does not change the atomic mass number of the element, but since there is one more proton created in this process, the atomic number increases by 1.

263. C. Halogens make pretty good leaving groups because they are happy in their ionic states. Carbon dioxide is often given off; what makes this such a good leaving group is the fact that it is a gas, so it is lost completely. Hydroxide is a weak conjugate acid, so it is stable in its ionic state, but hydrogen sulfide is a strong conjugate acid; it is not happy in its ionic state. Thus, it will form a stronger bond with carbon than the other choices.

264. B. This is Dalton's Law of Partial Pressures, which states that the total pressure of a mixture of gases is equal to the sum of the partial pressures of each component gas. Charles's law relates volume and temperature, Boyle's relates volume and pressure, and combined relates volume, temperature, and pressure.

265. A. The balanced reaction is 2 $Cr(NO_3)_3$ (aq) + 3 H_2SO_4 (aq) → $Cr_2(SO_4)_3$ (s) + 3 HNO_3 (aq).

266. B. A Lewis base acts by donating a lone pair of electrons, while an Arrhenius base acts by losing hydroxide.

267. A. Based on electronegativity, the carbon-oxygen bond is indeed polar, but since the molecule is linear (according to VSEPR), these dipoles will cancel out.

268. C. Whatever is being oxidized is the reducing agent. Oxidation means electrons are lost; mercury goes from a charge of 0 to +2, meaning it loses 2 electrons. Thus, mercury is the reducing agent.

269. A. sp hybridization is linear, sp^2 is trigonal planar, sp^3 is tetrahedral, sp^3d is trigonal bipyramidal, and sp^3d^2 is octahedral.

270. A. Changing the concentration does not seem to influence the reaction rate; thus, the rate law is r = k. First order would double the reaction rate as you double the concentration (r = k[A]), second order would quadruple the rate (r = k[A]^2), and third order would increase rate by a factor of 8 (r = k[A]^3).

Answer Sheet for PCAT Practice Test 2

(Remove This Sheet and Use It to Mark Your Answers)

Verbal Ability: Analogies

1 Ⓐ Ⓑ Ⓒ Ⓓ	11 Ⓐ Ⓑ Ⓒ Ⓓ	21 Ⓐ Ⓑ Ⓒ Ⓓ			
2 Ⓐ Ⓑ Ⓒ Ⓓ	12 Ⓐ Ⓑ Ⓒ Ⓓ	22 Ⓐ Ⓑ Ⓒ Ⓓ			
3 Ⓐ Ⓑ Ⓒ Ⓓ	13 Ⓐ Ⓑ Ⓒ Ⓓ	23 Ⓐ Ⓑ Ⓒ Ⓓ			
4 Ⓐ Ⓑ Ⓒ Ⓓ	14 Ⓐ Ⓑ Ⓒ Ⓓ	24 Ⓐ Ⓑ Ⓒ Ⓓ			
5 Ⓐ Ⓑ Ⓒ Ⓓ	15 Ⓐ Ⓑ Ⓒ Ⓓ	25 Ⓐ Ⓑ Ⓒ Ⓓ			
6 Ⓐ Ⓑ Ⓒ Ⓓ	16 Ⓐ Ⓑ Ⓒ Ⓓ	26 Ⓐ Ⓑ Ⓒ Ⓓ			
7 Ⓐ Ⓑ Ⓒ Ⓓ	17 Ⓐ Ⓑ Ⓒ Ⓓ	27 Ⓐ Ⓑ Ⓒ Ⓓ			
8 Ⓐ Ⓑ Ⓒ Ⓓ	18 Ⓐ Ⓑ Ⓒ Ⓓ	28 Ⓐ Ⓑ Ⓒ Ⓓ			
9 Ⓐ Ⓑ Ⓒ Ⓓ	19 Ⓐ Ⓑ Ⓒ Ⓓ	29 Ⓐ Ⓑ Ⓒ Ⓓ			
10 Ⓐ Ⓑ Ⓒ Ⓓ	20 Ⓐ Ⓑ Ⓒ Ⓓ				

Verbal Ability: Sentence Completions

30 Ⓐ Ⓑ Ⓒ Ⓓ	40 Ⓐ Ⓑ Ⓒ Ⓓ	50 Ⓐ Ⓑ Ⓒ Ⓓ
31 Ⓐ Ⓑ Ⓒ Ⓓ	41 Ⓐ Ⓑ Ⓒ Ⓓ	51 Ⓐ Ⓑ Ⓒ Ⓓ
32 Ⓐ Ⓑ Ⓒ Ⓓ	42 Ⓐ Ⓑ Ⓒ Ⓓ	52 Ⓐ Ⓑ Ⓒ Ⓓ
33 Ⓐ Ⓑ Ⓒ Ⓓ	43 Ⓐ Ⓑ Ⓒ Ⓓ	53 Ⓐ Ⓑ Ⓒ Ⓓ
34 Ⓐ Ⓑ Ⓒ Ⓓ	44 Ⓐ Ⓑ Ⓒ Ⓓ	54 Ⓐ Ⓑ Ⓒ Ⓓ
35 Ⓐ Ⓑ Ⓒ Ⓓ	45 Ⓐ Ⓑ Ⓒ Ⓓ	55 Ⓐ Ⓑ Ⓒ Ⓓ
36 Ⓐ Ⓑ Ⓒ Ⓓ	46 Ⓐ Ⓑ Ⓒ Ⓓ	56 Ⓐ Ⓑ Ⓒ Ⓓ
37 Ⓐ Ⓑ Ⓒ Ⓓ	47 Ⓐ Ⓑ Ⓒ Ⓓ	57 Ⓐ Ⓑ Ⓒ Ⓓ
38 Ⓐ Ⓑ Ⓒ Ⓓ	48 Ⓐ Ⓑ Ⓒ Ⓓ	58 Ⓐ Ⓑ Ⓒ Ⓓ
39 Ⓐ Ⓑ Ⓒ Ⓓ	49 Ⓐ Ⓑ Ⓒ Ⓓ	

Biology

59 Ⓐ Ⓑ Ⓒ Ⓓ	69 Ⓐ Ⓑ Ⓒ Ⓓ	79 Ⓐ Ⓑ Ⓒ Ⓓ	89 Ⓐ Ⓑ Ⓒ Ⓓ	99 Ⓐ Ⓑ Ⓒ Ⓓ	109 Ⓐ Ⓑ Ⓒ Ⓓ
60 Ⓐ Ⓑ Ⓒ Ⓓ	70 Ⓐ Ⓑ Ⓒ Ⓓ	80 Ⓐ Ⓑ Ⓒ Ⓓ	90 Ⓐ Ⓑ Ⓒ Ⓓ	100 Ⓐ Ⓑ Ⓒ Ⓓ	110 Ⓐ Ⓑ Ⓒ Ⓓ
61 Ⓐ Ⓑ Ⓒ Ⓓ	71 Ⓐ Ⓑ Ⓒ Ⓓ	81 Ⓐ Ⓑ Ⓒ Ⓓ	91 Ⓐ Ⓑ Ⓒ Ⓓ	101 Ⓐ Ⓑ Ⓒ Ⓓ	111 Ⓐ Ⓑ Ⓒ Ⓓ
62 Ⓐ Ⓑ Ⓒ Ⓓ	72 Ⓐ Ⓑ Ⓒ Ⓓ	82 Ⓐ Ⓑ Ⓒ Ⓓ	92 Ⓐ Ⓑ Ⓒ Ⓓ	102 Ⓐ Ⓑ Ⓒ Ⓓ	112 Ⓐ Ⓑ Ⓒ Ⓓ
63 Ⓐ Ⓑ Ⓒ Ⓓ	73 Ⓐ Ⓑ Ⓒ Ⓓ	83 Ⓐ Ⓑ Ⓒ Ⓓ	93 Ⓐ Ⓑ Ⓒ Ⓓ	103 Ⓐ Ⓑ Ⓒ Ⓓ	113 Ⓐ Ⓑ Ⓒ Ⓓ
64 Ⓐ Ⓑ Ⓒ Ⓓ	74 Ⓐ Ⓑ Ⓒ Ⓓ	84 Ⓐ Ⓑ Ⓒ Ⓓ	94 Ⓐ Ⓑ Ⓒ Ⓓ	104 Ⓐ Ⓑ Ⓒ Ⓓ	114 Ⓐ Ⓑ Ⓒ Ⓓ
65 Ⓐ Ⓑ Ⓒ Ⓓ	75 Ⓐ Ⓑ Ⓒ Ⓓ	85 Ⓐ Ⓑ Ⓒ Ⓓ	95 Ⓐ Ⓑ Ⓒ Ⓓ	105 Ⓐ Ⓑ Ⓒ Ⓓ	115 Ⓐ Ⓑ Ⓒ Ⓓ
66 Ⓐ Ⓑ Ⓒ Ⓓ	76 Ⓐ Ⓑ Ⓒ Ⓓ	86 Ⓐ Ⓑ Ⓒ Ⓓ	96 Ⓐ Ⓑ Ⓒ Ⓓ	106 Ⓐ Ⓑ Ⓒ Ⓓ	116 Ⓐ Ⓑ Ⓒ Ⓓ
67 Ⓐ Ⓑ Ⓒ Ⓓ	77 Ⓐ Ⓑ Ⓒ Ⓓ	87 Ⓐ Ⓑ Ⓒ Ⓓ	97 Ⓐ Ⓑ Ⓒ Ⓓ	107 Ⓐ Ⓑ Ⓒ Ⓓ	
68 Ⓐ Ⓑ Ⓒ Ⓓ	78 Ⓐ Ⓑ Ⓒ Ⓓ	88 Ⓐ Ⓑ Ⓒ Ⓓ	98 Ⓐ Ⓑ Ⓒ Ⓓ	108 Ⓐ Ⓑ Ⓒ Ⓓ	

Reading Comprehension

117 Ⓐ Ⓑ Ⓒ Ⓓ	127 Ⓐ Ⓑ Ⓒ	137 Ⓐ Ⓑ Ⓒ Ⓓ	147 Ⓐ Ⓑ Ⓒ Ⓓ	157 Ⓐ Ⓑ Ⓒ Ⓓ
118 Ⓐ Ⓑ Ⓒ Ⓓ	128 Ⓐ Ⓑ Ⓒ Ⓓ	138 Ⓐ Ⓑ Ⓒ Ⓓ	148 Ⓐ Ⓑ Ⓒ Ⓓ	158 Ⓐ Ⓑ Ⓒ Ⓓ
119 Ⓐ Ⓑ Ⓒ Ⓓ	129 Ⓐ Ⓑ Ⓒ Ⓓ	139 Ⓐ Ⓑ Ⓒ Ⓓ	149 Ⓐ Ⓑ Ⓒ Ⓓ	159 Ⓐ Ⓑ Ⓒ Ⓓ
120 Ⓐ Ⓑ Ⓒ Ⓓ	130 Ⓐ Ⓑ Ⓒ Ⓓ	140 Ⓐ Ⓑ Ⓒ Ⓓ	150 Ⓐ Ⓑ Ⓒ Ⓓ	160 Ⓐ Ⓑ Ⓒ Ⓓ
121 Ⓐ Ⓑ Ⓒ Ⓓ	131 Ⓐ Ⓑ Ⓒ Ⓓ	141 Ⓐ Ⓑ Ⓒ Ⓓ	151 Ⓐ Ⓑ Ⓒ Ⓓ	161 Ⓐ Ⓑ Ⓒ Ⓓ
122 Ⓐ Ⓑ Ⓒ Ⓓ	132 Ⓐ Ⓑ Ⓒ Ⓓ	142 Ⓐ Ⓑ Ⓒ Ⓓ	152 Ⓐ Ⓑ Ⓒ Ⓓ	162 Ⓐ Ⓑ Ⓒ Ⓓ
123 Ⓐ Ⓑ Ⓒ Ⓓ	133 Ⓐ Ⓑ Ⓒ Ⓓ	143 Ⓐ Ⓑ Ⓒ Ⓓ	153 Ⓐ Ⓑ Ⓒ Ⓓ	163 Ⓐ Ⓑ Ⓒ Ⓓ
124 Ⓐ Ⓑ Ⓒ Ⓓ	134 Ⓐ Ⓑ Ⓒ Ⓓ	144 Ⓐ Ⓑ Ⓒ Ⓓ	154 Ⓐ Ⓑ Ⓒ Ⓓ	164 Ⓐ Ⓑ Ⓒ Ⓓ
125 Ⓐ Ⓑ Ⓒ Ⓓ	135 Ⓐ Ⓑ Ⓒ Ⓓ	145 Ⓐ Ⓑ Ⓒ Ⓓ	155 Ⓐ Ⓑ Ⓒ Ⓓ	165 Ⓐ Ⓑ Ⓒ Ⓓ
126 Ⓐ Ⓑ Ⓒ Ⓓ	136 Ⓐ Ⓑ Ⓒ Ⓓ	146 Ⓐ Ⓑ Ⓒ Ⓓ	156 Ⓐ Ⓑ Ⓒ Ⓓ	

Quantitative Ability

166 Ⓐ Ⓑ Ⓒ Ⓓ	176 Ⓐ Ⓑ Ⓒ Ⓓ	186 Ⓐ Ⓑ Ⓒ Ⓓ	196 Ⓐ Ⓑ Ⓒ Ⓓ	206 Ⓐ Ⓑ Ⓒ Ⓓ
167 Ⓐ Ⓑ Ⓒ Ⓓ	177 Ⓐ Ⓑ Ⓒ Ⓓ	187 Ⓐ Ⓑ Ⓒ Ⓓ	197 Ⓐ Ⓑ Ⓒ Ⓓ	207 Ⓐ Ⓑ Ⓒ Ⓓ
168 Ⓐ Ⓑ Ⓒ Ⓓ	178 Ⓐ Ⓑ Ⓒ Ⓓ	188 Ⓐ Ⓑ Ⓒ Ⓓ	198 Ⓐ Ⓑ Ⓒ Ⓓ	208 Ⓐ Ⓑ Ⓒ Ⓓ
169 Ⓐ Ⓑ Ⓒ Ⓓ	179 Ⓐ Ⓑ Ⓒ Ⓓ	189 Ⓐ Ⓑ Ⓒ Ⓓ	199 Ⓐ Ⓑ Ⓒ Ⓓ	209 Ⓐ Ⓑ Ⓒ Ⓓ
170 Ⓐ Ⓑ Ⓒ Ⓓ	180 Ⓐ Ⓑ Ⓒ Ⓓ	190 Ⓐ Ⓑ Ⓒ Ⓓ	200 Ⓐ Ⓑ Ⓒ Ⓓ	210 Ⓐ Ⓑ Ⓒ Ⓓ
171 Ⓐ Ⓑ Ⓒ Ⓓ	181 Ⓐ Ⓑ Ⓒ Ⓓ	191 Ⓐ Ⓑ Ⓒ Ⓓ	201 Ⓐ Ⓑ Ⓒ Ⓓ	211 Ⓐ Ⓑ Ⓒ Ⓓ
172 Ⓐ Ⓑ Ⓒ Ⓓ	182 Ⓐ Ⓑ Ⓒ Ⓓ	192 Ⓐ Ⓑ Ⓒ Ⓓ	202 Ⓐ Ⓑ Ⓒ Ⓓ	212 Ⓐ Ⓑ Ⓒ Ⓓ
173 Ⓐ Ⓑ Ⓒ Ⓓ	183 Ⓐ Ⓑ Ⓒ Ⓓ	193 Ⓐ Ⓑ Ⓒ Ⓓ	203 Ⓐ Ⓑ Ⓒ Ⓓ	
174 Ⓐ Ⓑ Ⓒ Ⓓ	184 Ⓐ Ⓑ Ⓒ Ⓓ	194 Ⓐ Ⓑ Ⓒ Ⓓ	204 Ⓐ Ⓑ Ⓒ Ⓓ	
175 Ⓐ Ⓑ Ⓒ Ⓓ	185 Ⓐ Ⓑ Ⓒ Ⓓ	195 Ⓐ Ⓑ Ⓒ Ⓓ	205 Ⓐ Ⓑ Ⓒ Ⓓ	

Chemistry

214 Ⓐ Ⓑ Ⓒ Ⓓ	224 Ⓐ Ⓑ Ⓒ Ⓓ	234 Ⓐ Ⓑ Ⓒ Ⓓ	244 Ⓐ Ⓑ Ⓒ Ⓓ	254 Ⓐ Ⓑ Ⓒ Ⓓ	264 Ⓐ Ⓑ Ⓒ Ⓓ
215 Ⓐ Ⓑ Ⓒ Ⓓ	225 Ⓐ Ⓑ Ⓒ Ⓓ	235 Ⓐ Ⓑ Ⓒ Ⓓ	245 Ⓐ Ⓑ Ⓒ Ⓓ	255 Ⓐ Ⓑ Ⓒ Ⓓ	265 Ⓐ Ⓑ Ⓒ Ⓓ
216 Ⓐ Ⓑ Ⓒ Ⓓ	226 Ⓐ Ⓑ Ⓒ Ⓓ	236 Ⓐ Ⓑ Ⓒ Ⓓ	246 Ⓐ Ⓑ Ⓒ Ⓓ	256 Ⓐ Ⓑ Ⓒ Ⓓ	266 Ⓐ Ⓑ Ⓒ Ⓓ
217 Ⓐ Ⓑ Ⓒ Ⓓ	227 Ⓐ Ⓑ Ⓒ Ⓓ	237 Ⓐ Ⓑ Ⓒ Ⓓ	247 Ⓐ Ⓑ Ⓒ Ⓓ	257 Ⓐ Ⓑ Ⓒ Ⓓ	267 Ⓐ Ⓑ Ⓒ Ⓓ
218 Ⓐ Ⓑ Ⓒ Ⓓ	228 Ⓐ Ⓑ Ⓒ Ⓓ	238 Ⓐ Ⓑ Ⓒ Ⓓ	248 Ⓐ Ⓑ Ⓒ Ⓓ	258 Ⓐ Ⓑ Ⓒ Ⓓ	268 Ⓐ Ⓑ Ⓒ Ⓓ
219 Ⓐ Ⓑ Ⓒ Ⓓ	229 Ⓐ Ⓑ Ⓒ Ⓓ	239 Ⓐ Ⓑ Ⓒ Ⓓ	249 Ⓐ Ⓑ Ⓒ Ⓓ	259 Ⓐ Ⓑ Ⓒ Ⓓ	269 Ⓐ Ⓑ Ⓒ Ⓓ
220 Ⓐ Ⓑ Ⓒ Ⓓ	230 Ⓐ Ⓑ Ⓒ Ⓓ	240 Ⓐ Ⓑ Ⓒ Ⓓ	250 Ⓐ Ⓑ Ⓒ Ⓓ	260 Ⓐ Ⓑ Ⓒ Ⓓ	270 Ⓐ Ⓑ Ⓒ Ⓓ
221 Ⓐ Ⓑ Ⓒ Ⓓ	231 Ⓐ Ⓑ Ⓒ Ⓓ	241 Ⓐ Ⓑ Ⓒ Ⓓ	251 Ⓐ Ⓑ Ⓒ Ⓓ	261 Ⓐ Ⓑ Ⓒ Ⓓ	
222 Ⓐ Ⓑ Ⓒ Ⓓ	232 Ⓐ Ⓑ Ⓒ Ⓓ	242 Ⓐ Ⓑ Ⓒ Ⓓ	252 Ⓐ Ⓑ Ⓒ Ⓓ	262 Ⓐ Ⓑ Ⓒ Ⓓ	
223 Ⓐ Ⓑ Ⓒ Ⓓ	233 Ⓐ Ⓑ Ⓒ Ⓓ	243 Ⓐ Ⓑ Ⓒ Ⓓ	253 Ⓐ Ⓑ Ⓒ Ⓓ	263 Ⓐ Ⓑ Ⓒ Ⓓ	

Critical Thinking Essay

Write your essay on lined paper.

CUT HERE

Verbal Ability: Analogies

Directions: Select the word that best completes the analogy.

1. STAR : CONSTELLATION :: SKIRMISH:

   A. stellar
   B. compromise
   C. insurrection
   D. celestial

2. INDELIBLE : PERMANENT :: ENDURING:

   A. illegible
   B. pliable
   C. erasable
   D. fixed

3. EUPHORIC : HAPPINESS :: RAGE:

   A. unhappiness
   B. anger
   C. depression
   D. ardor

4. AUSPICIOUS : FAVORABLE :: COPIOUS:

   A. careful
   B. predictable
   C. diligent
   D. plentiful

5. CABAL : COLLUSION :: JUNTA:

   A. plan
   B. plot
   C. fight
   D. compromise

6. ARID : TASTE :: PUNGENT:

   A. sight
   B. sound
   C. touch
   D. smell

7. ACCEDE : ACQUIESCE :: CONCUR:

   A. create
   B. occur
   C. agree
   D. disagree

8. CRAVEN : COWARD :: WISE:

   A. benefactor
   B. philanderer
   C. misanthrope
   D. sage

9. VERBOSE : SUCCINCT :: IRRATIONAL:

   A. legal
   B. logical
   C. detailed
   D. salient

10. CAUSTIC : RUDE :: PETULANT:

   A. pertinent
   B. repetitious
   C. impervious
   D. impatient

11. ELATED : HAPPY :: TIRADE:

   A. critique
   B. exhaustive
   C. compliant
   D. impertinent

12. PHILANTHROPIST : MUNIFICENT :: TRAITOR:

   A. wise
   B. deceptive
   C. perfidious
   D. tyrannical

GO ON TO THE NEXT PAGE

13. EXPERT : SKILL :: NEOPHYTE:

- **A.** inexperience
- **B.** enthusiasm
- **C.** ambidexterity
- **D.** rigidity

14. SHOWY : FLAMBOYANT :: CAMPFIRE:

- **A.** candle
- **B.** match
- **C.** fragrance
- **D.** conflagration

15. GOURMAND : FOOD :: CONNOISSEUR:

- **A.** clothes
- **B.** wine
- **C.** music
- **D.** perfume

16. FACETIOUS : LAUGH :: LACHRYMOSE:

- **A.** grimace
- **B.** chortle
- **C.** guffaw
- **D.** cry

17. GREGARIOUS : ALOOF :: LOQUACIOUS:

- **A.** talkative
- **B.** intelligent
- **C.** repetitive
- **D.** reticent

18. INTREPID : DAUNTLESS :: INEXORABLE:

- **A.** unrelenting
- **B.** fearful
- **C.** fearless
- **D.** conciliatory

19. BOASTFUL : BRAGGART :: BIASED:

- **A.** pedagogue
- **B.** philanthropist
- **C.** anthropologist
- **D.** bigot

20. ARMORY : WEAPONS :: AVIARY:

- **A.** planes
- **B.** insects
- **C.** birds
- **D.** reptiles

21. THESAURUS : SYNONYMS :: ATLAS:

- **A.** antonyms
- **B.** pronunciations
- **C.** facts
- **D.** maps

22. LEGACY : WILL :: BEQUEST:

- **A.** law
- **B.** principles
- **C.** fee
- **D.** codicil

23. CANDID : DECEPTIVE :: FRANK:

- **A.** duplicitous
- **B.** doubtful
- **C.** caring
- **D.** friendly

24. CONTIGUOUS : ADJACENT :: ABUT:

- **A.** parallel
- **B.** juxtapose
- **C.** circle
- **D.** continue

25. INITIATE : CONSUMMATE :: COMMENCE:

- **A.** consumer
- **B.** graduate
- **C.** terminate
- **D.** continue

26. ODOMETER : DISTANCE :: SCALE:

- **A.** height
- **B.** length
- **C.** temperature
- **D.** weight

27. QUIXOTIC : IDEALISM :: REALISTIC:

    A. naturalism
    B. optimism
    C. pragmatism
    D. pessimism

28. DIVULGE : CONCEAL :: IMPART:

    A. release
    B. hide
    C. reveal
    D. talk

29. DILETTANTE : DABBLER :: EXPERT:

    A. teacher
    B. tinker
    C. master
    D. novice

GO ON TO THE NEXT PAGE

Verbal Ability: Sentence Completions

Directions: Select the word or words that best complete the sentence.

---

30. The pleasure derived from eating homegrown vegetables outweighs the _____ tasks of maintaining the garden.

    A. onerous
    B. delightful
    C. horrendous
    D. deciduous

31. The _____ of a wealthy family is proverbially born with a silver spoon in his mouth.

    A. bachelor
    B. descendent
    C. minister
    D. scion

32. A _____ feature of Frank Lloyd Wright's building was the use of cantilevers; however, lacking proper support, many of them are _____.

    A. modest . . . . . reliable
    B. grammatical . . . . . logical
    C. salient . . . . . unstable
    D. noticeable . . . . . delightful

33. Because of their _____, Minnesota and St. Paul are known as the Twin Cities.

    A. dissimilarity
    B. hostility
    C. consanguinity
    D. proximity

34. The governor's proposal for free universal health care for all residents of the state was _____ and _____.

    A. utopian . . . . . impractical
    B. welcome . . . . . hostile
    C. discouraging . . . . . useful
    D. conceptual . . . . . considerate

35. Because their personalities were not _____, their relationship did not last.

    A. derisive
    B. contemplative
    C. compatible
    D. cheerful

36. Although it is _____ to eat turkey for Thanksgiving dinner, the source of this custom is _____.

    A. customary . . . . . obvious
    B. unacceptable . . . . . mysterious
    C. gluttonous . . . . . eccentric
    D. traditional . . . . . unknown

37. Making _____ about someone's appearance demonstrates insensitivity and rudeness.

    A. pleasant
    B. gratuitous
    C. incongruous
    D. subtle

38. The Earth is not a perfect sphere; it _____ at the equator and slightly _____ at the poles.

    A. bulges . . . . . flattens
    B. moves . . . . . fattens
    C. connects . . . . . corrects
    D. retards . . . . . tumbles

39. The secret agent's mission required her to _____ the rebel's territory.

    A. compensate
    B. conquer
    C. infiltrate
    D. torture

40. Because Galileo's discoveries contradicted the teachings of religious authorities, he was condemned as a _____.

    A. heretic
    B. idolater
    C. zealot
    D. hedonist

41. When products in a category have similar features, price probably will _____ which brand _____ the market.

    A. determine . . . . . dominates
    B. conceal . . . . . lowers
    C. sell . . . . . enters
    D. produce . . . . . alters

42. Patience, a/an _____ part of a parent's role, does not come easily to some.

   A. articulate
   B. stoic
   C. indispensable
   D. glaring

43. A/an _____ of a home's contents, including appliances, furniture, clothing, jewelry, collectibles, and electronic items, should be completed for insurance purposes.

   A. inventory
   B. collection
   C. destruction
   D. memorandum

44. The committee voted to _____ the membership requirements, but the board of directors overruled the vote, and the requirements remained in place.

   A. consider
   B. remember
   C. rescind
   D. enhance

45. Studying mistakes and errors in logic can be _____ because the recognition and correction of errors provides _____ instruction.

   A. futile . . . . . philosophical
   B. instructive . . . . . remedial
   C. shameful . . . . . exacerbating
   D. pragmatic . . . . . determinate

46. The city council _____ vote on the zoning measure until the next meeting because two members were absent.

   A. determined
   B. deposited
   C. deferred
   D. directed

47. According to the United States Constitution, it is _____ that president be a person born in the United States.

   A. possible
   B. contemplated
   C. discussed
   D. mandatory

48. While raising the minimum wage by 25 cents per hour may seem to be a/an _____ amount, some employers _____ it will raise their costs excessively.

   A. inconsequential . . . . . contend
   B. expensive . . . . . lower
   C. minute . . . . . stabilize
   D. satisfactory . . . . . retard

49. Without both _____ and talent, _____ to a career as an opera singer is futile.

   A. perseverance . . . . . aspiring
   B. pretentiousness . . . . . clinging
   C. obscurity . . . . . pretending
   D. fortune . . . . . dedicating

50. After the cake collapsed in the oven, the cook _____ the recipe.

   A. increased
   B. fermented
   C. consolidated
   D. amended

51. High humidity and dropping barometric pressure were the _____ of the approaching hurricane.

   A. antithesis
   B. precursors
   C. meaning
   D. controls

52. The spring day's _____ atmosphere and sense of calm were _____ by the tragic events that would occur.

   A. benign . . . . . subverted
   B. restless . . . . . enhanced
   C. pleasant . . . . . complemented
   D. luxurious . . . . . noticed

53. In the novel *Great Expectations*, Pip searches for the _____ who has paid for his education.

   A. miser
   B. proletarian
   C. parvenu
   D. benefactor

PCAT Practice Test 2

GO ON TO THE NEXT PAGE

54. Although it appeared as if the amount of work to do was _____, that was a/an _____, since each task could be accomplished in a short time.

    A. troublesome . . . . . lie

    B. overwhelming . . . . . illusion

    C. minute . . . . . delusion

    D. voluminous . . . . . certitude

55. The glorious, gold-encrusted throne appearing on the stage was a/an _____, merely a wooden chair covered with metallic paint.

    A. relic

    B. idol

    C. antique

    D. sham

56. Having stuffed themselves with food and drink at the _____ dinner, the guests were _____.

    A. bountiful . . . . . replete

    B. generous . . . . . unsatisfied

    C. meager . . . . . nauseous

    D. delicious . . . . . concerned

57. Scorned by all who had known him, the gunfighter became a _____ on the western frontier.

    A. patriarch

    B. posse

    C. pariah

    D. potentate

58. She tried to budget her money, but her _____ for shopping led her into debt.

    A. talent

    B. predilection

    C. consideration

    D. distaste

Biology

Directions: Select the choice that best answers the following questions.

59. Which of the following statements best describes the process of photosynthesis?

   A. Chemical energy, in the form of starch, is converted to light energy.

   B. Chemical energy, in the form of glucose, is converted to light energy.

   C. Light energy is converted to chemical energy, in the form of glucose.

   D. Light energy is converted to chemical energy, in the form of starch.

60. Which of the following statements regarding cellular respiration is incorrect?

   A. Plants do not carry out cellular respiration; they use photosynthesis instead.

   B. Cellular respiration takes place in the mitochondria of cells.

   C. Cellular respiration produces energy (ATP) from the breakdown of glucose.

   D. Cellular respiration is most efficient when sufficient oxygen is present.

61. In a typical food chain, autotrophic organisms are referred to as _____, while heterotrophic organisms are referred to as

   _____.

   A. decomposers; producers

   B. producers; consumers

   C. producers; decomposers

   D. consumers; decomposers

62. When a toxin enters the food chain, it usually

   A. does not move up the food chain.

   B. becomes less and less concentrated as it moves up through the food chain.

   C. becomes more and more concentrated as it moves up through the food chain.

   D. is broken down immediately by the decomposers.

63. Most of the carbon in an ecosystem is cycled through in the form of

   A. coal.

   B. glucose.

   C. starch.

   D. carbon dioxide.

64. A tapeworm living inside a human intestine would be an example of which type of interspecific relationship?

   A. predation

   B. parasitism

   C. mutualism

   D. commnensalism

65. The DNA double helix is composed of

   A. a backbone of alternating sugars and nitrogenous bases held together by paired phosphate groups.

   B. a backbone of alternating phosphate groups and nitrogenous bases held together by paired sugars.

   C. a backbone of alternating phosphate groups and sugars held together by paired nitrogenous bases.

   D. a backbone of alternating deoxyribose and ribose sugars held together by paired nitrogenous bases.

66. The process in which the genetic information encoded in a DNA molecule is transferred to a messenger RNA molecule is referred to as

   A. DNA replication.

   B. transcription.

   C. translation.

   D. protein synthesis.

67. The genetic makeup of an individual is referred to as his or her

   A. genetic code.

   B. phenotype.

   C. genotype.

   D. gene pool.

GO ON TO THE NEXT PAGE

89

68. If a person has one allele coding for brown eye color and one allele coding for blue eye color, that person is said to be

    A. heterozygous for eye color.
    B. homozygous for eye color.
    C. dominant for eye color.
    D. recessive for eye color.

69. The existence of the "M," "N," and "MN" blood groups in humans is an example of

    A. complete dominance.
    B. complete recessiveness.
    C. incomplete dominance.
    D. co-dominance.

70. Which of the following combinations of children could be produced by a woman with type-AB blood and a man with type-O blood?

    A. AB only
    B. O only
    C. AB and O
    D. A and B

71. The characterization of an individual's DNA by restriction analysis and gel electrophoresis is referred to as a

    A. PCR product.
    B. DNA probe.
    C. DNA fingerprint.
    D. restriction blot.

72. A transgenic organism is

    A. an organism that has had all of its DNA removed and replaced with DNA from another organism.
    B. an organism in which genes from a different organism have been inserted into its DNA.
    C. an organism produced by in vitro fertilization.
    D. an organism that has undergone gene therapy.

73. Which of the following statements is NOT one of the observations upon which Darwin based his theory of evolution?

    A. Individuals in a population vary extensively in their characteristics.
    B. Variation among individuals in a population is non-heritable (cannot be passed on from parent to offspring).
    C. Natural resources are limited.
    D. When members of a population reproduce, they tend to produce more offspring than is necessary to maintain the population size over time.

74. Which of the following forces affecting evolution would most likely lead to a significant decrease in genetic diversity with a population?

    A. natural selection
    B. mutation
    C. genetic drift
    D. random mating

75. Which of the following statements regarding cell structure is incorrect?

    A. Eukaryotic cells tend to be more complex than prokaryotic cells.
    B. Eukaryotic cells contain a nucleus and well-defined organelles.
    C. Prokaryotic cells do not contain a nuclear membrane.
    D. Prokaryotic cells have well-defined organelles, including a nucleus.

76. If you were observing a piece of tissue of unknown origin under the microscope, which of the following characteristics would indicate the cell is most likely from plant tissue?

    A. lack of mitochondria
    B. presence of mitochondria
    C. lack of a cell wall
    D. presence of a large central vacuole

77. Human nerve cells are referred to as

    A. neurons.
    B. axons.
    C. dendrites.
    D. effectors.

78. If cells from human tissue were placed in saltwater, what would you most likely observe when viewing them under the microscope?

  A. The cells would swell and burst.
  B. The cells would swell until turgor pressure from the cell wall caused them to stop swelling.
  C. The cells would maintain their normal size and shape.
  D. The cells would shrivel up.

79. Which of the following represents the products of meiosis from a parent cell containing 36 chromosomes?

  A. 2 cells, each with 36 chromosome
  B. 2 cells, each with 18 chromosomes
  C. 4 cells, each with 36 chromosomes
  D. 4 cells, each with 18 chromosomes

80. Which of the following statements regarding mitosis is incorrect?

  A. Mitosis occurs in most somatic cells.
  B. Mitosis gives rise to unique daughter cells.
  C. Mitosis is involved in growth of an individual.
  D. Mitosis produces two daughter cells from one original parent cell.

81. After undergoing DNA replication (synthesis) in preparation for cell division, a cell that started out with four chromosomes would end up with

  A. two chromosomes, each consisting of four sister chromatids
  B. eight chromosomes, each consisting of one sister chromatid
  C. four chromosomes, each consisting of one sister chromatid
  D. four chromosomes, each consisting of two sister chromatids

82. Which of the following events does not lead to increased genetic variation in a population?

  A. crossing over during mitosis
  B. crossing over during meiosis I
  C. independent assortment of chromosomes during meiosis II
  D. random mutation

83. In animals, meiosis gives rise to _____, while in plants, meiosis gives rise to _____.

  A. spores; spores
  B. gametes; gametes
  C. gametes; spores
  D. spores; gametes

84. Which of the following conditions would improve the reproductive potential of a bacterial culture?

  A. greatly increasing the temperature
  B. greatly decreasing the temperature
  C. increasing the nutrient content of the culture
  D. adding salts to the culture

85. The normal bacteria that live in the human gut do which of the following?

  A. compete with foreign bacteria for food
  B. produce antimicrobial substances
  C. stimulate the immune system
  D. all of the above

86. Which of the following mechanisms of defense against microbes would be considered an active, rather than a passive, response?

  A. inflammation
  B. production of stomach acid
  C. presence of normal gut bacteria
  D. production of lysozyme in tears

87. Which of the following structures is nonessential for survival of Gram-negative bacteria?

  A. plasmid
  B. periplasm
  C. outer membrane
  D. mesosome

88. Which of the following diseases is not caused by a bacterial agent?

  A. botulism
  B. typhoid fever
  C. leprosy
  D. influenza

GO ON TO THE NEXT PAGE

PCAT Practice Test 2

89. The Gram stain, often used in the identification of bacterial strains, is considered to be a

    A. positive stain.
    B. negative stain.
    C. neutral stain.
    D. differential stain.

90. Which of the following sterilization methods is considered most effective?

    A. exposure to ultraviolet light
    B. autoclaving
    C. pasteurization
    D. soaking in 70% ethanol

91. The routine addition of antibiotics to cattle feed is controversial because

    A. the addition of antibiotics to feed is very expensive.
    B. it has the potential to lead to the development of antibiotic-resistant strains of bacteria.
    C. it reduces the supply of antibiotics available in developing countries.
    D. it often makes the animals ill.

92. How does human saliva help protect against bacterial infections?

    A. Human saliva is very acidic and kills potentially invading bacteria.
    B. Human saliva is very alkaline and kills potentially invading bacteria.
    C. Human saliva contains enzymes that destroy potentially invading bacteria.
    D. Human saliva provides an anaerobic environment in which potentially invading bacteria cannot survive.

93. Which of the following organisms is a normal, nonpathogenic inhabitant of the human gastrointestinal system?

    A. *Escherichia coli*
    B. *Streptococcus pneumoniae*
    C. *Staphylococcus aureus*
    D. *Haemophilus influenzae*

94. The tetanus vaccine uses a _____ for the immunizing agent.

    A. killed virus particle
    B. deactivated virus particle
    C. killed culture of weakened bacterial cells
    D. toxoid

95. When an opened bottle of wine has been exposed to air for a long period of time, which of the following is most likely to occur?

    A. The wine will expand in the bottle and begin to bubble out as the yeast continues to carry out cellular respiration.
    B. The wine will become alkaline and taste like sugar.
    C. The wine will become acidic and taste like vinegar.
    D. The wine will not be affected by long-term exposure to air.

96. Which of the following statements best describes the structure of the human heart?

    A. The human heart consists of four chambers: two atria and two ventricles.
    B. The human heart consists of four chambers called ventricles.
    C. The human heart consists of two chambers: one atria and one ventricle.
    D. The human heart consists of two chambers: the right and left ventricles.

97. The rhythmic stretching and relaxing of the arteries as blood is forced through them is referred to as the

    A. heart rate.
    B. pulse.
    C. blood pressure.
    D. systole.

98. Which of the following statements regarding red blood cells is incorrect?

    A. Red blood cells have a large, well-defined nucleus.
    B. Red blood cells are often referred to as erythrocytes.
    C. Red blood cells transport oxygen and carbon dioxide throughout the body.
    D. Red blood cells contain a pigmented protein called hemoglobin.

99. The primary function of the lymph nodes is to

    A. manufacture white blood cells.

    B. make antibodies.

    C. destroy red blood cells.

    D. filter the lymph and phagocytize foreign particles.

100. In the human respiratory system, exchange of gasses (oxygen and carbon dioxide) occurs between which of the following pairs of structures?

    A. white blood cells and bronchi

    B. red blood cells and bronchi

    C. red blood cells and alveoli

    D. red blood cells and white blood cells

101. Peristalsis refers to

    A. the initial softening of food by saliva in the mouth to form a bolus.

    B. the rhythmic muscular contractions that move a bolus of food through the esophagus.

    C. the opening and closing of the cardiac sphincter to let the bolus of food enter the stomach from the esophagus.

    D. the digestion of food by enzymes in the stomach.

102. Bile is emptied from the gall bladder into the small intestine to

    A. assist with the digestion of glucose.

    B. assist with the digestion of starch.

    C. assist with the digestion of fats.

    D. assist with the digestion of nucleic acids.

103. Which of the following statements regarding urine is incorrect?

    A. Urine contains urea, which is essential in high concentrations for normal body function.

    B. Urine contains urea, which in high doses can be toxic to humans.

    C. Urine is a watery solution of waste products, salts, and organic compounds.

    D. Urine is produced in the human kidney.

104. Which of the following hormone and function combinations is mismatched?

    A. human growth hormone; promotion of body growth

    B. lactogenic hormone; promotion of breast development and milk secretion in females

    C. thyroxine; regulation of body metabolism

    D. androgen; promotion of secondary female characteristics

105. Which of the following structures is NOT part of the human endocrine system?

    A. thyroid

    B. nephron

    C. pituitary

    D. pancreas

106. Which series of events depicted below best describes the proper order of the three interrelated processes that are active in the human nervous system?

    A. sensory input → motor output → integration

    B. motor output → sensory input → integration

    C. motor output → integration → sensory input

    D. sensory input → integration → motor output

107. The part of the brain responsible for coordinating motor activity and muscle contractions is the

    A. medulla.

    B. cerebrum.

    C. cerebellum.

    D. hypothalamus.

108. The human nervous system is divided into which of the following components?

    A. brain and spinal cord

    B. brain and peripheral nervous system

    C. spinal cord and central nervous system

    D. central nervous system and peripheral nervous system

GO ON TO THE NEXT PAGE

109. In humans, the function of the sympathetic nervous system is to

    A. prepare the body for emergencies.

    B. return the body to a normal state following an emergency.

    C. carry impulses from the external environment to the brain.

    D. control emotional responses to stimuli.

110. While the human body can manufacture some of the amino acids it needs, others must be obtained through the diet and are referred to as

    A. proper amino acids.

    B. needed amino acids.

    C. essential amino acids.

    D. supplemental amino acids.

111. Humans store excess kilocalories as glycogen in muscle and liver cells. Once the glycogen stores are full, an individual will begin storing excess kilocalories as

    A. glucose.

    B. starch.

    C. protein.

    D. fat.

112. In the human immune system, the skin, stomach acid, mucous membranes, and macrophages all represent

    A. specific immune responses.

    B. nonspecific immune responses.

    C. targeted immune responses.

    D. antigen-antibody responses.

113. When the human immune system is stimulated by coming in contact with a foreign _____, it responds by producing a specific _____.

    A. antigen; white blood cell

    B. antigen; antibody

    C. antibody; antigen

    D. invader; white blood cell

114. White blood cells that attack and destroy cancer cells and cells infected by viruses are referred to as

    A. phagocytes.

    B. macrophages.

    C. erythrocytes.

    D. natural killer cells.

115. Which of the following statements regarding vaccines is incorrect?

    A. Vaccines are likely to make you ill, because they are often made with killed virus particles.

    B. Vaccines stimulate the primary immune response.

    C. Vaccines stimulate the secondary immune response.

    D. Vaccines act like a foreign antigen stimulating the body to produce antibodies to it.

116. When the human body encounters a foreign agent for the second time, the immune response is typically much faster than when the foreign agent was first encountered. This is due to

    A. immune system memory.

    B. antibodies stored in red blood cells.

    C. stronger activity by the macrophages.

    D. the use of antibiotics.

Reading Comprehension

Directions: Read each of the following passages and answer the questions that follow.

Passage 1

(1) Most people get up in the morning and immediately turn on the radio or television to see what the temperature is and what the weather will be. This is how we plan our day. Likewise, the U.S. military relies on the scientists and programmers at the Navy's Fleet Meteorology and Oceanography Center (NFMOC) for timely, accurate weather data and maps to facilitate their missions. This is a very tall order for this group. Faced with having to create about 2.6 million oceanic and atmospheric charts, analyses, forecasts and related data sets daily, the center is in need of improving their processes. The task of keeping data in some sort of order is one challenge. To be able to retrieve and analyze it provides another challenge. Furthermore, having the space that such paper documentation uses is a further issue. To try to rectify this, the naval center has turned to a collaborative approach where there is an online forum. This cyberspace chat room is where scientists can communicate about their projects. The software, specially developed for this purpose allows military and civilian scientists, meteorologists and developers who discuss their objectives, strategies, and deadlines within the firewall. Users exchange open-source or proprietary codes within their own repositories. Unlike using e-mail, people can communicate in a single location, which facilitates project tracking. This increases efficiency for the meteorology and oceanography centers where the number of teams of programmers has dwindled due to budget cuts. Currently, there are 64 Navy projects and up to 200 registered users who spread out across multiple locations.

(2) It is too early to quantify how much this computer service has improved application-development process, but there is evidence of fewer meetings and exchanges of e-mails. Furthermore, all the documentation can be stored on the hard drive to eliminate the space problem. The retrieval of information is immediate and organized. The Navy is optimistic about transferring over 170 applications that were done manually to computer-generated activities.

117. The U.S. military relies on the NFMOC for

   A. only maps for indication of ocean currents.
   B. weather data for ground conditions of troop removal.
   C. maps and weather for military missions.
   D. help in deciding the next move in an important project.

GO ON TO THE NEXT PAGE

118. The biggest challenge for the NFMOC is

    A. creating 2.6 million oceanic and atmospheric charts.

    B. keeping data in one place.

    C. being able to retrieve the information.

    D. all of the above

119. Their cyberspace chat room is where

    A. scientists can exchange ideas about their project.

    B. naval officers can get good suggestions about maneuvers.

    C. weather reports are found.

    D. maps of ocean currents are available.

120. The new software

    A. is useful to all different groups of people.

    B. has complicated security codes.

    C. allows only the most important data to be stored easily.

    D. allows only the military to access the important information.

121. Project tracking is facilitated by

    A. meteorology and oceanography centers located near each other.

    B. the software that allows people to communicate in a single location.

    C. the dwindling number of teams of programmers.

    D. the 200 users spread out across multiple locations.

122. The word "quantify" in the first sentence of the last paragraph most closely means

    A. looking for positive data.

    B. determining how much something costs.

    C. examining the program for its bugs.

    D. predicting its future success.

123. Success will be measured by

    A. the number of e-mails and meetings that have to happen.

    B. the positive questionnaire that they receive.

    C. the success of naval missions.

    D. the happiness of 170 applications of the Navy workers.

Passage 2

(1)   Most people believe that mental illness is some form of psychological weakness or hereditary trait. However, some scientists at the National Institute of Mental Health, have extracted protein from spinal fluid of both healthy and schizophrenic people that indicate patterns that might identify viruses linked to some cases of the disease. Theories about the possible role of viral infections in schizophrenia have circulated in the psychiatric community for more than a century. Because there has only been indirect evidence, there is much controversy about this issue.

(2)   The term "schizophrenia" encompasses a number of disorders that are caused by genes, stress, early family interactions, chemical imbalance, infections, nutrition, or some combination of them. Symptoms include social withdrawal, incoherent speech, blunted emotions, delusions, and hallucinations. At least 2 million people in the United States are estimated to have some form of this mental disease.

(3)   In the past few years, other brain diseases like multiple sclerosis and Alzheimer's disease are being examined for evidence of viral infections. Researchers believe that this form of mental disease might also be related to viruses, because incidents may remain inactive for 20 years and then flare up.

(4)   One way to check for evidence of viruses is to examine the spinal fluid, which closely reflects brain proteins. More than 300 proteins have now been separated and identified by advanced staining and computer analysis processes. Since one-third of the patients had a pair of proteins that always surfaced together, and these proteins are also present in those suffering from herpes encephalitis or Creutzfeldt-Jakob disease, there is speculation that there might be a connection to schizophrenia. However, the problem remains as to whether the proteins represent a viral infection that precedes the disease or whether they are a result of the nervous system and immune system changes caused by the disease.

(5)   Continued research could unlock more information about the connections that might present medication that could help or prevent the onslaught of this mental illness. What has to happen is the collaboration between immunologists and biological psychiatrists so that theories can be more rigorously studied and tested.

124. Which of the following statements is true?

   A.   Mental illness is a hereditary trait.
   B.   Bacterial infections cause schizophrenia.
   C.   Protein in spinal fluid might be used as a determinant to causes of mental illness.
   D.   There are no recognizable patterns in types of mental illnesses.

125. Schizophrenia is a disorder that

   A.   could be linked to early family interactions.
   B.   is not a major illness in the United States.
   C.   only causes delusions and hallucinations.
   D.   is definitely caused by a chemical imbalance.

126. Doctors are examining spinal fluid because

   A.   it is easy to reach and cultivate in labs.
   B.   it resembles brain proteins.
   C.   it has over 200 proteins.
   D.   it can be easily stained and analyzed by a computer.

127. The commonality between herpes encephalitis and Creutzfeldt-Jakob disease is

   A.   people who have either disease possess similar blood proteins.
   B.   people who have either disease are also suffering from schizophrenia.
   C.   people who have either disease might have caught a bacteria infection.
   D.   people who have either disease are immune to certain antibiotics.

128. The major problem with the results of this study is whether the proteins are a result of

   A.   an infection that precedes the disease or changes in the immune system before the disease.
   B.   an infection that proceeds with the disease or nervous system infections.
   C.   an infection that precedes the disease or changes in the immune system due to the disease.
   D.   immunization or post-disease syndrome.

129. Scientists hope that the results of the research will be able to

   A.   find medications that could help or prevent the onslaught of the disease.
   B.   predict when the onslaught of the disease will happen.
   C.   unlock connections between medications and infections.
   D.   rebuild the nervous system after the onslaught of the disease.

GO ON TO THE NEXT PAGE

130. The attitude of the author of this article is:

    A. angry with the lack of money given for this type of research.

    B. annoyed that research is happening so slowly.

    C. encouraged that connections will help with a breakthrough in the next year or so.

    D. adamant that immunologists and biological psychiatrists need to work together in order for progress to be made.

Passage 3

(1)   Prostate cancer is the most common form of cancer in men. Although the causes of this disease are not truly understood, there is evidence that it is associated with age. The way to test for this disease is to take a biopsy, a microscopic examination of a tiny sample of prostate tissue. However, even if the results come back negative, as they do for the majority of the tests, this is not the end of the potential problem. As men age, they continue to be at risk. If there is a history of this disease in their family, then they are at higher risk. Furthermore, some of the symptoms of the disease continue even if the cancer is not there.

(2)   The existing treatment of this cancer can include hormonal therapy, radiation treatment, and surgery. All three conventional treatments are accepted widely. However, because there are significant side effects to each of the treatments, people are also turning to herbal remedies and nutritional supplements to alleviate symptoms or promote prostate health. The challenge to the consumer is to keep careful watch on the evidence of effectiveness of this ever-growing list of vitamins, herbs, and minerals.

(3)   While widely used drugs have gone through rigorous tests, many of the "natural" remedies have not. Thus, the need for appropriate lab tests and research is an expanding area of science. Preclinical tests include test-tube procedures, followed by cell-based assays, and ending with animal-based studies. For natural compounds, the primary question is whether these substances exhibit toxicity and to what extent. Studies on these elements will determine the effect the substance has for cell proliferation and whether their effect is tissue-specific. As more and more of these tests are taken, the cost of these "natural" remedies are going to increase, making them less appealing to patients and of greater concern to the insurance companies that will have to determine if they will pay for them.

131. In the third sentence, the word "biopsy" most closely indicates

    A. a type of minor, investigative surgery.

    B. a type of lab test on rat cells to figure out rate of tissue growth.

    C. a major type of surgery to correct the problem.

    D. an aggressive use of medication to cure the problem.

132. Which of the following statements is true?

- **A.** As men age, they are less likely to need to be tested as often.
- **B.** Even a negative test does not indicate the lack of cancer.
- **C.** These tests are easily done and completely accurate.
- **D.** Past family history does not affect the possibilities of getting the cancer.

133. Because of the negative side effects of traditional treatments of prostate cancer, patients are

- **A.** dying faster because patients are not following the regimen.
- **B.** seeking alternatives that might be less invasive.
- **C.** asking insurance companies to pay for their over-the-counter medications.
- **D.** watching TV for advice on how to treat the disease.

134. The danger with "natural" remedies is that

- **A.** they haven't had assays done.
- **B.** they are very expensive.
- **C.** their effectiveness is entirely false.
- **D.** their test-tube results are spurious.

135. Two areas of importance in determining the effectiveness of natural remedies are

- **A.** preclinical tests and cost.
- **B.** cell proliferation and tissue specificity.
- **C.** taste and toxicity.
- **D.** how they are marketed and who markets them.

136. These remedies might be less appealing because of

- **A.** the cost—more tests require higher prices.
- **B.** the availability—more people will want them.
- **C.** the taste—they are all natural.
- **D.** the lack of studies in comparison to the other treatments.

137. There is the suggestion that alternate treatments to diseases are partially controlled by

- **A.** news reports on TV.
- **B.** doctors and pharmacists.
- **C.** insurance companies.
- **D.** researchers and scientists.

Passage 4

(1)   College students are known for pulling "all-nighters" before exams. Business executives, preparing reports, might stay up all night before crucial presentations. Truck drivers might push through the night so that they can get their cargo to their destinations on time. You might have a caffeine drink to help you stay awake or loud music to keep those eyelids from drooping. But you cannot stifle a yawn, and that is the first sign that your brain is checking out for the night!

(2)   The yawn is the body's first external sign that you are losing your concentration. After 18 hours of no sleep, your reaction time begins to slow down from a quarter of a second to a half of a second and then longer. You begin to experience bouts of microsleep, moments when you zone out for 2 to 20 seconds. This is enough time for you to drift into another lane while driving or for you to have to reread a passage a second time. After 20 hours of sleep deprivation, you actually begin to nod off. Your reaction time is now equivalent to that of someone who has a blood alcohol level of 0.08, which is enough to get you arrested for driving under the influence in 49 states! Although you might feel that you get a second wind as the sun rises, your condition is continually deteriorating.

GO ON TO THE NEXT PAGE

(3)   All through the animal kingdom, sleep ranks up there among the other necessities like food, water, shelter, and air for survival. Yet scientists still don't know precisely what sleep is for. We immediately think of rejuvenation. However, except for the muscles—which need periodic relaxation, not necessarily sleep—the rest of our internal organs continue to chug along regardless of whether we are awake or asleep. Most researchers will agree that the part of the body that benefits us the most from sleep is our brain. Yet, scientists do not agree on what these benefits are. Some feel that sleep is the time that the brain reviews and consolidates all the streams of information it has gathered while awake. Others suggest that it is a time that allows the brain to refuel and slush out wastes. A third theory suggests that in some mysterious way, sleep helps the brain master various skills, such as how to play the piano or ride a bike.

138. A yawn is

   A.   the way to indicate who much sleep you need.
   B.   a sign that you are bored with the lecture.
   C.   an indication that your brain needs rest.
   D.   a rude thing to do in public.

139. The research shows that

   A.   no two people need the same amount of sleep.
   B.   as you get tired, your reflexes slow down at a rate of 2 seconds.
   C.   most people will be affected negatively after 18 hours without sleep.
   D.   all-nighters are not harmful if done only once a month.

140. The word "microsleep" in the third sentence of the second paragraph most closely means

   A.   that computer jargon is affecting medical words.
   B.   that automatically, your brain will zone out to rejuvenate itself.
   C.   cat naps.
   D.   that you are not dreaming.

141. The comparison between sleep deprivation and drinking alcohol is done to show that

   A.   drinking and driving is dangerous.
   B.   drinking will just speed up the need to sleep.
   C.   both situations severely impair your judgment.
   D.   there should be a law against sleepy people driving.

142. When you get your "second wind," it means that

   A.   you are now ready to continue work because you are awake again.
   B.   your condition is still deteriorating even though you don't know it.
   C.   your body is able to work harder now because you have gotten over the tiredness.
   D.   you can drive long distances now.

143. A contradictory fact to the concept of rejuvenation is that

   A.   only your muscles sleep.
   B.   sometimes you don't feel rested when you wake up.
   C.   none of your organs rest when you sleep.
   D.   all creatures—animals and humans—need sleep.

144. The article ends with three theories that

   A.   focus on sleep's effects on the brain.
   B.   indicate that sleep will help you perform better.
   C.   completely contradict each other in scope and depth.
   D.   are restatements of the basic tenet, sleep is necessary.

Passage 5

(1)   A slimy lump of green is clumped at the bottom of a plastic bucket, the contents of which are hardly distinguishable. This jellied mass is actually a dozen bullfrogs that have traveled thousands of miles to New York City's Chinatown to await their fate. Although they are native to North America, these particular suspicious specimens have been raised in South America and imported to the United States. The trafficking of bullfrogs is big business. The U.S. Fish and Wildlife Service has reported that in 2002, nearly 49 million amphibians were imported for trade. Although most of the creatures were brought in to be pets, many found their place on people's dinner plates. Their skins are discarded in the trash and become vehicles for the communication of disease.

(2)   Chytridiomycosis, an amphibious fungal plague, has cropped up throughout the world. These outbreaks have often led to the extinction of a species. Yet, not a single bullfrog or any other type of amphibian has been inspected at the U.S. border. Since September 11, our concern about biosecurity has been heightened. Tens of millions of dollars have been spent to try to protect the United States; all the while, foreign pathogens sail into the country hidden in the bodies of exotic wildlife and their accompanying fleas and ticks. An estimated $1.5 million dollars are spent in the legal business of U.S. wildlife imports, but there is an equally large illegal pet trade. However, there are fewer than 100 inspectors to investigate over 32 points of entry into the United States.

(3)   The U.S. Fish and Wildlife Service's aim is to protect endangered species and to assure humane transport of animals. The Department of Agriculture inspects only for diseases that threaten livestock and poultry. The Centers for Disease Control mandate public health issues so the idea of wildlife diseases falls through the cracks.

(4)   The result is that diseases spread easily among animals and through feeding stations that breed infection. Two-thirds of known human pathogens are zoonotic, able to pass from animals to humans and vice versa. West Nile virus, the bird flu, and Hendra-Nipah are recent examples of human diseases that started out in animals and birds. The problem is compounded by the fact that scientists have discovered that many of these animals host bacteria that are resistant to antibiotics. Thus the germs are not just cycling between wildlife, livestock, and humans, but they are becoming more dangerous with each pass. *Salmonella enterica* variant *Typhimurium DT104,* was a fairly common serotype first seen about 15 years ago. Now it is resistant to eight drugs. So even

GO ON TO THE NEXT PAGE

though there are fewer incidents of food-borne salmonella outbreaks, there are more instances of multi-drug-resistant bacteria. For most pathogens, there are no boundaries between animals and people, so the globe-trotting frogs are literally drops in the bucket when it comes to the modern spread of disease.

145. Bullfrogs are imported because

A.   they are not native to North America.
B.   they are needed for laboratory tests.
C.   they are part of the import trade business.
D.   they are easy to transport.

146. These frogs are mostly used for

A.   food.
B.   experiments.
C.   pets.
D.   high school science labs.

147. In the second paragraph, the word "chytridiomycosis" means

A.   a disease of the frogs.
B.   a chemical taken from the frogs.
C.   a medicine used for the frogs.
D.   a medicine made from the frogs.

148. The effect that September 11 had on our country has

A.   effectively decreased the infiltration of foreign pathogens.
B.   made inspectors look more closely at the import of frogs.
C.   increased the concern for biosecurity and, thus, uncovered numerous pathogens.
D.   had no effect on the import of amphibious creatures.

149. The purpose of the third paragraph is to show that

A.   despite all the agencies, things still fall through the cracks.
B.   the United States has many agencies that overlap their responsibilities.
C.   the United States cares greatly for wildlife.
D.   terrorists cannot infiltrate our livestock.

150. In the second sentence of the fourth paragraph, the word "zoonotic" most closely means

A.   able to pass from humans to animals.
B.   able to pass from animals to humans.
C.   able to pass back and forth between animals and humans.
D.   able to affect only humans or only animals but not both.

151. The inclusion of information about salmonella was to

A.   tell people to be careful of what they eat.
B.   make people more comfortable knowing that it is less frequently found.
C.   alert people to the fact that bacteria can become resistant to drugs.
D.   compare it to West Nile virus and Hendrah-Nipah.

Passage 6

(1)   The winter of 2005 in the Northern Hemisphere has provided much excitement to those who enjoy gazing at the heavens. Visible to the naked eye under a dark sky have been a string of comets. Comet c/2004 Q2, Machholz, can be seen during February in the northern sky as it slowly slides toward the North Star, Polaris. At the fifth magnitude, it is fainter than the Beehive star cluster, which, at this time, is beginning to rise in the east. If you are in the city, you will need binoculars to locate them. Like a baseball pop fly rounding the top of its arc, Machholz appears

to slow this month. Thus, from the earth's perspective, it lies almost straight up from the North Pole. This gives us a good sight line of its tail, which points away from the sun. In fact, you can see two tails: a tail that is slightly bluish in color due to the ionized gas blowing straight out in the solar wind of charged particles, and a yellow-white tail as ejected motes of dust begin tracing their own orbital paths. As these tails leave the brighter background of the Milky Way, they can become more distinguishable.

(2) Another glorious sight is Saturn with its rings. It can easily be located because it is the steady, pale-yellow "star" that is halfway up in the east as the sky grows dark. If the Earth's atmosphere is not too turbulent, you can detect the shadow of the planet on its rings. A couple of months ago, the shadow would have been seen on the opposite side, and in the afternoon it appears longer.

(3) Jupiter was seen the previous October and is always full of intrigue. As the planet rises before midnight, its view becomes very clear. Will the Great Red Spot begin a comeback. Are there any white ovals? Even though the moon lies closer to the Earth than Jupiter, the perspective makes it seem much closer to Jupiter. Thus, at a time during the winter cycle, Jupiter will obscure the red supergiant, Antares. In truth, what meets the eye in the sky can be deceiving but also exciting.

152. Machholz is

    A. a planet.

    B. a moon.

    C. a comet.

    D. a Beehive cluster.

153. The Macholtz and the Beehive star cluster

    A. can be seen at the same time.

    B. are moving away from each other.

    C. can never be seen at the same time.

    D. are names for the same comet.

154. The use of the baseball metaphor is

    A. to pique the reader's attention.

    B. to illustrate the placement and movement of the comet.

    C. to talk about its brightness and speed.

    D. to appeal to American sports fans.

155. The blue comet tail is due to

    A. the weather conditions.

    B. the type of binoculars you use.

    C. the time of night you see the comet.

    D. the amount of ions in the gas.

156. Jupiter's rings

    A. never change their placement to the viewer.

    B. never change their shape to the viewer.

    C. only change size in the afternoon.

    D. can only be seen at night.

157. The Great Red Spot and white ovals are

    A. part of cosmic mythology.

    B. characteristics of Mars.

    C. variable unexplained characteristics.

    D. traits of comets and stars.

158. Antares is

    A. a planet near Jupiter.

    B. a red supergiant.

    C. a large comet.

    D. a Greek giant.

GO ON TO THE NEXT PAGE

Passage 7

(1)   The spirit of adventure has always been basic to human nature both in the imagination and in reality. Jules Verne wrote about traveling the world in 180 days, a magical concept in a balloon. Captain Joshua Slocum, 100 years ago, sailed a vessel around the world alone. Now, a small ocean glider named *Spray* is the first autonomous underwater vehicle, or AUV, to cross the gulf stream underwater. This voyage has proven the viability of self-propelled gliders for long-distance scientific missions and providing new possibilities for the studies of the oceans.

(2)   The *Spray* was launched on September 11, 2004, about 100 miles south of Nantucket Island, Massachusetts. Looking like a model airplane, it is 6 feet long with a 4-foot wingspan and no visible moving parts. It journeyed between Cape Cod and Bermuda, traveling at one-half knot, or 12 miles a day. It surfaced three times a day to measure various properties of the ocean and then submerged to 1,000 meters in depth. During its 15-minute surfacing, the position in the ocean and conditions such as temperature and salinity are relayed back to Woods Hole, Massachusetts, and California via satellite.

(3)   The journey was not without its setbacks. Two malfunctions brought the *Spray* back to Woods Hole before its third successful venture. Even then, there were challenges. When it began to cross the gulf stream, the surface currents exceeded 6 miles per hour across the width of the glider, catapulting it on a fast ride north. In just two days, they lost two weeks of progress. However, the excellent communication with the vehicle from the command post allowed the glider to get back on track. Since the *Spray* has a range of 6,000 miles, it could probably cross the entire Atlantic Ocean. The major concern is whether the *Spray* can stay at sea for months at a relatively low cost. If so, this would allow observations of large-scale changes under the ocean that usually go unobserved.

(4)   The potential for the widespread use of gliders in all bodies of water are astounding. These gliders can look at entire sections of ocean basins like the Atlantic or serve as moorings for a keeping station at a single point. Unlike humans who need to stop for breaks, gliders can carry out missions from several weeks to as long as six months. Oceanographic gliders are now at the stage similar to the start of aviation. Within a few years, they will be as commonplace as air travel is now.

159. AUV is
A.   a new type of military submarine.
B.   a new type of four-wheel-drive car.
C.   a new type of unmanned water vehicle.
D.   a type of unexplained phenomenon.

160. Which of the following statements is true?

    A. There are no moving parts.
    B. The vehicle looks a bit like a plane.
    C. It is about the size of a superjet.
    D. It is considered a nuclear-powered glider.

161. The purpose of this vehicle is to

    A. take sightseeing trips between Cape Cod and Bermuda.
    B. examine fish underwater.
    C. measure the saltiness of the water.
    D. provide communication and to give reports.

162. The *Spray* is successful because

    A. it has excellent communication with the ground crew.
    B. it can travel across the Atlantic Ocean.
    C. it is easy to maneuver.
    D. it can ride the waves easily.

163. The only drawback about this invention is

    A. the cost.
    B. having to make enough vehicles so that they can be everywhere.
    C. the fact that it doesn't compete against regular submarines.
    D. convincing people of its worth.

164. The comparison to aviation is to

    A. identify that vehicle because it looks like a plane.
    B. go along with the term "glider" because it travels that way.
    C. show that although they are sparse now, they can become very common.
    D. provide another type of vehicle instead of planes.

165. The tone in the article is

    A. skeptical about unmanned research vehicles.
    B. excited about the global implications.
    C. afraid that money will be wasted in this venture.
    D. angry that it was not more commonly used.

GO ON TO THE NEXT PAGE

Quantitative Ability

Directions: Read each of the questions and select the choice that answers the question.

166. How many omelets can be made from two dozen eggs if an omelet contains three eggs?

   A. 1
   B. 3
   C. 6
   D. 8

167. A television is on sale for 20% off. If the sale price is $800, what was the original price?

   A. $160
   B. $640
   C. $960
   D. $1,000

168. A sweater originally priced at $40 is on sale for $30. What percent has the sweater been discounted?

   A. 25%
   B. 33%
   C. 70%
   D. 75%

169. Rachel ran $\frac{1}{2}$ mile in 4 minutes. At this rate, how many miles can she run in 15 minutes?

   A. $1\frac{7}{8}$
   B. 4
   C. 30
   D. 60

170. If $x^{\frac{2}{3}} = 9$, then what is the value of x?

   A. 3
   B. 18
   C. 27
   D. 81

171. The length of a rectangle is three times its width. If the perimeter of the rectangle is 48, what is its area?

   A. 108
   B. 96
   C. 54
   D. 48

172. The sum of 2 feet $2\frac{1}{2}$ inches, 4 feet $3\frac{3}{8}$ inches, and 3 feet $9\frac{3}{4}$ inches is

   A. 9 feet $\frac{7}{8}$ inches
   B. 9 feet $9\frac{5}{8}$ inches
   C. 10 feet $\frac{5}{8}$ inches
   D. 10 feet $3\frac{5}{8}$ inches

173. A 10-foot rope is to be cut into equal segments measuring 8 inches each. The total number of segments is

   A. 1
   B. 8
   C. 15
   D. 40

174. A restaurant bill without tax and tip comes to $38.40. If a 15% tip is included after a 6% tax is added to the bill, how much is the tip?

   A. $6.11
   B. $5.76
   C. $5.15
   D. $2.30

175. If $g(x) = 16^{-x}$, then $g\left(\frac{1}{2}\right) =$

   A. $\frac{1}{4}$
   B. $\frac{1}{2}$
   C. 2
   D. 4

176. An appliance originally costing $1,000 goes on sale one week for 25% off. The following week, it is discounted an additional 10%. What is the new sale price of the appliance?

   A. $650
   B. $675
   C. $750
   D. $900

177. A savings account earns $2\frac{1}{4}$ % interest each year. How much interest is earned on a $1,000 deposit after a five-year period?

    A. $22.50

    B. $100.00

    C. $112.50

    D. $150.00

178. 12 is 15% of what number?

    A. 1.8

    B. 18

    C. 36

    D. 80

179. $(3-1) \times 7 - 12 \div 2 =$

    A. 1

    B. −2

    C. 4

    D. 8

180. If $y = t^2 - 8t + 3$, then $\frac{dy}{dt} =$

    A. $2t - 8$

    B. $2t$

    C. $t^2 - 8$

    D. $2t + 3$

181. Simplify $\dfrac{9x^2 y^3 z - 12xy^2 z^2}{3yz}$.

    A. $3xy^2z - 4xyz$

    B. $3x^2y^2 - 12xyz$

    C. $3x^2y^2 - 4xyz$

    D. $3y^2 - 4xy^2z^2$

182. The expression of $\log_3 81$ is equal to

    A. 3

    B. 4

    C. 5

    D. 6

183. The angles of a triangle are in the ratio 3:4:5. What is the measure of the smallest angle?

    A. 15°

    B. 30°

    C. 45°

    D. 75°

184. How many distinct prime factors are there in 120?

    A. 2

    B. 3

    C. 4

    D. 5

185. Amelia casts a shadow 5 feet long. Her father, who is 6 feet tall, casts a shadow 8 feet long. How tall is Amelia?

    A. 6 feet 8 inches

    B. 4 feet 10 inches

    C. 4 feet 6 inches

    D. 3 feet 9 inches

186. What is the value of $-27^{\frac{2}{3}}$?

    A. −9

    B. −3

    C. 3

    D. 9

187. A blueprint has a scale of 3 feet per $\frac{1}{2}$ inch. If a bathroom is $1\frac{1}{2}$ inches × 2 inches, what are its actual dimensions?

    A. $4\frac{1}{2}$ feet × 6 feet

    B. 6 feet × $7\frac{1}{2}$ feet

    C. $7\frac{1}{2}$ feet × 9 feet

    D. 9 feet × 12 feet

188. What is the x-coordinate of the maximum value of $y = 7 + 6x - 3x^2$?

    A. −6

    B. 1

    C. 2

    D. 6

189. The volume of a cube is 343 cm³. The surface area of the cube is

    A. 7 cm²

    B. 49 cm²

    C. 294 cm²

    D. 2,401 cm²

GO ON TO THE NEXT PAGE

190. If $\log_{16} x = -2$, then $x =$

    A. $\dfrac{1}{256}$

    B. $\dfrac{1}{4}$

    C. $\dfrac{1}{2}$

    D. 2

191. A piece of wood measuring 16.5 inches long is cut into 2.75 inch pieces. How many smaller pieces of wood are there?

    A. 3

    B. 5

    C. 6

    D. 8

192. If $\sin b < 0$ and $\cos b < 0$, then $\angle b$ must lie in which quadrant?

    A. I

    B. II

    C. III

    D. IV

193. Tanya's bowling scores this week were 112, 156, 179, and 165. Last week, her average score was 140. How many points did her average improve?

    A. 18

    B. 13

    C. 11

    D. 8

194. Simplify $5(a - 2) - (4a - 6)$.

    A. $a - 4$

    B. $a - 8$

    C. $a - 10$

    D. $a + 4$

195. The product of two numbers is 117. If one of the numbers is 9, what is the other?

    A. 11

    B. 13

    C. 15

    D. 17

196. If $\log F = 36$, then $\log \sqrt{F} =$

    A. 4

    B. 6

    C. 12

    D. 18

197. The cube root of 512 is

    A. 8

    B. 56

    C. $170\dfrac{2}{3}$

    D. 1,536

198. If $\dfrac{m}{n} = \dfrac{3}{5}$, what is the value of $m + n$?

    A. 2

    B. 8

    C. $\dfrac{6}{5}$

    D. $\dfrac{9}{25}$

199. If $y = \sin x$, then $y'(x) =$

    A. $-\sin x$

    B. $\cos x$

    C. $-\cos x$

    D. 1

200. Which of the following expressions represents the cost of five books and three magazines if books cost twice as much as magazines?

    A. $8b$

    B. $8m$

    C. $11b$

    D. $13m$

201. For which of the following values of x is the function $h(x) = \tan 2x$ undefined?

    A. 0

    B. $\dfrac{\pi}{4}$

    C. $\dfrac{\pi}{2}$

    D. π

202. The diagonal of a square is 10 inches. What is the area of the square?

- A. 40 in^2
- B. 50 in^2
- C. 100 in^2
- D. 150 in^2

203. What is the first derivative of $f(x) = (\sin x)(\cos x)$?

- A. $2\cos^2 x$
- B. $2\sin^2 x$
- C. $\cos^2 x + \sin^2 x$
- D. $\cos^2 x - \sin^2 x$

204. $0.00525 \div 0.01 =$

- A. 5.25
- B. 0.525
- C. 0.0525
- D. 0.000525

205. What is the measure of $\angle A$?

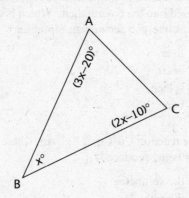

- A. 35°
- B. 60°
- C. 75°
- D. 85°

206. The expression $\tan\theta \cos\theta \sec\theta$ is equivalent to

- A. $\cot\theta$
- B. $\sec\theta$
- C. $\sin\theta$
- D. $\tan\theta$

207. Multiply $(5a^3bc^2)(-3a^2c)$

- A. $-15a^5bc^3$
- B. $15a^5bc^3$
- C. $-15a^6bc^2$
- D. $2abc$

208. Find the area of a regular hexagon whose sides measure 6 cm.

- A. 36
- B. $9\sqrt{2}$
- C. $54\sqrt{3}$
- D. 108

209. If C is used to represent the constant of integration, then $\int e^x \, dx =$

- A. $e^x + C$
- B. $xe^x + C$
- C. $lnx + C$
- D. $\frac{ex}{x} + C$

210. What is the slope of the line $x = -3y + 9$?

- A. -3
- B. $-\frac{1}{3}$
- C. 3
- D. 9

211. If $3^{4x+2} = 9^{x-1}$, then what is the value of x?

- A. -2
- B. -1
- C. 1
- D. 2

212. For which of the following sets of numbers is the median the same as the arithmetic mean?

- A. $\{-2, -1, 0, 2, 3\}$
- B. $\{0, 2, 3, 4, 5\}$
- C. $\{-1, 1, 4\}$
- D. $\{-2, -1, 0, 1, 2\}$

213. Which of the following values of x is a solution to the equation $\csc x = 2$?

- A. $x = 0°$
- B. $x = 30°$
- C. $x = 45°$
- D. $x = 60°$

GO ON TO THE NEXT PAGE

Chemistry

Directions: Select the choice that best answers the following questions. To consult the Periodic Table of the Elements, please go to the Appendix.

214. How many electrons does an isotope of uranium-235 have with a +2 charge?

- **A.** 90
- **B.** 92
- **C.** 143
- **D.** 94

215. Which part of an organic compound is likely to give a peak at 30 AMU on a mass spectrograph?

- **A.** CH_2O^+
- **B.** OH^+
- **C.** CH_3^+
- **D.** $C_6H_5^+$

216. Which thermodynamics quantity tends to increase in a spontaneous process?

- **A.** reaction rate
- **B.** enthalpy
- **C.** entropy
- **D.** free energy

217. What is the most advanced theory of molecular bonding?

- **A.** Valence Bond theory
- **B.** MO theory
- **C.** Lewis Dot structures
- **D.** VSEPR

218. The half-life for a second order decomposition reaction of the type aA→ products is given by the equation $t_{\frac{1}{2}} = \left(ak\left[A\right]_0 \right)^{-1}$. The half-life for a given compound is found to be 0.01 second with an initial concentration of 2.00 M. What is the value of *ak* for this compound?

- **A.** 0.02 M.sec
- **B.** 5/M.sec
- **C.** 50/M.sec
- **D.** 0.005 M.sec

219. In the infrared spectrum of an alcohol, the hydroxide functional group usually is shown how?

- **A.** a broad strong peak at 3,200–3,550 cm^{-1}
- **B.** a sharp peak at 1,630–1,780 cm^{-1}
- **C.** a medium peak at 2,220–2,260 cm^{-1}
- **D.** a medium-strong peak at 2,853–2,962 cm^{-1}

220. An apple is green. What does this statement show?

- **A.** a physical property
- **B.** a chemical property
- **C.** a chemical change
- **D.** a physical change

221. When the nuclear power plant in Chernobyl, Russia, melted down, radioactive strontium was released into the environment. Which body organ is most likely to accumulate strontium?

- **A.** liver
- **B.** heart
- **C.** spleen
- **D.** bone

222. In the reaction $Cu\left|Cu^{+2}\right\|Ag^+\left|Ag\right.$, where is the silver being produced?

- **A.** the voltmeter
- **B.** the cathode
- **C.** the salt bridge
- **D.** the anode

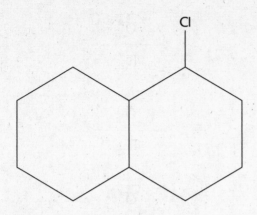

223. What is the correct IUPAC name for the compound in the above figure?

    A.   7-chloro [4.3.0] heptane

    B.   7-chloro [4.3.0] nonane

    C.   2-chloro [4.3.0] nonane

    D.   2-chloro [4.3.0] heptane

224. For the reaction, $2 NO_2F$ (g) $\longleftrightarrow$ N_2O_4 (g) $+ F_2$ (g), at some given set of conditions, we find that at equilibrium $[NO_2F] = 0.1$, $[N_2O_4] = 0.2$ and $[F_2] = 0.3$. What is the value of the equilibrium constant for this reaction at this set of conditions?

    A.   1.67

    B.   6

    C.   0.167

    D.   0.6

225. What best describes the electronic configuration $1s^2 2s^2 2p^5 3s^2$?

    A.   forbidden state

    B.   excited state

    C.   unknown state

    D.   ground state

226. In the reaction shown above, what is the role of the $AlCl_3$?

    A.   a Lewis acid

    B.   a Lewis base

    C.   a Bronsted-Lowry base

    D.   a Bronsted-Lowry acid

227. What is the coordination number of the coordination complex shown in the figure above?

    A.   2

    B.   4

    C.   6

    D.   3

228. Following is a list of ingredients from a cough medicine I happen to have in my cabinet. What is the solute?

    A.   saccharine sodium sweetener

    B.   pseudophedrine

    C.   FD&C red number 40

    D.   purified water

229. What type of reaction is $AgNO_3$ (aq) $+ LiCl$ (aq) $\rightarrow$ $LiNO_3$ (aq) $+ AgCl$ (s)?

    A.   decomposition

    B.   single replacement

    C.   addition

    D.   double replacement

230. What state is characterized as having a variable shape and a variable volume?

    A.   gas

    B.   liquid

    C.   solid

    D.   plasma

GO ON TO THE NEXT PAGE

231. At a given temperature, a saturated solution of calcium hydroxide will have a concentration of Ca^{+2} of 0.01 M. What is K_{sp} for calcium hydroxide at this temperature?

A. 2×10^{-4}

B. 1×10^{-6}

C. 4×10^{-6}

D. 1×10^{-4}

232. What will be the most likely product in the dehydrochlorination of 5,7,9-trichloro-1, 3-nonadiene (shown above)?

A. 7,9-dichloror-1,3,5-nonatriene

B. 5,9-dichloro-1,3,6-nonatriene

C. 5,9-dichloro-1,3,5-nonatriene

D. 5,7-dichloro-1,3,8-nonatriene

233. Calcium in teeth can be attacked by acids from foods because of hydroxide in calcium hydroxyphosphate:

$$2\ [Ca_5(OH)(PO_4)_3]\ (s) + 2\ H^+\ (aq) \rightarrow$$
$$3\ Ca_3(PO_4)_2\ (s) + Ca^{+2}\ (aq) + 2\ H_2O\ (l).$$

This reaction can be stemmed by replacing the fluoride ion with phosphate, in the equilibrium

$$[Ca_5(OH)(PO_4)_3]\ (s) + F^-\ (aq) \leftarrow$$
$$\rightarrow [Ca_5(F)(PO_4)_3]\ (s) + OH^-\ (aq).$$

Whose principle tells us that adding fluoride to our water and/or toothpaste will help in the formation of this fluoride form of calcium?

A. Heisenberg's

B. LeChatelier's

C. Bernoulli's

D. Dalton's

234. Given the molecular orbital diagram above, what form of oxygen will have the strongest oxygen-oxygen bond?

A. O_2^+

B. O_2

C. O_2^{-2}

D. O_2^{+2}

235. Heat released or absorbed in a chemical reaction is most directly related to what?

A. reaction rate

B. free energy

C. enthalpy

D. entropy

236. Of the following functional groups, what is the strongest meta director?

A. $-CO_2H$

B. $-NH_2$

C. $-OH$

D. $-CH_3$

237. Which is the only model of acids and bases that can apply to a non-protic environment?

A. Bronsted-Lowry

B. Lewis

C. Arrhenius

D. None

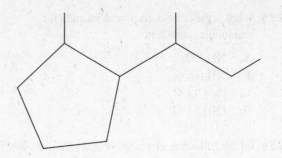

238. How many chiral carbons are in the above figure?

A. 1
B. 2
C. 0
D. 3

239. Which of the following would have to be 0.2N for a concentration of 0.1 M?

A. none
B. H_3PO_4
C. H_2SO_4
D. HCl

240. In a chemical reaction, what is the maximum amount of product that should in principle be able to be obtained?

A. theoretical yield
B. crude yield
C. actual yield
D. percent yield

241. Which functional group is the most highly oxidized?

A. alkene
B. ketone
C. alcohol
D. alkyne

242. We should be able to find a set of conditions in which the solubility product for each of these salts is 0.1. Which will be most soluble in these conditions?

A. KF
B. Al_2O_3
C. CaI_2
D. $AlCl_3$

243. Sodium hydroxide is what percent oxygen?

A. 40%
B. 33%
C. 77%
D. 60%

244. Chelation therapy is a relatively new way to reduce heavy metals, such as lead, in patients. In the following reaction, what term best describes the role of the lead?

$$Pb^{+2} + 6\ NH_3 \rightarrow [Pb(NH_3)_6]^{+2}$$

A. chelator
B. donor
C. acceptor
D. ligand

245. If we want to hold pressure and volume constant, what will we have to do with absolute temperature if we double the number of moles of gas?

A. Increase it by a factor of 2.
B. Decrease it by a factor of 2.
C. It is impossible to determine.
D. Keep it constant.

246. What molecular orbital configuration will give a bond order of $\frac{1}{2}$?

A. $\sigma_{1s}^2 \sigma *_{1s}^2 \sigma_{2s}^2 \sigma *_{2s}^2 \pi_{2p}^4 \sigma_{2p}^2 \pi *_{2p}^3$
B. $\sigma_{1s}^2 \sigma *_{1s}^2 \sigma_{2s}^2 \sigma *_{2s}^2 \pi_{2p}^4 \sigma_{2p}^2 \pi *_{2p}^4$
C. $\sigma_{1s}^2 \sigma *_{1s}^2 \sigma_{2s}^2 \sigma *_{2s}^2 \pi_{2p}^4 \sigma_{2p}^2 \pi *_{2p}^4 \sigma *_{2p}^2$
D. $\sigma_{1s}^2 \sigma *_{1s}^2 \sigma_{2s}^2 \sigma *_{2s}^2 \pi_{2p}^4 \sigma_{2p}^2 \pi *_{2p}^4 \sigma *_{2p}^1$

247. Which of the following is NOT matter?

A. preserves
B. heat
C. oxygen
D. humans

248. Which of the following would NOT constitute a chemical change?

A. damage to DNA by radiation
B. alkylosis (loss of acid from a person)
C. Distamycin (an antitumor drug) bonding to DNA
D. dehydration in a runner

GO ON TO THE NEXT PAGE

249. Which theory of bonding is the only one that predicts the possibility of fractional bonds?

- A. Molecular Orbital
- B. Valence Bond
- C. Lewis-Dot structure
- D. VSEPR

250. As a ligand, the cyanide anion, :C ≡ N:, can donate an electron pair either from the carbon or the nitrogen. If we have two different compounds where the only difference is the identity of the donor atom (that is, one is attached by N, the other by C), what type of isomer is this?

- A. stereoisomer
- B. linkage
- C. coordination
- D. hydrate

251. The dehydration reaction of a carboxylic acid with an alcohol yields what functional group?

- A. acid anhydride
- B. ether
- C. amide
- D. ester

252. Solutions based on which concentration unit are easiest to prepare in a lab, though this concentration unit is rarely used in chemical calculations?

- A. molality
- B. percent
- C. mole fraction
- D. molarity

253. Of the following free radicals, which will be the most stable?

- A. methyl carbon
- B. primary carbon
- C. tertiary carbon
- D. secondary carbon

254. What is the molar mass of calcium hydroxide, $Ca(OH)_2$?

- A. 114 g/mol
- B. 58 g/mol
- C. 74 g/mol
- D. 73 g/mol

255. What is the correct empirical formula for ammonium carbonate?

- A. NH_4CO_3
- B. $NH_4(CO_3)_2$
- C. $(NH_4)_3CO_3$
- D. $(NH_4)_2CO_3$

256. Of the following elements, which will most likely have the greatest electronegativity?

- A. As
- B. Sb
- B. Se
- D. Te

257. Of the following forms of radiation, which would have the most penetrating power?

- A. beta
- B. gamma
- C. neutrons
- D. alpha

258. Formaldehyde has the formula CH_2O. How many pi bonds would be present in this compound according to the Lewis-Dot structure?

- A. 0
- B. 1
- C. 3
- D. 2

259. Alklosis is caused by the decomposition of carbonic acid in the body: $H_2CO_3 (aq) \rightarrow H_2O (l) + CO_2 (g)$. What type of chemical reaction is this?

- A. addition
- B. single replacement
- C. decomposition
- D. double replacement

260. Which of the following functional groups will yield the greatest partial positive charge in carbon in the β position to the functional group?

- A. aldehyde
- B. alcohol
- C. alkene
- D. amine

261. In the redox equation 2 H$^+$ (aq) + 2 Fe^{+2} (aq) + NO$_3^-$ (aq) → 2 Fe^{+3} (aq) + NO$_2^-$ (aq) + H$_2$O (l), what is the oxidizing agent?

A. iron
B. nitrate ion
C. water
D. hydronium

262. What will lead to the formation of a free radical in an organic reaction?

A. dehydration
B. rearrangement
C. heterolytic cleavage
D. hemolytic cleavage

263. The solution of a salt that has the cation of a strong base and the anion of a weak acid (such as Na$_2$CO$_3$) will form what type of solution?

A. It cannot be determined.
B. acidic
C. basic
D. neutral

264. How many pi bonds are in a double bond?

A. 4
B. 3
C. 1
D. 2

265. For the neutralization reaction 2 NaOH (aq) + H$_2$SO$_4$ (aq) → Na$_2$SO$_4$ (aq) + 2 H$_2$O (l), what volume of acid at a concentration of 0.2 M will be needed to neutralize 10 mL of 0.1 M NaOH?

A. 2.5 mL
B. 5 mL
C. 7.5 mL
D. 10 mL

266. Patients with particularly high fever tend to display rapid shallow breathing, caused by the increase in the metabolic rate. Whose law tells us that at elevated temperatures, chemical reactions occur faster?

A. Dalton
B. Schroedinger
C. Arrhenius
D. LeChatelier

267. For the decomposition of a simple dipeptide (glycine-glycine) by hydrolysis, NH$_2$CH$_2$CO$_2$NHCH$_2$CO$_2$H (aq) + H$_2$O (l) → 2 NH$_2$CH$_2$CO$_2$H (aq), what would be the correct form of the equation for stating the rate of this reaction as a function of the formation of the monopeptide?

A. $rate = \dfrac{d\left[NH_2CH_2CO_2H\right]}{dt}$

B. $rate = 2\,\dfrac{d\left[NH_2CH_2CO_2H\right]}{dt}$

C. $rate = -\dfrac{1}{2}\dfrac{d\left[NH_2CH_2CO_2H\right]}{dt}$

D. $rate = \dfrac{1}{2}\dfrac{d\left[NH_2CH_2CO_2H\right]}{dt}$

268. What would be the correct IUPAC name for FePO$_4$?

A. Iron(III) Phosphate
B. Iron(II) Phosphate
C. Iron(I) Phosphate
D. Iron Phosphate

269. Hyperventilation leads to the breakdown of carbonic acid as follows.

$$H_2CO_3 \text{ (aq)} \rightarrow H_2O \text{ (l)} + CO_2 \text{ (g)}$$

In terms of this equation, the breakdown of carbonic acid should be accompanied by what kind of change in entropy?

A. It should increase.
B. It should decrease.
C. It should remain constant.
D. It would be impossible to tell.

270. Assuming complete dissociation of the solates, which of the following would be expected to have the highest vapor pressure at 25 degrees?

A. 0.1 M NaCl
B. 0.1 M CaCl$_2$
C. 0.1 M AlF$_3$
D. pure water

GO ON TO THE NEXT PAGE

Critical Thinking Essay

Directions: You will have 30 minutes in which to write an essay in response to the following statement. This essay will either require you to express an opinion or will present a problem that needs a solution.

Discuss a solution to the problem that as people rely more and more on technology to solve problems, we lose contact with our own abilities to be creative.

Answer Key for Practice Test 2

Verbal Ability: Analogies

1. C		11. C		21. D	
2. D		12. C		22. D	
3. B		13. A		23. A	
4. D		14. D		24. B	
5. B		15. B		25. C	
6. D		16. D		26. D	
7. C		17. D		27. C	
8. A		18. A		28. B	
9. B		19. D		29. C	
10. D		20. C			

Verbal Ability: Sentence Completions

30. A		40. A		50. D	
31. D		41. A		51. B	
32. C		42. C		52. A	
33. D		43. A		53. D	
34. A		44. C		54. B	
35. C		45. B		55. D	
36. D		46. C		56. A	
37. B		47. D		57. C	
38. A		48. A		58. B	
39. C		49. A			

Biology

59. C	**79.** D	**99.** D
60. A	**80.** B	**100.** C
61. B	**81.** D	**101.** B
62. C	**82.** A	**102.** C
63. D	**83.** C	**103.** A
64. B	**84.** C	**104.** D
65. C	**85.** D	**105.** B
66. B	**86.** A	**106.** D
67. C	**87.** A	**107.** C
68. A	**88.** D	**108.** D
69. D	**89.** D	**109.** A
70. D	**90.** B	**110.** C
71. C	**91.** B	**111.** D
72. B	**92.** C	**112.** B
73. B	**93.** A	**113.** B
74. C	**94.** D	**114.** D
75. D	**95.** C	**115.** A
76. D	**96.** A	**116.** A
77. A	**97.** B	
78. D	**98.** A	

Reading Comprehension

117. C	**134.** A	**151.** C
118. D	**135.** B	**152.** C
119. A	**136.** A	**153.** B
120. A	**137.** C	**154.** B
121. B	**138.** C	**155.** D
122. D	**139.** C	**156.** C
123. A	**140.** B	**157.** C
124. A	**141.** C	**158.** B
125. A	**142.** B	**159.** C
126. B	**143.** C	**160.** A
127. A	**144.** A	**161.** C
128. C	**145.** C	**162.** A
129. A	**146.** C	**163.** A
130. D	**147.** A	**164.** C
131. A	**148.** D	**165.** B
132. B	**149.** A	
133. B	**150.** C	

Quantitative Ability

166. D	**182.** B	**198.** B
167. D	**183.** C	**199.** B
168. A	**184.** B	**200.** D
169. A	**185.** D	**201.** B
170. C	**186.** A	**202.** B
171. C	**187.** D	**203.** D
172. D	**188.** B	**204.** B
173. C	**189.** C	**205.** D
174. A	**190.** A	**206.** D
175. A	**191.** C	**207.** A
176. B	**192.** C	**208.** C
177. C	**193.** B	**209.** A
178. D	**194.** A	**210.** B
179. D	**195.** B	**211.** A
180. A	**196.** D	**212.** D
181. C	**197.** A	**213.** B

Chemistry

214. A	**233.** B	**252.** B
215. A	**234.** D	**253.** C
216. C	**235.** C	**254.** C
217. B	**236.** A	**255.** D
218. C	**237.** B	**256.** C
219. A	**238.** D	**257.** B
220. A	**239.** C	**258.** B
221. D	**240.** A	**259.** C
222. B	**241.** B	**260.** A
223. B	**242.** A	**261.** B
224. B	**243.** A	**262.** D
225. B	**244.** C	**263.** C
226. A	**245.** B	**264.** C
227. C	**246.** D	**265.** A
228. B	**247.** B	**266.** C
229. D	**248.** D	**267.** D
230. A	**249.** A	**268.** A
231. C	**250.** B	**269.** B
232. A	**251.** D	**270.** D

Complete Answers and Explanations for Practice Test 2

Verbal Ability: Analogies

1. **C.** A star is part of a constellation. A skirmish is part of an insurrection or rebellion.

2. **D.** If something is indelible, it is permanent. If something is enduring, it is fixed and cannot be changed. All four words are similar.

3. **B.** To be euphoric is to be extremely happy. To have rage is to be extremely angry.

4. **D.** Something that is auspicious is something that is favorable. If something is copious, it means there is a lot, so it is plentiful.

5. **B.** A group of people who plot together are involved in collusion. Likewise, a junta is a group of people who get together and are involved in a plot.

6. **D.** Arid is related to taste; pungent is related to smell.

7. **C.** To accede is to acquiesce or give in and compromise. To concur is to agree.

8. **A.** A coward displays cowardice or being craven, as a sage would display being wise.

9. **B.** Something that is verbose is very wordy, while something succinct is very concise, so the words are opposite. The opposite of irrational is logical.

10. **D.** A caustic remark is a rude remark. A petulant person is an impatient person.

11. **C.** Being elated is extreme happiness. Having a tirade is showing extreme complaints.

12. **C.** A characteristic of a philanthropist is being munificent or giving money to charity. A characteristic of a traitor is being perfidious or very disloyal.

13. **A.** A quality of an expert is that he has skill. A quality of a neophyte or someone new to something is inexperience.

14. **D.** To be flamboyant is to be extremely showy. An extreme campfire is a conflagration.

15. **B.** An expert in food is a gourmand and an expert in wine is a connoisseur.

16. **D.** Something that is funny or facetious makes you laugh; something that is lachrymose or sad makes you cry.

17. **D.** A gregarious person likes to be with people; an aloof one stays away. A loquacious person loves to talk; a reticent one stays away from talking.

18. **A.** Someone who is intrepid has no fear and is dauntless or fearless. Someone who is inexorable will not give in and is unrelenting.

19. **D.** A braggart is a boastful person. A bigot is a biased or prejudiced person.

20. **C.** An armory is where you store weapons. An aviary is where you find birds.

21. **D.** You use a thesaurus to find a synonym for a word and an atlas to find maps.

22. **D.** When you leave things or legacies, you put it in a will. When you leave a bequest or legacy, you leave it in a codicil or addition to a will.

23. **A.** Someone who is candid does not hide anything and is not deceptive. Someone who is frank is very open and is not duplicitous or deceptive.

24. **B.** To be contiguous means to be next to or adjacent to something. To abut means to juxtapose or be next to something.

25. C. To initiate is to start something; to consummate is to end it. To commence means to begin; to terminate is to end.

26. D. An odometer measures distance. A scale measures weight.

27. C. Quixotic means to be unrealistic or having idealism. Being realistic is having pragmatism or a practical approach to life.

28. B. To divulge is not to conceal. To impart is not to hide.

29. C. A dilettante is someone who tries a lot of different hobbies and is the same as a dabbler. An expert is someone who focuses on one thing and is a master at it.

Verbal Ability: Sentence Completions

30. A. The word in the blank should have a negative connotation. Onerous means burdensome. Horrendous, Choice **C**, implies something terrifying, which is too strong a word to describe maintenance chores.

31. D. Scion means an heir or a descendant.

32. C. Salient means prominent or conspicuous; because the cantilevers lacked support, they had to be unstable.

33. D. Proximity means nearness. Consanguinity, although suggesting closeness, means related by blood.

34. A. Something utopian is idealistic and difficult to achieve; thus, it is impractical.

35. C. Compatible means capable of forming a harmonious combination.

36. D. Although customary, Choice **A**, might fit in the first blank, because the sentence begins with the word "although," the second blank requires a word that suggests something that is not as well known as a tradition or custom.

37. B. Gratuitous means unnecessary or uncalled for. The words insensitivity and rudeness in the sentence imply the word in the blank has a negative connotation.

38. A. The other choices include at least one word that creates a physical impossibility.

39. C. To infiltrate is to pass secretly into enemy territory. Because the subject of the sentence is a secret agent, conquer is not the best answer.

40. A. A heretic is one hold opinions contrary to those established by a religious belief.

41. A. The first blank requires a word that means decide; dominates means controls.

42. C. Indispensable means absolutely necessary.

43. A. An inventory is a detailed or itemized record or list. A memorandum suggests a short reminder or note.

44. C. To rescind means to take back or cancel.

45. B. The first blank requires a word with a positive connotation; in the second blank, remedial means supplying a remedy or improving deficient skills.

46. C. To defer means to put off until a later time. The word's next meaning in the sentence make this the correct choice.

47. D. Mandatory means required by authority or law. The U.S. Constitution is a set of laws.

48. A. The sentence suggests the word in the first blank denotes something small; inconsequential means unimportant or not causing serious effects. Contend means argue.

49. A. Perseverance means persistent effort; aspiring means having a goal or desire.

50. D. Amended means changes. If the cake collapsed, the recipe needed to be corrected.

51. B. Precursors are forerunners or events that come before another event. The word approaching in the sentence makes this the best choice.

52. A. The words tragic events require a word with positive connotations in the first blank. Benign means calm and peaceful. To subvert is to destroy or completely ruin.

53. D. A benefactor is one who provides aid, especially financial assistance.

54. B. The meaning of the sentence implies a contrast between the amount of work to be done and the fact that it was possible to do it quickly. Although Choice **A** might be considered, when something turns out not to be what it appeared to, that is not a lie.

55. D. Sham means false or fake.

56. A. Bountiful means generous or abundant, and replete means completely filled.

57. C. Because the gunfighter was scorned, the word in the blank must have a negative connotation. A pariah is an outcast.

58. B. Predilection means preference for or partiality toward.

Biology

59. C. During the process of photosynthesis, light energy from the sun is converted to chemical energy in the form of glucose.

60. A. Both plants and animals carry out the process of cellular respiration. This process, which takes place in the mitochondria of cells, breaks down glucose, producing energy in the form of ATP.

61. B. In any given food chain, the autotrophic organisms (organisms that are able to produce their own food) form the base. These organisms are referred to as producers. Organisms that feed on the producers are referred to as primary consumers; organisms that feed on the primary consumers are referred to as secondary consumers; and so forth. The consumers in the food chain are all heterotrophic (unable to produce their own food). The decomposers (fungi, bacteria, slime molds) break down dead organic matter and recycle it into the ecosystem. The decomposers operate at all levels of the food chain.

62. C. When consumed, toxins are usually sequestered and stored in the liver and fatty tissue of the organisms that consumed them. Thus, when a toxin enters the food chain, it becomes more and more concentrated at each trophic level. This increase in toxin concentration at subsequent levels of the food chain is referred to as biological magnification.

63. D. Most carbon is cycled through an ecosystem in the form of carbon dioxide, which is taken up by plants, algae, and cyanobacteria for use in photosynthesis and released by all organisms as a waste product of cellular respiration.

64. B. Parasitism involves one organism (e.g., tapeworm) living in or on a host organism (e.g., human). Predation (Choice **A**) involves one organism (e.g., mountain lion) killing and consuming another organism (e.g., deer). Mutualism (Choice **C**) is a type of symbiotic relationship in which both organisms benefit from the relationship (e.g., green algae and fungi living together as a lichen). Commensalism (Choice **D**) is a symbiotic relationship in which the symbiont benefits but the host is neither helped nor harmed.

65. C. The basic structure of the DNA double helix is composed of paired nucleotides held together by hydrogen bonds. Each nucleotide is composed of deoxyribose sugar, a phosphate group, and a nitrogenous base (adenine, thymine, guanine, or cytosine). Specifically, the DNA double helix consists of a backbone of alternating phosphate groups and sugars (deoxyribose), held together by paired nitrogenous bases.

66. B. The process in which the genetic code on the DNA molecule is copied onto a messenger RNA (mRNA) molecule is referred to as transcription. The process by which the code on the mRNA is converted into a polypeptide chain is referred to a translation (Choice **C**). Both transcription and translation are part of the overall process of protein synthesis (Choice **D**). DNA replication (Choice **A**) refers to the process by which a molecule of DNA synthesizes another copy of itself (for example, prior to cell division).

67. **C.** The genetic makeup of an individual is referred to as his genotype. The physical appearance of an individual is referred to as his phenotype (Choice **B**). The genetic code (Choice **A**) refers to the triplet of nitrogen bases that code for amino acids. A gene pool (Choice **D**) refers to the genetic constitution of a population.

68. **A.** An individual with two different alleles for a given trait (in this case, eye color) is said to be heterozygous for that trait. If both alleles for a given trait are the same (e.g., two alleles for blue eye color), the individual is said to be homozygous for the trait (Choice **B**). Dominance (Choice **C**) and recessiveness (Choice **D**) refer to the expression of alleles when present together in an individual. In this example, a person with one blue allele and one brown allele for eye color would have brown eyes because the brown allele is dominant over the blue allele.

69. **D.** The "M," "N," and "MN" blood groups in humans are an example of co-dominance, in which both alleles are expressed equally in the phenotype. With complete dominance (Choice **A**) the dominant allele masks the recessive allele. With incomplete dominance (Choice **C**), the phenotype is usually intermediate between the dominant and recessive phenotypes, with neither allele fully expressed. There is no condition referred to as complete recessiveness (Choice **B**).

70. **D.** A woman with type-AB blood and a man with type-O blood could produce children with either type-A or type-B blood. The woman would carry one A allele and one B allele for blood type, while the man would carry two O alleles. The A and B alleles are co-dominant, and the O allele is recessive to both the A and B alleles. Because the children would receive one allele from their mother and one allele from their father, the children could have the genotypes AO (with type-A blood) or BO (with type-B blood).

71. **C.** The characterization of an individual's DNA by restriction analysis and gel electrophoresis is referred to as a DNA fingerprint.

72. **B.** A transgenic organism is one in which DNA from another organism has been inserted into its DNA.

73. **B.** For evolution to take place, the genetic variation present in a population must be heritable (able to be passed on from parent to offspring).

74. **C.** Genetic drift involves a large reduction in population size, often accompanied by the loss of a large amount of genetic variation from the gene pool of a population. Both mutation (Choice **B**) and random mating (Choice **D**) act to enhance the amount of genetic variation present in the gene pool. Natural selection (Choice **A**) operates along with mutation, migration, and other forces affecting evolution, but does not in itself directly lead to an increase or decrease in the genetic variation present in the gene pool of a population.

75. **D.** Prokaryotic cells lack an organized nucleus and other well-defined organelles; whereas, eukaryotic cells have both a nucleus and well-defined organelles and, thus, are generally more complex than prokaryotic cells.

76. **D.** Plant cells tend to have a large central vacuole, while animal cells typically have several smaller vacuoles. A lack of mitochondria (Choice **A**) would indicate a bacterial (prokaryotic) cell. The presence of mitochondria (Choice **B**) would not distinguish between a plant cell and an animal cell, as both contain mitochondria. Plant cells have cell walls (Choice **C**), so lack of a cell wall would suggest the cell being observed is from animal tissue.

77. **A.** Human nerve cells are referred to as neurons. Axons (Choice **B**) and dendrites (Choice **C**) are nerve fibers extending from neurons that serve to conduct signals between neuron or between neurons and effectors (Choice **D**)—cells, tissues, or organs capable of carrying out a response to a nervous-system signal.

78. **D.** If cells forming animal tissue were placed in saltwater, they would lose water to their surrounding environment by osmosis. This would result in a shriveling up of the cell. If those same cells were placed in pure water (as opposed to a physiological saline solution) they would take up water and swell and burst.

79. **D.** Meiosis results in the production of four haploid daughter cells from each diploid parent cell. Thus, in this example, a parent cell containing 36 chromosomes would produce 4 daughter cells, each having 18 chromosomes, through the process of meiosis.

80. **B.** Mitosis produces two identical daughter cells from each original parent cell.

81. **D.** When a chromosome undergoes replication prior to cell division, the number of chromosome remains the same, but each chromosome will contain two copies of its DNA. These two DNA copies are referred to as sister chromatids.

82. A. Crossing over does not take place in mitosis.

83. C. In animals, meiosis gives rise directly to gametes, whereas in plants, meiosis gives rise to spores. The spores subsequently germinate to form a gametophyte stage, which produces the gametes.

84. C. Increasing the nutrient content of the culture would allow for greater reproductive potential in a bacterial colony. Most bacterial strains have an optimum temperature for growth and reproduction. Greatly increasing (Choice **A**) or decreasing (Choice **B**) the temperature would reduce the rate of growth and reproduction in the colony. Increasing the salt concentration of the media (Choice **D**) would likely kill most bacterial colonies, except perhaps halophytic (salt-loving) bacterial strains.

85. D. The normal bacterial strains that colonize the human gut serve to protect against invasion by foreign bacteria by competing with the foreign strains for food, producing antimicrobial substances that kill off the foreign strains, and stimulating the immune system to fight off invading microorganisms.

86. A. The inflammatory response is initiated following any kind of damage or physical injury, which triggers the release of chemical signals, such as histamine. These chemicals may induce nearby blood vessels to dilate and become leaky, causing more blood flow to the area. Other chemicals may attract phagocytes to the area, which consume any bacteria or cellular debris. The accumulated white blood cells and their breakdown products cause localized swelling of the infected tissue. The production of stomach acid (Choice **A**), the production of lysozymes in tears (Choice **D**), and the presence of a normal bacterial flora in the human gut (Choice **C**) are all examples of passive immune-system responses, as they are present continuously in the body, regardless of the presence of infectious agents.

87. A. Plasmids are small, extracellular structures present in most bacteria; however, they are not essential for survival or reproduction of the bacterial cell.

88. D. Influenza is a viral infection, and, thus, is not caused by a bacterial agent.

89. D. The Gram stain is used to distinguish between Gram-positive and Gram-negative bacterial strains based on the distinctive staining patterns of the two groups resulting from differences in the cell-wall components of each group. Thus, the Gram stain is considered to be a differential stain.

90. B. Autoclaving, which uses pressurized steam for sterilization, is considered the most effective sterilization technique currently available. The pressurized steam is able to penetrate bacterial spores and destroy them. UV radiation (Choice **A**) and 70% ethanol (Choice **D**) have very low sporicidal activity, while pasteurization (Choice **C**) has little to no sporicidal activity.

91. B. The development of antibiotic-resistant strains of bacteria can result from the inappropriate use of antibiotics (for example, not taking the entire course of a prescribed drug) and the routine addition of antibiotics to animal feed.

92. C. Human saliva contains enzymes that destroy many strains of invading bacteria. The pH of human saliva is close to neutral and is not sufficiently anaerobic to destroy invading bacterial strains.

93. A. The human gut contains a natural population of nonpathogenic *Escherichia coli*.

94. D. While some vaccines use killed or weakened viruses as an immunizing agent, the tetanus vaccine uses a toxoid as the immunizing agent.

95. C. If a bottle of wine is left open and exposed to air for a long period of time, acid-forming bacteria use the oxygen to convert the ethanol in the wine to acetic acid.

96. A. The human heart consists of four chambers: the right and left atria and the right and left ventricles.

97. B. The rhythmic stretching and relaxing of the arteries as blood is forced through them is referred to as the pulse. The pulse provides a measure of heart rate (Choice **A**). Blood pressure (Choice **C**) is the amount of force the blood exerts against the blood vessels. Systole (Choice **D**), is the phase of the cardiac cycle in which the atria briefly contract, filling the ventricles with blood.

98. A. Red blood cells do not have nuclei.

99. D. The primary function of the lymph nodes is to filter the lymph and phagocytize foreign particles.

100. C. In the human respiratory system, gas exchange occurs between the red blood cells and alveoli (small sacs at the termini of the bronchioles in the lungs).

101. B. Peristalsis, the rhythmic muscular contractions of smooth muscle that occur along the human digestive tract, helps to move a bolus of food through the esophagus and into the stomach, as well as helping to move chyme out of the stomach and into the small intestine. Peristalsis also helps move feces out of the large intestine.

102. C. Bile is made in the liver and stored in the gall bladder. It is emptied from the gall bladder into the small intestine to assist with the digestion of fats.

103. A. Urine contains urea, which is toxic to humans in large quantities.

104. D. Androgen is responsible for the production of secondary male (not female) characteristics.

105. B. The nephron is part of the human excretory system.

106. D. The human nervous system processes information in an organized manner, starting with sensory input, followed by integration of the signal, and finally ending with a response (motor output).

107. C. The part of the brain responsible for coordinating motor activity and muscle contractions is the cerebellum. The medulla (Choice **A**) is a small swelling at the tip of the hindbrain that serves as a passageway for nerves extending to and from the brain and controls automatic functions such as breathing, heart rate and digestion. The cerebrum (Choice **B**) is responsible for coordinating such activities as vision, hearing, smell, and speech. The hypothalamus (Choice **D**) regulates hunger, thirst, body temperature, and blood pressure, as well as synthesizes hormones that will be stored in the pituitary.

108. D. The human nervous system is divided into the central nervous system (brain and spinal cord) and the peripheral nervous system (nerves extending to and from the central nervous system).

109. A. In humans, the function of the sympathetic nervous system is to prepare the body for emergencies. The parasympathetic nervous system returns the body to a normal state following an emergency (Choice **B**). The sensory somatic system carries impulses from external stimuli to the brain (Choice **C**). The limbic system controls emotional responses to external stimuli (Choice **D**).

110. C. While the human body can manufacture many of its own amino acids, some must be obtained through the diet. Those amino acids needed by humans that cannot be manufactured by the body and, therefore, must be obtained through the diet, are referred to as essential amino acids.

111. D. Humans store excess kilocalories as glycogen in muscle and liver cells, as this is the most efficient source of energy utilized by the body. When the glycogen stores are full, an individual will begin storing excess kilocalories as fat that can be broken down for energy once all the glycogen stores are used up.

112. B. In the human immune system, the skin, stomach acid, mucous membranes, and macrophages all represent nonspecific immune responses, meaning they respond to any foreign invader. The production of specific antibodies to foreign molecules (antigens) represents a specific immune response.

113. B. When the human immune system is stimulated by coming in contact with a foreign antigen, it responds by producing a specific antibody.

114. D. White blood cells that attack and destroy cancer cells and cells infected by viruses are referred to as natural killer cells. Macrophages (Choice **B**) are a type of phagocyte (Choice **A**); these are cells that attack and destroy invading infectious agents, such as bacteria. Erythrocytes (Choice **C**) are red blood cells and are not considered a direct part of the human immune system.

115. A. Although many vaccines use killed or deactivated virus particles to stimulate the immune response, they will usually not cause one to become ill with the virus used in the vaccine.

116. A. When the human body encounters a foreign agent for the second time, the immune response is typically much faster than when the foreign agent was first encountered. This is due to immune system memory, which allows the immune system to recognize an invading agent as having been previously encountered.

Reading Comprehension

117. C. Choices **A** and **B** are too narrow. Choice **D** has no evidence in the text.

118. D. All those details are found in the first paragraph.

119. A. The sentence that states this fact is in the middle of the first paragraph.

120. A. The text states that military and civilian scientists, meteorologists, and developers all can use the system. Thus, it is useful to all people.

121. B. This statement is found at the end of the first paragraph.

122. D. Although looking for positive data (Choice **A**) and examining for bugs (Choice **C**) might be incorporated in analyzing its effectiveness, the word "quantify" suggests predicting its future success.

123. A. No questionnaires were mentioned (Choice **B**). There is no specific information about successes (Choice **C**), and the reference to 170 applications is talking about something else (Choice **D**).

124. A. It is stated in the first sentence.

125. A. The first sentence in the second paragraph states this.

126. B. This is stated in the first sentence of the fourth paragraph.

127. A. Evidence is found in paragraph four.

128. C. Evidence is found in paragraph four. Be careful of the difference between "precedes" (Choice **C**) and "proceeds" (Choice **B**).

129. A. Choices **B** and **C** are too narrow and Choice **D** has no evidence to support that idea.

130. D. The wording of the last sentence indicates a firm belief (adamant) about the need for collaboration. There is no evidence of anger (Choice **A**) or annoyance (Choice **B**), and the encouragement (Choice **C**) is due to the collaboration that is necessary.

131. A. It states that it is microscopic and uses only a tiny bit of tissue.

132. B. This is stated in the third sentence of the first paragraph.

133. B. Choices **A, C,** and **D** have no support within the article.

134. A. Tests include three steps and doing assays is one of them. Natural remedies have not gone through the extensive tests that the pharmaceuticals have.

135. B. This is stated at the end of the third paragraph. Cost (Choice **A**) is not mentioned. Taste (Choice **C**) is not mentioned, nor is marketing (Choice **D**).

136. A. The second to the last sentence of the article states this.

137. C. This is stated in the last sentence.

138. C. This is stated in the last sentence of the first paragraph.

139. C. There is no comparison between people (Choice **A**). The reflexes slow down at a quarter of a second (Choice **B**). There is no support for the idea in Choice **D**.

140. B. This is stated in the third sentence of the second paragraph.

141. C. Although you might agree with choices **A** and **D**, the article is not about this. There is no evidence of Choice **B**.

142. B. This is stated in the last sentence of the second paragraph.

143. C. Contradictory means opposite of what you expect. When you sleep, your organs don't sleep!

144. A. There is no contradiction (Choice **C**), and the information goes beyond the fact that sleep is necessary (Choice **D**). All statements include the affect of sleep on the brain.

145. C. This is stated in the first paragraph.

146. C. This is stated in the second to the last sentence of the first paragraph.

147. A. The first sentence of the second paragraph defines it as an amphibious fungal plaque.

148. D. Choice **A** is contradicted by the information in the text. The point of the article is that there is no inspection (Choice **B**). The first part of Choice **C** is true, but the second part of the statement is false.

149. A. The third paragraph explains the duties of various departments but none deals with the examination of imported creatures.

150. C. The second sentence of the last paragraph defines the word.

151. C. There is the statement that this disease is resistant to eight drugs in the last paragraph.

152. C. It is defined in the third sentence of the first paragraph.

153. B. In the first paragraph, there is the description of one comet moving north and the other one moving east.

154. B. The description of a fly ball allows us to think about the comet's motion.

155. D. At the end of the first paragraph, they state that the bluish color is from ionized gas.

156. C. The second paragraph discusses the movement and shape of the rings.

157. C. The third paragraph raises these questions about changes in the planet Jupiter.

158. B. The last sentence of the last paragraph defines Antares as a red supergiant.

159. C. The definition is given in the first paragraph, and the name is the abbreviation of autonomous underwater vehicle.

160. A. This is stated in the second sentence of the second paragraph.

161. C. The last sentence of the second paragraph states it measures salinity, which means the amount of salt in the water.

162. A. This is stated in the middle of the third paragraph.

163. A. This is stated at the end of the fourth paragraph.

164. C. The last sentence mentions that it will become commonplace like the airplane did, but it takes time.

165. B. The use of the word "astounding" in the first sentence of the last paragraph indicates excitement.

Quantitative Ability

166. D. There are 24 eggs in 2 dozen eggs. If 3 eggs are in an omelet, then $24 \div 3$, or 8 omelets can be made.

167. D. If an item is discounted 20%, the sale price is 80% of the original price. Let p represent the original price. Then $\$800 = 80\% \times p$ and $p = \frac{800}{80\%} = \frac{800}{.80} = \$1,000$.

168. A. The amount of discount is $\$40 - \$30 = \$10$. The percent of discount is the amount of discount divided by the original price: $\frac{10}{40} = \frac{1}{4} = 25\%$.

169. A. The proportion $\frac{\frac{1}{2}\,\text{mile}}{4\,\text{minutes}} = \frac{x\,\text{miles}}{15\,\text{minutes}}$ = models this situation. Cross-multiply.

$\frac{1}{2} \times 15 = 4x$ so $\frac{15}{2} = 4x$ and $x = \frac{15}{2} \cdot \frac{1}{4} = \frac{15}{8} = 1\frac{7}{8}$ miles.

170. C. In order to solve the equation for x, raise both sides of the equation to the $\frac{3}{2}$ power. Thus, $\left(x^{\frac{2}{3}}\right)^{\frac{3}{2}} = 9^{\frac{3}{2}}$, or $x = \left(\sqrt{9}\right)^3 = 3^3 = 27$.

171. C. The perimeter of a rectangle is $l + w + l + w = 48$. Since $l = 3w$, the perimeter is $3w + w + 3w + w = 48$ so $8w = 48$ and $w = 6$. Therefore, the length is 3×6 or 18 and the area of the rectangle is $l \times w = 18 \times 6 = 108$.

172. D. First add the number of feet together and then add the number of inches.

$$2 \text{ ft} + 4 \text{ ft} + 3 \text{ ft} = 9 \text{ ft}.$$

$$2\frac{1}{2} \text{ in} + 3\frac{3}{8} \text{ in} + 9\frac{3}{4} \text{ in} + \frac{5}{2} + \frac{27}{8} + \frac{39}{4} = \frac{20}{8} + \frac{27}{8} + \frac{78}{8} = \frac{125}{8} = 15\frac{5}{8} \text{ in}.$$

$15\frac{5}{8}$ in $= 1$ ft $3\frac{5}{8}$ in., so all together 9 ft $+ 1$ ft $3\frac{5}{8}$ in $= 10$ ft $3\frac{5}{8}$ in.

173. C. The total number of inches in a 10-foot rope is $10 \times 12 = 120$ inches. The number of 8-inch segments that can be cut is $\frac{120}{8} = 15$.

174. A. The tax on the bill is $\$38.40 \times 6\% = \$2.30$. The amount, including tax, is $\$38.40 + \$2.30 = \$40.70$. The tip is $\$40.70 \times 15\% = \$6.11$.

175. A. Since $g(x) = 16^{-x}$, it follows that $g\left(\frac{1}{2}\right) = 16^{-\frac{1}{2}} = \left(\frac{1}{16}\right)^{\frac{1}{2}} = \sqrt{\frac{1}{16}} = \frac{1}{4}$.

176. B. The discounted amount after the first week is $\$1,000 \times 25\% = \$250$ so the sale price is $\$1,000 - \$250 = \$750$. The discounted amount after the second week is $\$750 \times 10\% = \$75$, so the sale price is $\$750 - \$75 = \$675$.

177. C. Interest $=$ Principal $\times$ Rate $\times$ Time. Thus, Interest $= \$1,000 \times 2\frac{1}{4}\% \times 5 = \$1,000 \times 0.0225 \times 5 = \$112.50$.

178. D. Let n represent the number. If 12 is 15% of n, then $12 = 0.15n$. Divide both sides by 0.15. Therefore, $n = 80$.

179. D. Following the correct order of operations produces:

$$(3 - 1) \times 7 - 12 \div 2 = 2 \times 7 - (12 \div 2) = 14 - 6 = 8.$$

180. A. Using the properties of derivatives, if $y = t^2 - 8t + 3$, then $\frac{dy}{dt} = 2t - 8$.

181. C. $\dfrac{9x^2 y^3 z - 12xy^2 z^2}{3yz} = \dfrac{9x^2 y^3 z}{3yz} - \dfrac{12xy^2 z^2}{3yz} = 3x^2 y^2 - 4xyz$

182. B. Let $x = \log_3 81$. Then, by the definition of logarithm, $3^x = 81$, so $x = 4$.

183. C. Angles in a triangle add to $180°$. So $3x + 4x + 5x = 180°$ and $12x = 180°$. Dividing both sides by 12 results in $x = 15°$. The smallest angle is represented by $3x = 3(15°) = 45°$.

184. B. Prime factors of 120 are $2 \times 2 \times 2 \times 3 \times 5$. Distinct factors are 2, 3, and 5. Therefore, there are 3 distinct prime factors.

185. D. Using the ratio $\dfrac{\text{height}}{\text{shadow}}$, the proportion $\dfrac{x \text{ feet}}{5 \text{ feet}} = \dfrac{6 \text{ feet}}{8 \text{ feet}}$ can be used to find the unknown height. Cross-multiply. $8x = 5 \times 6$ so $8x = 30$ and $x = \dfrac{30}{8} = 3\frac{3}{4}$ feet. Convert $\frac{3}{4}$ feet to inches. $\frac{3}{4} \times 12 = 9$ inches. The height is therefore 3 feet 9 inches.

186. A. $-27^{\frac{2}{3}} = -\left(27^{\frac{2}{3}}\right) = 1\left(\sqrt[3]{27}\right)^2 = -(3)^2 = -9$.

187. D. If the blueprint shows $\frac{1}{2}$ inch for every 3 feet, then 1 inch represents 6 feet. The actual dimensions of a room $1\frac{1}{2}$ inches $\times$ 2 inches would be $\left(1\frac{1}{2} \times 6\right)$ by (2×6) or 9 feet by 12 feet.

188. B. To find the x-coordinate of the maximum value of the function, find the first derivative and set it equal to 0. The first derivative is $6 - 6x$, and this is 0 when $x = 1$. Note that, since the function represents a parabola that "opens down," there is only one maximum value, and it must be at $x = 1$.

189. C. The volume of a cube is s^3, where s represents the length of an edge. Surface area is $6s^2$. If the volume $= 343$ cm^3, then $s = \sqrt[3]{343} = \sqrt[3]{7 \cdot 7 \cdot 7} = 7$. So the surface area is $6 \cdot 7^2 = 6 \cdot 49 = 294$ cm^2.

190. A. The equation $\log_{16}x = -2$ is equivalent to $x = 16^{-2}$. Note that $16^{-2} = \left(\dfrac{1}{16}\right)^2 = \dfrac{1}{256}$.

191. C. The number of smaller pieces is $\dfrac{16.5}{2.75} = 6$.

192. C. The sine function is negative in quadrants III and IV, while the cosine function is negative in quadrants II and III. Therefore, they are both negative in the third quadrant.

193. B. The average is found by adding up all the scores and dividing by the total number of scores. The average this week is $\dfrac{112 + 156 + 179 + 165}{4} = \dfrac{612}{4} = 153$. The amount of improvement is $153 - 140 = 13$.

194. A. $5(a - 2) - (4a - 6) = 5a - 10 - 4a + 6 = a - 4$.

195. B. Let x be the unknown number. Then $9x = 117$ and $x = \dfrac{117}{9} = 13$.

196. D. Note that $\log \sqrt{F} = \log F^{\frac{1}{2}} = \dfrac{1}{2}\log F$. Since we are told that $\log F = 36$, $\dfrac{1}{2}\log F = 18$.

197. A. The cube root of 512 is $\sqrt[3]{512} = \sqrt[3]{8 \times 8 \times 8} = 8x$.

198. B. In the proportion $\dfrac{m}{n} = \dfrac{3}{5}$, let $m = 3$ and let $n = 5$. Therefore, $m + n = 3 + 5 = 8$.

199. B. The first derivative of $y = \sin x$ is $y'(x) = \cos x$.

200. D. If books are twice as much as magazines, then $b = 2m$. 5 books + 3 magazines $= 5b + 3m$. Substituting $2m$ for b gives $5(2m) + 3m = 10m + 3m = 13m$.

201. B. A good way to think about this problem is to recall that $\tan 2x = \dfrac{\sin 2x}{\cos 2x}$. Therefore, $\tan 2x$ will be undefined when $\cos 2x = 0$. Note that $\cos\left(\dfrac{\pi}{2}\right) = 0$, and, at $\dfrac{\pi}{4}$, $\cos 2x = \cos\left(\dfrac{\pi}{2}\right) = 0$. Thus, $\tan 2x$ is undefined at $\dfrac{\pi}{4}$.

202. B.

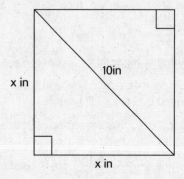

Let x represent a side of the square. The area of the square is x^2. To find the value of x^2, use the Pythagorean theorem. $x^2 + x^2 = 10^2$ so $2x^2 = 100$ and $x^2 = \dfrac{100}{2}$ or 50.

203. D. In order to find the derivative, it is necessary to use the product rule. Note that $f'(x) = (\cos x)(\cos x) + (\sin x)(-\sin x) = \cos^2 x - \sin^2 x$.

204. B. $0.00525 \div 0.01 = \dfrac{0.00525}{0.01} = 0.525$.

205. D. The sum of all angles in a triangle equal 180°. So $(3x - 20)° + x° + (2x - 10)° = 180°$.

$3x + x + 2x - 20 - 10 = 180$ and $6x - 30 = 180$. Then $6x = 210$ and $x = x = \dfrac{210}{6} = 35$.

Therefore, $\angle A$ is $3(35) - 20$ or 85°.

206. D. $\tan\theta\cos\theta\sec\theta = \dfrac{\sin\theta}{\cos\theta} \times \cos\theta \times \dfrac{1}{\cos\theta} = \tan\theta$.

207. A. $(5a^3bc^2)(-3a^2c) = 5 \cdot -3 \cdot a^{3+2}bc^{2+1} = -15a^5bc^3$.

208. C.

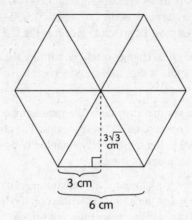

A regular hexagon is made up of six equilateral triangles. Find the area of one equilateral triangle and multiply that by 6 to find the area of the hexagon. The height, or altitude, of a triangle can be found by the Pythagorean theorem. The right triangle formed by the altitude has a hypotenuse of 6 and a shorter leg of $\frac{6}{2}$ or 3.

So $3^2 + h^2 = 6^2$ so $9 + h^2 = 36$ and $h^2 = 27$. Therefore, $h = \sqrt{27} = 3\sqrt{3}$. The area of one equilateral triangle is $\frac{1}{2} bh = \frac{1}{2} \cdot 6 \cdot 3\sqrt{3} = 9\sqrt{3}$ and the area of the hexagon is $6 \cdot 9\sqrt{3} = 54\sqrt{3}$.

209. A. By the properties of the integrals of exponential functions, $\int e^x dx = e^x + c$.

210. B. Begin by rewriting $x = -3y + 9$ in slope-intercept form as $y = -\frac{1}{3}x + 3$. The slope of the line is the coefficient of x, that is, $-\frac{1}{3}$.

211. A. Begin by rewriting 9 as 3^2, so that $3^{4x+2} = 9^{x-1}$ becomes $3^{4x+2} = 3^{2(x-1)}$. The only way this can be true is if $4x + 2 = 2(x - 1)$. This equation is true if $x = -2$.

212. D. The median of an odd number of numbers is the number in the middle when the numbers are put in numerical order. Note, then, that the median of this set is 0, which is also the mean.

213. B. Recall that the cosecant function is the reciprocal of the sine function. Thus, $\csc x = 2$ is the same as $\sin x = \frac{1}{2}$, which is true when $x = 30°$.

Chemistry

214. A. It does not matter what isotope of uranium we have, as this will influence the number of neutrons (in this case 143) not the number of electrons. Since uranium is atomic number 92, that means it has 92 protons and, in its elemental state, 92 electrons. However, since it has a +2 charge, it lost two electrons, giving it a total of 90 electrons.

215. A. A mass spectrograph smashes apart molecules creating positively charged components by smashing the molecules with high-energy electrons. This creates species that you are unlikely to find in ordinary circumstances (such as the hydroxide cation). However, the separation is based simply on atomic mass, and you calculate atomic masses of the pieces just as you would any molecule.

216. C. Entropy is usually thought of in terms of disorder, and in natural processes, it wants to be maximized. Internal energy (enthalpy) and Gibb's free energy both want to be minimized. Reaction rate deals with kinetics, not thermodynamics.

217. B. Although it is difficult to do by hand, MO theory will actually correct some misperceptions left by the other theories (such as the fact that oxygen is a di-radical, rather than having four lone pairs of electrons).

218. C. Kinetics is an important topic in medicine since we are concerned with how long medicines will remain in the human body after entering. For this equation, remember to invert the half-life (because of the −1 power), so 1/0.01=100. Then just divide by the initial concentration.

219. A. The broad strong hydroxide peak in an IR spectrograph at 3,200–3,550 cm^{-1} is one of the most easily recognized functional groups in infrared spectroscopy. A peak at 1,630–1,780 is a carbonyl, 2,220–2,260 is a nitrile, and 2,853–2,962 is common in most IR spectra since it is the C-H stretching peak.

220. A. Color is a physical property. A physical change might be turning the apple into applesauce (grinding), a chemical property might be that the apple is digestible, and a chemical change might be that the green apple ripens to red.

221. D. Looking at the periodic chart, we see that strontium (element number 38) is in the same family as calcium (element number 20), which is well known to build strong bones. The chemical and physical properties of these elements are so similar (since they are in the same family) that the body cannot distinguish between them, thus incorporating the strontium into the structure of bones.

222. B. The reaction written as Cu│Cu^{+2}║Ag^{+}│Ag means the reaction is occurring in an electrolytic cell. By convention, the oxidation (which occurs at the anode) is written on the left, and the reduction (which occurs at the cathode) on the right. The double lines (║) represent the salt bridge.

223. B. There are nine carbon atoms in the heterocycle, so it is a nonane. In addition, when numbering, you want the lowest possible number for functional groups, but by convention, you always number one of the bridgehead carbons as 1 and begin counting around the large ring first.

224. B. Two things to remember: First, it's always products over reactants, and second, in the equilibrium constant expression, the stoichiometric coefficient always becomes the superscript for the species. Thus, the equilibrium constant expression for this reaction is $K_{eq} = [N_2O_4][F_2]/[NO_2F]^2$.

225. B. The p subshell can hold a total of six electrons, so the ground state should be $1s^2 2s^2 2p^6 3s^1$ (the ground-state electronic configuration of sodium). However, since we are not breaking any of the orbital rules (such as putting too many electrons into a given orbital), this is, indeed, a legitimate electronic configuration and, therefore, is not forbidden. Since it is not ground state, it must be excited state.

226. A. There is no transference of a hydronium ion, so this is not acting according to the Bronsted-Lowry definition of acids and bases. In the Lewis definition, the lone pair donor is the base, and the lone pair acceptor is the acid.

227. C. The coordination number can be thought of as the number of coordinate covalent bonds on the central atom. This structure is tris(ethylenediamine) chromium (III), and while ethylenediamine is a bidentate ligand (and hence there are only three of them), there are six coordinate covalent bonds.

228. B. The solute is the reason we have the solution in the first place; it can be thought of as the "active ingredient." In this case, the solvent contains all the other components (and more); remember that even a solvent can be a mixture. Water is the foundation of the solvent, saccharine is a sweetener, and red is just for display.

229. D. You can imagine this as silver replacing lithium in lithium chloride and lithium replacing silver in silver nitrate. They are simply exchanging cations.

230. A. Gases expand to fill their container, thus both their shape and volume can change. Liquids assume the shape of their container but cannot significantly change their volume, while solids cannot change either their volume or their shape. The plasma state is defined as that state in which the kinetic energy is too high for even atoms themselves to hold together; thus, it is a gas of ions.

231. C. Calcium hydroxide has the formula Ca(OH)$_2$, so the solubility product expression will be $K_{sp} = [Ca^{+2}][OH^-]^2$. If the concentration of calcium is 0.01M (where M stands for Molarity), though, the concentration of hydroxide will be 0.02M because of the stoichiometric ratio. Thus, $K_{sp} = [0.01][0.02]^2$.

232. A. The significance of this compound is the conjugated diene, that can be used to help stabilize (through resonance) the cation formed in the loss of the carbon at the 5 position. Because this cation will be stabilized, we are likely to lose that carbon fastest, further propagating the conjugated pi system.

233. B. LeChatelier's principle is an important one in understanding physiological processes. It states that when a stress is applied to a system, the system will respond so as to relieve that stress. In this case, adding fluoride is a stress, so to remove fluoride, the equilibrium will shift to the right.

234. **D.** By looking at the bond order, you will find that the +2 ion has a bond order of 3, since the two electrons that you remove are from antibonding orbitals.

235. **C.** Enthalpy is the heat of reaction, determining if the reaction is exothermic or endothermic. Free energy (G) is related to whether or not the reaction is spontaneous and entropy is generally thought of as state of disorder.

236. **A.** Meta directors can help stabilize a positive charge on the meta position, as the carboxylic functional group can do via resonance.

237. **B.** Only the Lewis definition does not rely on the presence of hydronium or hydroxide ions; instead, it depends on lone pair electron donors (bases) and acceptors (acids).

238. **D.** There are two in the ring, plus one on the chain to the side. In rings, remember to "follow the path" around the ring; if there is any deviation, it counts toward chirality.

239. **C.** Sulfuric acid has two equivalents (that is, two acidic hydrogens per molecule), thus a 0.1 M solution will be 0.2 N.

240. **A.** Theoretical yield is what is found through standard stoichiometric calculations.

241. **B.** The order of oxidation for C is alkyne, alkene, alkane, alcohol, ketone or aldehyde, carboxylic acid, carbon dioxide.

242. **A.** Recall we can find the solubility product constants for each of these; $K_{SPKF} = [K^+][F^-] = [x] [x]_1$, $K_{SPCaI2} = [Ca^{+2}][I^-]^2 = [x] [2x]^2$, and so forth. Let x = solubility and substitute, and you will find the KF has the highest solubility when you solve for x.

243. **A.** The molecular mass of sodium hydroxide is 40 g/mol, and oxygen is 16 g/mol.

244. **C.** There are many terms to describe the donor, but the acceptor is typically the cation, accepting electron pair donated by the Lewis Bares.

245. **B.** The relationship for moles and absolute temperature can be derived from the ideal gas law.

246. **D.** Recall it's bonding electrons minus antibonding, divided by two. We could have discounted choices **B** and **C** immediately, since we will need an odd number of electrons to have a fractional bond order.

247. **B.** Matter has mass and volume; heat is a form of energy (with neither mass nor volume). Gases can be deceiving, because measuring the mass is a challenge, but they do, indeed, have mass.

248. **D.** Dehydration, caused in a runner primarily by perspiration, is essentially evaporation, making it a physical change rather than a chemical one.

249. **A.** The concept never even arises in the other theories. In fact, molecular orbital theory is such a powerful theory that it can even correct common errors propagated by the other theories, such as elemental oxygen. Using Lewis-Dot structures, it looks like diatomic oxygen has four lone pair electrons, but MO theory shows that one of these "lone pairs" is actually two unpaired electrons, making oxygen a di-radical and explaining its extreme reactivity.

250. **B.** Even flipping cyanide around leads to a new compound; the only difference is which atom is bonded to the central element.

251. **D.** Esters are generally very good smelling compounds frequently used in perfumes, and they also are the principle components in ear wax.

252. **B.** Percent is an easy concentration unit; for example, a saline solution of 0.5% w/v is simply 0.5 g of saline in 100 mL of solution. To use it in chemical calculations, however, we will need to know the density of the solution and molecular mass of the solute just to get to moles of the solution.

253. **C.** The more carbons on the free radical, the more stable the free radical will be. In addition, the more resonance to stabilize the free radical, the better as well.

254. **C.** Don't forget, OH has a mass of 17 g/mol, and you must double this and add the sum to the molar mass of Ca^H.

255. **D.** There are some polyatomic ions you should memorize. Ammonium has a charge of +1, carbonate –2. Be sure you know their formulas as well as their charges.

256. C. Electronegativity increases from left to right and bottom to top along the periodic chart.

257. B. Gamma radiation is not even a particle; it is pure energy and requires about an inch of lead to prevent penetration. Excessive exposure from the sun can lead to skin cancer.

258. B. The only double bond should be between carbon and oxygen, and a double bond is comprised of one sigma and one pi bond.

259. C. Alklosis is caused by hyperventilation, and this is the principle reaction responsible for it. This is why a paper bag is given to the victim; by capturing and reabsorbing the carbon dioxide, the loss of carbonic acid can be slowed.

260. A. An aldehyde is a double-bonded oxygen, and with its large electronegativity, there is a pull of electrons from adjacent carbons (the inductive effect). This same effect is seen with alcohols, but the presence of the hydrogen on the hydroxyl group will lessen the inductive effect in alcohol.

261. B. The oxidizing agent, if you recall, is always reduced. Here, nitrogen in the nitrate goes from +5 to +3 in the nitrous ion, thereby gaining electrons. Gaining electrons means it is reduced, which makes it the oxidizing agent.

262. D. Homolytic cleavage means the single bond is split with one electron going to each of the carbons involved in the bond. This breaks up the pair of electrons in the bond, leaving a free radical.

263. C. A weak acid forms a strong conjugate base, so the solution will be basic.

264. C. A single bond is a sigma bond, a double bond is one sigma and one pi bond, and a triple bond is one sigma and two pi bonds. Pi bonds are particularly important in organic reactions where electrophilic agents can easily break the weaker pi bond than they can a sigma bond.

265. A. 0.1 M * 10 mL gives 1 mmol of sodium hydroxide. It only requires 1 mole of sulfuric acid to neutralize the sodium hydroxide, so we need 0.5 mmol of acid; 0.5 mmol/0.2 M = 2.5 mL.

266. C. Arrhenius tells us that as temperature rises, reaction rates (as in metabolic processes) increase. As metabolism increases, the need to discard carbon dioxide and absorb oxygen increases, leading to an increase in respiration rate.

267. D. When measuring reaction rate using the formation of a product, use the positive change (no negative sign), and always divide by the stoichiometric coefficient.

268. A. You should know the charge of phosphate is –3, so to cancel the charge, iron must be +3. Since more than one oxidation state is possible for iron, you must include the roman numerals.

269. B. There are two big clues telling us that this is an increase in entropy. First, we have more moles of product than we have reactant. Second, and more important, notice the only gas we have is on the product side.

270. D. Remember your colligative properties; any solute will cause vapor pressure depression.

Answer Sheet for PCAT Practice Test 3

(Remove This Sheet and Use It to Mark Your Answers)

Verbal Ability: Analogies

1 Ⓐ Ⓑ Ⓒ Ⓓ
2 Ⓐ Ⓑ Ⓒ Ⓓ
3 Ⓐ Ⓑ Ⓒ Ⓓ
4 Ⓐ Ⓑ Ⓒ Ⓓ
5 Ⓐ Ⓑ Ⓒ Ⓓ
6 Ⓐ Ⓑ Ⓒ Ⓓ
7 Ⓐ Ⓑ Ⓒ Ⓓ
8 Ⓐ Ⓑ Ⓒ Ⓓ
9 Ⓐ Ⓑ Ⓒ Ⓓ
10 Ⓐ Ⓑ Ⓒ Ⓓ

11 Ⓐ Ⓑ Ⓒ Ⓓ
12 Ⓐ Ⓑ Ⓒ Ⓓ
13 Ⓐ Ⓑ Ⓒ Ⓓ
14 Ⓐ Ⓑ Ⓒ Ⓓ
15 Ⓐ Ⓑ Ⓒ Ⓓ
16 Ⓐ Ⓑ Ⓒ Ⓓ
17 Ⓐ Ⓑ Ⓒ Ⓓ
18 Ⓐ Ⓑ Ⓒ Ⓓ
19 Ⓐ Ⓑ Ⓒ Ⓓ
20 Ⓐ Ⓑ Ⓒ Ⓓ

21 Ⓐ Ⓑ Ⓒ Ⓓ
22 Ⓐ Ⓑ Ⓒ Ⓓ
23 Ⓐ Ⓑ Ⓒ Ⓓ
24 Ⓐ Ⓑ Ⓒ Ⓓ
25 Ⓐ Ⓑ Ⓒ Ⓓ
26 Ⓐ Ⓑ Ⓒ Ⓓ
27 Ⓐ Ⓑ Ⓒ Ⓓ
28 Ⓐ Ⓑ Ⓒ Ⓓ
29 Ⓐ Ⓑ Ⓒ Ⓓ

Verbal Ability: Sentence Completions

30 Ⓐ Ⓑ Ⓒ Ⓓ
31 Ⓐ Ⓑ Ⓒ Ⓓ
32 Ⓐ Ⓑ Ⓒ Ⓓ
33 Ⓐ Ⓑ Ⓒ Ⓓ
34 Ⓐ Ⓑ Ⓒ Ⓓ
35 Ⓐ Ⓑ Ⓒ Ⓓ
36 Ⓐ Ⓑ Ⓒ Ⓓ
37 Ⓐ Ⓑ Ⓒ Ⓓ
38 Ⓐ Ⓑ Ⓒ Ⓓ
39 Ⓐ Ⓑ Ⓒ Ⓓ

40 Ⓐ Ⓑ Ⓒ Ⓓ
41 Ⓐ Ⓑ Ⓒ Ⓓ
42 Ⓐ Ⓑ Ⓒ Ⓓ
43 Ⓐ Ⓑ Ⓒ Ⓓ
44 Ⓐ Ⓑ Ⓒ Ⓓ
45 Ⓐ Ⓑ Ⓒ Ⓓ
46 Ⓐ Ⓑ Ⓒ Ⓓ
47 Ⓐ Ⓑ Ⓒ Ⓓ
48 Ⓐ Ⓑ Ⓒ Ⓓ
49 Ⓐ Ⓑ Ⓒ Ⓓ

50 Ⓐ Ⓑ Ⓒ Ⓓ
51 Ⓐ Ⓑ Ⓒ Ⓓ
52 Ⓐ Ⓑ Ⓒ Ⓓ
53 Ⓐ Ⓑ Ⓒ Ⓓ
54 Ⓐ Ⓑ Ⓒ Ⓓ
55 Ⓐ Ⓑ Ⓒ Ⓓ
56 Ⓐ Ⓑ Ⓒ Ⓓ
57 Ⓐ Ⓑ Ⓒ Ⓓ
58 Ⓐ Ⓑ Ⓒ Ⓓ

Biology

59 Ⓐ Ⓑ Ⓒ Ⓓ
60 Ⓐ Ⓑ Ⓒ Ⓓ
61 Ⓐ Ⓑ Ⓒ Ⓓ
62 Ⓐ Ⓑ Ⓒ Ⓓ
63 Ⓐ Ⓑ Ⓒ Ⓓ
64 Ⓐ Ⓑ Ⓒ Ⓓ
65 Ⓐ Ⓑ Ⓒ Ⓓ
66 Ⓐ Ⓑ Ⓒ Ⓓ
67 Ⓐ Ⓑ Ⓒ Ⓓ
68 Ⓐ Ⓑ Ⓒ Ⓓ

69 Ⓐ Ⓑ Ⓒ Ⓓ
70 Ⓐ Ⓑ Ⓒ Ⓓ
71 Ⓐ Ⓑ Ⓒ Ⓓ
72 Ⓐ Ⓑ Ⓒ Ⓓ
73 Ⓐ Ⓑ Ⓒ Ⓓ
74 Ⓐ Ⓑ Ⓒ Ⓓ
75 Ⓐ Ⓑ Ⓒ Ⓓ
76 Ⓐ Ⓑ Ⓒ Ⓓ
77 Ⓐ Ⓑ Ⓒ Ⓓ
78 Ⓐ Ⓑ Ⓒ Ⓓ

79 Ⓐ Ⓑ Ⓒ Ⓓ
80 Ⓐ Ⓑ Ⓒ Ⓓ
81 Ⓐ Ⓑ Ⓒ Ⓓ
82 Ⓐ Ⓑ Ⓒ Ⓓ
83 Ⓐ Ⓑ Ⓒ Ⓓ
84 Ⓐ Ⓑ Ⓒ Ⓓ
85 Ⓐ Ⓑ Ⓒ Ⓓ
86 Ⓐ Ⓑ Ⓒ Ⓓ
87 Ⓐ Ⓑ Ⓒ Ⓓ
88 Ⓐ Ⓑ Ⓒ Ⓓ

89 Ⓐ Ⓑ Ⓒ Ⓓ
90 Ⓐ Ⓑ Ⓒ Ⓓ
91 Ⓐ Ⓑ Ⓒ Ⓓ
92 Ⓐ Ⓑ Ⓒ Ⓓ
93 Ⓐ Ⓑ Ⓒ Ⓓ
94 Ⓐ Ⓑ Ⓒ Ⓓ
95 Ⓐ Ⓑ Ⓒ Ⓓ
96 Ⓐ Ⓑ Ⓒ Ⓓ
97 Ⓐ Ⓑ Ⓒ Ⓓ
98 Ⓐ Ⓑ Ⓒ Ⓓ

99 Ⓐ Ⓑ Ⓒ Ⓓ
100 Ⓐ Ⓑ Ⓒ Ⓓ
101 Ⓐ Ⓑ Ⓒ Ⓓ
102 Ⓐ Ⓑ Ⓒ Ⓓ
103 Ⓐ Ⓑ Ⓒ Ⓓ
104 Ⓐ Ⓑ Ⓒ Ⓓ
105 Ⓐ Ⓑ Ⓒ Ⓓ
106 Ⓐ Ⓑ Ⓒ Ⓓ
107 Ⓐ Ⓑ Ⓒ Ⓓ
108 Ⓐ Ⓑ Ⓒ Ⓓ

109 Ⓐ Ⓑ Ⓒ Ⓓ
110 Ⓐ Ⓑ Ⓒ Ⓓ
111 Ⓐ Ⓑ Ⓒ Ⓓ
112 Ⓐ Ⓑ Ⓒ Ⓓ
113 Ⓐ Ⓑ Ⓒ Ⓓ
114 Ⓐ Ⓑ Ⓒ Ⓓ
115 Ⓐ Ⓑ Ⓒ Ⓓ
116 Ⓐ Ⓑ Ⓒ Ⓓ

Reading Comprehension

117 Ⓐ Ⓑ Ⓒ Ⓓ
118 Ⓐ Ⓑ Ⓒ Ⓓ
119 Ⓐ Ⓑ Ⓒ Ⓓ
120 Ⓐ Ⓑ Ⓒ Ⓓ
121 Ⓐ Ⓑ Ⓒ Ⓓ
122 Ⓐ Ⓑ Ⓒ Ⓓ
123 Ⓐ Ⓑ Ⓒ Ⓓ
124 Ⓐ Ⓑ Ⓒ Ⓓ
125 Ⓐ Ⓑ Ⓒ Ⓓ
126 Ⓐ Ⓑ Ⓒ Ⓓ

127 Ⓐ Ⓑ Ⓒ Ⓓ
128 Ⓐ Ⓑ Ⓒ Ⓓ
129 Ⓐ Ⓑ Ⓒ Ⓓ
130 Ⓐ Ⓑ Ⓒ Ⓓ
131 Ⓐ Ⓑ Ⓒ Ⓓ
132 Ⓐ Ⓑ Ⓒ Ⓓ
133 Ⓐ Ⓑ Ⓒ Ⓓ
134 Ⓐ Ⓑ Ⓒ Ⓓ
135 Ⓐ Ⓑ Ⓒ Ⓓ
136 Ⓐ Ⓑ Ⓒ Ⓓ

137 Ⓐ Ⓑ Ⓒ Ⓓ
138 Ⓐ Ⓑ Ⓒ Ⓓ
139 Ⓐ Ⓑ Ⓒ Ⓓ
140 Ⓐ Ⓑ Ⓒ Ⓓ
141 Ⓐ Ⓑ Ⓒ Ⓓ
142 Ⓐ Ⓑ Ⓒ Ⓓ
143 Ⓐ Ⓑ Ⓒ Ⓓ
144 Ⓐ Ⓑ Ⓒ Ⓓ
145 Ⓐ Ⓑ Ⓒ Ⓓ
146 Ⓐ Ⓑ Ⓒ Ⓓ

147 Ⓐ Ⓑ Ⓒ Ⓓ
148 Ⓐ Ⓑ Ⓒ Ⓓ
149 Ⓐ Ⓑ Ⓒ Ⓓ
150 Ⓐ Ⓑ Ⓒ Ⓓ
151 Ⓐ Ⓑ Ⓒ Ⓓ
152 Ⓐ Ⓑ Ⓒ Ⓓ
153 Ⓐ Ⓑ Ⓒ Ⓓ
154 Ⓐ Ⓑ Ⓒ Ⓓ
155 Ⓐ Ⓑ Ⓒ Ⓓ
156 Ⓐ Ⓑ Ⓒ Ⓓ

157 Ⓐ Ⓑ Ⓒ Ⓓ
158 Ⓐ Ⓑ Ⓒ Ⓓ
159 Ⓐ Ⓑ Ⓒ Ⓓ
160 Ⓐ Ⓑ Ⓒ Ⓓ
161 Ⓐ Ⓑ Ⓒ Ⓓ
162 Ⓐ Ⓑ Ⓒ Ⓓ
163 Ⓐ Ⓑ Ⓒ Ⓓ
164 Ⓐ Ⓑ Ⓒ Ⓓ
165 Ⓐ Ⓑ Ⓒ Ⓓ

Quantitative Ability

166 Ⓐ Ⓑ Ⓒ Ⓓ	176 Ⓐ Ⓑ Ⓒ Ⓓ	186 Ⓐ Ⓑ Ⓒ Ⓓ	196 Ⓐ Ⓑ Ⓒ Ⓓ	206 Ⓐ Ⓑ Ⓒ Ⓓ
167 Ⓐ Ⓑ Ⓒ Ⓓ	177 Ⓐ Ⓑ Ⓒ Ⓓ	187 Ⓐ Ⓑ Ⓒ Ⓓ	197 Ⓐ Ⓑ Ⓒ Ⓓ	207 Ⓐ Ⓑ Ⓒ Ⓓ
168 Ⓐ Ⓑ Ⓒ Ⓓ	178 Ⓐ Ⓑ Ⓒ Ⓓ	188 Ⓐ Ⓑ Ⓒ Ⓓ	198 Ⓐ Ⓑ Ⓒ Ⓓ	208 Ⓐ Ⓑ Ⓒ Ⓓ
169 Ⓐ Ⓑ Ⓒ Ⓓ	179 Ⓐ Ⓑ Ⓒ Ⓓ	189 Ⓐ Ⓑ Ⓒ Ⓓ	199 Ⓐ Ⓑ Ⓒ Ⓓ	209 Ⓐ Ⓑ Ⓒ Ⓓ
170 Ⓐ Ⓑ Ⓒ Ⓓ	180 Ⓐ Ⓑ Ⓒ Ⓓ	190 Ⓐ Ⓑ Ⓒ Ⓓ	200 Ⓐ Ⓑ Ⓒ Ⓓ	210 Ⓐ Ⓑ Ⓒ Ⓓ
171 Ⓐ Ⓑ Ⓒ Ⓓ	181 Ⓐ Ⓑ Ⓒ Ⓓ	191 Ⓐ Ⓑ Ⓒ Ⓓ	201 Ⓐ Ⓑ Ⓒ Ⓓ	211 Ⓐ Ⓑ Ⓒ Ⓓ
172 Ⓐ Ⓑ Ⓒ Ⓓ	182 Ⓐ Ⓑ Ⓒ Ⓓ	192 Ⓐ Ⓑ Ⓒ Ⓓ	202 Ⓐ Ⓑ Ⓒ Ⓓ	212 Ⓐ Ⓑ Ⓒ Ⓓ
173 Ⓐ Ⓑ Ⓒ Ⓓ	183 Ⓐ Ⓑ Ⓒ Ⓓ	193 Ⓐ Ⓑ Ⓒ Ⓓ	203 Ⓐ Ⓑ Ⓒ Ⓓ	213 Ⓐ Ⓑ Ⓒ Ⓓ
174 Ⓐ Ⓑ Ⓒ Ⓓ	184 Ⓐ Ⓑ Ⓒ Ⓓ	194 Ⓐ Ⓑ Ⓒ Ⓓ	204 Ⓐ Ⓑ Ⓒ Ⓓ	
175 Ⓐ Ⓑ Ⓒ Ⓓ	185 Ⓐ Ⓑ Ⓒ Ⓓ	195 Ⓐ Ⓑ Ⓒ Ⓓ	205 Ⓐ Ⓑ Ⓒ Ⓓ	

Chemistry

214 Ⓐ Ⓑ Ⓒ Ⓓ	224 Ⓐ Ⓑ Ⓒ Ⓓ	234 Ⓐ Ⓑ Ⓒ Ⓓ	244 Ⓐ Ⓑ Ⓒ Ⓓ	254 Ⓐ Ⓑ Ⓒ Ⓓ	264 Ⓐ Ⓑ Ⓒ Ⓓ
215 Ⓐ Ⓑ Ⓒ Ⓓ	225 Ⓐ Ⓑ Ⓒ Ⓓ	235 Ⓐ Ⓑ Ⓒ Ⓓ	245 Ⓐ Ⓑ Ⓒ Ⓓ	255 Ⓐ Ⓑ Ⓒ Ⓓ	265 Ⓐ Ⓑ Ⓒ Ⓓ
216 Ⓐ Ⓑ Ⓒ Ⓓ	226 Ⓐ Ⓑ Ⓒ Ⓓ	236 Ⓐ Ⓑ Ⓒ Ⓓ	246 Ⓐ Ⓑ Ⓒ Ⓓ	256 Ⓐ Ⓑ Ⓒ Ⓓ	266 Ⓐ Ⓑ Ⓒ Ⓓ
217 Ⓐ Ⓑ Ⓒ Ⓓ	227 Ⓐ Ⓑ Ⓒ Ⓓ	237 Ⓐ Ⓑ Ⓒ Ⓓ	247 Ⓐ Ⓑ Ⓒ Ⓓ	257 Ⓐ Ⓑ Ⓒ Ⓓ	267 Ⓐ Ⓑ Ⓒ Ⓓ
218 Ⓐ Ⓑ Ⓒ Ⓓ	228 Ⓐ Ⓑ Ⓒ Ⓓ	238 Ⓐ Ⓑ Ⓒ Ⓓ	248 Ⓐ Ⓑ Ⓒ Ⓓ	258 Ⓐ Ⓑ Ⓒ Ⓓ	268 Ⓐ Ⓑ Ⓒ Ⓓ
219 Ⓐ Ⓑ Ⓒ Ⓓ	229 Ⓐ Ⓑ Ⓒ Ⓓ	239 Ⓐ Ⓑ Ⓒ Ⓓ	249 Ⓐ Ⓑ Ⓒ Ⓓ	259 Ⓐ Ⓑ Ⓒ Ⓓ	269 Ⓐ Ⓑ Ⓒ Ⓓ
220 Ⓐ Ⓑ Ⓒ Ⓓ	230 Ⓐ Ⓑ Ⓒ Ⓓ	240 Ⓐ Ⓑ Ⓒ Ⓓ	250 Ⓐ Ⓑ Ⓒ Ⓓ	260 Ⓐ Ⓑ Ⓒ Ⓓ	270 Ⓐ Ⓑ Ⓒ Ⓓ
221 Ⓐ Ⓑ Ⓒ Ⓓ	231 Ⓐ Ⓑ Ⓒ Ⓓ	241 Ⓐ Ⓑ Ⓒ Ⓓ	251 Ⓐ Ⓑ Ⓒ Ⓓ	261 Ⓐ Ⓑ Ⓒ Ⓓ	
222 Ⓐ Ⓑ Ⓒ Ⓓ	232 Ⓐ Ⓑ Ⓒ Ⓓ	242 Ⓐ Ⓑ Ⓒ Ⓓ	252 Ⓐ Ⓑ Ⓒ Ⓓ	262 Ⓐ Ⓑ Ⓒ Ⓓ	
223 Ⓐ Ⓑ Ⓒ Ⓓ	233 Ⓐ Ⓑ Ⓒ Ⓓ	243 Ⓐ Ⓑ Ⓒ Ⓓ	253 Ⓐ Ⓑ Ⓒ Ⓓ	263 Ⓐ Ⓑ Ⓒ Ⓓ	

Critical Thinking Essay

Write your essay on lined paper.

CUT HERE

PCAT Practice Test 3

Verbal Ability: Analogies

Directions: Select the word that best completes the analogy.

1. ABSTRUSE : RECONDITE :: DIFFICULT :

   A. depressing
   B. accord
   C. pedantic
   D. dormant

2. OVERTURE : OPERA :: PREFACE :

   A. book
   B. play
   C. script
   D. score

3. BENEFACTOR : AID :: MISCREANT :

   A. knowledge
   B. help
   C. advice
   D. crime

4. MARRIAGE : JOINING :: DIVORCE :

   A. arguments
   B. result
   C. dissolution
   D. depression

5. DERISION : APPLAUD :: RIDICULE :

   A. acclaim
   B. encore
   C. remedy
   D. jeer

6. ALLAY : ANXIETY :: APPEASE :

   A. laughter
   B. meanness
   C. hysteria
   D. frustration

7. EPIC : LENGTHY :: EPITHET :

   A. anonymous
   B. ridiculous
   C. epitome
   D. succinct

8. AQUARIUM : FISH :: TERRARIUM :

   A. plants
   B. insects
   C. earth
   D. water

9. CAT : FELINE :: COW :

   A. spotted
   B. milk
   C. domestic
   D. bovine

10. LINE : STANZA :: SENTENCE :

    A. story
    B. poem
    C. paragraph
    D. chapter

11. PERFIDIOUS : TRAITOR : IMPETUOUS :

    A. gambler
    B. bigot
    C. hothead
    D. coach

12. TARDY : LAGGARD : ENERGETIC :

    A. dynamo
    B. bigot
    C. minister
    D. benefactor

GO ON TO THE NEXT PAGE

13. DISSEMBLER : PRETENTIOUS :: ZEALOT :

   A. rude
   B. courageous
   C. enthusiastic
   D. skillful

14. INTRACTABLE : COMPROMISE :: INEXORABLE :

   A. repeat
   B. listen
   C. relent
   D. compete

15. DESULTORY : DIRECTION :: NEFARIOUS :

   A. common sense
   B. fame
   C. virtue
   D. evil

16. EXORBITANT : MODERATION :: INSIPID :

   A. money
   B. goodness
   C. taste
   D. smell

17. ABDICATE : RESIGN :: RELEASE :

   A. rebel
   B. discharge
   C. retreat
   D. regret

18. FINESSE : INCOMPETENCE :: ADROITNESS :

   A. senselessness
   B. intelligence
   C. skillfulness
   D. clumsiness

19. DOCILE : SUBSERVIENT :: TRACTABLE :

   A. traceable
   B. threatening
   C. superfluous
   D. compliant

20. INTEREST : ARDOR :: ENVY :

   A. despair
   B. enjoyment
   C. curiosity
   D. avarice

21. VACCINATION : SMALLPOX :: ANTIDOTE :

   A. poison
   B. flu
   C. sneezing
   D. medicine

22. MONTAGE : PICTURE :: MOSAIC :

   A. table
   B. piece
   C. tile
   D. shape

23. DENTIST : TEETH :: PLUMBER :

   A. bones
   B. shovel
   C. drill
   D. pipes

24. PROFESSOR : LECTURE :: ACTOR :

   A. performs
   B. script
   C. tests
   D. stage

25. DUET : SOLO :: QUART :

   A. single
   B. trio
   C. pint
   D. gallon

26. FREEZE : COLD :: BOIL :

   A. steam
   B. ice
   C. smoke
   D. heat

27. DENY : CONTRADICT :: OBTAIN :

    A. acquire
    B. lose
    C. disagree
    D. stubborn

28. FOOD : NUTRITION :: SOAP :

    A. dirt
    B. suds
    C. cleanliness
    D. health

29. INFANT : TODDLER :: KID :

    A. goat
    B. baby
    C. joke
    D. calf

GO ON TO THE NEXT PAGE

Verbal Ability: Sentence Completions

Directions: Select the word or words that best complete the sentence.

30. Pouring water on burning grease will not put out the fire; instead, it will _____ the situation.

    A. quench
    B. improve
    C. exacerbate
    D. expiate

31. Before the test drive of the new model, we expected to be _____ by its performance, and that initial _____ makes it more remarkable that we ended up enjoying it after a week behind the wheel.

    A. underwhelmed . . . . . skepticism
    B. disappointed . . . . . hope
    C. impressed . . . . . certainty
    D. converted . . . . . impression

32. Rating in public opinion polls about elected officials tend to _____ with economic conditions, rising in _____ periods and falling when wealth is scarce.

    A. elevate . . . . . opulent
    B. descend . . . . . wealthy
    C. stabilize . . . . . deprived
    D. vacillate . . . . . prosperous

33. To avoid falling into debt, some people _____ the used of credit cards.

    A. embrace
    B. eschew
    C. contemplate
    D. lament

34. _____ hopes for the future are unlikely to be realized without specific means of achieving goals.

    A. descriptive
    B. nebulous
    C. foreseeable
    D. concupiscent

35. When the two old friends met after not having seen each other for ten years, they discovered they still had much in common in spite of their _____ lives during that period.

    A. disparate
    B. harmonious
    C. companionable
    D. amicable

36. The Surrealist artists _____ the everyday and _____; their paintings depicted the wild world of dreams.

    A. embraced . . . . . ordinary
    B. portrayed . . . . . commonplace
    C. contradicted . . . . . extraordinary
    D. renounced . . . . . banal

37. After new evidence showed that the original guilty verdict was an error, the defendant was _____.

    A. exonerated
    B. exorcised
    C. excommunicated
    D. exhibited

38. The ideals of the Founding Fathers of the United States _____ throughout the Constitution and Bill of Rights.

    A. resonate
    B. defer
    C. impel
    D. confound

39. A/An _____ impression of _____ was created by the starched linen tablecloths and crystal glasses, as well as by the formal bearing of the servers in the restaurant.

    A. traditional . . . . . gluttony
    B. exotic . . . . . hospitality
    C. indelible . . . . . propriety (customary, polite, appropriate)
    D. mediocre . . . . . opulence

40. Tidal waves called tsunamis, which may follow an earthquake, can cause as much damage as the original _____.

    A. counterattack
    B. deluge
    C. catastrophe
    D. explosion

41. The company's earnings were obtained by _____ in their contracts; as a result, it had to _____ the money to the buyers.

    A. chicanery . . . . . forfeit
    B. overproduction . . . . . apportion
    C. clauses . . . . . rescind
    D. legalities . . . . . default

42. Egotistical and insensitive, the man was _____ to criticism, and thus his rude manners never _____.

    A. liable . . . . . continued
    B. concomitant . . . . . softened
    C. faithful . . . . . offended
    D. impervious . . . . . altered

43. Verbal _____ between parents and children, especially conversation related to books and toys, is essential to a child's _____ development, providing a foundation for developing reading skills.

    A. confrontation . . . . . physical
    B. sorties . . . . . emotional
    C. contact . . . . . oracular
    D. interaction . . . . . cognitive

44. Although many of the wetlands and marshes of North America have disappeared, some of them are still _____; _____ efforts to make them flourish have been begun by conservation groups.

    A. viable . . . . . restoration
    B. defunct . . . . . ecological
    C. proliferating . . . . . destructive
    D. barren . . . . . conservation

45. When Jackie Robinson became the first African-American to play baseball in the major leagues, _____ criticism was directed at the owner of the team that hired him.

    A. strident
    B. felonious
    C. pacifist
    D. amenable

46. During the heat of the day, the animals moved _____, in contrast with their brisk activity early in the morning.

    A. frequently
    B. stupidly
    C. hungrily
    D. languidly

47. The contractor provided weekly reports on the construction project in order to keep the building's owner _____ about how the work was progressing.

    A. befuddled
    B. apprised
    C. distraught
    D. possessed

48. As gasoline prices declined, analysts _____ the decrease to lower demand and higher _____ resulting from increased production.

    A. affected . . . . . expenses
    B. purported . . . . . shortages
    C. contrasted . . . . . wages
    D. attributed . . . . . supplies

49. Because neither side was willing to modify its position, the negotiations were _____.

    A. fruitful
    B. minimal
    C. concise
    D. stagnant

50. The modestly decorated home's furnishings were _____, making visitors even more aware of the _____ views from its large windows.

    A. gorgeous . . . . . panoramic
    B. tawdry . . . . . restricted
    C. unobtrusive . . . . . spectacular
    D. mediocre . . . . . depressing

51. Neither passionate nor monotonous, the speaker's _____ voice helped the audience understand her views.

    A. dynamic
    B. minimal
    C. sentimental
    D. temperate

GO ON TO THE NEXT PAGE

52. Great literature _____ careful reading and study in order to _____ the art that has gone into its creation.

    A. rewards . . . . . deprecate

    B. warrants . . . . . appreciate

    C. enjoins . . . . . ignore

    D. requests . . . . . dispute

53. The game was tied, the potential winning run was at bat, and the fans became _____, jumping up from their seats, stamping their feet, and cheering.

    A. angry

    B. frenetic

    C. disillusioned

    D. outspoken

54. Practicing _____ every day, the student hoped that a career as a professional pianist could be achieved by mere _____.

    A. irregularly . . . . . infrequency

    B. conscientiously . . . . . tenacity

    C. rigorously . . . . . romanticism

    D. musically . . . . . harmony

55. Oliver Twist, unsatisfied by the _____ portion of porridge served at supper, asked "Please, sir, can I have some more?"

    A. meager

    B. munificent

    C. tasteless

    D. collateral

56. Scientific discoveries sometimes, surprisingly, derive from a/an _____ in an experiment which does not produce the _____ data.

    A. observation . . . . . unnecessary

    B. fatuity . . . . . traditional

    C. complication . . . . . unexpected

    D. anomaly . . . . . anticipated

57. Country music songs often describe people at the _____ of their lives; their dogs run away, their spouses leave them, and their pickup trucks break down.

    A. pyramid

    B. summit

    C. nadir

    D. confluence

58. Having only a _____ of acting talent, he was not selected for the leading role in the play.

    A. modicum

    B. plenitude

    C. quantity

    D. verisimilitude

Biology

Directions: Select the choice that best answers the following questions.

59. Which of the following statements regarding nucleic acids is incorrect?

    A. Messenger RNA is transcribed into DNA, which is then translated into protein.

    B. DNA carries the genetic code that is responsible for an individual's characteristics.

    C. DNA and RNA both contain the nitrogenous bases adenine, guanine, and cytosine.

    D. The sugars found in DNA and RNA are different from each other.

60. If a mutation occurs in a population resulting in a favorable trait, that trait is likely to increase in frequency in the population due to which of the following forces?

    A. evolution

    B. genetic drift

    C. natural selection

    D. genetic bottlenecking

61. Which of the following series of events represents the Central Dogma of Molecular Biology?

    A. protein → DNA → mRNA

    B. protein → mRNA → DNA

    C. DNA → protein → mRNA

    D. DNA → mRNA → protein

62. Which of the following lines of evidence in support of evolution is based in part on the fact that the genetic code is virtually identical in all living organisms?

    A. paleontology

    B. comparative embryology

    C. comparative biochemistry

    D. comparative anatomy

63. Which of the following groups of organisms is not considered to be protists?

    A. algae

    B. paramecia

    C. fungi

    D. slime molds

64. Bryophytes (mosses and liverworts) are members of which of the following groups of plants?

    A. vascular; fruit-producing

    B. vascular; seed-producing

    C. vascular; spore-producing

    D. non-vascular

65. Following fertilization in flowering plants, the _____ becomes the fruit and the _____ becomes the seed.

    A. ovule; ovary

    B. ovary; ovule

    C. ovule; egg

    D. egg; ovary

66. Which of the following phyla includes both members with backbones and members without backbones?

    A. Chordata

    B. Echinodermata

    C. Cnidaria

    D. Porifera

67. Which of the following groups of organisms spends part of its life on land and part of its life in water?

    A. sponges

    B. fishes

    C. amphibians

    D. reptiles

68. Which of the following structure–function pairs is mismatched?

    A. ribosome–protein synthesis

    B. mitochondrion–cellular respiration

    C. chloroplast–photosynthesis

    D. nucleus–ATP production

GO ON TO THE NEXT PAGE

69. During cell division, which of the following events takes place during the s-portion of interphase?

    A. Spindle fibers are formed.
    B. DNA molecules are replicated.
    C. DNA molecules are copied onto mRNA molecules.
    D. Sister chromatids separate from each other.

70. In the normal development of a human embryo, if the cells are separated in the two-cell stage, the result will be

    A. death for both cells.
    B. fraternal twins.
    C. identical twins.
    D. quadruplets.

71. The function of specialized cells, called nematocysts, in coelenterates (cnidaria) is to

    A. provide a rudimentary nervous system.
    B. produce digestive juices.
    C. sting and paralyze prey.
    D. rid the body of waste.

72. A critical process that took place during the evolutionary development of reptiles included

    A. the loss of scales from the body.
    B. the loss of a tail.
    C. the ability to reproduce on land.
    D. the ability to use fins for locomotion on land.

73. Unicellular animals, such as the paramecium, were first described by

    A. Linnaeus.
    B. Darwin.
    C. Hooke.
    D. Leeuwenhoek.

74. In order for a genetic mutation to have an evolutionary effect, it must occur in the

    A. germ cells.
    B. somatic cells.
    C. developing embryo.
    D. cytoplasm.

75. Which of the following statements regarding photosynthesis is incorrect?

    A. Photosynthesis occurs in the chloroplasts of plant cells.
    B. Photosynthesis converts light energy into chemical energy.
    C. Photosynthesis results in the production of ATP.
    D. Photosynthesis occurs in the cells of certain bacteria.

76. The dodo and the passenger pigeon became extinct a relatively short time ago. Which of the following was the most likely cause for their extinction?

    A. viral infection
    B. predation of eggs by snakes
    C. predation by humans
    D. nuclear waste

77. More complex life forms were able to evolve on Earth following the development of early photosynthetic organisms, which give off oxygen as a by-product of the process. This is because

    A. photosynthetic organisms are always more complex than non-photosynthetic organisms.
    B. organisms could now carry out aerobic respiration, which is nearly 20 times as efficient as anaerobic respiration at producing energy.
    C. life cannot exist in an oxygen-free environment.
    D. evolution cannot occur in an oxygen-free environment.

78. What is one of the primary functions of the Golgi apparatus in cells?

    A. to break up ingested food particles
    B. to prepare cell products for secretion
    C. to provide energy to the cell
    D. to enclose waste products

79. Which of the following genetic abnormalities can be detected by the use of amniocentesis?

    A. albinism
    B. muscular dystrophy
    C. Down's syndrome
    D. diabetes

80. An increase in which of the following factors would not allow for an increase in the rate of photosynthesis?

    A. oxygen
    B. carbon dioxide
    C. water
    D. sunlight

81. Red-green color-blindness is a sex-linked, recessive trait in humans. If a girl is born color-blind, which of the following statements <u>could be</u> true?

    A. Her father is color-blind.
    B. Her mother is color-blind.
    C. Her mother is a carrier for the allele coding for color-blindness.
    D. Any of the above statements could be true.

82. Humans have 46 chromosomes in each of their cells. How many chromosomes do human eggs and sperm contain?

    A. 46
    B. 23
    C. 92
    D. 45

83. If a red-flowered plant were crossed with a white-flowered plant and all of the offspring had pink flowers, what percentage of offspring from a cross between two of the pink-flowered plants would also have pink flowers?

    A. 100%
    B. 50%
    C. 75%
    D. 25%

84. Which of the following groups of organisms is NOT considered prokaryotic?

    A. cyanobacteria
    B. yeast
    C. chlamydia
    D. spirochetes

85. Which of the following characteristics is shared by bacteria, fungi, and protozoa?

    A. All include members that are photosynthetic.
    B. All include members that are eukaryotic.
    C. All contain members that are prokaryotic.
    D. All contain members with the potential to cause disease.

86. A bacterial cell that has picked up foreign DNA from its environment, for example, by taking up a plasmid while in culture, is said to have been

    A. conjugated.
    B. transduced.
    C. transformed.
    D. phagocytized.

87. Which of the following is not a respiratory tract disease of bacterial origin?

    A. typhoid fever
    B. pertussis
    C. diphtheria
    D. tuberculosis

88. Which of the following gastrointestinal disorders is not caused by a protozoan?

    A. amoebiasis
    B. shigellosis
    C. giardiasis
    D. cryptosporidiosis

89. Plague, Lyme disease, spotted fever, and tularemia are all blood-borne diseases caused by

    A. viruses.
    B. ticks.
    C. bacteria.
    D. protozoa.

90. Which type of immunity does an individual develop in response to the polio vaccine?

    A. artificially-acquired; active
    B. artificially-acquired; passive
    C. naturally-acquired; active
    D. naturally-acquired; passive

GO ON TO THE NEXT PAGE

91. The presence of coliform bacteria in the drinking water supply suggests that

    A. the water supply is relatively clean and safe to drink, because coliform bacteria are natural inhabitants of the human gut.

    B. the water supply is probably downstream from a chemical processing plant.

    C. the water supply contains deadly protozoans.

    D. the water supply is contaminated with sewage.

92. Which of the following types of microorganisms is used in the wine and beer-making industries?

    A. bacteria

    B. fungi

    C. protozoans

    D. viruses

93. The capsid surrounding a virus particle is composed of

    A. DNA.

    B. RNA.

    C. protein.

    D. cellulose.

94. The bacterial genome consists of

    A. one double-stranded, circular molecule of DNA.

    B. one single-stranded, circular molecule of DNA.

    C. one double-stranded, circular molecule of RNA.

    D. one single-stranded, circular molecule of RNA.

95. The enzyme produced by retroviruses that enables them to produce a strand of DNA from an RNA template is

    A. DNA polymerase.

    B. RNA polymerase.

    C. ribozyme.

    D. reverse transcriptase.

96. Which of the following best represents the correct order of structures through which food travels in the human digestive system?

    A. mouth → duodenum → esophagus → stomach → large intestine

    B. mouth → pancreas → stomach → small intestine

    C. mouth → esophagus → stomach → large intestine

    D. mouth → esophagus → stomach → small intestine

97. Oxygen-poor blood enters the human heart through the _____, is pumped to the lungs where it picks up oxygen, and returns to the heart through the _____.

    A. right atrium; left atrium

    B. left atrium; right atrium

    C. left ventricle; right ventricle

    D. pulmonary artery; vena cava

98. If an individual's pancreas were surgically removed, the individual would

    A. have trouble digesting fat.

    B. be unable to properly regulate his blood sugar level.

    C. have trouble breathing.

    D. not be able to produce adrenaline.

99. In human males, meiosis occurs in the

    A. Cowper's gland.

    B. nephron tubules.

    C. penis.

    D. seminiferous tubules.

100. Several of the latest fad diets rely on the consumption of high levels of protein, high levels of fat, and low levels of carbohydrates. Metabolic changes associated with such diets include increased production of ketoacids, acetone breath, and acidic urine. Similar metabolic changes take place in individuals with which of the following disorders?

    A. PKU

    B. diabetes mellitus

    C. Tay-Sachs disease

    D. lactose intolerance

101. The pH of human blood is approximately 7.4. Thus, human blood is

A. slightly acidic.
B. neutral.
C. slightly alkaline.
D. extremely alkaline.

102. What is the major artery located on each side of the neck called?

A. carotid artery
B. pulmonary artery
C. vena cava
D. pulmonary cava

103. In the human body, red blood cells are made in the

A. lymph nodes.
B. heart.
C. bone marrow.
D. liver.

104. Which part of the human eye does not have a blood supply flowing to it?

A. retina
B. lens
C. iris
D. cornea

105. In which part of the human body are the rotator cuffs located?

A. elbows
B. knees
C. shoulders
D. hips

106. A collection of nerves located outside the central nervous system is referred to as a/an

A. nerve fiber.
B. ganglion.
C. dendrite.
D. axon.

107. What is the proper term for the "windpipe"?

A. larynx
B. pharynx
C. trachea
D. epiglottis

108. The "Islets of Langerhans" refers to a group of cells located in the

A. pancreas.
B. liver.
C. gall bladder.
D. small intestine.

109. In which part of the brain is memory coordinated?

A. hypothalamus
B. hippocampus
C. cerebellum
D. medulla

110. The most common type of white blood cell found in humans is the

A. macrophage.
B. erythrocyte.
C. monocyte.
D. neutrophil.

111. The tissue that builds up in the uterus, which could be used to nourish a developing embryo should fertilization take place, is referred to as

A. uterine tissue.
B. fallopian tissue.
C. endometrial tissue.
D. ovarian tissue.

112. The human heart is controlled by nerves that originate on the right side in the upper region of the atrium at a node referred to as the

A. pacemaker.
B. atrial node.
C. ventricular node.
D. heart regulation node.

113. In the human circulatory system, which of the following represents the part of the blood that serves to begin the blood clotting mechanism?

A. red blood cells
B. plasma
C. leukocytes
D. platelets

GO ON TO THE NEXT PAGE

114. The primary function of the Eustachian tubes, which lead from the pharynx to the middle ear in humans is to

    A. drain fluid from the ears into the throat.

    B. trap and filter out microorganisms entering the body through the mouth, nose, or ears.

    C. equalize pressure.

    D. exchange gas with red blood cells.

115. Which of the following statements regarding the Fallopian tubes of human females is incorrect?

    A. Fertilization occurs in the Fallopian tubes.

    B. Meiosis takes place in the Fallopian tubes to produce eggs.

    C. The Fallopian tubes lead from the ovaries to the uterus.

    D. The Fallopian tubes serve as a passageway for the eggs that are produced by the ovaries.

116. The primary function of the ureters in the human excretory system is to

    A. carry waste products from the kidneys to the large intestine.

    B. carry waste products from the kidneys to the small intestine.

    C. carry waste products from the bladder to the kidneys.

    D. carry waste products from the kidneys to the bladder.

Reading Comprehension

Directions: Read each of the following passages and answer the questions that follow.

Passage 1

(1)   Can anyone make a blind man see? Scientists at the University of California, Berkeley, have given "blind" nerve cells the ability to detect light. This might pave the way to an innovative therapy that would restore sight to those who have lost it through diseases such as retinitis pigmentosa, or age-related macular degeneration.

(2)   People who have lost the light-sensitive rods and cones in their eyes have photoreceptors that are dead. However, other nerve cells downstream of the photoreceptors are still alive. Importantly, the retinal ganglion cells, which are the third cells in the path from the photoreceptor to the brain could take over some of the functions of the photoreceptors if they could be genetically engineered to respond to light. In the experiment, the researchers inserted a light-activated switch into brain cells normally insensitive to light, enabling researchers to turn the cells on with green light and turn them off with ultraviolet light. The way that this process would work for people is the creation of a device that resembles that type of eyepiece worn by the blind Geordi La Forge in *Star Trek: The Next Generation*. Using laser scanning to trace on and off patterns on the retina, it could allow people to see visual patterns.

(3)   This process might have more advantages than the common approach to solving blindness, that of the bionic eye. This is done by the insertion of electrodes into the optic nerve to simulate the cell firings that a visual scene might normally excite. The parallel process, that of cochlear implants for deafness, works very well in the ear. However, the eye is much more complicated. Electrodes are large and tend to stimulate an entire bank of cells at once, which would limit the resolution of the image. Furthermore, there is the problem of biocompatibility. The effectiveness of this technique depends on how well you match the density of the electrodes with the neural elements underneath.

(4)   The newer approach will allow doctors to cover the entire retina with light-sensitive cells. If each nerve responds individually, there could be a very fine scan of the retinal field resulting in a much better spatial resolution. The current attempts at restoring sight with electrodes in the retinal ganglion cells, only allows the patients to see little more than patches of dark and light.

GO ON TO THE NEXT PAGE

117. The new research for restoring sight to blind people affects

- **A.** only those who have lost their sight in infancy.
- **B.** only those who have lost their sight during old age degeneration.
- **C.** only those who have lost a particular ability to sensor light.
- **D.** anyone and everyone who is blind.

118. Evidence has shown

- **A.** that certain cells can take on the responsibilities of the photoreceptors.
- **B.** that ultraviolet light causes people to see better.
- **C.** that there are two sets of cells that work to send messages to the rods and cones.
- **D.** that dead photoreceptors means permanent blindness.

119. The eyepiece that is used in this research would allow patients

- **A.** to see only visual patterns.
- **B.** to discriminate among colors.
- **C.** to distinguish shapes and sizes.
- **D.** to identify outlines and profiles.

120. By studying the process of cochlear implants, doctors have

- **A.** perfected the implant of the bionic eye.
- **B.** stimulated the optic nerve with the same success.
- **C.** decided that the two processes are vastly different.
- **D.** concluded that more testing needs to happen.

121. The issue of biocompatibility is related to

- **A.** the problem that too many cells might be fired up at once.
- **B.** the fact that each person's biology is different and might not tolerate the electrodes.
- **C.** the lack of complexity of the eye's structure.
- **D.** the match of the density of the electrodes with the neural elements of the patient.

122. The new approach effectively addressed the problem of

- **A.** better spatial resolution.
- **B.** cosmetic appeal to the eye.
- **C.** broader scan of the retinal field.
- **D.** neural rejection of electrodes.

123. Current research allows patients to

- **A.** determine distance of objects.
- **B.** distinguish between dark and light patches.
- **C.** recognize faces and shapes.
- **D.** see setting but not people.

Passage 2

(1)   Extinction is forever, and those creatures whose habitats are destroyed through either man-made or natural disasters and hang on in remaining patches of deforested areas are not survivors. This is the conclusion of researchers who examined the coastal region harboring the greatest number of threatened birds in America, Brazil's Atlantic Forest. This area has now been reduced to 119,540 square kilometers or 10 percent of its original extent. There are more species threatened with extinction in this coastal strip of rain forest than anywhere else in the Americas. People started moving inland about 75 years ago, leaving the coastal forest in the lowlands mainly impenetrable mountains. The deforestation of about 800 miles along the coast has contributed to the drying out of the highlands farther west. As the lowlands are cleared away, they become hot. This affects the uplands because there are not getting the flow of moist air off the land. The entire

area's geography and environmental conditions are changed and, thus, the habitat for these creatures has likewise been altered.

(3)   A study of threatened birds was done based on the diminishing habits for these birds. Researchers estimated the forest's original extent by consulting data from remote sensing technologies and a simple rule of thumb: if there are 4 feet of rain a year and it's warm and the rain falls every month, you're going to have a lush, tropical foliage. By checking numbers of varieties of birds that lived in the region before deforestation and creating maps that used dry season satellite imagery, they were able to create and superimpose bird range maps on their current forest map. What emerged was their own estimate of remaining distributions of two categories of birds species: those that were forest-obligate which cannot exist outside the woods and those that were survivor birds, which can exist marginally in secondary habitats. Some of these birds could be seen in other environments like gardens, plantations, and golf courses. However, the results were disturbing. The data showed that habitat loss threatens forest-obligate and those using secondary habitats equally. Thus, if a species has lost 95 percent of its range, irrespective of whether it uses human habitats or not, it is still considered to be on the brink of extinction.

124. Researchers concluded that

A. creatures that can adapt to several environments will escape extinction.
B. birds in coastal regions can live on golf courses.
C. only natural disasters cause extinction due to habitat destruction.
D. there are no survivors of habitat destruction.

125. The highlands are arid in the west of the Atlantic Forest because

A. there has been no rainfall for months.
B. the lack of trees allows the sun to dry out the land.
C. the moisture just runs off the land.
D. deforestation has allowed for brush to grow there instead.

126. The clearing away of forests leads to extinction because

A. the animals run away.
B. the animals' predators can more easily attack them.
C. the habitat has changed so the animals cannot survive.
D. the temperature gets too high.

127. In the second sentence of the second paragraph, "rule of thumb" most closely means

A. a simple rule can be followed easily.
B. that you can use your thumb to measure the rainfall.
C. the mathematical equation is easier than it looks.
D. it is similar to the idea of having a green thumb, like a gardener.

128. Forest-obligate means

A. a category of bird.
B. any creature that can only live in the forest.
C. a bird that must find a new habitat.
D. a creature whose environment has been destroyed by fire.

GO ON TO THE NEXT PAGE

129. Birds that were found in gardens, plantations, and golf courses

    A. were more likely to survive the habitat destruction.

    B. were domesticated and treated like pets.

    C. were equally doomed because of their lost habitat.

    D. needed to move into and adapt to a new environment.

130. One indication of possible extinction is

    A. constant destruction of forests.

    B. loss of 95% of its living space.

    C. decrease in repopulation.

    D. lack of food and water.

Passage 3

(1)   What do rhinoceroses, supersonic aircraft, hurricanes, and pipe organs have in common? They all emit a silent infrasound, a long sound wave with a frequency below 20 hertz. People can't hear anything below that level for good reason: We would be constantly distracted by the din of the wind, the groaning of the earth, and any distant explosion, natural or man-made. However, scientists are anxiously listening to volcanoes, avalanches, earthquakes, and meteorites to see what a study of infrasound might reveal.

(2)   Just as seismic waves travel through the Earth, infrasonic waves travel through the air. The lower the frequency of the waves, the farther they can travel without losing strength. Scientists first detected infrasound in 1883 when the eruption of the Krakatoa volcano erupted and sent inaudible sounds around the world, noticeably affecting the barometric readings. In the 1950s, the monitoring of these sounds became an important tool for both the United States and the Soviet Union because it was a way of detecting atmospheric nuclear testing. The decrease in interest of this science came in 1963 with the Limited Test Ban Treaty. However, since 1996, there has been a renewed interest in infrasound because of the Comprehensive Test Ban Treaty adopted by the United Nations. A monitoring section in the treaty calls for a global network of 60 stations to search for violations. Each station is equipped with specialized monitoring microphones that can detect the strength of a sound, its frequency, and its direction. This data is sent 20 times a second to the headquarters in Vienna where scientists determine the course of the sound. However, scientists are also using this network and others like these to study a variety of events in the atmosphere. Stations in the United States and Canada recorded the explosion of the space shuttle *Columbia*. They were able to defuse the rumors that either lightning or meteors stuck the craft because there were no recordings that indicated that.

(3)   Although this science is still young, it has been used in weather tracking. Ocean storms and waves are two of the big generators of infrasound. They act

like giant loudspeakers in pushing the air at high frequencies. The swirling winds of hurricanes generate a different type of infrasound. Knowledge of this has helped weather-prediction systems. Furthermore, by examining the patterns of infrasound in the atmosphere, scientists might be able to determine common places of turbulence and relay this information to pilots. Using the infrasound readings of gas-filled bubbles in volcano lakes allows researchers to estimate the size of bubbles and the amount of gas they contain. After reading the sensors on the Sakurajima volcano in Japan, the scientists have determined that the increasing amplitude of a wave relates to how often rumblings occur. Tests are also under way to use infrasound data as a warning signal for avalanches since, when snow rushes down mountains, it pushes air before it and creates infrasound at frequencies below 8 hertz. Studies are being conducted on the effect that infrasound has on human response to audible sound. Preliminary work indicates the use of infrasound along with music causes more intense reactions to the music.

131. The measurement of sound is in

    A. loudness or softness.
    B. decibel tones.
    C. wave frequency.
    D. length of waves.

132. Seismic waves pertain to

    A. the air.
    B. the water.
    C. the Earth.
    D. the sound.

133. Interest in infrasound by the United States and Russia revolved around

    A. the need for better clarity of hearing.
    B. the use of infrasound as a tool for nuclear testing.
    C. ways to incorporate its use in military training.
    D. the warning by the Limited Test Ban Treaty.

134. The study of infrasound is most useful in

    A. detecting how far and fast it can travel to determine missile strength.
    B. detecting trouble with space travel.
    C. defusing rumors of disasters that can be identified.
    D. improving the sound of music played through the airwaves.

135. Ocean storms and waves generate infrasound that allows scientists to

    A. predict types of weather.
    B. detect types of weather.
    C. map places of turbulence.
    D. all of the above.

136. If this science of infrasound becomes perfected it could

    A. serve as an early warning of a tsunami.
    B. allow satellites to become more efficient.
    C. make space travel safer.
    D. prevent avalanches.

137. The final two sentences serve to

    A. show the limitations of this kind of study.
    B. indicate new applications of this kind of study.
    C. warn about the impracticality of this kind of study.
    D. encourage people to fund this kind of study.

Practice Test 3

GO ON TO THE NEXT PAGE

Passage 4

(1)   On a moonless January night in 2003, a French sailor was racing across the Atlantic Ocean when his boat came to a sudden and mysterious halt. There was no land for hundreds of miles. Yet the boat teetered and rattled as if it had run aground. To the astonishment of his first mate, they saw a limb-like structure with suckers on it. This seemingly huge tentacle had wrapped its arm around the boat's rudder. Just as suddenly as it appeared, it un-wrapped itself from the boat and sunk into the depths of the ocean. As it slipped away, the sailor estimated that the whole animal must have been nearly 30 feet long. What he claimed he saw, was a giant squid, an architeuthis, the largest invertebrate on earth. Its tentacles can sometimes be as long as a city bus and its eyes are about the size of a human head. Unfortunately, no scientist has yet to see a living specimen. Scientists have only studied car-casses that have washed ashore or floated to the surface of the ocean.

(2)   While some squid hunters are spending millions of dollars in underwater equipment and submarines in search of a giant squid, one marine biologist from New Zealand is on the hunt for a paralarva. He hopes to grow this baby, the size of a cricket, in cap-tivity. In 2001, this biologist caught a group of baby giant squid, but by the time he reached the docks, they had all died. He was so upset that he actually climbed into the tank in tears to retrieve the dead bodies himself. This defeat stifled his enthusiasm for nearly three years. Then, in late 2004, he decided to sail to the Southern Hemisphere where the giant squid release their babies during the summer nights.

(3)   His expedition was very modest, consisting of himself, a photojournalist, and a grad student. His boat was old and rickety and his nets were hand-repaired. He sailed into the night until he ventured into waters that might be ripe for hunting. With his own devised nets studded with glow sticks because the squid are attracted to light, he lowered the nets and waited. A half-hour later, the nets were swarm-ing with krill and shrimp but no squid. Three days of disappointment were finally punctuated with the discovery of one baby squid amidst the krill and shrimp. However, when the scientist searched for it amid the muck, it had disappeared. To this day, his search goes on with the hope that one day he will be able to study a live architeuthis.

138. An architeuthis is
A.   a mythical beast.
B.   a type of octopus.
C.   a giant squid.
D.   a large boat.

139. The evidence of the existence of the architeuthis is

    A. the tales of sailors.

    B. the in-depth study of deep-sea divers.

    C. the large eyes and long tentacles.

    D. the dead specimens that scientists have received.

140. Paralarva are

    A. insects before they turn into adults.

    B. small relatives who are descended from the architeuthis.

    C. baby architeuthis.

    D. squid only found in New Zealand.

141. Evidence that the marine biologist from New Zealand was passionate about his work is the fact that

    A. he got little help from his friends.

    B. he was willing to use old equipment.

    C. he personally dealt with the failures of his missions.

    D. he was willing to travel far from his homeland.

142. The first sentence of the last paragraph uses the word "modest." What does it mean in this context?

    A. being very self-effacing

    B. not wanting much publicity

    C. not using a lot of money and expensive equipment

    D. not bragging

143. The use of glow sticks indicates that

    A. there was no electricity on the boat.

    B. they were more practical on a low budget.

    C. light scares the fish away.

    D. baby squid like light.

144. The article leaves the reader with

    A. complete understanding of the architeuthis.

    B. a sense of mystery about this creature.

    C. amazement at the size of these sea creatures.

    D. curiosity about the validity of the sea tales.

Passage 5

(1) What is a SpeechEasy? It is not a nightclub of the 1920s or a place to get bootleg alcohol. Instead, it is an electronic device that help people who stutter speak more fluently. The company that manufactures these devises has awarded more than $500,000 in devices and therapy to 100 recipients through its outreach program. There were over a thousand ap-

(2) plicants who were interested in the free or reduced-cost fluency devices. Their selection was based on financial need, potential for academic and career advancement, and consideration expressed in a written essay. The process was similar to those that students are subjected to for university acceptance and financial aid.

(2) Stuttering affects people from all walks of life. It is a speech fluency disorder characterized by frequent repetitions, pauses and prolongations that interfere with the normal flow of speech. It affects over three million Americans. While stuttering most frequently occurs in childhood, it can affect people at any age. Therefore the outreach program included people ranging from preteens to retired grandparents. Each had a compelling story of battling against an often debilitating condition that can turn even routine tasks such as speaking on the

GO ON TO THE NEXT PAGE

phone into a horror show. Simple tasks, such as ordering from a menu, or life-crises, such as giving information in a 911 call, become unbearable. The SpeechEasy device is a promise of more effective communication.

(3)   Similar in appearance to a hearing aid, the device is worn in or around the ear. It does not amplify sound. Instead, it alters the way the user hears his/or her own voice by re-creating a natural phenomenon know as the "choral effect." This occurs when a person's stutter is dramatically reduced or even eliminated as the person speaks or sings in unison with others. Although this effect has been documented for ages, even with famous actors like Jim Nabors, scientists have only recently been able to re-create it in a small device that is wearable in everyday life. It uses a technology called altered auditory feedback (AAF) to create and optimize the choral effect. When someone is wearing the device and speaks, the words are digitally replayed with a slight delay and frequency modification in the person's ear. The brain, however, perceives that the speaking in unison is another person, thus creating the choral effect. Again the age of digitalization has proven to better the quality of life.

145. A SpeechEasy is

    A. a place in the 1920s.
    B. a device to help the hearing impaired.
    C. another type of movie theater.
    D. a place for debates.

146. Selection of candidates for these devices was compared to a university application process because

    A. it was a needs-based program.
    B. it combined many factors, including an essay.
    C. it only took a small number of the applicants.
    D. The applicants had to be personally interviewed.

147. Stuttering

    A. is a speech fluidity disorder that only affects the young.
    B. is not very prevalent in the United States.
    C. is not a life threatening illness.
    D. affects communication.

148. The device to assist the patient is

    A. worn like a hearing aid.
    B. worn around the neck like a microphone.
    C. surgically implanted behind the ear.
    D. a hand-held device.

149. The "choral effect"

    A. is something positive about the disorder.
    B. refers to their ability to sing completely on tune.
    C. is what causes stutters to repeat words or phrases.
    D. is similar to an echoing in the ear.

150. The AAF was used to

    A. determine the cause of stuttering.
    B. create and amplify the "choral effect."
    C. manufacture the microchip in the device.
    D. experiment with low-level sound frequencies.

151. The author's last sentence indicates that

    A. technology should all be digitalized.

    B. inventions can both harm and help people.

    C. technical advances can lead to better mental conditions in people who stutter.

    D. some of the new uses of digitalization are too avant-garde.

Passage 6

(1)   An idea that was mere fantasy just a few years ago, growing new tissues to replace damaged or diseased heart muscle, is now one of the hottest areas of cardiology research. Teams around the world are trying to mend broken hearts by injecting or infusing primitive stem cells or muscle cells into the heart or by rousing the heart to repair itself. How quickly these efforts become accepted and universal is hard to predict since there are daunting scientific, technical, and ethical hurdles. But the excitement of these possibilities is growing since 5 million Americans and 23 million people worldwide have heart failure, and half of them die within five years. Treating heart failure costs $40 billion a year.

(2)   Drugs and devices can ease symptoms and prevent heart attacks or sudden death by reducing the heart's workload, regulating its electrical signals, and even assisting with some of the pumping. What they don't do is reverse the damage. Dead muscle and scar tissues left behind by a heart attack weaken the heart's pumping ability, making it difficult for the heart to deliver enough blood to meet the body's demands. In theory, growing new, healthy tissues could give the heart the extra kick it needs and eliminate some expensive and not always effective treatments.

(3)   A number of so-called lower animals are able to repair serious damage or sprout new parts. Sliced-up flatworms grow into identical worms. Salamanders that lose their tails grow new ones. They can even replace a damaged or partially amputated heart. The zebrafish, a striped denizen of many home fish tanks, can also repair damages to its body. But humans aren't so plastic. Although our cuts and scrapes can heal through effective skin regeneration and our bodies can repair damaged livers, bones, and muscles tissues, the damage to the heart can be fatal. However, since the 1980s, new experiments have suggested the possibility of heart regrowth.

(4)   All human life begins with a single cell that multiplies. At first, these cells are identical. Each has the potential to grow into a fully formed child. However, gradually, small clusters of cells set off onto separate paths, morphing into the 200 or so different cell types that begin specialization. This is known as differentiation. There are small groups of cells that remain unspecialized called stem cells. Given the right chemical and genetic signals, stem cells can develop into many different types of differentiated cells.

GO ON TO THE NEXT PAGE

Stem cells can be injected into the heart to replace the dead tissue. This can improve the heart's ability to provide oxygenated blood.

(5) Immature muscle cells called myoblasts may be an alternative to stem cells captured from bone marrow and blood. They are harvested from a marble-sized chunk of thigh muscle and allowed to grow and divide in number over a few days. When injected into the heart, they adopt the characteristics of heart cells and begin to act like them. Although this is an exciting breakthrough, the procedure isn't without risks. They might not fit seamlessly into the precise architecture of the heart. However, continued research in this area can also benefit the cure of other diseases like Parkinson's and Alzheimer's.

152. This passage could be titled

   A. "How to Mend a Broken Heart."
   B. "Heart Replacement Therapy."
   C. "The Growing American Killer."
   D. "End to Heartaches and Attacks."

153. What do drugs and devices NOT do?

   A. regulate electrical signals
   B. reduce the heart's workload
   C. reverse the damage
   D. assist in the pumping

154. In the third paragraph, the word "plastic" is used in reference to humans. What that means is

   A. you can't see through people as well.
   B. people can't generate another tail.
   C. our skin has pigmentation in it that gives us color.
   D. our skin is not as stretchable.

155. Stem cells

   A. have not differentiated yet.
   B. have numerous specialization places.
   C. haven't matured yet.
   D. remain unspecialized.

156. Myoblasts

   A. are similar to stem cells because they come from the blood and bone.
   B. could be used like stem cells because they can modify their specialization.
   C. are easier to harvest than stem cells.
   D. are better than stem cells because there are no risks.

157. The second to the last sentence uses the term "architecture of the heart." It most closely means

   A. the size of the heart.
   B. the shape of the heart.
   C. the particular structure of the heart.
   D. the placement of the heart.

158. The article ends with

   A. reassurances of the stem cell research continuing.
   B. the further expansion of research into other areas.
   C. the importance of effective research for heart disease eradiation.
   D. the futility of continuing this type of study.

Passage 7

(1) Mary Shelley wrote the story that first dealt with the creation of life in her novel *Frankenstein*. The monster's creator was tormented by his creation for the rest of his life. He believed that he was being punished for going beyond what humans should be able to do. Now the recent success in freezing the spermatogonial stem cells of mice, cells that produce sperm cells in all male mammals, raises the possibility of cloning people. It also raises the

possibility of marketing genetic material, which worries bioethicists.

(2) Researchers from the University of Pennsylvania's School of Veterinary Medicine have frozen the sperm cells of mice. They then thawed the cells and replanted them into other mice and even rats. Implications of this act are that different species can act as hosts for the sperm of endangered species. While freezing sperm cells is nothing new, the freezing of stem cells has dramatic implications. If this new technique were successful in humans, a man who was undergoing chemotherapy, which destroys cells, could freeze some of his own stem cells for later regeneration. Because stem cells regenerate themselves indefinitely, they can provide an unlimited supply from a single donor. In the animal world, this could be the answer to protecting and repopulating endangered species. Furthermore, sperm from a previous generation can be introduced to improve the diversity of the species. The frightening aspect of this is its potential application to humans. What this would mean is that a father whose stem cells were stored, can father children long after his death. Copies of people would be possible. The worst case is the possible consumer market for genetic material. In fact, in the field of in vitro fertilization, this is happening where people can "shop" for the characteristics they most want their child to inherit along

with culling any unwanted hereditary traits. Bioethicists believe that laws need to be established to maintain what is in our best interest in managing our genetic traits. Others are concerned with a premature rush to control science in a way that will limit further studies. Society must decide what limits, if any, should be placed on technology but to not talk about these questions is to answer them in a certain way.

159. The concept of man creating life

- **A.** is a relatively new idea.
- **B.** raises important ethical questions.
- **C.** is only found in fiction books.
- **D.** has little impact on everyday life.

160. Marketing genetic material means

- **A.** sending out flyers about gene therapy.
- **B.** advertising sperm banks.
- **C.** selling cells that have the best qualities to the highest bidder.
- **D.** being part of capitalistic societies.

161. Implications of freezing and thawing sperm include

- **A.** using hosts to keep alive endangered species.
- **B.** being able to do tests on a control set over a period of years.
- **C.** establishing businesses that will add to research funding.
- **D.** making new advancements in retrieval of sperm.

162. A positive aspect of this research is that

- **A.** it is very inexpensive.
- **B.** there can be unlimited regeneration of cells from a single donor.
- **C.** the procedure can be processed in any hospital.
- **D.** people can "buy" the type of child they want.

GO ON TO THE NEXT PAGE

163. A negative aspect of having the choice of when to use the sperm cells is that

    A. men with prostrate cancer can still reproduce.

    B. genes that carry disease can be eliminated.

    C. people can "buy" the traits they want in their children.

    D. endangered species can be saved.

164. Bioethicists are concerned about

    A. the idea of playing God with human creation.

    B. the cost of in vitro fertilization.

    C. the lack of human emotion about creation.

    D. the limits that are not being placed on science.

165. The ending of this article is one of

    A. warning about the need to reflect on consequences.

    B. amazement at the ingenuity of scientists.

    C. scorn because too many negative issues have been raised.

    D. happiness because the true importance of science is being confirmed.

Quantitative Ability

Directions: Read each of the questions and select the choice that answers the question.

166. Two runners finished a race in 80 seconds, another runner finished the race in 72 seconds, and the final runner finished in 68 seconds. The average of these times is

    A. 73 seconds
    B. 74 seconds
    C. 75 seconds
    D. 76 seconds

167. Staci earns $9.50 an hour plus 3% commission on all sales made. If her total sales during a 30-hour workweek were $500, how much did she earn?

    A. $15
    B. $250
    C. $285
    D. $300

168. $\log_5 5 =$

    A. $\frac{1}{5}$
    B. 1
    C. 5
    D. 25

169. A cardboard box has a length of 3 feet, a height of $2\frac{1}{2}$ feet, and a depth of 2 feet. If the length and depth are doubled, by what percent does the volume of the box change?

    A. 200%
    B. 300%
    C. 400%
    D. 600%

170. What is the value of $(-8)^{\frac{2}{3}}$?

    A. -4
    B. -2
    C. 2
    D. 4

171. Tiling costs $2.89 per square foot. What is the cost to tile a kitchen with dimensions of 4 yards by 5 yards?

    A. $57.80
    B. $173.40
    C. $289.00
    D. $520.20

172. A machine can produce 8,000 widgets in 3 hours. How many widgets are produced in one day?

    A. 96,000
    B. 64,000
    C. 32,000
    D. 8,000

173. Doug earns 15% commission on all sales over $5,000. Last month, his sales totaled $12,500. What were Doug's earnings?

    A. $750
    B. $1,125
    C. $1,875
    D. $2,625

174. Three boxes are needed to hold 18 reams of paper. How many boxes are needed for 90 reams?

    A. 5
    B. 6
    C. 9
    D. 15

GO ON TO THE NEXT PAGE

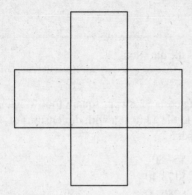

175. The figure above contains five equal squares. If the area is 405, what is the perimeter?

    A. 81

    B. 90

    C. 108

    D. 144

176. Dennis ran a race in 2.2 minutes. Kayla ran the same race in 124 seconds. What is the difference between these two times?

    A. 2 seconds

    B. 8 seconds

    C. 14 seconds

    D. 22 seconds

177. Stanley can type 35 words per minute. If it takes him a half-hour to type a document, about how many words are in the document?

    A. 900

    B. 1,050

    C. 1,500

    D. 2,100

178. Evaluate $3x + 7$ when $x = -3$.

    A. −2

    B. 10

    C. 16

    D. 21

179. Solve the following equation for x: $5^9 = 5^{4x+1}$

    A. −2

    B. 1

    C. 2

    D. 4

180. The greatest common factor of 24 and 36 is

    A. 6

    B. 12

    C. 36

    D. 60

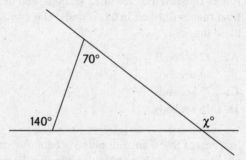

181. See the above figure. The value of x is

    A. 70°

    B. 110°

    C. 140°

    D. 180°

182. Subtract $(2x^3 - 3x + 1) - (x^2 - 3x - 2)$

    A. $2x^3 - x^2 + 3$

    B. $2x^3 - x^2 - 6x - 1$

    C. $x^3 - 6x - 1$

    D. $x^2 + 3$

183. What percent of $\frac{3}{4}$ is $\frac{1}{8}$?

    A. $9\frac{3}{8}\%$

    B. 12%

    C. $16\frac{2}{3}\%$

    D. 20%

184. A recipe calls for 3 cups of wheat and white flour combined. If $\frac{3}{8}$ of this is wheat flour, how many cups of white flour are needed?

    A. $1\frac{1}{8}$

    B. $1\frac{7}{8}$

    C. $2\frac{3}{8}$

    D. $2\frac{5}{8}$

185. Which of the following is a solution to the equation $\frac{dy}{dx} = 3x^2 + 1$?

    A. $x^3 + x$

    B. $6x^3 + x + 4$

    C. $x^3 + 1$

    D. $x^3 + x^2 + x + 3$

186. A barrel holds 60 gallons of water. If a crack in the barrel causes $\frac{1}{2}$ gallon to leak out each day, how many gallons of water remain after 2 weeks?

    A. 30

    B. 53

    C. $56\frac{1}{2}$

    D. 59

187. If $h(y) = 4^y$, then $h(0) =$

    A. 0

    B. 1

    C. 2

    D. 4

188. Melodi eats $\frac{3}{8}$ of a pizza and divides the rest among her two friends. What percent of the pizza do her friends each receive?

    A. 62.50%

    B. 37.50%

    C. 31.25%

    D. 18.75%

189. While dining out, Chad spent $25.00. If the bill totaled $21.00 before the tip was added, approximately what percent tip did Chad leave?

    A. 16%

    B. 19%

    C. 21%

    D. 25%

190. Felix buys three books for $8.95 each. How much does he owe if he uses a $12.73 credit toward his purchase?

    A. $39.58

    B. $26.85

    C. $21.68

    D. $14.12

191. The expression $\sec^2\theta - 1$ is equivalent to

    A. $\tan^2\theta$

    B. $\csc^2\theta$

    C. $\sin^2\theta$

    D. $\cos^2\theta$

192. If $y = (a - 3)(a + 2)$, then $\frac{dy}{dx} =$

    A. $2a - 1$

    B. $2a$

    C. a

    D. $a^2 - a - 6$

193. What is the diameter of a circle with a circumference equivalent to its area?

    A. 2

    B. 3

    C. 4

    D. 6

194. Simplify $\left(\frac{a^{-3}b^2}{2ab^{-1}}\right)^{-3}$

    A. $\frac{2a^6}{b}$

    B. $\frac{8a^{12}}{b^9}$

    C. $\frac{a^8}{8b^3}$

    D. $\frac{a^{12}}{8b^9}$

195. What is the probability of rolling a sum of 9 using two dice?

    A. $\frac{1}{4}$

    B. $\frac{1}{9}$

    C. $\frac{5}{12}$

    D. $\frac{7}{36}$

196. If $\log_{11} x = -1$, then $x =$

    A. -11

    B. $-\frac{1}{11}$

    C. $\frac{1}{11}$

    D. 11

GO ON TO THE NEXT PAGE

Practice Test 3

197. Floor tiling costs $13.50 per square yard. What would it cost to tile a room 15 feet long by 18 feet wide?

    A. $20

    B. $405

    C. $1,350

    D. $3,645

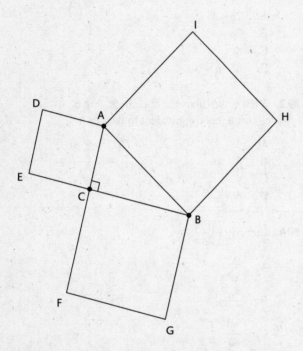

198. Squares ADEC, BCFG, and ABHI are shown above. If the area of ADEC is 81 and the area of BCFG is 144, what is the perimeter of $\triangle ABC$?

    A. 36

    B. 72

    C. 225

    D. 450

199. If $\csc \theta > 0$ and $\cos \theta < 0$, then what quadrant is the angle θ in?

    A. I

    B. II

    C. III

    D. IV

200. A car travels 20 miles in 30 minutes. At this rate, how far will the car travel in two hours?

    A. 40 miles

    B. 60 miles

    C. 80 miles

    D. 100 miles

201. $\dfrac{3}{4} \div \dfrac{4}{3} =$

    A. 0

    B. 1

    C. $\dfrac{9}{16}$

    D. $\dfrac{16}{9}$

202. Which of the following values of x is a solution of the equation $\cot x = 1$?

    A. $x = 0°$

    B. $x = 30°$

    C. $x = 45°$

    D. $x = 60°$

203. If $w - 3 = 3 - w$, what is the value of w^2?

    A. 0

    B. 1

    C. 3

    D. 9

204. If $y = e^x$, then $y'(x) =$

    A. x^{ex-1}

    B. e^x

    C. $-e^x$

    D. $\dfrac{1}{e^x}$

205. Simplify $\dfrac{x^2 - 25}{5 - x}$

    A. $x + 5$

    B. $x - 5$

    C. $-(x + 5)$

    D. $5 - x$

206. If $y^{-\frac{3}{4}} = 8$, what is the value of y?

    A. $-\dfrac{1}{8}$

    B. $-\dfrac{1}{16}$

    C. $\dfrac{1}{16}$

    D. $\dfrac{1}{8}$

207. The girl's basketball team won three times as many games as they lost. How many games were won if they played a total of 24 games?

  A. 6
  B. 8
  C. 12
  D. 18

208. What is the period of the function $b(x) = -7 + 3\cos \pi x$?

  A. 0
  B. 1
  C. 2
  D. π

209. If $\log G = \frac{1}{49}$, then $\log \left(\frac{1}{G}\right) =$

  A. $-\frac{1}{49}$
  B. $-\frac{1}{7}$
  C. $\frac{1}{7}$
  D. 7

210. A line parallel to the line $y = 5x + 9$ has a slope of

  A. -5
  B. $-\frac{1}{5}$
  C. $\frac{1}{5}$
  D. 5

211. Which of the following is the first derivative of $x\sin x$?

  A. $x(\sin x + \cos x)$
  B. $\sin x$
  C. $x\cos x - \sin x$
  D. $x\cos x + \sin x$

212. What is the mode of the set of numbers $\{1, 1, 1, 2, 2, 3, 3, 3, 3, 4, 4, 4, 5, 6, 6, 6\}$?

  A. 1
  B. 3
  C. 4
  D. 5

213. Which of the following is an extreme point of $y = x^3 - 3x^2 + 9$?

  A. $(1, 7)$
  B. $(3, 9)$
  C. $(-1, 5)$
  D. $(2, 5)$

GO ON TO THE NEXT PAGE

Chemistry

Directions: Select the choice that best answers the following questions. To consult the Periodic Table of the Elements, please go to the Appendix.

214. In the figure above, what is the VB hybridization for the carbon?

A. sp^2

B. sp^3

C. sp^3d

D. sp

215. Which of the following organic acids will be the strongest?

A. C_2H_2 $pK_a = 25$

B. CF_3CO_2H $pK_a = 0.18$

C. H_2CO_3 $pK_a = 3.7$

D. CH_3CO_2H $pK_a = 4.8$

216. What functional group is RCHO?

A. Alcohol

B. Aldehyde

C. Ketone

D. Carboxylic acid

217. What will form when ^{205}Pb undergoes alpha decay?

A. ^{204}Bi

B. ^{205}Bi

C. ^{201}Hg

D. ^{203}Hg

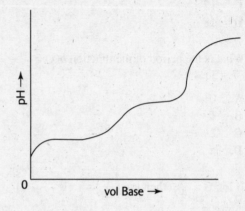

218. In the figure above, what type of acid titration is represented?

A. diprotic

B. monoprotic

C. none, this is the titration curve of a base

D. triprotic

219. In the electrolysis of water, hydrogen gas is collected by water displacement. If the pressure of the collected gas is 726 torr, and if water vapor has a pressure of 32 torr, what is the pressure of only the hydrogen gas?

A. 726 torr

B. 798 torr

C. 32 torr

D. 694 torr

220. In the electrochemical reaction $Zn|Zn^{+2}||Cu^{+2}|Cu$, what is the chemical reaction at the cathode?

A. $Zn \rightarrow Zn^{+2} + 2\,e^-$

B. $Zn^{+2} + 2e^- \rightarrow Zn$

C. $Cu^{+2} + 2\,e^- \rightarrow Cu$

D. $Cu \rightarrow Cu^{+2} + 2\,e^-$

221. What form of spectroscopy is generally best suited for detection with a conjugate pi compound?

    A. FT-IR
    B. MS
    C. UV-Vis
    D. NMR

222. The net equation for the oxidation of glucose is $C_6H_{12}O_6$ (aq) + 6 O_2 (g) → 6 CO_2 (g) + 6 H_2O (l). For every 2 moles of glucose, how many moles of oxygen are required?

    A. 3
    B. 2
    C. 12
    D. 6

223. One mole of electrons is usually symbolized as what?

    A. 1 Ohm
    B. 1 Faraday
    C. 1 Coulomb
    D. 1 Ampere

224. What state has the middle density for just about every compound or element?

    A. liquid
    B. solid
    C. gas
    D. plasma

225. The explosion of TNT is represented in the following equation.

4 $C_7H_5N_3O_6$ (s) + 21 O_2 (g) → 28 CO_2 (g) + 6 N_2 (g) + 10 H_2O (g) + heat

What can be said about this reaction?

    A. It is enthalpy driven.
    B. It is driven by both enthalpy and entropy.
    C. It is driven by neither enthalpy or entropy.
    D. It is entropy driven.

226. Which colligative properties will cause most bacteria to die when they come into contact with honey?

    A. boiling point elevation
    B. vapor pressure depression
    C. osmotic pressure
    D. freezing point depression

227. In the formation of a polymer, what step brings the reaction to an end?

    A. propagation
    B. initiation
    C. termination
    D. dissociation

228. Which set of conditions would make a real gas behave like an ideal gas?

    A. high temperature/low pressure
    B. high temperature/high pressure
    C. low temperature/low pressure
    D. low temperature/high pressure

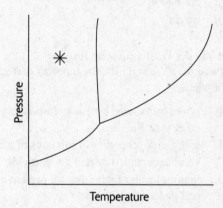

229. In the above phase diagram, what is represented by the asterisk?

    A. gas
    B. the triple point
    C. liquid
    D. solid

230. What type of reactant is most likely to react with an aromatic compound?

    A. electrophile
    B. nucleophile
    C. hydrophobic
    D. acidic

231. What type of alcohol will most rapidly undergo a dehydration reaction?

    A. methanol
    B. primary
    C. tertiary
    D. secondary

GO ON TO THE NEXT PAGE

232. There are two forms of calcium in bones. For infants, calcium is primarily in the more soluble form $Ca_3(PO_4)_2$, while for adults, it tends to be in the less soluble form $Ca_5(OH)(PO_4)_3$. Recently, a study has indicated that an elevated intake of phosphates (such as from some soft drinks) can cause the decalcification of bones. The equilibrium is represented as follows:

$3\ Ca_5(OH)(PO_4)_3\ (s) + PO_4^{-3}\ (aq) \leftarrow \rightarrow 5\ Ca_3(PO_4)_2\ (aq) + 3\ OH^-\ (aq)$

Whose principle supports this finding?

A. LeChatelier's
B. Dalton's
C. Aufbau's
D. Boyle's

233. In Van der Waal's equation for gases, $(P+an^2/V^2)(V-nb) = nRT$, the term "a" corrects for what?

A. errors introduced by using temperature scales other than Kelvin
B. colligative properties of mixtures of gases
C. volume occupied by real gas particles
D. intermolecular forces that are present in real gases

234. What volume of water is necessary to produce 100 mL of a 0.1% NaCl solution from a 2% stock solution?

A. 5 mL
B. 95 mL
C. 100 mL
D. 10 mL

235. If it were to dissociate completely, how many ions (total) would be produced by one formula unit of $Ca_3(PO_4)_2$?

A. 3
B. 13
C. 4
D. 5

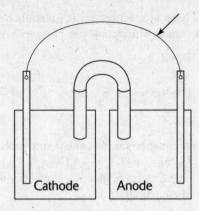

236. In the above diagram of an electrochemical setup, what is the arrow pointing to?

A. electrical connection
B. salt bridge
C. cathode
D. anode

237. What type of elimination mechanism would be expected if the intermediate is very stable?

A. E2
B. E1
C. S_N2
D. S_N1

238. To balance the half-equation $MnO_4^- \rightarrow MnO_2$ in an acidic solution, how many electrons will we have to add and to which side?

A. 1 to the product side
B. 2 to the reactant side
C. 3 to the reactant side
D. 2 to the product side

239. When writing molecular orbital electron configuration, what does the asterisk denote for any given orbital?

A. It is a bonding orbital.
B. It is a forbidden orbital.
C. It is an antibonding orbital.
D. It is a nonbonding orbital.

240. In what representation of a chemical reaction do we neglect to write the spectator ions?

A. total ionic
B. net ionic
C. traditional
D. decomposition

241. What salt would form from the reaction of nitric acid with ammonium hydroxide?

A. $(NH_4)_2NO_3$
B. $(NH_4)_3NO_3$
C. NH_4NO_3
D. $NH_4(NO_3)_2$

242. What is the only type of nuclear decay that can increase the atomic number?

A. α decay
B. γ decay
C. $n°$ decay
D. β decay

243. What is the only factor that can never influence solubility?

A. stirring
B. pressure
C. temperature
D. the nature of the solvent and solute

244. Which of the following functional groups involve nitrogen?

A. carboxylic acid
B. alcohol
C. amine
D. ether

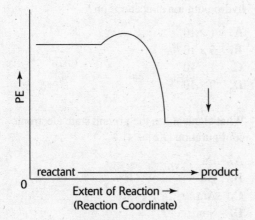

reactant ——————→ product

Extent of Reaction →
(Reaction Coordinate)

245. In the above diagram, what is the arrow denoting?

A. energy of reaction
B. activation energy
C. transition state
D. products

246. If we hold the number of moles of a gas and the temperature constant, what will happen to volume if we double the pressure?

A. It could do anything.
B. It will not change.
C. It will double.
D. It will halve.

247. In the Nernst equation, $E = E^0 - (RT/nF)\ln Q$, what information does Q contain?

A. standard potential
B. the reaction quotient
C. temperature effects
D. electrons per mole

248. Short of producing carbon dioxide, which of the following functional groups cannot be further oxidized?

A. aldehydes
B. alkane
C. alcohol
D. ketone

249. In 1,1,2 trichloroethane, $CHCl_2CH_2Cl$, what type of peak will we see for first hydrogen (as written) in the ^2H–NMR spectrum?

A. higher than triplet
B. singlet
C. triplet
D. doublet

250. For the reaction $2\,NO_2\,(g) \longleftrightarrow N_2O_4\,(g)$, what is the reaction quotient if $[NO_2]_o = 0.1$ and $[N_2O_4]_o = 1.0$?

A. 0.1
B. 10
C. 100
D. 0.01

251. What type of reaction is $C\,(s) + O_2\,(g) \rightarrow CO_2\,(g)$?

A. decomposition
B. single replacement
C. addition
D. double replacement (or combination, or synthesis)

GO ON TO THE NEXT PAGE

252. What term represents the energy gained by giving an electron to an element?

    A. electronegativity

    B. ionization energy

    C. electron affinity

    D. electron energy

253. In the reaction Ag^+ (aq) + I^- (aq) ←→ AgI (s), what can we add to remove more silver from the solution?

    A. $AgNO_3$

    B. KI

    C. water

    D. heat

254. What is the rate law expression for the reaction $2 C_8H_{18}$ (l) + $25 O_2$ (g) → $16 CO_2$ (g) + $18 H_2O$ (g)?

    A. rate = $[C_8H_{18}(l)]^2[O_2(g)]^{25}/[CO_2(g)]^{16}[H_2O(g)]^{18}$

    B. rate = $k[C_8H_{18}(l)]^x[O_2(g)]^y$

    C. rate = $k[C_8H_{18}(l)]^2[O_2(g)]^{25}$

    D. rate = $[CO_2(g)]^{16}[H_2O(g)]^{18}/[C_8H_{18}(l)]^2[O_2(g)]^{25}$

255. From the following list, what should be the strongest acid?

    A. HSO_4^-

    B. H_2SO_3

    C. H_2SO_4

    D. HSO_3^-

256. What is the proper equilibrium constant expression of H_2SO_3 (aq) + $2 H_2O$ (l) ←→ $2 H_3O^+$ (aq) + SO_3^{-2} (aq)?

    A. $K_{eq} = \{2[H_3O^+(aq)]+[SO_3^{-2}(aq)]\}/\{[H_2SO_3(aq)]+2[H_2O(l)]\}$

    B. $K_{eq} = [H_3O^+(aq)]^2[SO_3^{-2}(aq)]/[H_2SO_3(aq)]$

    C. $K_{eq} = [H_3O^+(aq)]^2[SO_3^{-2}(aq)]/[H_2SO_3(aq)][H_2O(l)]^2$

    D. $K_{eq} = \{2[H_3O^+(aq)]+[SO_3^{-2}(aq)]\}/[H_2SO_3(aq)]$

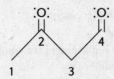

257. In the above figure, which carbon will most likely form a carbanion?

    A. carbon 2

    B. carbon 1

    C. carbon 4

    D. carbon 3

258. Which of the following gases will behave most like an ideal gas?

    A. H_2S

    B. CH_3OH

    C. Xe

    D. Ar

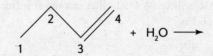

259. According to Markonikov's rule, which carbon will the hydroxide go on in the formation of alcohol from the following hydration reaction? (See above figure.)

    A. 1

    B. 2

    C. 4

    D. 3

260. If the pOH of a solution is 9.0, what is the hydronium ion concentration?

    A. 1×10^{-5}

    B. 5×10^{-10}

    C. 1×10^{-9}

    D. 9×10^{-10}

261. What element has the ground state electronic configuration $[Xe]6s^24f^7$?

    A. Eu

    B. Gd

    C. Am

    D. Sm

262. How does atomic radius tend to increase on the periodic chart?

    A. from left to right, and from top to bottom

    B. from right to left, and from bottom to top

    C. from right to left, and from top to bottom

    D. from left to right, and from bottom to top

263. Which of the following ring structures will be aromatic?

A.

B.

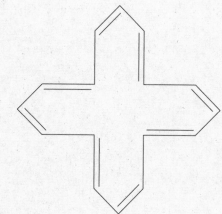

C.

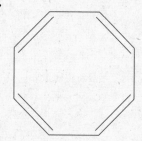

D.

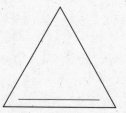

264. At equilibrium, which of the following must be true?

A. $\triangle H = \triangle S$
B. $\triangle G = 0$
C. $K_{eq} = 1$
D. $E^0 = 1$

265. What is the process that best describes the forming of ice crystals on a windshield on a cold morning?

A. sublimation
B. freezing
C. decomposition
D. deposition

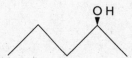

266. What is the proper IUPAC name for the alcohol shown above?

A. S-2-pentanol
B. R-2-pentanol
C. R-4-pentanol
D. S-4-pentanol

267. According to the Arrhenius equation, if temperature has any effect on a chemical reaction, what will that effect be?

A. increased reaction rate
B. a shift of equilibrium
C. increased product formation
D. more molecular collisions

268. Cuprous nitrate has what chemical formula?

A. $Cu(NO_3)_3$
B. Cu_2NO_3
C. $Cu(NO_3)_2$
D. $CuNO_3$

269. In the reaction $4\ H^+$ (aq) + $3\ Fe^{+2}$ (aq) + MnO_4^- (aq) $\rightarrow$ $3\ Fe^{+3}$ (aq) + MnO_2 (s) + $2\ H_2O$ (l), what is the reducing agent?

A. iron (II) ion
B. water
C. permanganate ion
D. hydronium ion

270. A clear blue liquid containing water and copper (II) sulfate can be best described by which term?

A. solution
B. compound
C. element
D. mixture

GO ON TO THE NEXT PAGE

Critical Thinking Essay

Directions: You will have 30 minutes in which to write an essay in response to the following statement. This essay will either require you to express an opinion or will present a problem that needs a solution.

"Politicians and other government officials are usually well-informed and therefore, major policy decisions should be left to them, rather than to the general public."

Answer Key for Practice Test 3

Verbal Ability: Analogies

1. C	**11.** C	**21.** A
2. A	**12.** A	**22.** C
3. D	**13.** C	**23.** D
4. C	**14.** C	**24.** B
5. A	**15.** C	**25.** C
6. C	**16.** C	**26.** D
7. D	**17.** B	**27.** A
8. A	**18.** D	**28.** C
9. D	**19.** D	**29.** A
10. C	**20.** D	

Verbal Ability: Sentence Completions

30. C	**40.** C	**50.** C
31. A	**41.** A	**51.** D
32. D	**42.** D	**52.** B
33. B	**43.** D	**53.** B
34. B	**44.** A	**54.** B
35. A	**45.** A	**55.** A
36. D	**46.** D	**56.** D
37. A	**47.** B	**57.** C
38. A	**48.** D	**58.** A
39. C	**49.** B	

Biology

59. A	**79.** C	**99.** D
60. C	**80.** A	**100.** B
61. D	**81.** D	**101.** C
62. C	**82.** B	**102.** A
63. C	**83.** B	**103.** C
64. D	**84.** B	**104.** D
65. B	**85.** D	**105.** C
66. A	**86.** C	**106.** B
67. C	**87.** A	**107.** C
68. D	**88.** B	**108.** A
69. B	**89.** C	**109.** B
70. C	**90.** A	**110.** D
71. C	**91.** D	**111.** C
72. C	**92.** B	**112.** A
73. D	**93.** C	**113.** D
74. A	**94.** A	**114.** C
75. C	**95.** D	**115.** B
76. C	**96.** D	**116.** D
77. B	**97.** A	
78. B	**98.** B	

Reading Comprehension

117. C	**134.** C	**151.** C
118. A	**135.** D	**152.** A
119. A	**136.** A	**153.** C
120. B	**137.** B	**154.** B
121. D	**138.** C	**155.** D
122. A	**139.** D	**156.** B
123. B	**140.** C	**157.** C
124. D	**141.** C	**158.** B
125. B	**142.** C	**159.** B
126. D	**143.** D	**160.** C
127. A	**144.** B	**161.** A
128. B	**145.** B	**162.** B
129. C	**146.** B	**163.** C
130. B	**147.** D	**164.** A
131. C	**148.** A	**165.** A
132. C	**149.** A	
133. B	**150.** B	

Quantitative Ability

166. C	**182.** A	**198.** A
167. D	**183.** C	**199.** B
168. B	**184.** B	**200.** C
169. B	**185.** A	**201.** C
170. D	**186.** B	**202.** C
171. D	**187.** B	**203.** D
172. B	**188.** C	**204.** B
173. B	**189.** B	**205.** C
174. D	**190.** D	**206.** C
175. C	**191.** A	**207.** D
176. B	**192.** A	**208.** C
177. B	**193.** C	**209.** A
178. A	**194.** B	**210.** D
179. C	**195.** B	**211.** D
180. B	**196.** C	**212.** B
181. B	**197.** B	**213.** D

Chemistry

214. A	**234.** B	**254.** B
215. B	**235.** D	**255.** C
216. B	**236.** A	**256.** B
217. C	**237.** B	**257.** D
218. A	**238.** C	**258.** D
219. D	**239.** C	**259.** D
220. C	**240.** B	**260.** A
221. C	**241.** C	**261.** A
222. C	**242.** D	**262.** B
223. B	**243.** A	**263.** B
224. A	**244.** C	**264.** B
225. B	**245.** D	**265.** D
226. C	**246.** D	**266.** A
227. C	**247.** B	**267.** A
228. A	**248.** D	**268.** D
229. D	**249.** C	**269.** A
230. A	**250.** C	**270.** A
231. C	**251.** C	
232. A	**252.** C	
233. D	**253.** B	

Complete Answers and Explanations for Practice Test 3

Verbal Ability: Analogies

1. **C.** Abstruse is difficult to understand or recondite. Something that is difficult is also pedantic.

2. **A.** The opening part of an opera is the overture, and the opening part of the book is the preface.

3. **D.** A benefactor is a good person who gives aid. A miscreant is a bad person who does crime.

4. **C.** The act of joining together happens in a marriage; the act of dissolving or pulling apart something is a divorce.

5. **A.** Derision is making fun of something and is the opposite of applaud. Ridicule is making fun of something and the opposite is acclaim, which means to praise.

6. **C.** To lessen the anxiety is to allay one's fears. To lessen hysteria is to appease one's crying.

7. **D.** An epic is a lengthy text; an epithet is a very succinct text.

8. **A.** An aquarium is where you find fish. A terrarium is where you find plants.

9. **D.** The adjective to describe cats is feline; the adjective to describe cows is bovine.

10. **C.** A part of a stanza is a line; a part of a paragraph is a sentence.

11. **C.** A quality of a traitor is disloyalty or being perfidious. A quality of a hothead is being impetuous or acting before thinking.

12. **A.** A laggard is someone who is slow and always tardy and a dynamo is someone who is energetic.

13. **C.** A dissembler pretends to be more than he is; a zealot is someone who is enthusiastic.

14. **C.** Someone who is intractable will not compromise; someone who is inexorable will not relent or give in.

15. **C.** Desultory is lack of direction; nefarious is lack of virtue because the person is so bad.

16. **C.** An extreme of moderation is exorbitant. An extreme of taste is insipid.

17. **B.** To abdicate means to resign or give up. To release means to discharge or let go.

18. **D.** Finesse means having grace and skill, which is the opposite of incompetence. Adroitness means having skill, and the opposite is clumsiness.

19. **D.** Docile is giving in or being subservient. Tractable is also giving in or being compliant.

20. **D.** An extreme of interest is ardor. An extreme of envy is avarice.

21. **A.** You get a vaccination so you don't get smallpox. You get an antidote so you don't get poisoned.

22. **C.** Many pictures make up a montage. Many tiles make up a mosaic.

23. **D.** A dentist works on teeth, and a plumber works on pipes.

24. **B.** A professor reads lectures and an actor reads scripts. Choice **A,** although it sounds likely, is not a good choice because performing is what the actor does, not what the actor reads.

25. **C.** The relationship is from more to less or greater to smaller.

26. **D.** The relationship is effect to cause. Choices **A** and **C** would be cause to effect.

27. **A.** The words are synonyms.

28. **C.** The relationship is purpose. Food is eaten for nutrition; soap is used to maintain cleanliness.

29. **A.** You may not know that a kid is a baby goat. But the relationship of the first two words is from younger to older. None of the other choice would fit that sequence.

Verbal Ability: Sentence Completions

30. C. Exacerbate means to make worse.

31. A. The second half of the sentence requires that the word in the first blank creates the meaning that enjoyment was not expected. The phrase underwhelmed by its performance suggests doubt, skepticism.

32. D. Vacillate means to go back and forth, and prosperous means wealthy. Because the sentence includes prices that both rise and fall, Choice **A** is not a good answer, even though opulent would fit in the second blank.

33. B. To eschew is to shun or avoid.

34. B. Nebulous means cloudy, misty, or hazy.

35. A. The phrase "in spite of" suggests the words in the blank denotes difference. Disparate means dissimilar.

36. D. That the paintings depicted wildness means they contrasted with the everyday. The second blank requires a synonym for everyday. Banal means ordinary or commonplace. Since that was what they did not paint, the first blank requires a word meaning gave up—renounced.

37. A. To exonerate means to free from blame.

38. A. To resonate is to echo.

39. C. Because the description is favorable, the words in both blanks must have positive connotations. Indelible means inerasable, and propriety means customary and polite—appropriate.

40. C. A catastrophe is a great disaster. The other choices, while they may imply problems, are inappropriate to describe an earthquake.

41. A. Chicanery means trickery or fraud; to forfeit is to give up.

42. D. The sentence uses cause-and-effect logic. Because he was egotistical and insensitive, he was impossible to affect (impervious), and his behavior did not change (alter).

43. D. A conversation is a form of interaction. Cognitive means relating to acquiring knowledge. While contact, Choice **C,** might make sense, oracular, meaning able to foretell the future, would not.

44. A. The first half of the sentence requires a contrast between something disappearing and something that may continue. Viable means able to live or develop under favorable conditions. To make something flourish is to restore it.

45. A. Strident means loud and harsh.

46. D. Languidly means slowly and sluggishly.

47. B. To apprise means to keep informed.

48. D. To attribute means to explain the cause of.

49. B. Minimal means the smallest possible amount. The logic of the sentence is that neither side was willing to bargain; as a result, there could be little negotiation.

50. C. The sentence suggests a contrast between the view (spectacular) and the furnishings (unobtrusive—not intruding on one's vision) because the home was decorated modestly.

51. D. Temperate means moderate—neither passionate nor monotonous.

52. B. Choice **A** doesn't make sense because if something is rewarding, it would not deprecate (disparage) what follows. Warrants means justifies.

53. B. Frenetic means wildly excited.

54. B. Conscientiously means with deliberate regard to principles, or thoroughly; tenacity means holding steadily to a course of action.

55. A. Meager means scanty.

56. D. An anomaly is something that is irregular or difficult to classify. Since the result of the experiment was an anomaly, it was not anticipated.

57. C. The nadir is the lowest point of something.

58. A. A modicum is a small amount.

Biology

59. A. DNA is transcribed onto mRNA, which is then translated into proteins.

60. C. Natural selection will help to increase the frequency of favorable traits in a population. Evolution (Choice **A**) is the result of changes in the genetic makeup of a population over time. The rate of evolution is affected by the degree of natural selection operating on various traits. Genetic drift (Choice **B**) and genetic bottlenecking (Choice **D**) are both associated with small population size and a decrease in the amount of genetic variation within a population.

61. D. The Central Dogma of Biology refers to the fact that genetic information encoded in the DNA of an individual is transcribed onto mRNA, which is then translated into the proteins that give rise to the characteristics of the individual.

62. C. The field of comparative biochemistry supports the theory of evolution by showing that virtually all living organisms share the same genetic code. Paleontology (Choice **A**) supports the theory of evolution by evaluating evolutionary relationships through analysis of the fossil record. Comparative embryology (Choice **B**) supports the theory of evolution through the study of similarities that occur during embryo development among a diverse array of organisms. Comparative anatomy (Choice **D**) supports the theory of evolution by evaluating similarities in anatomical structure among a diverse array of organisms.

63. C. The fungi are in their own kingdom. The other organisms listed are all protists.

64. D. The bryophytes do not have xylem and phloem and, therefore, are nonvascular in nature.

65. B. Following fertilization in flowering plants, the ovary becomes the fruit and the ovule becomes the seed.

66. A. The Chordata includes members both with and without backbones. None of the other groups listed include members that have backbones.

67. C. Amphibians spend part of their life cycle on land and part of their life cycle in water. Sponges (Choice **A**) and fishes (Choice **B**) spend their entire lives in the water. While many reptiles (Choice **D**) live in moist habitats and occasionally spend time in water, as a group, reptiles do not spend entire portions of their life cycle living in the water.

68. D. The nucleus houses the genetic information of an individual. ATP production is a result of cellular respiration, which takes place in the mitochondria.

69. B. During the s-portion (synthesis) of interphase, DNA is replicated within each chromosome.

70. C. Separation of cells at the two-cell stage during normal development of a human embryo will result in the production of identical twins.

71. C. Coelenterates (cnidaria) use nematocysts to sting and paralyze prey.

72. C. The ability to reproduce on land was an important evolutionary step in the development of reptiles, as these organisms were no longer dependent on water for reproduction.

73. D. Leeuwenhoek developed a primitive microscope and was the first person to observe unicellular organisms.

74. A. In order for a genetic mutation to have an evolutionary effect, it must be able to be passed from parent to offspring and, thus, must occur in the germ cells giving rise to eggs or sperm.

75. C. The process of cellular respiration, not photosynthesis, results in the production of ATP.

76. C. Predation by humans, in the form of hunting, is the most likely cause of extinction for both the dodo and the passenger pigeon.

77. B. Complex life forms would most likely evolve in an aerobic environment because aerobic respiration is nearly 20 times as efficient as anaerobic respiration at producing energy.

78. B. One of the primary function of the Golgi apparatus is to prepare cell products for secretion. The Golgi apparatus may also serve as a center of manufacturing, storage, sorting and shipping. In cells specialized for secretion the Golgi apparatus is very extensive.

79. C. Down's syndrome is cause by a chromosomal aberration and, therefore, can be detected with routine amniocentesis.

80. A. In photosynthesis, light energy is used to convert water and carbon dioxide into glucose molecules, with oxygen produced as a byproduct. Therefore, increasing the reactants in the photosynthetic reactions (carbon dioxide and water), or increasing the source of energy that drives the reactions (light) would increase the rate of photosynthesis, but increasing the oxygen concentration would not cause an increase in the rate of photosynthesis.

81. D. Red-green color-blindness is a sex-linked, recessive trait carried on the X chromosome. A girl with red-green color-blindness must, therefore, have a recessive allele on both of her X-chromosomes. Girls inherit one X from their dad and one X from their mom. A girl could inherit red-green colorblindness from either of the following combinations: color-blind dad and color-blind mom; or color-blind dad and carrier (heterozygous) mom.

82. B. Human somatic cells contain 46 chromosomes. When meiosis occurs in human germ cells, giving rise to eggs or sperm, the chromosome number is reduced by half, to 23, in the resulting egg or sperm cells.

83. B. If a cross between a red-flowered plant and a white-flowered plant produces all pink offspring, the parent plants must have been homozygous for red and white flowers, respectively, and the offspring must all be heterozygous for flower color. A cross between two of the heterozygous pink-flowered plants would produce offspring in the following proportions: 25% homozygous red-flowered, 50% heterozygous pink-flowered, and 25% homozygous white-flowered.

84. B. Yeast are in the Kingdom Fungi and are eukaryotic organisms.

85. D. Certain strains of fungi, bacteria, and protozoa are capable of causing disease.

86. C. A bacterial cell that has picked up foreign DNA from its environment, for example, by taking up a plasmid while in culture, is said to have been transformed. Conjugation (Choice **A**) involves genetic exchange between two bacterial cells that are temporarily joined together by a conjugation tube. Transduction (Choice **B**) involves the introduction of foreign DNA into a bacterial cell through infection by a phage. Phagocytosis (Choice **D**) involves the engulfing and destroying of bacterial cells by certain cells in the human immune system (e.g., macrophages).

87. A. Typhoid fever is a bacterial disease affecting the gastrointestinal tract.

88. B. Shigellosis is caused by a bacterial infection.

89. C. Plague, Lyme disease, spotted fever, and tularemia are all blood-borne diseases caused by bacteria.

90. A. Vaccines artificially introduce an antigen (as opposed to being exposed to the disease by an infected individual), initiating an immune response to produce antibodies. The production of antibodies to an antigen is considered an active immune response.

91. D. The presence of coliform bacteria in the drinking water supply indicates the presence of human feces, suggesting that the water supply has been contaminated by sewage.

92. B. Yeast, which is used in the fermentation process leading to the production of alcohol, is a member of the Kingdom Fungi.

93. C. The capsid surrounding a virus particle is composed of protein.

94. A. The bacterial genome consists of one double-stranded, circular molecule of DNA.

95. D. Retroviruses produce the enzyme reverse transcriptase, which enables them to make a strand of DNA from an RNA template.

96. **D.** The order in which food travels through the human digestive system is as follows: mouth → esophagus → stomach → small intestine. Nutrients from the digested food are absorbed into the bloodstream. Any undigested material (waste) moves on to the large intestine and is eliminated from the body as feces.

97. **A.** Oxygen-poor blood enters the human heart at the right atrium, is pumped to the lungs where it picks up oxygen, and returns to the heart at the left atrium.

98. **B.** An individual would have trouble regulating their blood sugar levels if their pancreas were surgically removed.

99. **D.** In human males, meiosis occurs in the seminiferous tubules, where sperm are made.

100. **B.** Many of the metabolic changes that occur in the bodies of individuals consuming diets high in protein and fat, but low in carbohydrates, are similar to those that occur in individuals with diabetes mellitus.

101. **C.** A pH of 7.4 is slightly alkaline, with a pH of 7.0 being neutral. pH values below 7 are acidic and those above 7 are alkaline.

102. **A.** The major artery located on each side of the neck in humans is referred to as the carotid artery.

103. **C.** In humans, both red and white blood cells are made in the bone marrow.

104. **D.** The cornea of the human eye does not have a blood supply flowing to it.

105. **C.** The rotator cuff is located in the human shoulder.

106. **B.** A ganglion consists of a collection of nerves located outside the central nervous system.

107. **C.** In humans, the trachea is sometimes referred to as the windpipe.

108. **A.** The "Islets of Langerhans" refers to a group of cells located in the pancreas.

109. **B.** In the human brain, memory is coordinated in the hippocampus. The hypothalamus (Choice **A**) controls hunger, thirst, body temperature, and blood pressure, as well as produces hormones that will be stored in the pituitary. The cerebellum (Choice **C**) coordinates motor activity and muscle contractions. The medulla (Choice **D**) serves as a passageway for nerves extending to and from the brain and controls automatic functions such as breathing, heart rate and digestion.

110. **D.** Neutrophils are the most common type of white blood cell found in humans.

111. **C.** Endometrial tissue builds up in the uterus and could be used to nourish a developing embryo should fertilization take place.

112. **A.** The human heart is controlled by nerves that originate on the right side in the upper region of the atrium at a node referred to as the pacemaker.

113. **D.** In the human circulatory system, the platelets serve to begin the blood clotting mechanism.

114. **C.** The primary function of the Eustachian tubes, which lead from the pharynx to the middle ear in humans is to equalize pressure.

115. **B.** Meiosis takes place in the ovaries, producing eggs.

116. **D.** The primary function of the ureters in the human excretory system is to carry waste products from the kidneys to the bladder.

Reading Comprehension

117. **C.** In the second paragraph, it states that the rods and cones are dead but that they have other cells down the line that still are alive.

118. **A.** This is stated in the second paragraph when it is mentioned that they can share the responsibility if they can be engineered to respond to light.

119. **A.** This is stated in the last sentence of the second paragraph.

120. B. This is stated in the second sentence of the third paragraph.

121. D. This is stated in the last sentence of the third paragraph.

122. A. This is stated in the second sentence of the last paragraph.

123. B. This is stated in the last sentence of the article.

124. D. This is the topic sentence of the first paragraph.

125. B. (Choice **A**) There is not talk about amount of rainfall nor what happens to the water (**C**). Deforestation (Choice **D**) means the destruction of all vegetation.

126. D. When there are no trees for protection from the sun, it gets too hot and the land dries out.

127. A. In the second paragraph, they state the rule of thumb, which is a way to determine the type of land.

128. B. In the middle of the last paragraph, the definition of forest-obligate is one that "cannot exist outside of the woods."

129. C. The fact is the stated in the second to the last sentence of the article.

130. B. This is stated in the last sentence of the article.

131. C. The second sentence indicates the frequency of sound waves in hertz.

132. C. The first sentence of the second paragraph states this.

133. B. There is no discussion of hearing (Choice **A**) nor ways to use it for military training (Choice **C**). The Limited Test Ban Treaty made the use of infrasound less necessary (Choice **D**).

134. C. There is no discussion of space travel (Choice **B**) nor missile strength (Choice **A**), nor anything about music (Choice **C**).

135. D. These facts are all found in the last paragraph.

136. A. Since the infrasound can help with weather predictions and volcanic action, it would make sense that it could predict a tsunami.

137. B. There is the introduction of music and infrasound waves so this is a new application.

138. C. It is defined in the first paragraph.

139. D. It is stated in the last sentence of the first paragraph.

140. C. In the second paragraph, following the word paralarva is the word "baby."

141. C. The second paragraph describes how he himself went into the nets to retrieve the dead squid.

142. C. His boat is described as old and rickety and he made his own nets.

143. D. This is stated in the middle of the last paragraph.

144. B. At the end of the article, he still hasn't caught a live paralarva and scientists have not studied a live one.

145. B. In the first paragraph, it is referred to as a device.

146. B. There is no mention of an interview (Choice **D**) and items in choices **A** and **C** are just part of the entire process. Choice **B** incorporates this information.

147. D. Within the second paragraph, the facts in choices **A**, **B**, and **C** are all proven wrong.

148. A. This is stated in the first sentence of the third paragraph.

149. A. Because of this effect, the device can help the person not stutter.

150. B. This is stated in the middle of the last paragraph.

151. C. Because this device can improve the quality of life, it must also help the people's mental conditions, too.

152. A. The article is talking about regeneration of heart tissues.

153. C. This is stated in the second sentence of the second paragraph.

154. B. The other creature mentioned all can regrow some part of their bodies.

155. D. This is found in paragraph four. Be aware that the use of "yet" (Choice **A**) implies that it will eventually differentiate.

156. B. This is explained in the last paragraph.

157. C. The combination of size and shape indicates structure.

158. B. By relating the research to other diseases, it demonstrates an expansion of this concept.

159. B. This is the main idea of the first paragraph.

160. C. At the end of the second paragraph, they mention that people could "shop" for traits that they wanted in their offspring.

161. A. This is stated in the third sentence of the second paragraph.

162. B. This is stated in the middle of the second paragraph.

163. C. It would be negative because then there would be little diversity and people might reject children that are not perfect.

164. A. By playing God, people would be making choices about every aspect of what it means to be human.

165. A. The last sentence warns that the discussion of ethics must happen or else consequences will be dire.

Quantitative Ability

166. C. Since two runners finished in 80 seconds, the average of 80, 80, 72, and 68 must be found. This average is $\frac{80 + 80 + 72 + 68}{3} = \frac{300}{4} = 75$ seconds.

167. D. For a 30 hour week with $500 in sales, total earnings are $(30 \times \$9.50) + (3\% \times \$500) = \$285 + \$15 = \$300$.

168. B. Let $\log_5 5 = x$. Then, by the definition of logarithms, $5 = 5x$, so $x = 1$.

169. B. The volume of the original box is $3 \times 2\frac{1}{2} \times 2 = 15$. The volume of the box with the length and depth doubled is $6 \times 2\frac{1}{2} \times 4 = 60$. The amount of change in volume is $60 - 15 = 45$. The percent change is the amount of change in volume divided by the original volume. $\frac{45}{15} = 3 = 300\%$.

170. D. $(-8)^{\frac{2}{3}} = \left(\sqrt[3]{-8}\right)^2 = (-2)^2 = 4$

171. D. There are 3 feet in a yard, so a kitchen 4 yards by 5 yards is equivalent to (4×3) feet by (5×3) feet, or 12 feet by 15 feet. The area of the kitchen is $12 \times 15 = 180$ square feet. The cost to tile is $\$2.89 \times 180 = \$520.20$.

172. B. If a machine produces 8,000 widgets in three hours, it produces $\frac{8000}{3}$ widgets in one hour. There are 24 hours in a day, so $\frac{8000}{3} \times 24$ or 64,000 widgets are produced in one day.

173. B. The amount of commissions over $5,000 is $12,500 - \$5,000 = \$7,500$. Earning are $\$7,500 \times 15\% = \$1,125$.

174. D. The proportion $\frac{3 \text{ boxes}}{18 \text{ reams}} = \frac{x \text{ boxes}}{90 \text{ reams}}$ can be used to find the number of boxes. Cross-multiply. $3 \times 90 = 18x$ so $270 = 18x$ and $x = \frac{270}{18} = 15$ boxes.

175. C. The area of one square is $\frac{405}{5} = 81$. So the length of each side is $\sqrt{81} = 9$. The total number of sides in the figure is 12, so the perimeter is $9 \times 12 = 108$.

176. B. Convert 2.2 minutes to seconds. $2.2 \times 60 = 132$ seconds. The difference in the two times is $132 - 124 = 8$ seconds.

177. B. There are 30 minutes in a half-hour. $30 \times 35 = 1,050$ words.

178. A. Substitute -3 for x. Then $3(-3) + 7 = -9 + 7 = -2$.

179. C. This equation can only be true if $9 = 4x + 1$, that is, if $x = 2$.

180. B. Factors of 24 are $2 \times 2 \times 2 \times 3$. Factors of 36 are $2 \times 2 \times 3 \times 3$. The greatest common factor is $2 \times 2 \times 3 = 12$.

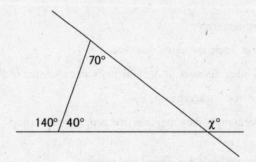

181. B. (See above figure.)

The angle adjacent to the 140° angle is 40° since supplementary angles add to 180°. The angles of a triangle add to 180° so the angle adjacent to angle x is $180° - 70° - 40° = 70°$. Angle x and 70° are supplementary, so $x = 180° - 70° = 110°$.

182. A. Subtraction can be changed to addition by changing the signs in the entire term being subtracted. $(2x^3 - 3x + 1) - (x^2 - 3x - 2) = (2x^3 - 3x + 1) + (-x^2 + 3x + 2)$.

Combine like terms. $2x^3 - x^2 - 3x + 3x + 1 + 2 = (x^2 - 3x - 2) = 2x^3 - x^2 + 3$

183. C. Let p represent the unknown percent. Then $p \times \frac{3}{4} = \frac{1}{8}$. Solve for p by multiplying by the reciprocal of $\frac{3}{4} \times p \times \frac{3}{4} \times \frac{4}{3} = \frac{1}{8} \times \frac{4}{3} = \frac{4}{24} = \frac{1}{6}$. As a percent, $\frac{1}{6}$ is $16\frac{2}{3}\%$.

184. B. If $\frac{3}{8}$ is wheat flour, then $1 - \frac{3}{8}$ or $\frac{5}{8}$ is white flour. So $3 \times \frac{5}{8} = \frac{15}{8} = 1\frac{7}{8}$ cups of white flour is needed.

185. A. In this problem, we are looking for the function whose first derivative is equal to $3x^2 + 1$. The first term of the function must be x^3, since the derivative of x^3 is $3x^2$. The second term of the function must be x, since the derivative of x is 1. Overall, then, the solution must be $x^3 + x$.

186. B. In 2 weeks, or 14 days, $\frac{1}{2} \times 14 = 7$ gallons leak out, leaving $60 - 7 = 53$ gallons.

187. B. Note that $h(0) = 40 = 1$.

188. C. If $\frac{3}{8}$ of the pizza is eaten, then $1 - \frac{3}{8} = \frac{5}{8}$ remains. If that is divided by 2, then each receives $\frac{5}{8} \div 2 = \frac{5}{8} \times \frac{1}{2} = \frac{5}{16} = 0.3125 = 31.25\%$.

189. B. The percent tip is the amount of tip over the total before tip. The amount of the tip is $\$25.00 - \$21.00 = \$4.00$. The percent of the tip is $\frac{4}{21} = 0.19 = 19\%$.

190. D. The total cost of the purchase is $\$8.95 \times 3 = \$26.85$. With a $12.73 credit, the amount owed is $\$26.85 - \$12.73 = \$14.12$.

191. A. One of the Pythagorean identities in Trigonometry is $\tan^2\theta + 1 = \sec^2\theta$. Thus, $\tan^2\theta = \sec^2\theta - 1$.

192. A. The quickest way to solve this problem is to begin by performing the multiplication to obtain $y = a^2 - a - 6$. The first derivative of this function is $2a - 1$.

193. C. The circumference of a circle is given by the formula $C = 2\pi r$ and the area of a circle is given by $A = \pi r^2$. If the circumference is equal to the area, then $2\pi r = \pi r^2$. Solving for r, $\frac{2\pi r}{\pi r} = \frac{\pi r^2}{\pi r}$ and $2 = r$. The diameter is $2r$, or 4.

194. B. $\left(\dfrac{a^{-3}b^2}{2ab^{-1}}\right)^{-3} = \dfrac{a^9 b^{-6}}{2^{-3}a^{-3}b^3} = 2^3 a^{9-(-3)}b^{-6-3} = 8a^{12}b^{-9} = \dfrac{8a^{12}}{b^9}$.

195. B. There are 4 possible ways to roll a 9 using 2 dice: 3 and 6, 4 and 5, 5 and 4, 6 and 3. The total number of possible outcomes when rolling 2 dice is 6^2 or 36. Therefore, the probability of rolling a 9 is $\dfrac{4}{36} = \dfrac{1}{9}$.

196. C. $\log_{11}x = -1$ can be rewritten as $x = 11^{-1}$. Therefore, $x = \dfrac{1}{11}$.

197. B. The area of a room 15 feet wide by 18 feet long is $15 \times 18 = 270$ square feet. Since there are 3 feet in a yard, there are 3×3 or 9 feet in a square yard. Convert 270 square feet to square yards. $\dfrac{270}{9} = 30$ square yards. Since the cost is \$13.50 per square yard, the total cost is \$13.50 $\times$ 30 or \$405.

198. A. Since the area of ADEC is 81, AC $= \sqrt{81} = 9$. Since the area of BCFG is 144, BC $= \sqrt{144} = 12$. Use the Pythagorean theorem to find the length of the remaining side AB. $AB^2 = 9^2 + 12^2$ so $AB^2 = 81 + 144 = 225$ and AB $= \sqrt{225} = 15$. Therefore, the perimeter of the triangle $= 9 + 12 + 15 = 36$.

199. B. The cosecant function is positive in quadrants I and II. The cosine function is negative in quadrants II and III. Thus, the angle must be in the second quadrant.

200. C. There are 120 minutes in 2 hours. Setting up a proportion yields $\dfrac{20 \text{ miles}}{30 \text{ minutes}} = \dfrac{x \text{ miles}}{120 \text{ minutes}}$. Cross-multiplying results in $30x = 20 \times 120$ or $30x = 2{,}400$. Dividing both sides by 30 gives $x = \dfrac{2400}{30} = 80$ miles.

201. C. $\dfrac{3}{4} \div \dfrac{4}{3} = \dfrac{3}{4} \times \dfrac{3}{4} = \dfrac{9}{16}$.

202. C. Recall that $\cot x = \dfrac{\cos x}{\sin x}$ and so $\cot x$ will equal 1 when $\sin x$ and $\cos x$ have the same value. In the first quadrant, the only place where this happens is when $x = 45°$.

203. D. Solve for w by adding w to both sides. $w - 3 + w = 3 - w + w$ so $2w - 3 = 3$. Adding 3 to both sides gives $2w = 6$. So $\dfrac{2w}{2} = \dfrac{6}{2}$ and $w = 3$. Therefore, $w^2 = 3^2 = 9$.

204. B. The function $y = ex$ is equal to its own derivative. That is, $y(x) = e$.

205. C. $\dfrac{x^2 - 25}{5 - x} = \dfrac{(x+5)(x-5)}{5-x} = \dfrac{(x+5)(x-5)}{-(x-5)} = \dfrac{(x+5)}{-1} = -(x+5)$.

206. C. To solve the equation, raise both sides to the $-\dfrac{4}{3}$ power. Then, $\left(y^{-\frac{3}{4}}\right)^{-\frac{4}{3}} = 8^{-\frac{4}{3}}$ or $y = 8^{-\frac{4}{3}} = \left(\sqrt[3]{\dfrac{1}{8}}\right)^4 = \left(\dfrac{1}{2}\right)^4 = \dfrac{1}{16}$.

207. D. Let w represent the games won and l represent the games lost. Then $w = 3 \times l = 3l$. The total number of games played is $w + l = 24$. Substituting $3l$ in for w yields $3l + l = 24$ or $4l = 24$. The number of losses is $\dfrac{24}{4} = 6$ and the number of wins is $24 - 6 = 18$.

208. C. To find the period, set πx equal to 2π and solve for x. Clearly, the period is $x = 2$.

209. A. By the properties of logarithms, $\left(\dfrac{1}{G}\right) = \log\left(G^{-1}\right) = -\log G = -\dfrac{1}{49}$, since we are told that $\log G = -\dfrac{1}{49}$.

210. D. Parallel lines have the same slope. Since the given line is in the slope-intercept form, the slope is the coefficient of the x term, which is 5. This must also be the slope of a parallel line.

211. D. We will need to use the product rule to find the derivative. The derivative will be
$x\left(\dfrac{d\sin x}{dx}\right) + \sin x\left(\dfrac{dx}{dx}\right) = x\cos x + \sin x$.

212. B. The mode is the number that occurs the most often, which is, in this case, 3.

213. D. To find the extreme points, determine the first derivative and set it equal to 0. The first derivative is $y'(x) = 3x^2 - 6x$. Now, solve $3x^2 - 6x = 0$.

$3x^2 - 6x = 0$ Factor the left-hand side

$3x(x - 2) = 0$ This is true when $x = 0$ or 2.

Note that when $x = 2$ then $y = 5$, and so $(2, 5)$ is an extreme point.

Chemistry

214. A. Remember, we need one orbital for each sigma bond. Thus, 1 s and 2 p orbitals.

215. B. Remember, pKa = –log(K_a); because of the negative sign, the smaller the pK_a, the stronger the acid.

216. B. In shorthand notation, an alcohol would be RCH_2OH, a ketone would be RCOR, and a carboxylic acid would be RCO_2H.

217. C. Remember, alpha decay reduced the atomic number by two and the atomic mass by four (two protons and two neutrons lost in the form of helium).

218. A. There are two equivalence points here, so either there are two acids present, or it is a single diprotic acid.

219. D. Dalton's Law of Partial Pressures tell us the pressure just adds. So, we have 726 = x + 32.

220. C. In the electrochemistry shorthand, oxidation is shown on the left, so zinc is being oxidized (the anode is where oxidation occurs). Copper here is being reduced at the cathode.

221. C. Explanation of the answer: FT-IR is best for functional groups, MS for molecular fragments, and NMR for bonding structure.

222. C. The oxygen/glucose mole ratio is 6:1.

223. B. This is Faraday's law.

224. A. Density goes gas < liquid < solid for every known substance with two well-known exceptions. One is Germanium, and the other is very unfortunate: water. Because water is so common to us as humans, it is easy to get this problem wrong, but it is this self-same *very* peculiar property of water that makes life on Earth possible. Otherwise, the oceans would freeze from the bottom up and no life could have developed on the ocean surface.

225. B. Here, because heat is released, enthalpy is decreased, but since we form more moles of gas in the product side than we do on the reactant side, the entropy is increasing as well. These are the two things natural processes want.

226. C. The concentration of sugar in honey is so high, that the osmotic pressure of honey will be enormous. Therefore, the honey will literally draw the water out of bacteria, thereby "cool-pasteurizing" itself.

227. C. In polymerization, the first step is initiation. In the lab, this is done by adding something that can easily dissociate into free radicals, such as benzoyl peroxide. The propagation step is the chain lengthening step, until the polymer meets with something that can absorb the free radical without forming a new one (such as another strand of the polymer, or oxygen). In the body, these same steps are used to form proteins, DNA, and RNA.

228. A. The two principle assumptions of an ideal gas that do not correspond to real gases is that the gas particles have no volume themselves and no intermolecular forces. At high temperature, the intermolecular forces present in real gases are less important than at lower temperatures, and at low pressure, the volume of the atoms is less significant since there will be fewer gas particle collisions.

229. D. Solids occur at lower temperatures and higher pressures.

230. A. Aromatic compounds have a free flowing electrons above and below the aromatic carbons, and even though they are made very stable by the resonance, they are subject to attack by electrophilic reagents.

231. C. Explanation of the answer: A tertiary alcohol will have the most stable carbocation intermediate.

232. A. When a stress is applied to a system, the system will shift to alleviate the stress. Excess phosphate will shift this equilibrium to the right.

233. D. The term b corrects for the assumption that gas particles have no volume.

234. B. There is a simple formula, $C_iV_i = C_fV_f$, so (2%)V_i = (0.1%)(100 mL). This tells us that we will need 5 mL of stock solution, and, therefore, we need (100 mL – 5 mL = 95 mL) of water.

235. D. The phosphate polyatomic ion will not dissociate; thus, we will have two phosphate and three calcium ions.

236. A. For the reaction in a redox cell to occur, you need not only a way for counter ions to flow from one side to another, but electrons as well. This is why we can store batteries as long as we do.

237. B. E1 implies the reaction begins by loss of a functional group without outside interference.

238. C. Start by adding two waters to the product side, and four hydronium ions to the reactant side. Then add electrons to balance the charge, or compare okay numbers.

239. C. Non-bonding orbitals are simply carried across from the atomic orbitals without splitting.

240. B. Spectator ions don't participate in the reaction, but rather are present to balance the positive and negative charges in a solution (sometimes they are called "counterions"). Many biochemical reactions are written as net ionic equations.

241. C. The charge of nitrate is −1, and ammonium is +1. You should know some of the more common polyatomic ions by name, charge, and formula.

242. D. Beta decay increases the atomic number by one but has no effect on the atomic mass number.

243. A. Neglecting heating due to the mechanic action, stirring does not influence solubility, which is the maximum amount of solute that can dissolve in a given volume of a solvent. People often miss this question because to get something to dissolve (like sugar in tea), we stir, but the stirring only influences the rate of dissolution, not the total solubility.

244. C. Amine is $R\text{-}NH_2$ (primary amine only). You should be familiar with the types of functional groups; amine compounds often display physiological activity and are used in pharmaceuticals.

245. D. This is an exothermic reaction. The order in which we write the reactants and products for these diagrams are the same as we would write the reaction.

246. D. This is Boyle's law, but it can also be deduced from the ideal gas law.

247. B. This is the reaction quotient, of the same form as that used in equilibrium calculations, except initial concentrations are used for the reaction quotient, and the equilibrium concentrations are used in the equilibrium constant.

248. D. The position of the carbonyl oxygen is important, which is why we distinguish between aldehydes (terminal carbonyls) and ketones (non-terminal carbonyls). Aldehydes can be oxidized to carboxylic acid, which is a common property that chemists use to distinguish between different types of sugars (aldoses versus ketoses).

249. C. The hydrogen on this carbon is adjacent to two hydrogens, causing a triplet in the NMR spectrum.

250. C. The reaction quotient would be $Q = [N_2O_4(g)]//[NO_2(g)]^2$.

251. C. Addition reactions always have only one product.

252. C. Ionization energy is the energy required to force an electron away from an atom, and electronegativity is more of a generic concept relating to how much an element wants an electron.

253. B. This is the common ion effect, and is related to LeChateliere's principle.

254. B. Don't confuse equilibrium constant expressions with rate law expressions, and remember that the superscripts x and y must be determined experimentally and are not necessarily equal to the stoichiometric coefficients.

255. C. In oxyacids, the more oxygen present, the stronger the acid. In polyprotic acids, the more hydrogen bonds of oxygen lost hydronium ions, the stronger the acid. Thus, the acid with the most oxygen and the lowest charge will be the strongest.

256. B. Remember in equilibrium constant expressions, we do not include water since its concentration will remain essentially constant.

257. D. Recall that carbons 2 and 4 have no hydrogen, and being flanked by carbonyls, the hydrogens on carbon 3 will be far more acidic than those on carbon 1.

258. D. Argon would have the weakest intermolecular forces. The London forces for Argon is less than those for Xenon because it has fewer electrons per atom.

259. D. Remember, Markonikov's rule, sometimes known as "the rich get richer," says that the hydrogen will go onto the carbon that already has the most hydrogen, Carbon 4 in this case.

260. A. Recall, pH + pOH = 14, so for pOH = 9, pH = 5. Then, $[H^+] = 10^{-pH}$.

261. A. Remember that in the periodic chart, La is in the man body to remind us that the entire series belongs there. An easier way to do this might be to figure out the atomic number from the total number of electrons.

262. B. Top to bottom makes sense, but right to left throws some people. Remember that the charge of the nucleus increases as we go from left to right, but the additional electrons are going into the same shell. Thus, atomic radius decreases from left to right.

263. B. Remember Hukel's rule; a system with $4n + 2\pi$ electrons can be aromatic.

264. B. If the Gibb's free energy were not zero, the equilibrium would shift.

265. D. Deposition is the opposite of sublimation; the formation of solid directly from a gas.

266. A. The rotation from highest to lowest priority is counterclockwise (S), and always name compounds so the numbers are the lowest possible.

267. A. The higher the temperature, the greater the average kinetic energy for collisions between reactants, and the greater the kinetic energy, the higher the fraction of these collisions with enough energy to overcome the activation energy.

268. D. In the IUPAC nomenclature, this would be copper (I) nitrate. In this older convention, the *–ous* ending means copper has the smaller of its more common oxidation states.

269. A. Iron is losing electrons, so it is being oxidized. Whatever is oxidized is the reducing agent.

270. A. A solution is also a mixture, but a mixture can be heterogeneous. Clear solutions, even if they have color, are homogeneous.

Answer Sheet for PCAT Practice Test 4

(Remove This Sheet and Use It to Mark Your Answers)

Verbal Ability: Analogies

1 Ⓐ Ⓑ Ⓒ Ⓓ	11 Ⓐ Ⓑ Ⓒ Ⓓ	21 Ⓐ Ⓑ Ⓒ Ⓓ
2 Ⓐ Ⓑ Ⓒ Ⓓ	12 Ⓐ Ⓑ Ⓒ Ⓓ	22 Ⓐ Ⓑ Ⓒ Ⓓ
3 Ⓐ Ⓑ Ⓒ Ⓓ	13 Ⓐ Ⓑ Ⓒ Ⓓ	23 Ⓐ Ⓑ Ⓒ Ⓓ
4 Ⓐ Ⓑ Ⓒ Ⓓ	14 Ⓐ Ⓑ Ⓒ Ⓓ	24 Ⓐ Ⓑ Ⓒ Ⓓ
5 Ⓐ Ⓑ Ⓒ Ⓓ	15 Ⓐ Ⓑ Ⓒ Ⓓ	25 Ⓐ Ⓑ Ⓒ Ⓓ
6 Ⓐ Ⓑ Ⓒ Ⓓ	16 Ⓐ Ⓑ Ⓒ Ⓓ	26 Ⓐ Ⓑ Ⓒ Ⓓ
7 Ⓐ Ⓑ Ⓒ Ⓓ	17 Ⓐ Ⓑ Ⓒ Ⓓ	27 Ⓐ Ⓑ Ⓒ Ⓓ
8 Ⓐ Ⓑ Ⓒ Ⓓ	18 Ⓐ Ⓑ Ⓒ Ⓓ	28 Ⓐ Ⓑ Ⓒ Ⓓ
9 Ⓐ Ⓑ Ⓒ Ⓓ	19 Ⓐ Ⓑ Ⓒ Ⓓ	29 Ⓐ Ⓑ Ⓒ Ⓓ
10 Ⓐ Ⓑ Ⓒ Ⓓ	20 Ⓐ Ⓑ Ⓒ Ⓓ	

Verbal Ability: Sentence Completions

30 Ⓐ Ⓑ Ⓒ Ⓓ	40 Ⓐ Ⓑ Ⓒ Ⓓ	50 Ⓐ Ⓑ Ⓒ Ⓓ
31 Ⓐ Ⓑ Ⓒ Ⓓ	41 Ⓐ Ⓑ Ⓒ Ⓓ	51 Ⓐ Ⓑ Ⓒ Ⓓ
32 Ⓐ Ⓑ Ⓒ Ⓓ	42 Ⓐ Ⓑ Ⓒ Ⓓ	52 Ⓐ Ⓑ Ⓒ Ⓓ
33 Ⓐ Ⓑ Ⓒ Ⓓ	43 Ⓐ Ⓑ Ⓒ Ⓓ	53 Ⓐ Ⓑ Ⓒ Ⓓ
34 Ⓐ Ⓑ Ⓒ Ⓓ	44 Ⓐ Ⓑ Ⓒ Ⓓ	54 Ⓐ Ⓑ Ⓒ Ⓓ
35 Ⓐ Ⓑ Ⓒ Ⓓ	45 Ⓐ Ⓑ Ⓒ Ⓓ	55 Ⓐ Ⓑ Ⓒ Ⓓ
36 Ⓐ Ⓑ Ⓒ Ⓓ	46 Ⓐ Ⓑ Ⓒ Ⓓ	56 Ⓐ Ⓑ Ⓒ Ⓓ
37 Ⓐ Ⓑ Ⓒ Ⓓ	47 Ⓐ Ⓑ Ⓒ Ⓓ	57 Ⓐ Ⓑ Ⓒ Ⓓ
38 Ⓐ Ⓑ Ⓒ Ⓓ	48 Ⓐ Ⓑ Ⓒ Ⓓ	58 Ⓐ Ⓑ Ⓒ Ⓓ
39 Ⓐ Ⓑ Ⓒ Ⓓ	49 Ⓐ Ⓑ Ⓒ Ⓓ	

Biology

59 Ⓐ Ⓑ Ⓒ Ⓓ	69 Ⓐ Ⓑ Ⓒ Ⓓ	79 Ⓐ Ⓑ Ⓒ Ⓓ	89 Ⓐ Ⓑ Ⓒ Ⓓ	99 Ⓐ Ⓑ Ⓒ Ⓓ	109 Ⓐ Ⓑ Ⓒ Ⓓ
60 Ⓐ Ⓑ Ⓒ Ⓓ	70 Ⓐ Ⓑ Ⓒ Ⓓ	80 Ⓐ Ⓑ Ⓒ Ⓓ	90 Ⓐ Ⓑ Ⓒ Ⓓ	100 Ⓐ Ⓑ Ⓒ Ⓓ	110 Ⓐ Ⓑ Ⓒ Ⓓ
61 Ⓐ Ⓑ Ⓒ Ⓓ	71 Ⓐ Ⓑ Ⓒ Ⓓ	81 Ⓐ Ⓑ Ⓒ Ⓓ	91 Ⓐ Ⓑ Ⓒ Ⓓ	101 Ⓐ Ⓑ Ⓒ Ⓓ	111 Ⓐ Ⓑ Ⓒ Ⓓ
62 Ⓐ Ⓑ Ⓒ Ⓓ	72 Ⓐ Ⓑ Ⓒ Ⓓ	82 Ⓐ Ⓑ Ⓒ Ⓓ	92 Ⓐ Ⓑ Ⓒ Ⓓ	102 Ⓐ Ⓑ Ⓒ Ⓓ	112 Ⓐ Ⓑ Ⓒ Ⓓ
63 Ⓐ Ⓑ Ⓒ Ⓓ	73 Ⓐ Ⓑ Ⓒ Ⓓ	83 Ⓐ Ⓑ Ⓒ Ⓓ	93 Ⓐ Ⓑ Ⓒ Ⓓ	103 Ⓐ Ⓑ Ⓒ Ⓓ	113 Ⓐ Ⓑ Ⓒ Ⓓ
64 Ⓐ Ⓑ Ⓒ Ⓓ	74 Ⓐ Ⓑ Ⓒ Ⓓ	84 Ⓐ Ⓑ Ⓒ Ⓓ	94 Ⓐ Ⓑ Ⓒ Ⓓ	104 Ⓐ Ⓑ Ⓒ Ⓓ	114 Ⓐ Ⓑ Ⓒ Ⓓ
65 Ⓐ Ⓑ Ⓒ Ⓓ	75 Ⓐ Ⓑ Ⓒ Ⓓ	85 Ⓐ Ⓑ Ⓒ Ⓓ	95 Ⓐ Ⓑ Ⓒ Ⓓ	105 Ⓐ Ⓑ Ⓒ Ⓓ	115 Ⓐ Ⓑ Ⓒ Ⓓ
66 Ⓐ Ⓑ Ⓒ Ⓓ	76 Ⓐ Ⓑ Ⓒ Ⓓ	86 Ⓐ Ⓑ Ⓒ Ⓓ	96 Ⓐ Ⓑ Ⓒ Ⓓ	106 Ⓐ Ⓑ Ⓒ Ⓓ	116 Ⓐ Ⓑ Ⓒ Ⓓ
67 Ⓐ Ⓑ Ⓒ Ⓓ	77 Ⓐ Ⓑ Ⓒ Ⓓ	87 Ⓐ Ⓑ Ⓒ Ⓓ	97 Ⓐ Ⓑ Ⓒ Ⓓ	107 Ⓐ Ⓑ Ⓒ Ⓓ	
68 Ⓐ Ⓑ Ⓒ Ⓓ	78 Ⓐ Ⓑ Ⓒ Ⓓ	88 Ⓐ Ⓑ Ⓒ Ⓓ	98 Ⓐ Ⓑ Ⓒ Ⓓ	108 Ⓐ Ⓑ Ⓒ Ⓓ	

Reading Comprehension

117 Ⓐ Ⓑ Ⓒ Ⓓ	127 Ⓐ Ⓑ Ⓒ Ⓓ	137 Ⓐ Ⓑ Ⓒ Ⓓ	147 Ⓐ Ⓑ Ⓒ Ⓓ	157 Ⓐ Ⓑ Ⓒ Ⓓ
118 Ⓐ Ⓑ Ⓒ Ⓓ	128 Ⓐ Ⓑ Ⓒ Ⓓ	138 Ⓐ Ⓑ Ⓒ Ⓓ	148 Ⓐ Ⓑ Ⓒ Ⓓ	158 Ⓐ Ⓑ Ⓒ Ⓓ
119 Ⓐ Ⓑ Ⓒ Ⓓ	129 Ⓐ Ⓑ Ⓒ Ⓓ	139 Ⓐ Ⓑ Ⓒ Ⓓ	149 Ⓐ Ⓑ Ⓒ Ⓓ	159 Ⓐ Ⓑ Ⓒ Ⓓ
120 Ⓐ Ⓑ Ⓒ Ⓓ	130 Ⓐ Ⓑ Ⓒ Ⓓ	140 Ⓐ Ⓑ Ⓒ Ⓓ	150 Ⓐ Ⓑ Ⓒ Ⓓ	160 Ⓐ Ⓑ Ⓒ Ⓓ
121 Ⓐ Ⓑ Ⓒ Ⓓ	131 Ⓐ Ⓑ Ⓒ Ⓓ	141 Ⓐ Ⓑ Ⓒ Ⓓ	151 Ⓐ Ⓑ Ⓒ Ⓓ	161 Ⓐ Ⓑ Ⓒ Ⓓ
122 Ⓐ Ⓑ Ⓒ Ⓓ	132 Ⓐ Ⓑ Ⓒ Ⓓ	142 Ⓐ Ⓑ Ⓒ Ⓓ	152 Ⓐ Ⓑ Ⓒ Ⓓ	162 Ⓐ Ⓑ Ⓒ Ⓓ
123 Ⓐ Ⓑ Ⓒ Ⓓ	133 Ⓐ Ⓑ Ⓒ Ⓓ	143 Ⓐ Ⓑ Ⓒ Ⓓ	153 Ⓐ Ⓑ Ⓒ Ⓓ	163 Ⓐ Ⓑ Ⓒ Ⓓ
124 Ⓐ Ⓑ Ⓒ Ⓓ	134 Ⓐ Ⓑ Ⓒ Ⓓ	144 Ⓐ Ⓑ Ⓒ Ⓓ	154 Ⓐ Ⓑ Ⓒ Ⓓ	164 Ⓐ Ⓑ Ⓒ Ⓓ
125 Ⓐ Ⓑ Ⓒ Ⓓ	135 Ⓐ Ⓑ Ⓒ Ⓓ	145 Ⓐ Ⓑ Ⓒ Ⓓ	155 Ⓐ Ⓑ Ⓒ Ⓓ	165 Ⓐ Ⓑ Ⓒ Ⓓ
126 Ⓐ Ⓑ Ⓒ Ⓓ	136 Ⓐ Ⓑ Ⓒ Ⓓ	146 Ⓐ Ⓑ Ⓒ Ⓓ	156 Ⓐ Ⓑ Ⓒ Ⓓ	

CUT HERE

Quantitative Ability

166 Ⓐ Ⓑ Ⓒ Ⓓ	176 Ⓐ Ⓑ Ⓒ Ⓓ	186 Ⓐ Ⓑ Ⓒ Ⓓ	196 Ⓐ Ⓑ Ⓒ Ⓓ	206 Ⓐ Ⓑ Ⓒ Ⓓ
167 Ⓐ Ⓑ Ⓒ Ⓓ	177 Ⓐ Ⓑ Ⓒ Ⓓ	187 Ⓐ Ⓑ Ⓒ Ⓓ	197 Ⓐ Ⓑ Ⓒ Ⓓ	207 Ⓐ Ⓑ Ⓒ Ⓓ
168 Ⓐ Ⓑ Ⓒ Ⓓ	178 Ⓐ Ⓑ Ⓒ Ⓓ	188 Ⓐ Ⓑ Ⓒ Ⓓ	198 Ⓐ Ⓑ Ⓒ Ⓓ	208 Ⓐ Ⓑ Ⓒ Ⓓ
169 Ⓐ Ⓑ Ⓒ Ⓓ	179 Ⓐ Ⓑ Ⓒ Ⓓ	189 Ⓐ Ⓑ Ⓒ Ⓓ	199 Ⓐ Ⓑ Ⓒ Ⓓ	209 Ⓐ Ⓑ Ⓒ Ⓓ
170 Ⓐ Ⓑ Ⓒ Ⓓ	180 Ⓐ Ⓑ Ⓒ Ⓓ	190 Ⓐ Ⓑ Ⓒ Ⓓ	200 Ⓐ Ⓑ Ⓒ Ⓓ	210 Ⓐ Ⓑ Ⓒ Ⓓ
171 Ⓐ Ⓑ Ⓒ Ⓓ	181 Ⓐ Ⓑ Ⓒ Ⓓ	191 Ⓐ Ⓑ Ⓒ Ⓓ	201 Ⓐ Ⓑ Ⓒ Ⓓ	211 Ⓐ Ⓑ Ⓒ Ⓓ
172 Ⓐ Ⓑ Ⓒ Ⓓ	182 Ⓐ Ⓑ Ⓒ Ⓓ	192 Ⓐ Ⓑ Ⓒ Ⓓ	202 Ⓐ Ⓑ Ⓒ Ⓓ	212 Ⓐ Ⓑ Ⓒ Ⓓ
173 Ⓐ Ⓑ Ⓒ Ⓓ	183 Ⓐ Ⓑ Ⓒ Ⓓ	193 Ⓐ Ⓑ Ⓒ Ⓓ	203 Ⓐ Ⓑ Ⓒ Ⓓ	213 Ⓐ Ⓑ Ⓒ Ⓓ
174 Ⓐ Ⓑ Ⓒ Ⓓ	184 Ⓐ Ⓑ Ⓒ Ⓓ	194 Ⓐ Ⓑ Ⓒ Ⓓ	204 Ⓐ Ⓑ Ⓒ Ⓓ	
175 Ⓐ Ⓑ Ⓒ Ⓓ	185 Ⓐ Ⓑ Ⓒ Ⓓ	195 Ⓐ Ⓑ Ⓒ Ⓓ	205 Ⓐ Ⓑ Ⓒ Ⓓ	

Chemistry

214 Ⓐ Ⓑ Ⓒ Ⓓ	224 Ⓐ Ⓑ Ⓒ Ⓓ	234 Ⓐ Ⓑ Ⓒ Ⓓ	244 Ⓐ Ⓑ Ⓒ Ⓓ	254 Ⓐ Ⓑ Ⓒ Ⓓ	264 Ⓐ Ⓑ Ⓒ Ⓓ
215 Ⓐ Ⓑ Ⓒ Ⓓ	225 Ⓐ Ⓑ Ⓒ Ⓓ	235 Ⓐ Ⓑ Ⓒ Ⓓ	245 Ⓐ Ⓑ Ⓒ Ⓓ	255 Ⓐ Ⓑ Ⓒ Ⓓ	265 Ⓐ Ⓑ Ⓒ Ⓓ
216 Ⓐ Ⓑ Ⓒ Ⓓ	226 Ⓐ Ⓑ Ⓒ Ⓓ	236 Ⓐ Ⓑ Ⓒ Ⓓ	246 Ⓐ Ⓑ Ⓒ Ⓓ	256 Ⓐ Ⓑ Ⓒ Ⓓ	266 Ⓐ Ⓑ Ⓒ Ⓓ
217 Ⓐ Ⓑ Ⓒ Ⓓ	227 Ⓐ Ⓑ Ⓒ Ⓓ	237 Ⓐ Ⓑ Ⓒ Ⓓ	247 Ⓐ Ⓑ Ⓒ Ⓓ	257 Ⓐ Ⓑ Ⓒ Ⓓ	267 Ⓐ Ⓑ Ⓒ Ⓓ
218 Ⓐ Ⓑ Ⓒ Ⓓ	228 Ⓐ Ⓑ Ⓒ Ⓓ	238 Ⓐ Ⓑ Ⓒ Ⓓ	248 Ⓐ Ⓑ Ⓒ Ⓓ	258 Ⓐ Ⓑ Ⓒ Ⓓ	268 Ⓐ Ⓑ Ⓒ Ⓓ
219 Ⓐ Ⓑ Ⓒ Ⓓ	229 Ⓐ Ⓑ Ⓒ Ⓓ	239 Ⓐ Ⓑ Ⓒ Ⓓ	249 Ⓐ Ⓑ Ⓒ Ⓓ	259 Ⓐ Ⓑ Ⓒ Ⓓ	269 Ⓐ Ⓑ Ⓒ Ⓓ
220 Ⓐ Ⓑ Ⓒ Ⓓ	230 Ⓐ Ⓑ Ⓒ Ⓓ	240 Ⓐ Ⓑ Ⓒ Ⓓ	250 Ⓐ Ⓑ Ⓒ Ⓓ	260 Ⓐ Ⓑ Ⓒ Ⓓ	270 Ⓐ Ⓑ Ⓒ Ⓓ
221 Ⓐ Ⓑ Ⓒ Ⓓ	231 Ⓐ Ⓑ Ⓒ Ⓓ	241 Ⓐ Ⓑ Ⓒ Ⓓ	251 Ⓐ Ⓑ Ⓒ Ⓓ	261 Ⓐ Ⓑ Ⓒ Ⓓ	271 Ⓐ Ⓑ Ⓒ Ⓓ
222 Ⓐ Ⓑ Ⓒ Ⓓ	232 Ⓐ Ⓑ Ⓒ Ⓓ	242 Ⓐ Ⓑ Ⓒ Ⓓ	252 Ⓐ Ⓑ Ⓒ Ⓓ	262 Ⓐ Ⓑ Ⓒ Ⓓ	
223 Ⓐ Ⓑ Ⓒ Ⓓ	233 Ⓐ Ⓑ Ⓒ Ⓓ	243 Ⓐ Ⓑ Ⓒ Ⓓ	253 Ⓐ Ⓑ Ⓒ Ⓓ	263 Ⓐ Ⓑ Ⓒ Ⓓ	

Critical Thinking Essay

Write your essay on lined paper.

CUT HERE

Verbal Ability: Analogies

Directions: Select the word that best completes the analogy.

1. TIGHT : LOOSE :: GRITTY :

   A. coarse
   B. relaxed
   C. pavement
   D. smooth

2. ROTOR : HELICOPTER :: TUNER :

   A. radio
   B. piano
   C. airplane
   D. dial

3. SLOW : SNAIL :: THIN :

   A. skinny
   B. kitten
   C. heavy
   D. twig

4. HAMBURGER : COW :: PORK CHOP :

   A. cat
   B. fish
   C. pig
   D. bird

5. TELEVISION : RADIO :: NEWSPAPER :

   A. telephone
   B. town crier
   C. bell
   D. movie projector

6. EGG : CHICKEN :: ROSEBUD :

   A. flower
   B. tree
   C. petal
   D. leaf

7. EAGLE : ROBIN :: SHARK :

   A. small fish
   B. snake
   C. swan
   D. whale

8. WRENCH : MECHANIC :: HOSE :

   A. firefighter
   B. axe
   C. mail deliverer
   D. judge

9. APPLE : PEAR ::

   A. sandwich : cookie
   B. roll : frankfurter
   C. corn : carrot
   D. vine : grapes

10. HAT : CAP ::

    A. glove : ring
    B. pearl : necklace
    C. cotton : socks
    D. pants : shirt

11. CIRCUS TENT : TRAPEZE ARTIST ::

    A. fishing : rod
    B. lion tamer : lion
    C. hospital : doctor
    D. secretary : computer

12. COOKIE : BOX OF COOKIES ::

    A. tree : hedge
    B. biscuit : cake
    C. rain cloud : white cloud
    D. flower : bouquet

GO ON TO THE NEXT PAGE

13. JACK O'LANTERN : SKELETON ::

- **A.** Christmas tree : Santa Claus
- **B.** rabbit : Easter Bunny
- **C.** broom : witch
- **D.** bank : firecracker

14. BOLD : TAME :: POLITE :

- **A.** gentle
- **B.** brave
- **C.** rude
- **D.** dirty

15. GREEN : PLANT :: CREATIVE :

- **A.** imaginative
- **B.** monkey
- **C.** flower
- **D.** inventor

16. CLUMSY : TRIP :: LATE :

- **A.** walk
- **B.** early
- **C.** forgive
- **D.** hurry

17. FALL : WINTER :: BUD :

- **A.** leaf
- **B.** spring
- **C.** root
- **D.** curl

18. RUIN : SPOIL :: JUMP :

- **A.** surprise
- **B.** leap
- **C.** run
- **D.** stand

19. BAY : OCEAN :: PEBBLE :

- **A.** dust
- **B.** rock
- **C.** lake
- **D.** salt

20. MATHEMATICS : ALGEBRA :: BIOLOGY :

- **A.** alive
- **B.** animals
- **C.** botany
- **D.** science

21. LEAD : HEAVY :: WATER :

- **A.** wet
- **B.** light
- **C.** ice
- **D.** solid

22. MANUAL : EXPLAIN :: STAPLER :

- **A.** staples
- **B.** fasten
- **C.** define
- **D.** paper

23. DEPTH : TRENCH :: HEIGHT :

- **A.** empty
- **B.** size
- **C.** hole
- **D.** hill

24. ANKLE : LEG :: WRIST :

- **A.** foot
- **B.** finger
- **C.** arm
- **D.** pair of socks

25. APRON : CHEF :: ROBE :

- **A.** nurse
- **B.** judge
- **C.** dress
- **D.** oven

26. EYES : NOSE :: ROOF :

- **A.** mouth
- **B.** carpet
- **C.** house
- **D.** chair

27. LION : CAT :: WOLF :

- **A.** tiger
- **B.** bird
- **C.** fish
- **D.** dog

28. BOUQUET : VASE :: GARBAGE :

- **A.** trash pail
- **B.** sink
- **C.** glass of water
- **D.** carton

29. BUTTON : SNAP :: KEY :

- **A.** zipper
- **B.** locket
- **C.** screen
- **D.** can opener

GO ON TO THE NEXT PAGE

Verbal Ability: Sentence Completions

Directions: Select the word or words that best complete the sentence.

30. In classical mythology, the _____ of Aphrodite, the Greek goddess of love, was the Roman love goddess Venus; their _____ were similar.

    A. nephew . . . . . countenances
    B. manager . . . . . futures
    C. counterpart . . . . . attributes
    D. opposite . . . . . wonders

31. Although the book is intended to explain philosophical ideas to the general reader, its vocabulary is so _____ that it will add little to their _____.

    A. recondite . . . . . edification
    B. lucid . . . . . confidence
    C. abstruse . . . . . lunacy
    D. concise . . . . . religiosity

32. The referee gave the tennis player a/an _____, stating the match would be forfeited if her inappropriate reactions to the line calls continued.

    A. illustration
    B. admonition
    C. default
    D. victory

33. The shy student _____ the idea of giving an oral presentation in speech class.

    A. enjoyed
    B. misconstrued
    C. dreaded
    D. applauded

34. In the decision ending school segregation, the United States Supreme Court concluded that separate facilities were _____ unequal by their very nature.

    A. inherently
    B. desperately
    C. simultaneously
    D. inconsolably

35. A _____ atmosphere _____ in the opening scene of Charles Dickens's novel *Great Expectations:* The winter air is raw; the clouds lower; the fog looms.

    A. festive . . . . . descends
    B. cantankerous . . . . . expands
    C. desolate . . . . . prevails
    D. meticulous . . . . . contracts

36. Having paid a high price for the automobile, the buyer felt great _____ when it frequently needed repairs.

    A. indigestion
    B. indecision
    C. indignation
    D. indolence

37. The report about the situation was _____; no facts supported its conclusions.

    A. speculative
    B. improving
    C. special
    D. prophetic

38. Completely _____ after losing the last game of the season, the football team hoped that their prospects would improve in the future.

    A. disingenuous
    B. demoralized
    C. inundated
    D. misapprehended

39. So many factors are involved in trying to decide which house to purchase that home buyers often find themselves in a _____.

    A. directory
    B. solution
    C. quandary
    D. question

40. The _____ fisherman in *The Old Man and the Sea,* who never gives up and struggles until he has achieved his goal, is the _____ of courage.

- **A.** stupendous . . . . . morality
- **B.** sacrificial . . . . . contrary
- **C.** sadistic . . . . . elegy
- **D.** stalwart . . . . . epitome

41. To _____ support for its policies, the political group began a campaign of speeches and advertisements.

- **A.** nurture
- **B.** destroy
- **C.** clarify
- **D.** change

42. Because the strange events had been very _____, the man was _____ by insomnia.

- **A.** familiar . . . . . confronted
- **B.** detrimental . . . . . cured
- **C.** callous . . . . . inundated
- **D.** disconcerting . . . . . plagued

43. The newspaper article praised the rescue efforts as being _____.

- **A.** reckless
- **B.** valorous
- **C.** extraordinary
- **D.** unorganized

44. A _____ sound came from the room as the entire audience joined the singers.

- **A.** muffled
- **B.** strange
- **C.** jubilant
- **D.** angry

45. The offhand remark by the politician _____ the audience, who took umbrage at his lack of _____ for the situation.

- **A.** incensed . . . . . consideration
- **B.** puzzled . . . . . amusement
- **C.** discouraged . . . . . wonderment
- **D.** bemused . . . . . enjoyment

46. To her credit, during the crisis, the young flight attendant showed extreme _____ during the crisis.

- **A.** fatigue
- **B.** desperation
- **C.** carelessness
- **D.** fortitude

47. As if unconcerned with the _____ of the situation, the witness responded _____ to questions from the prosecutor.

- **A.** pleasure . . . . . quickly
- **B.** severity . . . . . languidly
- **C.** location . . . . . abruptly
- **D.** style . . . . . weakly

48. For many years, despite the growth of the surrounding area, the family lived in their _____ cabin.

- **A.** rustic
- **B.** spacious
- **C.** weather-beaten
- **D.** lonely

49. There was no question that his old computer disks just were not _____ with his new system.

- **A.** organized
- **B.** victorious
- **C.** logical
- **D.** compatible

50. The charging lion was felled with one shot of a _____ tranquilizer.

- **A.** potent
- **B.** healthy
- **C.** predictable
- **D.** pleasant

51. We couldn't wait for him to leave the party; he was so _____, nobody wanted to be around him.

- **A.** ridiculous
- **B.** obstinate
- **C.** obnoxious
- **D.** fearful

GO ON TO THE NEXT PAGE

52. As soon as the new band began to play, the patrons left in _____.

    A. fear
    B. droves
    C. teams
    D. disagreement

53. Coming from a third-world country, the tourist was _____ by his _____ surroundings.

    A. inspired . . . . . local
    B. overwhelmed . . . . . affluent
    C. pleased . . . . . happy
    D. puzzled . . . . . spacious

54. She was able to get by with her story since there was a _____ of truth to what she told them.

    A. splash
    B. radius
    C. shape
    D. kernel

55. He faced an uncomfortable _____: Should he accept the invitation, or plead illness?

    A. dilemma
    B. punishment
    C. weariness
    D. morning

56. They had no choice but to _____ him—he was too _____ in his views to fit in with their comfortable situation.

    A. praise . . . . . open
    B. encourage . . . . . confusing
    C. discharge . . . . . militant
    D. help . . . . . joyful

57. He was an apprentice, and therefore required to be _____ with the needs of his boss.

    A. careful
    B. compliant
    C. construed
    D. quixotic

58. Don't let that poor grade _____ you too much—you'll do better the next time.

    A. fail
    B. please
    C. calculate
    D. perturb

Biology

Directions: Select the choice that best answers the following questions.

59. A DNA molecule containing 30% guanine will also contain

    A. 30% adenine, 20% thymine, and 20% cytosine.
    B. 20% adenine, 20% thymine, and 30% cytosine.
    C. 40% adenine, 40% thymine, and 30% cytosine.
    D. 20% adenine, 30% thymine, and 20% cytosine.

60. The process by which a polypeptide is made from an mRNA template is referred to as

    A. DNA replication.
    B. protein synthesis.
    C. transcription.
    D. translation.

61. Which of the following best describes the components of the DNA molecule?

    A. deoxyribose sugar, phosphate groups, four nitrogenous bases
    B. deoxyribose sugar, nitrate groups, four phosphorous bases
    C. deoxyribose sugar, hydrogen groups, four nitrogenous bases
    D. deoxyribose sugar, nitrate groups, four hydrogenous bases

62. The process of protein synthesis takes place

    A. in the nucleus on DNA molecules.
    B. in the nucleus on ribosomes.
    C. in the cytoplasm on ribosomes.
    D. in the cytoplasm on mitochondria.

63. In which of the following organisms would you expect to find the greatest number of mitochondria per cell?

    A. corn plant
    B. oak tree
    C. snail
    D. cheetah

64. Which of the following sets of structures are you likely to find in plant cells but not in animal cells?

    A. chloroplasts, plasma membranes, numerous small vacuoles
    B. chloroplasts, plasma membranes, large central vacuole
    C. chloroplasts, cell wall, large central vacuole
    D. chloroplasts, cell wall, numerous small vacuoles

65. Which of the following statements regarding cellular respiration is incorrect?

    A. Cellular respiration occurs in animals, but not in plants, algae, or bacteria.
    B. Cellular respiration takes place in the mitochondria of cells.
    C. Cellular respiration produces energy in the form of ATP.
    D. Cellular respiration can take place aerobically or anaerobically (fermentation).

66. A diploid organism with a somatic cell chromosome number of 64 would produce eggs and sperm containing how many chromosomes?

    A. 64
    B. 32
    C. 128
    D. 16

67. A mutation that takes place during mitosis would affect

    A. the individual in which it occurs, as well as the offspring of that individual.
    B. the offspring of the individual in which it occurs, but not the individual themselves.
    C. the individual in which it occurs, but not their offspring.
    D. the individual in which it occurs and all subsequent children, grandchildren, and so on.

GO ON TO THE NEXT PAGE

68. If coat color in cows showed incomplete dominance, a cross between a homozygous dominant black cow and a homozygous recessive white cow would most likely produce

    A. all black offspring.

    B. half black offspring and half white offspring.

    C. offspring that are white with black spots.

    D. brown offspring.

69. What proportion of offspring resulting from a cross between a squirrel that was homozygous dominant for round ears and a squirrel that is heterozygous for round and pointed ears would have pointed ears?

    A. 0%

    B. 25%

    C. 50%

    D. 75%

70. Which of the following statements regarding sex-linked traits is incorrect?

    A. Daughters will always show dominant sex-linked traits if their father has the trait.

    B. Sons will always show the sex-linked trait if their mother is homozygous for the trait.

    C. Sons cannot inherit a sex-linked trait from their father.

    D. Daughters cannot inherit a sex-linked trait; only sons can inherit sex-linked traits.

71. Which of the following forces affecting evolution is the result of a very small population size?

    A. mutation

    B. natural selection

    C. genetic drift

    D. random mating

72. A change in the genetic composition of a population over time is referred to as

    A. genetic drift.

    B. mutation.

    C. natural selection.

    D. evolution.

73. Angiosperms fall under which of the following groups of plants?

    A. non-vascular; reproduce by spores

    B. vascular; reproduce by spores

    C. non-vascular; reproduce by seeds

    D. vascular; reproduce by seeds

74. The "producers" form the base of all food chains because

    A. they can produce energy in the form of ATP.

    B. they can produce their own food.

    C. they break down dead matter and recycle it back into the ecosystem.

    D. they consume the microbes and protozoa to obtain energy.

75. Which of the following interspecific relationships is considered beneficial to both organisms involved?

    A. predator-prey

    B. host-parasite

    C. mutualism

    D. competition

76. Over-fertilization of some agricultural and urban lands has led to the runoff of excess nitrogen and phosphorous into the lakes and streams. The excess fertilizer in turn results in excessive plant growth that often leads to a depletion of oxygen in the lake or stream, and subsequent death of the organisms inhabiting it. The excess plant growth caused by runoff of large quantities of nitrogen and phosphorous is referred to as

    A. eutrophication.

    B. nitrification.

    C. toxification.

    D. pollution.

77. The combustion of fossil fuels may lead to a global change in climate due to the release of excessive amounts of

    A. carbon monoxide.

    B. carbon dioxide.

    C. oxygen.

    D. hydrogen.

78. The restriction enzymes used in the production of DNA fingerprints were isolated from various strains of bacteria, where their natural role is to

A. produce mRNA from the bacterial DNA template.
B. produce amino acids from the bacterial mRNA template.
C. stimulate the replication of the bacterial DNA.
D. destroy foreign DNA molecules that invade the bacterial cells.

79. Osmosis refers to

A. the movement of particles across a differentially permeable membrane from a region of high concentration to a region of low concentration.
B. the movement of particles across a differentially permeable membrane from a region of low concentration to a region of high concentration.
C. the movement of water across a differentially permeable membrane from a region of high concentration to a region of low concentration.
D. the movement of water across a differentially permeable membrane from a region of low concentration to a region of high concentration.

80. During photosynthesis,

A. oxygen is consumed and carbon dioxide is released.
B. carbon dioxide is consumed and oxygen is released.
C. oxygen is both consumed and released.
D. ATP is produced from the breakdown of glucose.

81. If plant cells were removed from leaf tissue and placed in saltwater, what would you most likely observe under the microscope?

A. The cells would swell and burst.
B. The cells would swell until turgor pressure from the cell wall prevented them from swelling any further.
C. The cells would lose water and the cell walls would collapse.
D. The cells would lose water and the plasma membrane would pull away from the cell walls, which would remain intact.

82. Biological magnification refers to

A. the increase in toxin concentration at successive levels of a food chain.
B. the increase in available energy at successive levels of a food chain.
C. the increase in size of organisms at successive levels of a food chain.
D. the viewing of microorganisms under a microscope.

83. Each of the terrestrial and aquatic ecosystems of the world is referred to as a

A. geographic region.
B. community.
C. biome.
D. biosphere.

84. Which of the following organisms is a photosynthetic strain of bacteria?

A. cyanobacteria
B. photobacteria
C. chlorobacteria
D. autobacteria

85. Which of the following diseases of bacterial origin affects the gastrointestinal tract?

A. tuberculosis
B. pertussis
C. typhoid fever
D. diphtheria

86. Bacterial cells may exchange genetic information with each other by forming a tube connecting the cells with each other. This type of genetic exchange is referred to as

A. transduction.
B. transformation.
C. budding.
D. conjugation.

87. Yeast, which is used in the wine- and beer-making industries, belongs to which of the following groups of organisms?

A. plants
B. bacteria
C. fungi
D. animals

GO ON TO THE NEXT PAGE

88. Bacterial DNA is organized into

A. several double-stranded chromosomes.

B. a single linear, double-stranded chromosome.

C. a single circular, single-stranded chromosome.

D. a single circular, double-stranded chromosome.

89. The first photosynthetic bacteria, which evolved between 3 billion and 3.5 billion years ago, allowed for which of the following conditions?

A. an increase in the level of carbon dioxide in the atmosphere

B. an increase in the level of oxygen in the atmosphere

C. a decrease in the level of oxygen in the atmosphere

D. a decrease in the level of water vapor in the atmosphere

90. Using raw eggs to make eggnog is no longer recommended because

A. raw eggs are often contaminated with *Escherichia coli.*

B. raw eggs are often contaminated with tapeworms.

C. raw eggs are often contaminated with *Salmonella.*

D. raw eggs are often contaminated with liver flukes.

91. Against which of the following diseases would the use of antibiotics not be helpful?

A. influenza

B. leprosy

C. typhoid fever

D. botulism

92. Autoclaving is considered the most effective method for the sterilization of medical instruments. The process of autoclaving relies on the use of

A. pasteurization.

B. exposure to radiation.

C. sub-freezing temperatures.

D. pressurized steam.

93. Which of the following mechanisms of defense against invading microorganisms would be considered a passive, rather than an active, response?

A. production of stomach acid

B. inflammation

C. phagocytosis

D. production of antibodies

94. Genetic transformation of bacterial cells involves

A. the injection of DNA into the bacterial cells by a bacteriophage.

B. the transfer of genetic information between bacterial cells through the formation of a tube temporarily connecting the cells with each other.

C. the uptake of DNA, often in the form of a plasmid, from the surrounding culture medium.

D. the loss of DNA from bacterial cells into the surrounding culture medium.

95. Retroviruses use the enzyme reverse transcriptase to

A. make mRNA from a DNA template.

B. make tRNA from a DNA template.

C. make DNA from a DNA template.

D. make DNA from an RNA template.

96. The primary function of human red blood cells is to

A. phagocytize invading microorganisms.

B. transport oxygen and carbon dioxide throughout the body.

C. recognize antigens and produce antibodies against them.

D. stimulate the passive immune response.

97. In the human respiratory system, the alveoli function to

A. exchange gases with the red blood cells.

B. filter out microorganisms.

C. control the rate of breathing.

D. allow an individual to hold his breath for long periods of time.

98. In the human digestive system, the digestion of fat is aided by

   A. the emptying of bile from the pancreas into the stomach.

   B. the emptying of bile from the pancreas into the small intestine.

   C. the emptying of bile from the gall bladder into the stomach.

   D. the emptying of bile from the gall bladder into the small intestine.

99. The cerebrum is the part of the human brain responsible for

   A. coordinating taste, smell, vision, and hearing.

   B. coordinating motor activity and muscle contractions.

   C. controlling breathing, heart rate, and blood pressure.

   D. controlling the production of hormones that will be stored in the pituitary gland.

100. Essential amino acids refer to those amino acids that

   A. are coded for by the genetic code.

   B. the body can manufacture itself.

   C. must be obtained through the diet.

   D. are the building blocks of proteins.

101. The hormone thyroxin regulates which of the following functions in the human body?

   A. development of secondary female characteristics

   B. development of secondary male characteristics

   C. promotion of muscle development

   D. metabolic processes

102. In humans, the function of the parasympathetic nervous system is to

   A. prepare the body for emergencies.

   B. return the body to a normal state following an emergency.

   C. control emotional responses.

   D. carry signals between the external environment and the brain.

103. Which of the following would be considered a specific immune response in humans?

   A. production of antibodies

   B. production of stomach acid

   C. presence of mucous membranes

   D. destruction of invading microorganisms by macrophages

104. Vaccines function by

   A. stimulating the primary immune response only.

   B. stimulating the secondary immune response only.

   C. stimulating both the primary and secondary immune responses.

   D. stimulating red blood cell activity.

105. In the human digestive system, the primary function of the large intestine is to

   A. absorb nutrients from the digested food particles.

   B. reabsorb water and create waste for expulsion.

   C. digest fats and proteins.

   D. break down nucleic acids into their component sugars and phosphates.

106. It is efficient for the human heart to have four chambers because

   A. each receives oxygen-poor blood and can supply the blood with four times more oxygen than if there was only one chamber.

   B. each has its own pacemaker and, thus, they operate independently from one another.

   C. they help keep oxygen-poor blood separated from oxygen-rich blood.

   D. they all perform the same function; therefore, if one chamber is diseased, the heart will still function normally.

107. In human females, meiosis results in the production of

   A. additional cells needed for normal growth and development.

   B. ovaries.

   C. endometrial tissue.

   D. eggs.

GO ON TO THE NEXT PAGE

108. An increase in the production of ketoacids and acidic urine are symptoms of which of the following disorders?

   A. Tay-Sachs disease

   B. PKU

   C. gallstones

   D. diabetes

109. The function of platelets in the human circulatory system is to

   A. begin the blood clotting process.

   B. exchange oxygen with tissue in the lungs.

   C. provide a watery solution in which the red blood cells travel throughout the body.

   D. thin the blood so that it flows more smoothly through the blood vessels.

110. In human females, fertilization of the egg by the sperm takes place in the

   A. vagina.

   B. cervix.

   C. uterus.

   D. Fallopian tube.

111. In the human excretory system, waste is carried

   A. from the kidneys to the bladder through the nephrons.

   B. from the bladder to the kidneys through the nephrons.

   C. from the kidneys to the bladder through the ureters.

   D. from the bladder to the kidneys through the ureters.

112. Oxygen and carbon dioxide are moved throughout the human body by the

   A. respiratory system.

   B. circulatory system.

   C. excretory system.

   D. endocrine system.

113. When an individual is lacking an adequate number of kilocalories in their diet, that person is said to be

   A. malnourished.

   B. poorly nourished.

   C. undernourished.

   D. impoverished.

114. Which of the following organs is responsible for the production of insulin in humans?

   A. liver

   B. gallbladder

   C. appendix

   D. pancreas

115. Which of the following is likely to lead to the development of antibiotic-resistant strains of bacteria?

   A. taking antibiotics to fight influenza

   B. not taking the entire amount of antibiotic prescribed for a bacterial infection

   C. the routine use of antibiotics in livestock feed

   D. all of the above

116. The human endocrine system is responsible for

   A. chemical coordination of the body's systems.

   B. movement of oxygen and carbon dioxide throughout the body.

   C. the breakdown of fats and proteins.

   D. the removal of waste products from the body.

Reading Comprehension

Directions: Read each of the following passages and answer the questions that follow.

Passage 1

(1)   The Commons Health Committee of Great Britain reported that children allergic to peanuts have risen from one in 200 in 1996 to one in 70 in 2002. This increase in numbers is alarming because although 20 percent spontaneously outgrow the allergy by their sixth birthday, after that age, remission is rare. It is not clear how and why some redevelop the allergy later in life when most avoid the food even after being given the all-clear. A reaction may be triggered by as little as a thousandth of a peanut and can lead to life-threatening anaphylaxis.

(2)   A new study, which can be found in the *Journal of Allergy and Clinical Immunology,* followed 68 people aged 5 to 21 who outgrew a peanut allergy. The results showed that 34 children who consumed concentrated peanut products frequently and 13 children who ate them in limited amounts continued to tolerate peanuts. Three children who said they infrequently ate peanut products experience a recurrence of the allergy and the remaining 18 were unable to trace any specific results. The interpretations of these results are mixed.

(3)   Some researchers recommend that children who outgrow their allergy should eat concentrated peanuts such as peanut butter at least once a month to maintain a tolerance. For some reason, they believed that continuing the contact with the substance would cause the body not to reject it. However, other interpretations suggest that the children who did not continue eating peanuts avoided them because they had not properly outgrown the allergy and did not like the taste that occurred when histamine was released in their mouths. The results of their allergy test might indicate that they have not outgrown the allergy, but rather their reaction threshold may have shifted.

(4)   Finally, advocates of a balanced diet for children state that children declared allergy free should regularly eat products that contain the allergens because continued exposure does maintain a state of immunological and clinical tolerance. However, these children should carry around an adrenaline injection kit for about a year after being claimed allergy free, as a precautionary tool. It is also good for children to eat non-exclusive diets for social reasons. However, a good sign that something is wrong is when a child starts to avoid a particular food. Then the situation should be reassessed by a clinician.

GO ON TO THE NEXT PAGE

117. The number of children allergic to peanuts is alarming because

A. so many foods are made with some sort of peanut byproduct.

B. no one outgrows this type of allergy.

C. only 20 percent of people outgrow this type of allergy.

D. remission becomes slower as people age.

118. The danger associated with peanut allergies is

A. irritating hives and skin rashes.

B. intense abdominal pain.

C. inability to breathe.

D. heart palpitations.

119. The study published in the *Journal of Allergy and Clinical Immunology* can be considered inconclusive because

A. the study was too small.

B. the number of children who did not react to the peanuts was equal to those who did react.

C. the majority of the subjects were untraceable.

D. the interpretations of the results were too varied.

120. When interpreting the data, one conclusion was

A. continued exposure to the substance built up a tolerance of it.

B. once the subject had refrained from the substance intake, the body adjusted to it and then was able to tolerate it.

C. the subjects only ate the substance in moderation so it was not as concentrated in form.

D. the subjects eventually grow out of the allergy.

121. From this study, there is evidence that histamines

A. have an odd taste.

B. are released to counteract the allergic substance.

C. smell aromatically.

D. can be taken as an antidote to the allergy.

122. From reading the article, the following conclusions can be made:

A. Once a child reaches a certain age and still has an allergy, it will be with him the rest of his life.

B. Once a child has refrained from the contact with an allergic substance, the child can slowly increase this contact until the allergy reappears.

C. Children can regularly eat substances that contain an allergen because the exposure will build up an immunity.

D. Children who have exhibited allergies should always be wary of unexpected recurrences.

123. The second to last sentence of the article indicates

A. that children can be fastidious eaters.

B. that children's eating habits can trigger concern about possible allergies.

C. that fussy eaters should be brought to a clinician for constant monitoring.

D. that there is no correlation between children's eating preferences and possible allergies.

Passage 2

(1)   A patient has chronic pain. The usual route for relief is being seen by a physician who takes a few tests, orders pain medication and physical therapy. But what would it mean if the prescription were to have energy work done by a *qigong* healer. Does this sound futuristic? This type of medical care might easily happen in the near future.

(2)   The concept of bioenergy is common to most culturally based medical systems. Asian countries have used qigong as a foundation for good health for over 5,000 years. Its name is the combination of two Chinese words: *qi* meaning "energy" and *gong* (*kung*) meaning "skill or practice." This practice of

cultivating energy leads to improved physical and mental health. It reduces stress, lowers blood pressure, and establishes a better attitude about life through physical exercise and mental concentration. This enhancement of the mind/body connection increases your awareness of where your body needs work and where changes should occur—for instance diet, exercise, and sleep. The ancient Chinese believed that good health is the result of a free-flowing, well-balanced energy system. With regular practice, this can get rid of toxins in the body.

(3) Although there has yet to be a way to measure *qi,* there has been observable evidence from the qigong masters of external *qi* that changes have happened to the structure of water and aqueous solutions; they alter behavior of dipalmitoyl phosphatidyl chline (DPPC) leposomes and enable the growth of Fab protein crystals.

(4) A study of 39 subjects who suffered from major depression, dystheymia, or bipolar disorder were used in a study where they were given *qi* emissions and took part in the exercises for two months. Although there was not a noticeable change with the exposure to the *qi* emissions in combination with the exercises, there was recordable improvement in both the chemical and behavioral aspects of the patients' problems. Thus, the conclusion is that *qigong* is an effective complimentary medical

approach to healing and can even be considered an alternative treatment for many physical problems.

(5) With more exposure of this concept of bioenergy, physicians will begin to encourage its use. After a two part lecture to clinicians by a notable doctor and a *qigong* master, the physicians were able to personally experience the *qiqong* energy that emanated from their hands. As continued studies reveal that the effects are measurable, are repeatable, and can be intentionally directed toward a specific target or person, this practice will become more widespread in the Western world.

124. Bioenergy is

A. a type of medicinal therapy used by most doctors.
B. used by a *qigong* healer.
C. a mystical, unexplainable healing done by primitive tribes.
D. a fallacy.

125. *Qigong* is the practice of cultivating energy that

A. makes the patient feel better but has no measurable results.
B. reduces stress as seen by the lowering of blood pressure.
C. only improves the patient's mental health.
D. can only work if it is coupled with physical exercise.

126. Ancient Chinese healers believed that ill health was due to

A. germs.
B. body toxins.
C. evil feelings.
D. lack of exercise.

GO ON TO THE NEXT PAGE

127. The behavior of dipalmitol phosphatidl chline (DPPC) leposomes indicates

    A. that *qi* can be measured.
    B. that water can change into crystals
    C. that there is observable evidence of the power of *qi*.
    D. that the entire concept of *qi* is a hoax.

128. The study in the use of *qi* on patients with various mental illnesses show

    A. that *qi* must be used in conjunction with exercise in order to be effective.
    B. that *qi* can be most effective when combined with other medical approaches.
    C. that there is no place for *qi* in the treatment of physical problems.
    D. that *qi* alone can cure patients with bipolar disorders.

129. An event that convinced doctors of the actual presence of *qi* was

    A. energy emanating from the doctor and master's hands.
    B. the sound that started reverberating in the room.
    C. an aura of light that was seen around the master's head.
    D. a hypnotic smell that put everyone into a relaxed mood.

130. The attitude of the author about this subject could best be described as

    A. extremely cynical.
    B. mildly curious.
    C. aloof and distant.
    D. direct and informative.

Passage 3

(1)   For Luciano Pavarotti or Julie Andrews, losing their voices was a major disruption to their lives and careers. However, it is not until the average person loses his voice that you realize just what a commodity it is. For most of us, sounding hoarse is no more than an inconvenience. But for a growing number of people—teachers, broadcasters, barristers, and call-center staff—the voice is a crucial tool of their trade. Damaged vocal cords can mean the end of a career. According to a recent report, one worker in three in the world's modern economies relies on their voice to carry out their jobs. Up to one quarter of them have experienced voice problems. One in five teachers miss work with voice problems, five times the national average.

(2)   As there is a shift to a service-based economy, more people are going to suffer from repetitive voice injury. Besides the physical strain, bad weather, low humidity, heated rooms, colds, and infections all contribute to voice stress. There is increasing evidence that more people are taking time off because they can't use their voices. Eventually, these absences mean more problems and expenses for their companies. Thus, the care of the voice is a critical concern.

(3)   A government document, *Fitness to Teach,* acknowledges that those who have had voice training seem to experience fewer problems. Thus, the training of speech therapists is including an understanding of these voice strains and ways to prevent them. Furthermore, the Voice Care Network, whose members are voice teachers and speech and language therapists, are beginning to offer workshops and private lessons to help train and look after the

voice. It's easy to fall into bad habits that can be damaging to the voice, but these can be corrected with a little forethought.

(4)   First of all, you should think about your body as a six-cylinder vehicle. You need to breathe properly using your whole chest to support your voice. If you only use your upper chest to breathe, you are running on only three cylinders and putting unnecessary strain on the voice box. The practice of drinking plenty of water is encouraged for overall health, but it also lubricates the vocal cords. People should consciously relax. Keeping your shoulders low and easy helps lessen the tension in your face. Yawning and sighing before speaking opens the voice and relieves stress. Coughing and clearing your throat causes vocal fatigue and sometimes irritation. If there is persistent need to clear your throat, you might have acid reflux and should consult a doctor. Coffee, tea, and spicy food can be further irritants. Lower pitches are more soothing than higher ones. Speakers should never try to talk over background noise. It is better to be silent, to punctuate the need for attention, than to attempt to be louder than the noise. Above all, throat infections need to be dealt with immediately to prohibit any permanent damage to the larynx and pharynx.

131. The use of the word "commodity" in the second sentence can best be translated as

    A. possession.
    B. worthwhile talent.
    C. a saleable item.
    D. a nuisance.

132. Statistics in this article indicate that today's economy

    A. relies heavily on the use of complicated machines.
    B. depends strongly on interpersonal, verbal interactions.
    C. is based on what computers can do.
    D. is driven by the entertainment business.

133. The major cause of voice stress is

    A. physical strain.
    B. poor working conditions.
    C. infectious diseases.
    D. a combination of many factors.

134. A probable way to help prevent voice problems is

    A. private voice training.
    B. singing in your free time.
    C. altering heating and air-conditioning structures.
    D. using telephones less frequently.

135. The use of the vehicle metaphor is effective because

    A. everyone has a vehicle so they know how they work.
    B. it gives a vivid picture of how breathing affects your speaking.
    C. it adds variety to the piece.
    D. it explains why you should drink water.

136. After reading this article, when you see someone yawning and sighing you might

    A. think about the fact that they are preparing to give a speech.
    B. assume they have been up too late the night before.
    C. be annoyed that they are showing their boredom.
    D. wonder why they are being so rude.

GO ON TO THE NEXT PAGE

137. Silence can

    A. be an effective way to punctuate a point.

    B. be a way to give yourself a chance to catch your breath.

    C. be uncomfortable to the audience.

    D. contribute to infections of the pharynx.

Passage 4

(1)   As the Baby Boomers age and the population of elderly patients increases, many questions and challenges face physicians. In addition to the cognitive deficits associated with this neurodegenerative condition, AD patients, frequently experience non-cognitive symptoms, notably psychosis. The question that is raised is what is the best way to treat these patients. Most doctors believe that the most important thing is to give medication when the benefits exceed the risks.

(2)   There is, however, a lack of published evidence on the use of atypical antipsychotic in elderly patients with dementia. This makes it difficult to fully assess the associated risks and benefits of medications. The psychosis associated with dementia is generally thought to be different from other psychoses due to disease's like Parkinson's or schizophrenia. However, it is unclear whether the delusions and behaviors of AD patients are true psychotic delusions or are due to cognitive deficits due to neurodegeneration. In many cases, the behavior could be triggered by something in the environment and may respond favorable to simply removing the trigger. Thus, before treating with medication, it is important to assess the environmental impact on the patient by examining their unmet needs and determining whether subtle changes to their surrounding could minimize psychotic behaviors. Psychosocial and psychotherapeutic interventions should always be considered first before psychopharmaceutical treatments. For example, if a patient is physically attacking someone, perhaps medication should be used first to treat the aggression, but if someone is shouting and pacing, other interventions that offer the same benefits but are less risky would be preferable.

(3)   When pharmaceuticals are needed, evidence has shown that risperidone, olanzapine, quetiapine, and aripiprazole are effective. Risperidone seems particularly effective in improving behavioral pathology and diminishing aggressive behavior. However, it failed to diminish kicking or pushing, the making of strange noises, negativism, visual hallucinations, and suspicious or paranoid behaviors. Furthermore, risperidone and to some extent olanzapine has been shown to increase extrapyramidal symptoms (EPS). The newer atypical antipsycholitics have not been shown to cause EPS.

(4)   Researchers specializing in the treatment of elderly patients are hoping that the results from the Clinical Antipsycholitic Trials of Intervention Effectiveness (CATIE) will provide necessary data that compares the uses of various drugs along with behavioral conditioning and environmental adjustments to assist decisions on clinical courses. To date, the advocacy is to fine-tune the environment of the elderly to give a better fit between the person and the environment. To do this, there needs to be increased caregiver training programs to educate these people on how to recognize and avoid situations that may lead to catastrophic reactions.

138. The increase in the population of the elderly raises questions about

A.   how to pay for increased health costs.
B.   how to treat the mental deterioration of the population.
C.   whether there will be enough doctors to treat these patients.
D.   how many people have cognitive deficits.

139. A main problem in treating the psychosis of these patients is

A.   their inability to articulate clearly.
B.   their slowness in getting things done.
C.   the question as to whether it is caused by neurodegeneration or true delusions.
D.   to decide where to start.

140. The primary way to treat the behavior is

A.   to increase their medication.
B.   to change their environment.
C.   to withdraw their medication.
D.   to ignore their behavior.

141. From the example given in the text, the treatment of inappropriate behavior

A.   should always be dealt with pharmaceutically first.
B.   should be analyzed for its rudimentary cause.
C.   should use the easiest intervention first.
D.   should be treated simultaneously with drugs and psychosocial patterning.

142. Risperdone is effective in

A.   treating all symptoms equally in aggressive behavior.
B.   curtailing hitting and pushing.
C.   diminishing aggressive behavior and visual hallucinations.
D.   improving behavioral pathology.

143. EPS indicates that

A.   the drug increases its effectiveness each time it is given.
B.   it is a newer drug with fewer side effects.
C.   the drug might address one symptom but aggravates other symptoms.
D.   is an antipsycholitic drug.

144. The article indicates that training programs should be given to caregivers because

A.   it is important for them to recognize which drugs are most effective.
B.   there are not enough nurses to make the diagnosis.
C.   the environment of these patients should be more compatible with their personalities.
D.   they need to have more input on clinical decisions.

Passage 5

(1)   What would you say if you heard of a frantic mother's plea for help because her son had been expelled from nursery school? At 2 years old, he has managed to disrupt the family household since he was an infant. He has few friends because he hits,

GO ON TO THE NEXT PAGE

shoves, pushes, and screams at them, which frightens them away. In the house, he is able to climb up on countertops and unscrews or unlatches everything. Another parent speaks of her son who cannot sit still in class and leaves the classroom without permission; although he has above-average intelligence, he has trouble reading and writing and talks so fast that most people can't understand him. A third father spoke of his son who was constantly found wandering the neighborhood. When the child got tall enough to open the door—and because he would not sleep at night—he was found in the middle of the street. His explorations cause him to get cuts and scrapes so that he looks like an abused child!

(2) Childhood hyperactivity has been in the medical literature since the 1880s. However, it is still a disorder that baffles doctors because of its complexity in diagnosing, treating, and naming it. Since the symptoms of this disease are often associated with other disorders, such as mental retardation and drug/poison-related illnesses, misdiagnoses and misunderstanding results. Furthermore, the disorder has been labeled in so many ways that the general public is confused. It has been called hyperkinetic reaction, hyperkinetic syndrome, learning disability, minimal brain dysfunction, minor cerebral dysfunction, and hyperactive child syndrome. The American Psychiatric Association (APA) has labeled this disease Attention Deficit Disorder based on the results of the standard diagnostic reference tests. Because it has no single cause and manifests a cluster of symptoms, it is categorized as a syndrome. APA criteria for this syndrome includes the following: excessive motor activity, short attention span, impulsive behavior for a child's age, usual onset before the age of 7, duration of at least six months, and a proven absence of illness or mental retardation.

(3) This syndrome appears in boys more than girls. The statistics displaying the numbers of school-age children afflicted vary, but it can range from 1 to 15 percent of the school-age population. Traditional therapy for children with the condition has included medication, behavioral modification, educational techniques, and psychotherapy.

145. Hyperactivity
   A. can be diagnosed by very basic behavior problems.
   B. is a relatively new behavior issue.
   C. has been around for over a century.
   D. affects only adolescent boys.

146. The challenge of treating hyperactivity comes
   A. in the complexity of figuring out exactly whether it is hyperactivity.
   B. in determining the right dosage of medication.
   C. in creating an effective behavioral system.
   D. in identifying the possible causes.

147. The APA uses standard reference tests to

    A. decide which name is appropriate.
    B. indicate whether the cause is justified.
    C. diagnose the syndrome.
    D. evaluate the treatment procedures.

148. It is called a syndrome because

    A. the symptoms are not always noticeable.
    B. it has a cluster of symptoms.
    C. it is difficult to evaluate.
    D. it has various effective treatments.

149. It is important that, when diagnosing the syndrome, there is the absence of

    A. illness or mental retardation.
    B. impulsive behavior for at least six months.
    C. excessive motor activity.
    D. short attention spans.

150. Given the information in the article, one could conclude that

    A. this syndrome is not the problem of schools.
    B. there is only one main way to deal with this syndrome.
    C. teachers must be wary of reasons for girls acting out in class.
    D. complex plans must exist to treat this syndrome effectively.

151. The attitude of the author in this article is one of

    A. extreme concern.
    B. frustration.
    C. distance and objectivity.
    D. amazement.

Passage 6

(1)   Career development activities by professional school counselors at the elementary, middle, and high school levels can help students with mental retardation make meaningful career choices as adults. However, existing research on the career development of people with moderate to severe mental retardation focuses on occupational choice rather than career development. Occupational choice reflects a person's vocational decision at any point in time, whereas career development reflects an ongoing process that incorporates and integrates personal and environmental information. The latter is a dynamic process that requires individuals to engage in the ongoing assessment, analysis, and synthesis of information about the world of work and self.

(2)   Early exposure of children to career development activities allows students the time to explore and acquire the necessary skills for vocational success in a preferred occupation. Furthermore, these activities lead to job satisfaction and promote sustained patterns of employment among people diagnosed with mental retardation. Although people involved in these programs attest to their success, there is a paucity of controlled outcome research that can scientifically claim success. The heterogeneity of characteristics and the life circumstances of students with developmental disorders make it difficult to establish a causal relationship between early interventions and adult employment outcomes. There was one study that investigated the adult employment status of 153 students who were educable mentally

GO ON TO THE NEXT PAGE

retarded and 81 students who were severely learning disabled and who, as grade-school students, all received a competency-based, life-centered career education curriculum. Completion of the career education curriculum in grade school was significantly related to the future employment levels of all students with mental retardation and of females with severe learning disabilities. More recently, a survey of 713 young adults who had been students in special education programs found that career development activities such as work opportunities, the intensity of vocational preparation, and the percentage of time spent in career education courses were predictors of increased employment, self-esteem, independence, and job security.

(3)   People with developmental disabilities may lack realistic information about occupation and career on which to base their interest. These interests can be stimulated through short-term job tryout experiences and job shadowing experiences. Information regarding the student's preferences of activities, work environments, emotional and monetary rewards, and supervision can help students and parents to identify possible avenues for the future. Moreover, using strategies that help identify, develop, and maintain a vocational skill set that will transfer over to a successful employment opportunity is the goal of this type of education. For instance, a vocational skill set

that will transfer to employment in clerical and reception occupations may include social skills such as appropriate socialization with peers and customers, mechanical skills like the operation of office machines, safety skills like seeking assistance, communication skills like telephone etiquette, and hygiene skills like dressing appropriately. The development of skills congruent with abilities, aptitudes and aspirations within multiple vocational contexts can promote employability and career advancement.

152. A criticism of the treatment of mentally challenged students is

A.   that their future is relegated to only what they can manipulate rather than what they might be able to do.

B.   that college is never considered for them.

C.   that they are given too many options for employment.

D.   that they are never given meaningful choices.

153. Successful programs are not extolled because

A.   there is no research on the outcomes that can be scientifically documented.

B.   there are too many of them to keep track of.

C.   none of the employers are satisfied with their help.

D.   the students are not adequately prepared for the world of work.

154. The word "causal" in the middle of the second paragraph best refers to

A.   connection between success in the workplace and a good home life.

B.   the relationship between the teacher and pupil.

C.   the interactions between the employer and the employee.

D.   the link between early career preparation and success on the job.

155. Three factors that lead to success on the job for these people are

    A. good jobs, job security, and self-esteem.

    B. appropriate job preparatory activities, intense experiences, and amount of time spent on career programs.

    C. safety skills, independence, and peer evaluations.

    D. good educational curriculum, high pay, and mechanical skills.

156. The major benefit of job shadowing is

    A. acquiring realistic information about types of jobs.

    B. the ability of it being only short term.

    C. the stimulation of interest in a job.

    D. the free labor that the company receives.

157. A vocational skill set is

    A. a strategy to identify a particular skill needed for a job.

    B. occupational knowledge and talent.

    C. the set of skills that are congruent with job expectations.

    D. the ability to work with your hands in manual labor.

158. The last sentence of this article indicates that

    A. people who are mentally challenged can only expect entry-level jobs.

    B. people with mental handicaps can be successful in jobs only if they are matched to their knowledge and personal abilities.

    C. career programs should only focus on certain basic social skills.

    D. there is little hope of finding jobs for the majority of mentally challenged people.

Passage 7

(1)   According to a 2001 study by the National Institute of Child Health and Human Development, about three in ten children are affected as bullies, victims, or both. However, the knowledge base pertaining to the relationship between bullying and students with disabilities is relatively new and sparse. Still, researchers feel that there is a dyad to be studied. People are more aware of the problem of bullying because of the media coverage of school violence and high-profile tragedies. Statistics indicate that 160,000 children skip school in the United States each day because of intimidation by their peers. Furthermore, studies also indicate that 25% of elementary and high school students and 40% of middle school students report being bullied at least once per week. According to a study done in 1994, students with disabilities are more likely to be involved in a bullying situation. Bullies may have bad tempers and come from family situations where parents are distant, exhibit inconsistent discipline, and use violence as punishment. Characteristics such as these are indicative of children with conduct-disordered patterns of behaviors; thus, the student with a disability is more likely to be the bully or both the bully and victim.

(2)   To begin to research this problem, a working definition of "bully" and "bullying" needs to be established because different cultures have varying terms to describe the activity. The dictionary states that, to bully a person means to browbeat a

GO ON TO THE NEXT PAGE

person—especially one habitually cruel to others who are weaker. Educators have established a bully as one who demonstrates repetitive aggressive behavior that purposefully hurts another person and ultimately results in a systematic abuse of power. Together, these definitions identify three distinct attributes of a bully: harassment of the victim occurs over time, the intent is nocuous, the result is the imbalance of power.

(3)   Although a profile of the bully has been displayed in the media, there are other mitigating factors like age, gender, and environment. However, generalities include the fact that more males rather than females seem to bully, they come from unsafe neighborhoods, and they are likely to be involved in substance abuse. The victims appear to be those students who are on the fringes of a school culture. Therefore, children with disabilities are prime candidates because they lack self-esteem, tend to look to others for cues and guidance, and lack the awareness of potentially dangerous situations. Furthermore, moderate to low functioning children are more likely to have observable physical impairments that mark them for the bullies as weaker victims.

(4)   The most common suggestion for decreasing bullying involves the establishment of a school intervention program that begins in the elementary schools and extends throughout the 12 years of schooling. Effective programs allow children to establish rules, and include social skills training and parental involvement. To address the particular issues with special-needs children, administrators need to be able to identify variables in the school environment that will ensure a safe setting for all students.

159. The word "dyad," found in the third sentence of the first paragraph, most closely means

   A.   problem.
   B.   connection.
   C.   complexity.
   D.   situation.

160. The assumption that students with learning disabilities are more likely to be involved in bullying situations is based on

   A.   a prejudice that these students are different.
   B.   the inability of these students to know right from wrong.
   C.   the fact that these students have low IQs.
   D.   poor patterns of behavior that have developed in homes with absent parents.

161. A working definition of a bully does not include

   A.   harmful intent.
   B.   short-term annoyances.
   C.   imbalance of power.
   D.   repetition of aggression.

162. The word "nocuous" in the last sentence of the second paragraph most closely means

   A.   harmful.
   B.   obnoxious.
   C.   repetitive.
   D.   fearful.

163. The third paragraph focuses on the importance of

   A.   clear structure in the schools.
   B.   consistent discipline at home.
   C.   peer pressure in developing self-esteem.
   D.   punitive action to bullies.

164. A key component to a successful intervention program is

    A. emphasis on the middle years of school.
    B. parental involvement
    C. rules established by experts.
    D. focus on expected behavior patterns.

165. The author concludes the article with

    A. a desperate cry for attention to this issue.
    B. rational ways to combat the problem.
    C. cynical predictions for the future of this problem.
    D. humor to lighten the somberness of the problem.

GO ON TO THE NEXT PAGE

Quantitative Ability

Directions: Read each of the questions and select the choice that answers the question.

---

166. If 400 people can be seated in 8 subway cars, how many people can be seated in 5 subway cars?

    A. 200
    B. 250
    C. 300
    D. 350

167. The area of one circle is 4 times as large as a smaller circle with a radius of 3 inches. The radius of the larger circle is

    A. 12 inches
    B. 9 inches
    C. 8 inches
    D. 6 inches

168. Mr. Triber earns a weekly salary of $300 plus 10% commission on all sales. If he sold $8,350 last week, what were his total earnings?

    A. $835
    B. $865
    C. $1,135
    D. $1,835

169. One-eighth of a bookstore's magazines are sold on a Friday. If $\frac{1}{4}$ of the remaining magazines are sold the next day, what fractional part of the magazines remains at the end of the second day?

    A. $\frac{1}{32}$
    B. $\frac{1}{8}$
    C. $\frac{7}{32}$
    D. $\frac{21}{32}$

170. If $\log A = 8$, then $\log A^2 =$

    A. 16
    B. 24
    C. 48
    D. 64

171. Devin throws a football $7\frac{1}{3}$ yards. Carl throws it $2\frac{1}{2}$ times farther. How much farther did Carl's throw travel than Devin's?

    A. $2\frac{1}{2}$ yards
    B. $7\frac{1}{3}$ yards
    C. 11 yards
    D. $18\frac{1}{3}$ yards

172. Fencing costs $4.75 per foot. Posts cost $12.50 each. How much will it cost to fence a garden if 10 posts and 34 feet of fencing are needed?

    A. $472.50
    B. $336.50
    C. $315.50
    D. $286.50

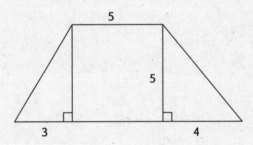

173. The area of the figure above is

    A. 42.5
    B. 47
    C. 52.5
    D. 60

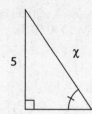

174. Find the length of x in the above figure.

- **A.** $6\frac{2}{3}$
- **B.** $7\frac{1}{3}$
- **C.** $8\frac{1}{4}$
- **D.** $\frac{15}{4}$

175. A taxi ride costs \$3 for the first mile and \$1 each additional half mile. What is the cost of a 10-mile ride?

- **A.** \$10
- **B.** \$12
- **C.** \$13
- **D.** \$21

176. If $\sin x > 0$ and $\sec x < 0$, then which quadrant must $\angle x$ lie in?

- **A.** I
- **B.** II
- **C.** III
- **D.** IV

177. Sandy bought $4\frac{1}{2}$ pounds of apples and 6 kiwi fruits. Brandon bought $3\frac{1}{4}$ pounds of apples and 9 kiwi fruits. If apples cost \$1.39 per pound and kiwis are 2 for \$1, how much more money did Sandy spend than Brandon?

- **A.** \$0.24
- **B.** \$0.94
- **C.** \$1.54
- **D.** \$2.32

178. Find the diagonal of a square whose area is 36.

- **A.** 6
- **B.** $6\sqrt{2}$
- **C.** 9
- **D.** $9\sqrt{2}$

179. If $7^{2x-1} = 7^{5x+8}$, what is the value of x?

- **A.** −3
- **B.** −1
- **C.** 3
- **D.** 9

180. Solve for m: $3m - 12 = -6$

- **A.** −6
- **B.** 0
- **C.** 2
- **D.** 4

181. $\dfrac{\cos\theta}{\sin\theta}$

- **A.** $\tan\theta$
- **B.** $\cot\theta$
- **C.** $\sec\theta$
- **D.** $\csc\theta$

182. In a standard deck of playing cards, a king of hearts is drawn and not replaced. What is the probability of drawing another king from the deck?

- **A.** $\frac{1}{4}$
- **B.** $\frac{1}{13}$
- **C.** $\frac{1}{17}$
- **D.** $\frac{3}{52}$

183. If the area of a square is 400, what is the length of its side?

- **A.** 20
- **B.** 40
- **C.** 100
- **D.** 200

184. If $j(z) = \left(\frac{1}{2}\right)^z$, then $j(-1) =$

- **A.** −1
- **B.** $-\frac{1}{2}$
- **C.** $\frac{1}{2}$
- **D.** 2

GO ON TO THE NEXT PAGE

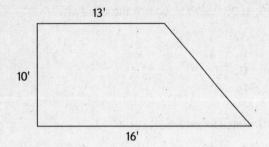

13'

10'

16'

185. What is the area of the figure shown above?

A. 130 ft^2

B. 145 ft^2

C. 154 ft^2

D. 160 ft^2

186. Jared rents three videos for $8. What would the cost of two video rentals be?

A. $1.33

B. $5

C. $5.33

D. $6

187. log$_5$625 =

A. 2

B. 4

C. 6

D. 8

188. If $a^{\frac{1}{3}} = 2$, then what is the value of a?

A. 4

B. 8

C. 16

D. 32

189. How many blocks 6" × 4" × 4" can fit in a box 8' × 6' × 4'?

A. 2

B. 48

C. 576

D. 3,456

190. If $y = 5x^2 - 8x + 1$, then $\frac{dy}{dx}$

A. $5x - 8$

B. $2x - 8$

C. $10x - 8$

D. $-3x$

191. Roger collects bottle caps. Each cap can be traded for 5 cents. If Roger receives $40.50, how many bottle caps did he trade?

A. 810

B. 405

C. 200

D. 8

192. A right triangle has an area of 24 feet. If one leg is three times as long as the other, what is the length of the longest side?

A. 12.6

B. 12

C. 8.4

D. 6.3

193. What is the value of $64^{-\frac{1}{3}}$?

A. $-\frac{1}{4}$

B. $-\frac{1}{8}$

C. $\frac{1}{8}$

D. $\frac{1}{4}$

194. Multiply $(2x + 1)(2x + 1)$.

A. $2x^2 + 1$

B. $4x^2 + 1$

C. $4x^2 + 2x + 1$

D. $4x^2 + 4x + 1$

195. The cube of 8 is

A. 2

B. 24

C. 512

D. 8,000

196. There are five more boys in the kindergarten class than girls. If there are 27 children altogether, how many are boys?

A. 10

B. 11

C. 16

D. 22

197. What is the amplitude of the function $f(x) = 3 + 2\sin(7x)$?

  A. 2
  B. 3
  C. 5
  D. 7

198. What is the maximum number of extreme points that a function of the form $f(x) = ax^4 + bx^3 + cx^2 + dx + e$ can have, if a, b, c, d, and e are constants and $a \neq 0$?

  A. 2
  B. 3
  C. 4
  D. 5

199. If the diameter of a circle is increased by 100%, the area is increased by

  A. 50%
  B. 100%
  C. 200%
  D. 400%

200. A rope is made by linking beads that are $\frac{1}{2}$" in diameter. How many feet long is a rope made from 60 beads?

  A. $2\frac{1}{2}$ ft
  B. 10 ft
  C. 30 ft
  D. 120 ft

201. Find the product of $(3 - 4x)$ and $(3 + 4x)$.

  A. 9
  B. $9 + 12x - 16x^2$
  C. $9 - 16x^2$
  D. $9 + 16x^2$

202. If $\log_x 125 = -3$, then $x =$

  A. $-\frac{1}{5}$
  B. $\frac{1}{25}$
  C. $\frac{1}{5}$
  D. 5

203. Which of the following values of x is a solution to the equation $\sin x = \frac{1}{2}$?

  A. $x = 30°$
  B. $x = 45°$
  C. $x = 60°$
  D. $x = 90°$

204. If C represents the constant of integration, then $\int \cos x \, dx =$

  A. $\sin x + C$
  B. $-\cos x + C$
  C. $-\sin x + C$
  D. $x\sin x + C$

205. Simplify $\dfrac{15\sqrt{3}}{\sqrt{5}}$.

  A. $3\sqrt{3}$
  B. $3\sqrt{15}$
  C. $15\sqrt{15}$
  D. $75\sqrt{3}$

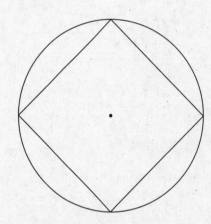

206. If the area of the circle is 121π, find the area of the square. (See above figure.)

  A. 121
  B. 242
  C. 363
  D. 484

207. If $y = -\cos x$, then $y'(x) =$

  A. $\cos x$
  B. $\sin x$
  C. $-\sin x$
  D. -1

GO ON TO THE NEXT PAGE

208. $\dfrac{24}{96} - \dfrac{8}{12} =$

   A. $\dfrac{1}{4}$

   B. $\dfrac{5}{96}$

   C. $-\dfrac{5}{12}$

   D. $\dfrac{4}{21}$

209. Given that the point $(x, 1)$ lies on a line with a slope of $-\dfrac{3}{2}$ and a y-intercept of -2, find the value of x.

   A. -2
   B. -1
   C. 1
   D. 2

210. Which of the following is an equation of a line parallel to the line $4x + 2y = 12$?

   A. $y = 2x + 6$
   B. $y = -2x + 7$
   C. $y = \dfrac{1}{2}x + 4$
   D. $y = -\dfrac{1}{2}x + 4$

211. What is the median of the set $\{1, 2, 2, 4, 4, 4\}$?

   A. 2
   B. 2.83
   C. 3
   D. 4

212. How many different 4-digit numbers can be formed from the digits 6, 7, 8, and 9 if no digits are repeated?

   A. 12
   B. 24
   C. 128
   D. 256

213. Which of the following is the first derivative of $x(\log x)$?

   A. $1 + \log x$
   B. $\log x$
   C. xe^x
   D. 1

Chemistry

Directions: Select the choice that best answers the following questions. To consult the Periodic Table of the Elements, please go to the Appendix.

214. Which of the following is a redox reaction?

    A. $2\ NaHCO_3\ (s) \rightarrow Na_2CO_3\ (aq) + H_2O\ (l) + CO_2\ (g)$

    B. $AgNO_3\ (aq) + HCl\ (aq) \rightarrow AgCl\ (s) + HNO_3\ (aq)$

    C. $H_2O\ (l) + CO_2\ (g) \rightarrow H_2CO_3\ (aq)$

    D. $H_2\ (g) + C_6H_6\ (l) \rightarrow C_6H_8\ (l)$

215. What type of isomer will rotate plane polarized light?

    A. enantiomer
    B. diastereomer
    C. constitutional
    D. hydration

216. Causing a reaction to occur by increasing the temperature increases the influence of what?

    A. entropy
    B. enthalpy
    C. electronegativities
    D. bond energies

217. The formation of acid rain can be expressed by the following set of chemicals:

$2\ S\ (s) + 3\ O_2\ (g) \rightarrow 2\ SO_3\ (g)$

$SO_3\ (g) + H_2O\ (l) \rightarrow H_2SO_4\ (aq)$

If we start with 15 moles of sulfur, how many moles of sulfuric acid will form?

    A. 7.5 moles
    B. 30 moles
    C. 10 moles
    D. 15 moles

218. What is the proper name for the compound shown in the figure above?

    A. Z-1-bromo-2-fluoropropene
    B. E-1-bromo-2-fluoropropene
    C. Z-3-bromo-2-fluoropropene
    D. E-3-bromo-2-fluoropropene

219. What type of change is sublimation?

    A. chemical
    B. physical
    C. energy
    D. nuclear

220. What type of amine will be the most alkaline in water?

    A. primary
    B. secondary
    C. tertiary
    D. quaternary

GO ON TO THE NEXT PAGE

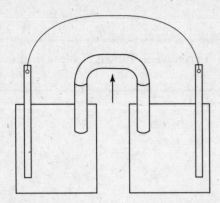

221. In the diagram above, what is the arrow pointing to?

    A. anode
    B. salt bridge
    C. electrical connection
    D. cathode

222. A Claisen Rearrangement yields what type of compound?

    A. an amine derivative
    B. a phenol derivative
    C. a carboxylic acid derivative
    D. alkyne derivative

223. From the following reactions, what is the enthalpy change for the reaction H_2O (l) + CO_2 (g) $\rightarrow$ H_2CO_3 (aq)?

$$2\,H_2\,(g) + O_2\,(g) \rightarrow 2\,H_2O\,(l) \qquad \Delta H = -285.8 \text{ kJ}$$

$$C\,(s) + O_2\,(g) \rightarrow CO_2\,(g) \qquad \Delta H = -393.5 \text{ kJ}$$

$$H_2\,(g) + C\,(s) + O_2\,(g) \rightarrow H_2CO_3\,(aq) \quad \Delta H = -691.1 \text{ kJ}$$

    A. +11.8 kJ
    B. +1307.4 kJ
    C. −1307.4 kJ
    D. −11.8 kJ

224. How many neutrons does ^{238}U have?

    A. 238
    B. 146
    C. 328
    D. 92

225. When we need to know the exact concentration of a base, we react it with a known amount of KHP (potassium hydrogen phthalate). Measuring the exact concentration of a solution is best known as?

    A. an indicator
    B. the endpoint
    C. a titration
    D. a standardization

226. Following are standard electrode potential for two half reactions:

$$I_2 + 2\,e^- \rightarrow 2\,I^- \qquad E^0 = 0.535 \text{ V}$$

$$Ag^+ + e^- \rightarrow Ag \qquad E^0 = 0.799 \text{ V}$$

What is the standard electrode potentials for the reaction $I^-|I_2\|Ag^+|Ag$?

    A. 0.264 V
    B. 1.334V
    C. −0.270 V
    D. 1.063 V

227. The most stable electronic configuration $1s^2 2s^2 2p^4$ can best be described?

    A. forbidden state
    B. excited state
    C. ground state
    D. thermal state

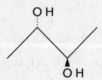

228. What is the name of the above compound?

    A. meso-2,3-butadiol
    B. R, S-2,3-butadiol
    C. S,S-2,3-butadiol
    D. R,R-2,3-butadiol

229. Which of the following groups cannot be further oxidized without oxidizing completely to carbon dioxide?

    A. ether
    B. aldehyde
    C. alkane
    D. alcohol

230. According to the assumptions of an ideal gas, what is temperature most directly related to for a mixture of gases?

    A. the average number of collisions
    B. the average velocity
    C. the average kinetic energy
    D. the average volume

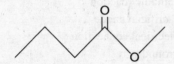

231. What functional group is shown in the figure above?

    A. ether
    B. ketone
    C. aldehyde
    D. ester

232. In this ionic equation H_2O (l) + CO_2 (g) + Pb^{+2} (aq) + NO_3^- (aq) → $PbCO_3$ (s) + 2 H^+ (aq) + NO_3^- (aq), what is the spectator ion?

    A. NO_3^-
    B. CO_2
    C. H_2O
    D. Pb^{+2}

233. Hyponatremia is a medical condition caused by excessive drinking of water. It leads to the loss of minerals and nutrients. What colligative property is the cause of this condition?

    A. boiling point elevation
    B. freezing point depression
    C. vapor pressure depression
    D. osmotic pressure

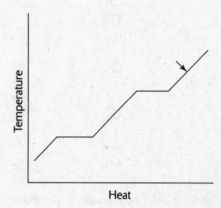

234. In the above diagram, what is the arrow pointing to?

    A. freezing
    B. heating of a solid
    C. boiling
    D. heating of a gas

235. What is the molar mass of calcium acetate?

    A. 84 g/mol
    B. 158 g/mol
    C. 139 g/mol
    D. 99 g/mol

GO ON TO THE NEXT PAGE

$$\overline{\underset{2p}{\sigma^*}}$$

$$\underset{2p}{\pi^*}$$

$$\underset{}{\uparrow\downarrow}$$

$$\underset{}{\uparrow\downarrow}\ \underset{2p}{\sigma}\ \underset{}{\uparrow\downarrow}$$

$$\underset{2p}{\pi}$$

$$\underset{}{\uparrow\downarrow}$$

$$\underset{2s}{\sigma^*}$$

$$\underset{}{\uparrow\downarrow}$$

$$\underset{2s}{\sigma}$$

$$\underset{}{\uparrow\downarrow}$$

$$\underset{1s}{\sigma^*}$$

$$\underset{}{\uparrow\downarrow}$$

$$\underset{1s}{\sigma}$$

236. What bond order corresponds to the above molecular orbital diagram?

    A. 2
    B. 3
    C. 0
    D. 1

237. "Reducing sugars" contain a carbonyl that can be further oxidized (without oxidizing completely to carbon dioxide). What functional group would reducing sugars have?

    A. carboxylic acid
    B. aldehyde
    C. alcohol
    D. ketone

238. What term from quantum mechanics is associated with the shell number?

    A. n (the principle quantum number)
    B. l (the angular momentum number)
    C. m_s (the spin quantum number)
    D. m_l (the magnetic quantum number)

239. In a chemical reaction, what will stop the reaction by running out first?

    A. the limiting reagent
    B. the products
    C. the theoretical yield
    D. the percent yield

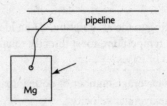

240. In the above diagram of a pipeline, what is the arrow pointing to?

    A. cathodic reaction
    B. sacrificial anode
    C. electrical connection
    D. ground wire

241. Of the following gases, what will have the fasted rate of diffusion?

    A. carbon dioxide
    B. argon
    C. oxygen
    D. nitrogen

242. Which of the following represents a physical change?

    A. digestion
    B. melting
    C. rusting
    D. burning

243. What is the reaction mechanism of an organic decomposition that is caused by the presence of another substance that gets the reaction started by removing an element from the parent chain?

    A. S_N1
    B. E1
    C. S_N2
    D. E2

244. In the Lewis Dot structure for carbonate ion, CO_3^{-2}, how many sigma bonds are present?

   A. 1
   B. 2
   C. 4
   D. 3

245. What type of nuclear particle must be released to convert uranium into thorium in a single step?

   A. alpha
   B. gamma
   C. beta
   D. neutron

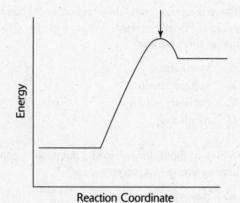

Energy

Reaction Coordinate

246. In the above diagram, what is the arrow pointing to?

   A. reactants
   B. transition state
   C. products
   D. energy released by the reaction

247. Which definition of acids and bases is based on the donation and acceptance of lone pairs of electrons?

   A. Arrhenius
   B. Dalton
   C. Lewis
   D. Bronsted-Lowry

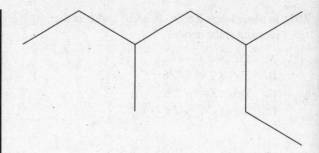

248. What is the correct name for the compound shown in the figure above?

   A. 2-ethyl-4-methylhexane
   B. 2-ethyl-5-methylhexane
   C. 5-ethyl-3-methylhexane
   D. 3,5-dimethylheptane

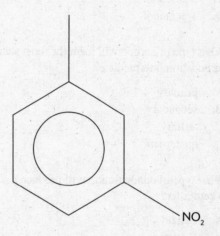

249. What is the name of the above compound?

   A. m-methyl-nitrobenzene
   B. o-methyl-nitrobenzene
   C. m-nitrotoluene
   D. o-nitrotoluene

250. In the presence of sulfuric acid, sugar undergoes a simple decomposition reaction in which the volume of the product is much greater than the volume of the reactant. The reaction is $C_6H_{12}O_6$ (s) $\rightarrow$ 6 C (s) + 6 H_2O (l). What will happen to the density of the product as it is related to the reactants?

   A. It increases.
   B. It changes, but unpredictably.
   C. It decreases.
   D. It remains constant.

GO ON TO THE NEXT PAGE

251. In the reaction $Zn|Zn^{+2}||Cu|Cu^{+2}$, what is the reaction at the anode?

   A. $Cu^{+2} + 2\,e^- \rightarrow Cu$

   B. $Zn^{+2} + 2\,e^- \rightarrow Zn$

   C. $Zn \rightarrow Zn^{+2} + 2\,e^-$

   D. $Cu \rightarrow Cu^{+2} + 2\,e^-$

$+ H_2O \longrightarrow$

252. According to Markonikov's rule, what alcohol should form from the above reaction?

   A. 1-pentanol

   B. 5-pentanol

   C. 2-pentanol

   D. 4-pentanol

253. What type of carbon will form the most stable carbocation intermediate?

   A. primary

   B. secondary

   C. tertiary

   D. quaternary

254. What type of condensation will produce a β keto ester?

   A. Zaitzev

   B. Huckel

   C. Claisen

   D. Markonikov

255. Of the following elements, which is a metalloid?

   A. Cl

   B. Ar

   C. As

   D. Cu

256. The reaction of a carboxylic acid with an alcohol will yield what type of compound?

   A. ether

   B. amide

   C. ester

   D. aldehyde

257. What is the bond order for the MO configuration $\sigma_{1s}^{2}\sigma^{*}{}_{12}^{2}\sigma_{2s}^{2}\sigma^{*}{}_{2s}^{2}\sigma_{2p}^{2}\pi_{2p}^{2}$?

   A. 2

   B. 3

   C. 1

   D. 4

258. What type of compound has two or more internal chiral carbons that cancel out rotation of light?

   A. meso

   B. chiral

   C. racemic

   D. enantiomer

259. There is an old "trick" in which a needle can be made to "float" on water. What property of fluids makes this possible?

   A. viscosity

   B. surface tension

   C. capillary action

   D. meniscus

260. Which of the following would not make a good leaving group in aqueous media?

   A. methyl

   B. hydroxide

   C. halides

   D. nitrate

261. What type of functional group is RCOOR'?

   A. ketone

   B. ester

   C. ether

   D. alcohol

262. The atomic number can best be thought of in terms of the number of what particle in a form or monatomic ion?

   A. proton

   B. nucleus

   C. electron

   D. neutron

263. When balanced, the stoichiometric coefficient for phosphoric acid in the equation [H_3PO_4 (aq) + $Ca(OH)_2$ (aq) → products] will be what?

    A. 1
    B. 3
    C. 2
    D. 4

264. With very few exceptions, which state generally has the highest density?

    A. liquid
    B. solid
    C. unable to determine
    D. gas

265. What is the mass of 1 mole of calcium?

    A. 6.02×10^{23}
    B. 1
    C. 40 g
    D. impossible to determine

266. What does it mean if the reaction quotient is less than the equilibrium constant for a reversible reaction, $Q < K_{eq}$?

    A. Reactant concentration is too high.
    B. Reactant concentration is higher than the product concentration.
    C. Product concentration is higher than the reactant concentration.
    D. Product concentration is too high.

267. Rusting is what type of reaction?

    A. double replacement
    B. equilibrium
    C. decomposition
    D. redox

268. Which of the following functional groups would be most acidic?

    A. terminal alkenes
    B. terminal alkynes
    C. alkanes
    D. non-terminal alkenes

269. If we double both the absolute temperature and the volume of a fixed quantity of gas, what will happen to the pressure?

    A. It will double.
    B. It will change, but it is impossible to tell how.
    C. It will halve.
    D. It will remain constant.

270. What is name given to the amount of energy required to remove an electron from an atom?

    A. electronegativity
    B. ionic radii
    C. ionization energy
    D. electron affinity

271. Which is the only alkaline functional group in the following list?

    A. amide
    B. alcohol
    C. amine
    D. alkyne

GO ON TO THE NEXT PAGE

Critical Thinking Essay

Directions: You will have 30 minutes in which to write an essay in response to the following statement. This essay will either require you to express an opinion or will present a problem that needs a solution.

Discuss a solution to the problem of government's restrictions on scientific research and development.

Answer Key for Practice Test 4

Verbal Ability: Analogies

1. D	11. C	21. A
2. A	12. D	22. B
3. D	13. A	23. D
4. C	14. C	24. C
5. B	15. D	25. B
6. A	16. D	26. C
7. A	17. A	27. D
8. A	18. B	28. A
9. C	19. B	29. D
10. D	20. C	

Verbal Ability: Sentence Completions

30. C	40. D	50. A
31. A	41. A	51. C
32. B	42. D	52. B
33. C	43. B	53. B
34. A	44. C	54. D
35. C	45. A	55. A
36. C	46. D	56. C
37. A	47. B	57. B
38. B	48. A	58. D
39. C	49. D	

Biology

59. B	**79.** C	**99.** A
60. D	**80.** B	**100.** C
61. A	**81.** D	**101.** D
62. C	**82.** A	**102.** B
63. D	**83.** C	**103.** A
64. C	**84.** A	**104.** C
65. A	**85.** C	**105.** B
66. B	**86.** D	**106.** C
67. C	**87.** C	**107.** D
68. D	**88.** D	**108.** D
69. A	**89.** B	**109.** A
70. D	**90.** C	**110.** D
71. C	**91.** A	**111.** C
72. D	**92.** D	**112.** B
73. D	**93.** A	**113.** C
74. B	**94.** C	**114.** D
75. C	**95.** D	**115.** D
76. A	**96.** B	**116.** A
77. B	**97.** A	
78. D	**98.** D	

Reading Comprehension

117. C	**134.** A	**151.** B
118. C	**135.** B	**152.** A
119. D	**136.** A	**153.** A
120. A	**137.** A	**154.** D
121. A	**138.** B	**155.** B
122. D	**139.** C	**156.** A
123. B	**140.** B	**157.** C
124. B	**141.** B	**158.** B
125. B	**142.** D	**159.** B
126. B	**143.** C	**160.** D
127. C	**144.** C	**161.** B
128. B	**145.** C	**162.** A
129. A	**146.** A	**163.** C
130. D	**147.** C	**164.** B
131. C	**148.** B	**165.** B
132. B	**149.** A	
133. D	**150.** D	

Quantitative Ability

166. B	**182.** C	**198.** B
167. D	**183.** A	**199.** D
168. C	**184.** D	**200.** A
169. D	**185.** B	**201.** C
170. A	**186.** C	**202.** C
171. C	**187.** B	**203.** A
172. D	**188.** B	**204.** A
173. A	**189.** D	**205.** B
174. A	**190.** C	**206.** B
175. D	**191.** A	**207.** A
176. B	**192.** A	**208.** C
177. A	**193.** D	**209.** A
178. B	**194.** D	**210.** B
179. A	**195.** C	**211.** C
180. C	**196.** C	**212.** B
181. B	**197.** A	**213.** A

Chemistry

214. D	**234.** D	**254.** C
215. A	**235.** B	**255.** C
216. A	**236.** B	**256.** C
217. D	**237.** B	**257.** A
218. A	**238.** A	**258.** A
219. B	**239.** A	**259.** B
220. C	**240.** B	**260.** A
221. B	**241.** B	**261.** B
222. B	**242.** B	**262.** A
223. D	**243.** D	**263.** C
224. B	**244.** D	**264.** B
225. D	**245.** A	**265.** C
226. A	**246.** B	**266.** D
227. C	**247.** C	**267.** D
228. A	**248.** D	**268.** B
229. A	**249.** C	**269.** D
230. C	**250.** C	**270.** C
231. D	**251.** C	**271.** C
232. A	**252.** C	
233. D	**253.** C	

Complete Answers and Explanations for Practice Test 4

Verbal Ability: Analogies

1. **D.** The relationship is opposites.

2. **A.** The relationship is part to whole.

3. **D.** The relationship is characteristic. A snail is slow, and a twig is a thin branch of a tree.

4. **C.** Hamburger is made of beef, which comes from cattle, and pork chops come from pigs.

5. **B.** The relationship is of opposites: new and old. Just as television is a newer way to communicate information than radio is, a newspaper is a newer way to communicate information than a town crier.

6. **A.** An egg becomes a chicken as a bud becomes a flower.

7. **A.** The relationship is one of degree, large to small.

8. **A.** The relationship is one of function. A wrench is used by a mechanic; a hose is used by a firefighter.

9. **C.** Apples and pears are parts of the whole category fruit; corn and carrots are part of the whole category vegetables.

10. **D.** Both hats and caps are worn on the head; both gloves and rings are worn on the hand.

11. **C.** The relationship is the characteristic place of work of a specific job.

12. **D.** The relationship is that of a part to whole.

13. **A.** Jack-o'-lanterns and skeletons are associated with Halloween; a decorated tree and Santa Claus are associated with Christmas.

14. **C.** The relationship is opposites.

15. **D.** To be green is a characteristic of plants, and to be creative is characteristic of an inventor.

16. **D.** The relationship is cause to effect. To be clumsy can cause one to trip, and to be late can cause one to hurry.

17. **A.** The relationship is sequence. Fall comes before winter, and a bud appears before a leaf opens.

18. **B.** The words are synonyms.

19. **B.** A bay is a small body of salt water, and an ocean is a large body of salt water. A pebble is small, and a rock is large.

20. **C.** Whole to part is the relationship. Algebra is a branch of mathematics; botany is a branch of biology.

21. **A.** What is characteristic is the key to this analogy. Lead is heavy; water is wet.

22. **B.** The function of a manual is to explain something, and the function of a stapler is to fasten things.

23. **D.** Depth is a characteristic of a trench, and height is characteristic of a hill.

24. **C.** The arm is located between the wrist and the hand; the ankle is located between the leg and the foot.

25. **B.** The relationship is what a person in this job usually wears.

26. **C.** The relationship is location. Eyes are above a nose; a roof is above a house.

27. **D.** The relationship is that they are part of the same family of animals. Lions and cats are felines; wolves and dogs are canines.

28. **A.** Location explains the answer. What is the appropriate place to put the object?

29. **D.** Buttons and snaps close things; keys and can openers open things.

Verbal Ability: Sentence Completions

30. **C.** Choice **A** cannot be correct since both were goddesses (female). Since both were goddesses of love, Choice **D**, opposites, is unlikely. Counterparts means something having the same functions and characteristics. Attributes are characteristics.

31. **A.** Because the book will not add to something, the first blank requires a negative word. Recondite means not easily understood. Although abstruse, Choice **C**, has a similar meaning, lunacy, meaning insanity, is not logical for the second blank. Edification means intellectual improvement.

32. **B.** An admonition is a warning. Choice **C** is not correct because the match has not yet been ended by the referee.

33. **C.** If a person is shy, he would probably fear (dread) speaking before a group.

34. **A.** Something inherent is an essential or intrinsic characteristic.

35. **C.** The description in the second clause of the sentence indicates that desolate, meaning barren and gloomy, is the best choice.

36. **C.** Indignation means anger caused by unfairness or injustice.

37. **A.** Speculative means based on inconclusive data, not based on evidence.

38. **B.** To be demoralized is to lack confidence, a probable effect of losing a game.

39. **C.** A quandary is a dilemma or state of perplexity.

40. **D.** The word in the first blank must have a positive connotation. Stalwart means strong and steadfast. An epitome is a symbol of something.

41. **A.** To nurture means to help to grow or develop.

42. **D.** Since the person described in the sentence suffers from insomnia, something must be troubling him. Disconcerting means upsetting one's sense of self-possession. To be plagued is to be persistently annoyed.

43. **B.** Valorous means brave, and that is implied by the words "praise" and "rescue."

44. **C.** Jubilant means joyful, and none of the other choices really fits the situation.

45. **A.** The word "umbrage" is the clue. It means to take offense. Thus, the audience would be angered, or incensed, by the remark. Offhand also means unthinking, and demonstrates a lack of consideration.

46. **D.** It's important to look for clues. In this sentence, the word "credit" indicates something positive. The only positive word here is Choice **D**, which means strength. The other choices are negative words.

47. **B.** Some of the word choices just don't make sense in the context of the sentence. Choice **B** is correct since severity means serious, which is something one would find in a courtroom, and languidly means lazily, which indicates his lack of concern.

48. **A.** It often helps to rewrite the sentence with each of the words. The only word that makes sense is rustic, which means rural, and this is implied by the growth of the surrounding area. The area blossomed, but their cabin did not.

49. **D.** Compatible means getting along with, or agreeable. It also means capable of integrating with a system. In this case, the disks did not integrate with the new system.

50. **A.** Potent means strong, or having a strong chemical effect.

51. **C.** Obnoxious means extremely unpleasant, which was the reason they wanted him to leave the part—he was obnoxious. Choices **A** and **B** don't fit, and Choice **D** makes no sense in this context.

52. **B.** Droves means large groups. It's not likely they feared the music, and they certainly weren't teams. And although they may have disliked the music, disagreement is not the correct word here.

53. B. Someone from a poor country (third-world) would likely be overwhelmed—affected deeply by his surroundings—especially if they were wealthy (affluent).

54. D. A kernel is a small bit, or an element of truth in what she said.

55. A. A dilemma is usually a two-sided problem. There were two situations that he faced, either accept the invitation or plead illness.

56. C. The sentence sets up a negative situation, and choices **A, B,** and **D** are somewhat positive, with words like "praise," "encourage," and "help." Only Choice **C** makes sense here.

57. B. One must be submissive to one's boss, thus only compliant is correct.

58. D. Perturb means bother, and is the only correct choice in this sentence.

Biology

59. B. In a DNA molecule, guanine pairs with cytosine and adenine pairs with thymine to hold the two sugar-phosphate backbones together. Therefore, a DNA molecule composed of 30% guanine must also contain 30% cytosine. The remaining 40% of the bases will be evenly split between adenine (20%) and thymine (20%).

60. D. Protein synthesis (Choice **B**) is comprised of two steps. The first step, transcription (Choice **C**), involves the making of an mRNA template from a molecule of DNA. The second step, translation (Choice **D**), involves the making of a polypeptide chain from an mRNA template. DNA replication (Choice **A**) involves a doubling of the DNA content of a chromosome in preparation for cell division.

61. A. The DNA molecule consists of paired nucleotides arranged to form a backbone of alternating deoxyribose sugars and phosphate groups, with paired nitrogenous bases facing inward and joined by hydrogen bonds.

62. C. Protein synthesis takes place in the cytoplasm of cells, with the mRNA molecules held in position on ribosomes.

63. D. The more energy an organism expends, the more mitochondria it is likely to have per cell.

64. C. Plant cells contain a cell wall, chloroplasts, and a large central vacuole. Animal cells do not have a cell wall or chloroplasts, and they typically have one or more small vacuoles, rather than a large central vacuole.

65. A. Cellular respiration occurs in most living organisms, including bacteria, algae, plants, and animals.

66. B. Eggs and sperm are produced through the process of meiosis, which reduces the chromosome number in half. Therefore, a diploid organism with 64 chromosomes in each of its somatic cells would produce eggs or sperm containing 32 chromosomes.

67. C. A mutation that occurs in a somatic cell cannot be passed on to the offspring of the individual in which it occurs. Only mutations that occur in germ cells, which give rise to eggs and sperm, can be passed on to one's offspring.

68. D. With incomplete dominance, neither allele masks the presence of the other allele; thus, heterozygous individuals will usually have a phenotype intermediate to that of the homozygous dominant and homozygous recessive individuals.

69. A. All of the offspring would inherit at least one dominant allele for round ears from the homozygous dominant parent.

70. D. Both daughters and sons can inherit sex-linked traits.

71. C. Genetic drift occurs when a population undergoes a significant decrease in size, resulting in the loss of much genetic variation in the population.

72. D. Evolution refers to the change in the genetic composition of a population over time.

73. D. Angiosperms are the group of plants with vascular tissue (xylem and phloem) that reproduce by seeds enclosed in fruits.

74. B. The producers, which form the base of all food chains, are autotrophic organisms that are able to produce their own food, usually by the process of photosynthesis.

75. C. In a mutualistic relationship, both organisms benefit from the arrangement. A predator-prey (Choice **A**) or a host-parasite (Choice **B**) relationship benefits one organism and is detrimental to the other organism. With competition (Choice **D**), neither organism benefits from the relationship.

76. A. The excess plant growth caused by runoff of large quantities of nitrogen and phosphorous from over-fertilization of agricultural and urban lands is referred to as eutrification.

77. B. The combustion of fossil fuels releases very large quantities of carbon dioxide into the atmosphere, upsetting the carbon balance of the world's ecosystems. The buildup of carbon dioxide in the atmosphere is leading to a global change in climate.

78. D. The restriction enzymes used in the production of DNA fingerprints were isolated from various strains of bacteria, where their natural role is to destroy foreign DNA molecules that invade the bacterial cells.

79. C. Osmosis refers to the movement of water across a differentially permeable membrane from a region of high concentration to a region of low concentration. The movement of particles across a differentially permeable membrane, from a region of high concentration to a region of low concentration (Choice **A**), is referred to as diffusion. The movement of particles (Choice **B**) or water (Choice **D**) from a region of low concentration to a region of high concentration requires the input of energy (ATP) and is referred to as active transport.

80. B. During photosynthesis, plants take in carbon dioxide and water and use light energy to produce chemical energy in the form of glucose. Oxygen is given off as a by-product of the photosynthetic reactions.

81. D. If plant cells were removed from leaf tissue and placed in saltwater, the cells would lose water and the plasma membrane would pull away from the cell walls, which would remain intact.

82. A. The increase in toxin concentration at successive levels of a food chain is referred to as biological magnification.

83. C. Each of the terrestrial and aquatic ecosystems of the world is referred to as a biome. The biosphere (D) is the sum of all of the Earth's ecosystems.

84. A. The cyanobacteria are photosynthetic species of bacteria.

85. C. Typhoid fever is a bacterial disease affecting the human gastrointestinal tract. Tuberculosis (Choice **A**), pertussis (Choice **B**), and diphtheria (Choice **D**) are all bacterial diseases affecting the human respiratory tract.

86. D. Bacterial cells may exchange genetic information with each other by forming a tube connecting the cells with each other. This type of genetic exchange is referred to as conjugation. Transduction (Choice **A**) involves the introduction of foreign DNA into bacterial cells through the use of a bacteriophage. Transformation (Choice **B**) occurs when bacterial cells take up foreign DNA, usually in the form of a plasmid, from their surrounding medium in culture. Budding (Choice **C**) refers to a type of asexual reproduction in which a piece of cytoplasm is pinched off of the parent cell.

87. C. Yeast, which is used in the wine and beer making industries, belongs to the Kingdom Fungi.

88. D. Bacterial DNA is organized into a single circular, double-stranded chromosome.

89. B. Oxygen is a by-product of the process of photosynthesis. Thus, the first photosynthetic bacteria, which evolved between 3 billion and 3.5 billion years ago, allowed for an increase in the level of oxygen in the atmosphere.

90. C. Using raw eggs to make eggnog is no longer recommended because raw eggs are often contaminated with *Salmonella*.

91. A. The use of antibiotics would not be helpful against influenza, which is caused by a virus. Leprosy (Choice **B**), typhoid fever (Choice **C**), and botulism (Choice **D**) are all diseases of bacterial origin, against which antibiotics would be helpful.

92. D. The process of autoclaving relies on the use of pressurized steam for sterilization and is considered to be the most effective sterilization technique currently available.

93. **A.** The production of stomach acid, which occurs continuously, not just when invading microorganisms are present, would be considered a passive immune response.

94. **C.** Genetic transformation of bacterial cells involves the uptake of DNA, often in the form of a plasmid, from the surrounding culture medium.

95. **D.** Retroviruses use the enzyme reverse transcriptase to make DNA from an RNA template.

96. **B.** The primary function of human red blood cells is to transport oxygen and carbon dioxide throughout the body.

97. **A.** In the human respiratory system, the alveoli function to exchange gases with the red blood cells.

98. **D.** In the human digestive system, the emptying of bile (which is manufactured in the liver and stored in the gall bladder) from the gall bladder into the small intestine aids in the digestion of fats.

99. **A.** In the human brain, the cerebrum serves as the site for coordinating taste, smell, vision, and hearing. The cerebellum is responsible for the coordination of motor activity and muscle contractions (Choice **B**). The hypothalamus is responsible for the coordination of breathing, heart rate, and blood pressure (Choice **C**), as well as serving as the site for the production of several hormones that are stored in the pituitary gland.

100. **C.** Essential amino acids refer to those that humans cannot synthesize and must be obtained through the diet.

101. **D.** In the human body, metabolic processes are regulated by the hormone thyroxine. The development of secondary female characteristics (Choice **A**) is controlled by the hormone estrogen, while the development of secondary male characteristics (Choice **B**) is controlled by the hormone androgen. Human growth hormone is responsible for promoting normal growth in the human body (Choice **C**).

102. **B.** In humans, the function of the parasympathetic nervous system is to return the body to a normal state following an emergency. The sympathetic nervous system prepares the body for emergencies (Choice **A**). The limbic system controls emotional responses (Choice **C**), and the somatic sensory system carries signals from the external environment to the brain (Choice **D**).

103. **A.** In humans, the production of specific antibodies in response to exposure to a specific antigen is an example of a specific immune response, where the response is different for each target invader. While stomach acid (Choice **B**), mucous membranes (Choice **C**), and macrophage (Choice **D**) all help protect the human body from invading microorganisms, they are nondiscriminatory and, therefore, considered to be nonspecific immune responses.

104. **C.** Vaccines stimulate both the primary and secondary immune responses in humans, as well as the production of specific antibodies.

105. **B.** In the human digestive system, the primary function of the large intestine is to reabsorb water and create waste for expulsion.

106. **C.** The presence of a four-chambered heart in humans is quite efficient, as it keeps oxygen-poor blood separated from oxygen-rich blood.

107. **D.** In human females, meiosis takes place in the ovaries, resulting in the production of eggs.

108. **D.** An increase in the production of ketoacids and acidic urine are symptoms of diabetes.

109. **A.** In the human circulatory system, the platelets initiate the blood-clotting process.

110. **D.** In human females, fertilization of the egg by the sperm takes place in the Fallopian tube.

111. **C.** In the human excretory system, waste is carried from the kidneys to the bladder through the ureters.

112. **B.** Oxygen and carbon dioxide are moved throughout the human body by the circulatory system. The respiratory system (Choice **A**) allows the exchange of oxygen and carbon dioxide between the body and the external environment. The excretory system (Choice **C**) allows for the removal of waste, in the form of urine, from the body through the kidneys. The endocrine system (Choice **D**) produces and regulates the hormones responsible for conducting chemical signals throughout the body.

113. C. When an individual is lacking an adequate number of kilocalories in their diet, that person is said to be undernourished. A person who is missing certain nutrients from their diet is said to be malnourished (Choice **A**) or poorly nourished (Choice **B**). An impoverished individual (Choice **D**) may or may not be either malnourished or undernourished, depending on his particular circumstances. Impoverishment is an economic classification rather than a nutritional classification.

114. D. In humans, the pancreas is responsible for the production of insulin.

115. D. Taking antibiotics when they are not necessary, as for a viral infection (Choice **A**), failing to take the entire amount of an antibiotic prescribed for a bacterial infection (Choice **B**), and the routine use of antibiotics in livestock feed (Choice **C**) may all lead to the development of antibiotic-resistant strains of bacteria.

116. A. The human endocrine system is responsible for chemical coordination of the body's systems. The human circulatory system is responsible for moving oxygen and carbon dioxide throughout the body (Choice **B**). The human digestive system is responsible for the breakdown of food, including fats and proteins, and absorption of nutrients (Choice **C**). The excretory system is responsible for the removal of waste products, in the form of urine, from the body through the kidneys (Choice **D**).

Reading Comprehension

117. C. It states this in the first paragraph and indicates that after age 6, remission is rare.

118. C. The danger is life-threatening anaphylaxis, which means the closing of the muscles in your throat.

119. D. The last sentence in paragraph two states, "The interpretations of these results are mixed."

120. A. The first sentence of paragraph three suggests eating peanuts at least once a month maintains a tolerance to them.

121. A. Paragraph three states that children did not like the taste that occurred when histamines were released in their mouths.

122. D. In paragraph four it is suggested that injection kits should be carried as precaution even if the child hasn't shown signs of allergies recently.

123. B. The last two sentences indicate that a change in eating habits should be assessed by a clinician.

124. B. The first sentence describes bioenergy as found in culturally based medical systems.

125. B. In the middle of paragraph one, it lists all the improvement including stress reduction and lower blood pressure.

126. B. This is stated in the last sentence of the first paragraph.

127. C. The second paragraph explains changes seen in the structure of water and aqueous solutions.

128. B. The fact is stated in paragraph three.

129. A. Doctors were able to personally experience the energy from the master's hands.

130. D. This text states observable facts. There is not evidence of negative opinions (cynicism) nor does the author ask questions or seem removed from the issues.

131. C. The voice is later called a "crucial tool of their trade."

132. B. Statistics say that one of three people use their voice to carry out their jobs.

133. D. Paragraph two lists all the causes of voice strain.

134. A. Paragraph three states that people who have voice training experience fewer problems with their voices.

135. B. The use of only your upper chest is equated to using only three cylinders in a car engine.

136. A. Paragraph four states that yawning and sighing relieves stress before speech making.

137. **A.** The second to last sentence states, "It is better to be silent, to punctuate the need for attention, than to talk about the noise."

138. **B.** This is stated in the third sentence of the first paragraph.

139. **C.** In paragraph two, it talks about the difficulty of determining the true cause of psychosis in the fourth sentence.

140. **B.** A situation is described at the end of paragraph two where it is suggested that "subtle changes to their surroundings" could minimize bad behavior.

141. **B.** A rudimentary cause means basic reason for behavior. The article states that psychosocial and psychotherapeutic interventions should be considered first.

142. **D.** This is stated in the second sentence of the third paragraph.

143. **C.** EPS stands for extra pyramidal symptoms, which means behaviors that result from medications.

144. **C.** Paragraph four talks about "fine-tuning the environment . . . to give a better fit" for patients.

145. **C.** In paragraph two, it states that hyperactivity has been around since the 1880s.

146. **A.** The second sentence of the second paragraph states the difficulty as diagnosing, treating, and naming the disorder.

147. **C.** Paragraph two includes the statement that the APA "has leveled this disease . . . based on standard diagnostic reference tests."

148. **B.** The text states that because there are a cluster of symptoms, it is called a syndrome.

149. **A.** The last sentence of paragraph two states this.

150. **D.** The last sentence in the article addressed help, which includes medicine, behavior modifications, educational technologies and psychotherapy.

151. **B.** The introduction presents three frantic parents and their need for help and the ending states the percentage of afflicted students as varying.

152. **A.** The third sentence of the first paragraph says the emphasis is on occupational choice rather than career development.

153. **A.** Paragraph two talks about the lack of controlled research to indicate success in scientific terms.

154. **D.** The sentence states a relationship between "early intervention and adult employment outcomes."

155. **B.** The last sentence of paragraph two lists work opportunities, vocational preparation, and time in career education as predictors of success.

156. **A.** It is stated in the first sentence of paragraph three.

157. **C.** Congruent means linked or applied to similar expectations that will transfer to successful employment.

158. **B.** There is discussion of matching skills with employability.

159. **B.** The second sentence in the first paragraph states relationship between bullying and students with disabilities so there is a connection.

160. **D.** The last two sentences of the first paragraph talk about family situations where parents are distant.

161. **B.** All indications are that bullying happens over a period of time.

162. **A.** If the result is the imbalance of power, then that is harmful.

163. **C.** "Victims . . . are on fringes of the school culture," which means they don't feel they belong to any group.

164. **B.** The last paragraph states the needs to include parents.

165. **B.** All suggestions in the last paragraph with school intervention programs and the need to address school environments indicate a rational way to deal with the problem.

Quantitative Ability

166. B. If 400 people fit in 8 subway cars, then $400 \div 8$, or 50, people fit in one subway car. Therefore, 50×5, or 250, people fit in 5 subway cars.

167. D. The area of the circle with a radius of 3 is $\pi r^2 = \pi \times 3^2 = 9\pi$. The area of the larger circle is $4 \times 9\pi = 36\pi$. Therefore, $r^2 = 36$ so $r = \sqrt{36} = 6$. The radius of the larger circle is 6.

168. C. The amount of commission is $10\% \times \$8,350 = \$835$. Total earnings are $\$300 + \$835$ commission $= \$1,135$.

169. D. At the end of the first day, there are $1 - \frac{1}{8} = \frac{7}{8}$ of the magazines remaining. $\frac{7}{8} \times \frac{1}{4} = \frac{7}{32}$ sold the next day. So at the end of the second day, there are $\frac{7}{8} - \frac{7}{32} = \frac{28}{32} - \frac{7}{32} = \frac{21}{32}$ of the magazines remaining.

170. A. By the properties of logarithms, $\log A^2 = 2\log A$. Since $\log A = 8$, $2\log A = 16$.

171. C. Carl's throw went $7\frac{1}{3} \times 2\frac{1}{2} = \frac{22}{3} \times \frac{5}{2} = \frac{110}{6} = 18\frac{1}{3}$ yards. The difference between the two throws is $18\frac{1}{3} - 7\frac{1}{3} = 11$ yards.

172. D. The total cost for the posts and fencing is $(10 \times \$12.50) + (34 \times \$4.75) = \$125.00 + \$161.50 = \$286.50$.

173. A. Add the areas of the two triangles and the square to find the total area. The area of the square is $5^2 = 25$. Both triangles have a height of 5. The area of one triangle is $\frac{1}{2}bh = \frac{1}{2} \cdot 3 \cdot 5 = \frac{15}{2} = 7.5$. The area of the other triangle is $\frac{1}{2}bh = \frac{1}{2} \cdot 4 \cdot 5 = \frac{20}{2} = 10$. The total area is $25 + 7.5 + 10 = 42.5$.

174. A. The proportion $\frac{5}{3} = \frac{x}{4}$ can be used to find x. Cross-multiply. $5 \times 4 = 3x$ so $20 = 3x$ and $x = \frac{20}{3} = 6\frac{2}{3}$.

175. D. In a 10-mile trip, after the first mile, there are 9 additional miles. If each additional half mile is $1, then an additional mile is $2. The cost of the trip is $3 for the first mile + ($2 \times 9$) for the additional miles. $\$3 + \$18 = \$21$.

176. B. The sine function is positive in the first and second quadrants, and the secant function is negative in the second and third quadrants. Thus, $\angle x$ must lie in the second quadrant.

177. A. The cost of Sandy's purchase is $(4\frac{1}{2} \times \$1.39) + (6 \times \$0.50) = \$9.26$. The cost of Brandon's purchase is $(3\frac{1}{4} \times \$1.39) + (9 \times \$0.50) = \$9.02$. Sandy spent $\$9.26 - \$9.02 = \$0.24$ more.

178. B. The area of a square is s^2 where s is a side of the square. If $s^2 = 36$, then $s = 6$. The diagonal of a square forms two right triangles; d is the hypotenuse and the two legs are 6 units long.

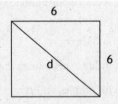

Using the Pythagorean theorem, $d^2 = 6^2 + 6^2 = 36 + 36 = 72$. Therefore, $d = \sqrt{72} = 6\sqrt{2}$.

179. A. For this equation to be true, it must be the case that $2x - 1 = 5x + 8$. This is true when $x = -3$.

180. C. $3m - 12 + 12 = -6 + 12$. $3m = 6$. Dividing both sides by 3 results in $m = 2$.

181. B. One of the fundamental trigonometric identities is that $\frac{\cos\Theta}{\sin\Theta} = \cot\Theta$.

182. C. Probability is $\frac{\text{number of expected outcomes}}{\text{number of possible outcomes}}$. Since one king was drawn and not replaced, three kings remain in the deck of 51 cards. So the probability of drawing another king is $\frac{3}{51} = \frac{1}{17}$.

183. A. The area of a square is s^2 where s is a side of the square. If $s^2 = 400$, then $s = \sqrt{400} = 20$.

184. D. Since $j(z) = \left(\frac{1}{2}\right)^z$, it follows that $j(-1) = \left(\frac{1}{2}\right)^{-1} = 2$.

185. B. Divide the figure into a rectangle and triangle as shown.

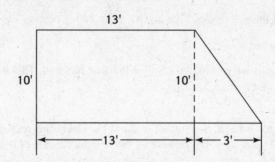

The area of the figure equals the area of the rectangle plus the area of the triangle. The rectangle = length × width or $10 \times 13 = 130$ ft²; the triangle = $\frac{1}{2}$ base × height or $\frac{1}{2} \times 3 \times 10 = 15$ ft². Together, the area is $130 + 15 = 145$ ft².

186. C. Using the ratio $\frac{\text{price}}{\text{video}}$, the proportion $\frac{8}{3} = \frac{x}{2}$ can be used to find the cost to rent two videos. Cross-multiply. $8 \times 2 = 3x$ so $16 = 3x$ and $x = \frac{16}{3} = \$5.33$.

187. B. Let $x = \log_5 625$. Then, by the definition of logarithms, $5^x = 625$. This means that $x = 4$.

188. B. This equation is solved by the number whose cube root is 2. The number with this property is 8.

189. D. Convert the dimensions of the box from feet to inches. $8' \times 6' \times 4'$ is equivalent to $(8 \times 12 \text{ in}) \times (6 \times 12 \text{ in}) \times (4 \times 12 \text{ in}) = 96 \text{ in} \times 72 \text{ in} \times 48 \text{ in}$. The volume = $96 \times 72 \times 48 = 331{,}776$. The volume of each block is $6 \times 4 \times 4 = 96$. The number of blocks that fit in the box is $\frac{331{,}776}{96} = 3456$.

190. C. Using the properties of derivatives of polynomial functions, if $y = 5x^2 - 8x + 1$, then $\frac{dy}{dx} = 10x - 8$.

191. A. Let c represent the number of caps traded in. Then $0.05c = 40.50$ and $c = \frac{40.50}{0.05} = 810$ caps.

192. A. The area of a triangle is $\frac{1}{2} bh$. Let b represent the length of one leg. Then $h = 3b$ so the area is $\frac{1}{2} bh = \frac{1}{2} \cdot b \cdot 3b = \frac{3}{2} b^2 = 24$ so $\frac{2}{3} \cdot \frac{3}{2} b^2 = \frac{2}{3} \cdot 24$ and $b^2 = 16$. $b = \sqrt{16} = 4$ and $h = 3 \times 4 = 12$. The longest side of a right triangle is the hypotenuse. Using the Pythagorean theorem, $\text{leg}^2 + \text{leg}^2 = \text{hypotenuse}^2$ so $4^2 + 12^2 = c^2$ and $16 + 144 = c^2$. Therefore, $160 = c^2$ and $c = \sqrt{160} = 12.6$.

193. D. $64^{-\frac{1}{3}} = \sqrt[3]{\frac{1}{64}} = \frac{1}{4}$.

194. D. Using the distributive property, $(2x + 1)(2x + 1) = 4x^2 + 2x + 2x + 1 = 4x^2 + 4x + 1$.

195. C. The cube of 8 is $8 \times 8 \times 8 = 512$.

196. C. Let b represent the number of boys in the class and g represent the number of girls. Then $b + g = 27$. If $b = g + 5$, then $(g + 5) + g = 27$. $2g + 5 = 27$ and $2g = 22$ so $g = 11$. Therefore, the number of boys is $27 - 11$ or 16.

197. A. The amplitude of a sine curve is the coefficient of the sine term, which in this case is 2.

198. B. In order to find the extreme points, you need to find the first derivative and set it equal to 0. Since this function is a quartic function, the derivative will be a cubic, which will have, at most, three solutions.

199. D. The radius $r = \frac{d}{2}$. The area of the circle is $\pi r^2 = \pi \left(\frac{d}{2}\right)^2 = \frac{\pi d^2}{4}$. If the diameter is increased 100%, the diameter is $2d$ and $r = \frac{2d}{2} = d$. The area of the enlarged circle is $\pi r^2 = \pi d^2$. The enlarged circle is $\frac{\pi d^2}{\frac{\pi d^2}{4}} = \pi d^2 \div \frac{\pi d^2}{4} = \pi d^2 \cdot \frac{4}{\pi d^2} = 4$ or 400% bigger.

200. A. 60 beads $\times \frac{1}{2}" = 30$ inches. Converting this to feet gives 30 inches $\times \frac{1 \ foot}{12 \ inches} = \frac{30}{12} = 2\frac{1}{2}$ feet.

201. C. $(3 - 4x)(3 + 4x) = 9 + 12x - 12x - 16x^2 = 9 - 16x^2$.

202. C. We are given that $\log_x 125 = -3$. By the definition of logarithms, this means that $x^{-3} = 125$. To solve this equation, raise both sides to the $-\frac{1}{3}$ power. That is, $\left(x^{-3}\right)^{-\frac{1}{3}} = 125^{-\frac{1}{3}}$ or $x = \left(\frac{1}{125}\right)^{\frac{1}{3}} = \sqrt[3]{\frac{1}{125}} = \frac{1}{5}$.

203. A. The value of $\sin x$ is $\frac{1}{2}$ when $x = 30°$.

204. A. When the cosine function is integrated, the result is the sine function. That is, $\int \cos x\, dx = \sin x + c$.

205. B. $\frac{15\sqrt{3}}{5} = \frac{15\sqrt{3}}{5} \cdot \frac{\sqrt{5}}{\sqrt{5}} = \frac{15\sqrt{15}}{5} = 3\sqrt{15}$.

206. B. The area of the circle is $\pi r^2 = 121\pi$. So $r^2 = 121$ and $r = 11$. The radius represents half the diagonal of the square, so the diagonal is 22 units long. If x represents the length of a side of the square, then x^2 is the area of the square. Using the Pythagorean theorem, $x^2 + x^2 = 22^2$ and $2x^2 = 484$. Therefore $x^2 = \frac{484}{2} = 242$.

207. A. The derivative of the cosine function is the negative of the sine function. Thus, $y'(x) = -(-\sin x) = \cos x$.

208. C. The least common denominator of 96 and 12 is 96 so $\frac{24}{96} - \frac{8}{12} = \frac{24}{96} - \frac{64}{96} = \frac{-40}{96} = -\frac{5}{12}$.

209. A. The equation of a line with a slope of $-\frac{3}{2}$ and a y-intercept of -2 is $y = -\frac{3}{2}x - 2$. To find the value of x in the point $(x, 1)$, substitute 1 for y and solve the equation for x. Then $1 = -\frac{3}{2}x - 2$ and $3 = -\frac{3}{2}x$. So $(3)\left(-\frac{2}{3}\right) = \left(-\frac{2}{3}\right)\left(-\frac{3}{2}\right)x$ and $x = -\frac{6}{3}$ or -2.

210. B. Begin by writing the line $4x + 2y = 12$ is slope-intercept form as $y = -2x + 6$. The slope of this line is the coefficient of the x-coordinate, which is -2. Since parallel lines have the same slope, we need to find an equation with a slope of -2. All the answer choices are in slope-intercept form, and the choice with x coefficient of -2 is Choice **B**.

211. C. The set contains an even number of numbers, so the median of the numbers is the arithmetic mean of the two numbers in the middle. The numbers in the middle are 2 and 4, and the arithmetic mean of these numbers is 3.

212. B. There are four choices for the first digit of the number. After this, there are three choices for the second digit, two for the third digit, and one for the final digit. Overall, then, there are $4 \times 3 \times 2 \times 1 = 24$ possible numbers.

213. A. In order to find this derivative, we need to use the product rule. The derivative of $x(\log x)$ would be
$$x\left(\frac{d\log x}{dx}\right) + \log x\left(\frac{dx}{dx}\right) = \frac{x}{x} + \log x = 1 + \log x.$$

Chemistry

214. D. Here is a hint; if anything appears in its elemental state, either as a reactant or a product, then the reaction is redox. This must be because the oxidation state of any element is zero, but as part of a compound, it is not zero.

215. A. A diastereomer has chiral carbons, but they cancel the rotation out on each other.

216. A. Remember Gibb's equation, $\triangle G = \triangle H - T\triangle S$. Changing temperature only changes the importance of entropy.

217. D. For each mole of sulfur, we form one mole of sulfur dioxide, and each mole of sulfur dioxide produces one mole of sulfuric acid.

218. A. The higher priority elements are on the same side (hence Z), and in propenes, the numbering of carbon is always such that the pi bond starts at the lowest number carbon as possible.

219. B. Sublimation is a state change, a change from solid to gas without going through the liquid state.

220. C. Quaternary amines cannot be alkaline because these salts have no lone pair electrons. The more functional groups on the nitrogen, the more stable the resulting ion will be on absorbing a hydroxide ion; thus, tertiary amines are stronger than secondary and so on.

221. B. The salt bridge allows for counter ions to flow from one side to the other as the redox reaction proceeds to maintain charge balance in both solutions.

222. B. The Claisen Rearrangement causes phenyl-ethers to undergo an internal rearrangement to form o-substituted phenols.

223. D. Hess's law tells us that the heat of reaction is independent of pathway. By reversing the first two reactions, we can add these up to get our net reaction.

224. B. Uranium is element number 92. With an atomic mass number of 238, there are $238 - 92 = 146$ neutrons.

225. D. The indicator is what we add to see the endpoint, which hopefully is very near the equivalence point (when the moles of acid and base are equal in a titration; we choose indicators carefully to try to ensure that the endpoint and equivalence point are very nearly the same).

226. A. We have to reverse the iodine reaction, which will change the sign. However, even though we have to multiply the reaction by ½, we do not change the potential. Thus, $0.7994 - 0.535 = 0.2644$ V.

227. C. An excited state is possible but does not follow Hund's rule, and a forbidden state is not possible (for example, having three electrons in an s orbital).

228. A. The two alcohol groups will cancel out rotation, making this a meso compound. It would not be B, because this would be no different than S, R 2,3 butadiol, and by IUPAC convention, a single compound cannot have more than one name.

229. A. Aldehydes can be oxidized to carboxylic acid, alkanes to alcohols, and alcohols to aldehydes or ketones.

230. C. Velocity is related to kinetic energy but is also a function of the mass of the gas.

231. D. Esters are derivatives of carboxylic acids.

232. A. Nitrate does not change, in form or charge, from reactant to product side. Since it does not change, it does not really participate in the reaction.

233. D. Too much water would dilute out the ions in the solution between cells. This would lead to diffusion of ions out of the cells.

234. D. Phase changes do not have temperature changes, and the gas is the state with the highest internal energy.

235. B. You should know the common polyatomic ions by formula, name and charge. The formula for calcium acetate is $Ca(CH_3CO_2)_2$.

236. B. Remember that bond order is (bonding electrons – antibonding electrons) ÷ 2. Here we have ten bonding electrons, and four antibonding electrons.

237. B. Alcohol has no carbonyl (C = O) group, and carboxylic acids are oxidized as far as possible short of carbon dioxide. Ketones cannot be further oxidized.

238. A. The subsidiary quantum number is the subshell (s, p, d, etc.) and the magnetic quantum number are the orbitals.

239. A. A reaction stops when the first reactant runs out, and that is the limiting reagent.

240. B. A sacrificial anode is made of a metal that is easily oxidized, thus providing electrons to provide the metal in the pipeline.

241. B. The lower the molecular or atomic weight, the higher the rate of diffusion.

242. B. State changes are always physical changes.

243. D. Decomposition is an elimination (say the dehydration of alcohols to form alkenes).

244. D. All three oxygens will be bonded to carbon, and whether the bond is single, double, or triple, one (and only one) bond of each will be a sigma bond.

245. A. Alpha decay reduces atomic number by 2, beta decay increases the atomic number. Gamma and neutron decomposition does not affect the atomic number.

246. B. The transition state is a high energy transitory complex between reactants and products.

247. C. Both Arrhenius and Bronsted-Lowry definitions are based on hydronium (H^+) ions.

248. D. Remember that the parent is the longest continuous carbon chain, in this case, seven carbon atoms.

249. C. Methylbenzene is known as toluene, and the positions around the ring from the methyl group goes ortho, meta, and para.

250. C. Loss of mass and increase in volume both will lead to lower density.

251. C. Oxidation occurs at the anode, and oxidation is loss of electrons. Zinc, in this reaction, is losing electrons.

252. C. Remember, Markonikov tells us that the hydrogen will go to the carbon that already has the most hydrogens. Correct nomenclature requires us to locate the hydroxyl group with the smallest number.

253. C. The more carbons on the carbocation, the more stable the carbocation. A quaternary carbocation cannot exist.

254. C. This is the reaction of esters in the presence of sodium ethoxide.

255. C. Metalloids lie on the border between metals and non-metals, and they tend to display properties of both.

256. C. Esters are created by dehydration reactions between an alcohol and carboxylic acid. Amides are also formed by dehydration reactions with carboxylic acids, only with amines rather than alcohols. This is the reaction that is used by the body in protein synthesis.

257. A. There are eight bonding and four antibonding electrons.

258. A. In a meso compound, there is always a plane of symmetry. A racemic mixture will also show no plane polarized light rotation, but this is because there is an equal mixture of two different enantiomers.

259. B. Surface tension is caused by asymmetric distribution of intermolecular forces at the surface of a liquid.

260. A. A good leaving group would be stable in ionic form in water; methyl does not form a stable cation or anion.

261. B. A ketone would be RCOR', ether ROR' and alcohol R-OH in shorthand notation.

262. A. Electrons are most important for the behavior of elements, but they are subject to change as electrons are exchanged or shared. The number of protons will never change and are equal to the number of electrons for the element; thus, for element identification, the number of protons is the most logical choice.

263. C. The products, based on the charges, will be $Ca_3(PO_4)_2$ and water.

264. B. Water is an unfortunate example; it is one of only two known substances that expand on freezing. Unfortunately, since we are so familiar with water, it tends to mislead us into thinking that the solid state is generally lower density than the liquid. For all other compounds (and all but one element), solid is the highest density state. Don't let your experience with water throw you on questions like this.

265. C. This is what atomic mass means.

266. D. Remember that Q is products/reactants. Thus, if Q is less than K, equilibrium is achieved by converting more reactant to product.

267. D. "Oxidation" historically came from "reaction with oxygen," which is what rusting is.

268. B. The excess pi bond electrons in the alkyne helps to stabilize the resulting carbanion by the loss of the terminal hydrogen. The alkene is not stabilized as well because there are fewer pi electrons.

269. D. Doubling the absolute temperature counteracts the doubling in volume. This can be determined from the ideal gas law.

270. C. Electron affinity is energy released when you add an electron to an atom.

271. C. You might think that an amide is alkaline because of the presence of the nitrogen, but resonance makes it slightly acidic.

Answer Sheet for PCAT Practice Test 5

(Remove This Sheet and Use It to Mark Your Answers)

Verbal Ability: Analogies

1 Ⓐ Ⓑ Ⓒ Ⓓ	11 Ⓐ Ⓑ Ⓒ Ⓓ	21 Ⓐ Ⓑ Ⓒ Ⓓ
2 Ⓐ Ⓑ Ⓒ Ⓓ	12 Ⓐ Ⓑ Ⓒ Ⓓ	22 Ⓐ Ⓑ Ⓒ Ⓓ
3 Ⓐ Ⓑ Ⓒ Ⓓ	13 Ⓐ Ⓑ Ⓒ Ⓓ	23 Ⓐ Ⓑ Ⓒ Ⓓ
4 Ⓐ Ⓑ Ⓒ Ⓓ	14 Ⓐ Ⓑ Ⓒ Ⓓ	24 Ⓐ Ⓑ Ⓒ Ⓓ
5 Ⓐ Ⓑ Ⓒ Ⓓ	15 Ⓐ Ⓑ Ⓒ Ⓓ	25 Ⓐ Ⓑ Ⓒ Ⓓ
6 Ⓐ Ⓑ Ⓒ Ⓓ	16 Ⓐ Ⓑ Ⓒ Ⓓ	26 Ⓐ Ⓑ Ⓒ Ⓓ
7 Ⓐ Ⓑ Ⓒ Ⓓ	17 Ⓐ Ⓑ Ⓒ Ⓓ	27 Ⓐ Ⓑ Ⓒ Ⓓ
8 Ⓐ Ⓑ Ⓒ Ⓓ	18 Ⓐ Ⓑ Ⓒ Ⓓ	28 Ⓐ Ⓑ Ⓒ Ⓓ
9 Ⓐ Ⓑ Ⓒ Ⓓ	19 Ⓐ Ⓑ Ⓒ Ⓓ	29 Ⓐ Ⓑ Ⓒ Ⓓ
10 Ⓐ Ⓑ Ⓒ Ⓓ	20 Ⓐ Ⓑ Ⓒ Ⓓ	

Verbal Ability: Sentence Completions

30 Ⓐ Ⓑ Ⓒ Ⓓ	40 Ⓐ Ⓑ Ⓒ Ⓓ	50 Ⓐ Ⓑ Ⓒ Ⓓ
31 Ⓐ Ⓑ Ⓒ Ⓓ	41 Ⓐ Ⓑ Ⓒ Ⓓ	51 Ⓐ Ⓑ Ⓒ Ⓓ
32 Ⓐ Ⓑ Ⓒ Ⓓ	42 Ⓐ Ⓑ Ⓒ Ⓓ	52 Ⓐ Ⓑ Ⓒ Ⓓ
33 Ⓐ Ⓑ Ⓒ Ⓓ	43 Ⓐ Ⓑ Ⓒ Ⓓ	53 Ⓐ Ⓑ Ⓒ Ⓓ
34 Ⓐ Ⓑ Ⓒ Ⓓ	44 Ⓐ Ⓑ Ⓒ Ⓓ	54 Ⓐ Ⓑ Ⓒ Ⓓ
35 Ⓐ Ⓑ Ⓒ Ⓓ	45 Ⓐ Ⓑ Ⓒ Ⓓ	55 Ⓐ Ⓑ Ⓒ Ⓓ
36 Ⓐ Ⓑ Ⓒ Ⓓ	46 Ⓐ Ⓑ Ⓒ Ⓓ	56 Ⓐ Ⓑ Ⓒ Ⓓ
37 Ⓐ Ⓑ Ⓒ Ⓓ	47 Ⓐ Ⓑ Ⓒ Ⓓ	57 Ⓐ Ⓑ Ⓒ Ⓓ
38 Ⓐ Ⓑ Ⓒ Ⓓ	48 Ⓐ Ⓑ Ⓒ Ⓓ	58 Ⓐ Ⓑ Ⓒ Ⓓ
39 Ⓐ Ⓑ Ⓒ Ⓓ	49 Ⓐ Ⓑ Ⓒ Ⓓ	

Biology

59 Ⓐ Ⓑ Ⓒ Ⓓ	69 Ⓐ Ⓑ Ⓒ Ⓓ	79 Ⓐ Ⓑ Ⓒ Ⓓ	89 Ⓐ Ⓑ Ⓒ Ⓓ	99 Ⓐ Ⓑ Ⓒ Ⓓ	109 Ⓐ Ⓑ Ⓒ Ⓓ
60 Ⓐ Ⓑ Ⓒ Ⓓ	70 Ⓐ Ⓑ Ⓒ Ⓓ	80 Ⓐ Ⓑ Ⓒ Ⓓ	90 Ⓐ Ⓑ Ⓒ Ⓓ	100 Ⓐ Ⓑ Ⓒ Ⓓ	110 Ⓐ Ⓑ Ⓒ Ⓓ
61 Ⓐ Ⓑ Ⓒ Ⓓ	71 Ⓐ Ⓑ Ⓒ Ⓓ	81 Ⓐ Ⓑ Ⓒ Ⓓ	91 Ⓐ Ⓑ Ⓒ Ⓓ	101 Ⓐ Ⓑ Ⓒ Ⓓ	111 Ⓐ Ⓑ Ⓒ Ⓓ
62 Ⓐ Ⓑ Ⓒ Ⓓ	72 Ⓐ Ⓑ Ⓒ Ⓓ	82 Ⓐ Ⓑ Ⓒ Ⓓ	92 Ⓐ Ⓑ Ⓒ Ⓓ	102 Ⓐ Ⓑ Ⓒ Ⓓ	112 Ⓐ Ⓑ Ⓒ Ⓓ
63 Ⓐ Ⓑ Ⓒ Ⓓ	73 Ⓐ Ⓑ Ⓒ Ⓓ	83 Ⓐ Ⓑ Ⓒ Ⓓ	93 Ⓐ Ⓑ Ⓒ Ⓓ	103 Ⓐ Ⓑ Ⓒ Ⓓ	113 Ⓐ Ⓑ Ⓒ Ⓓ
64 Ⓐ Ⓑ Ⓒ Ⓓ	74 Ⓐ Ⓑ Ⓒ Ⓓ	84 Ⓐ Ⓑ Ⓒ Ⓓ	94 Ⓐ Ⓑ Ⓒ Ⓓ	104 Ⓐ Ⓑ Ⓒ Ⓓ	114 Ⓐ Ⓑ Ⓒ Ⓓ
65 Ⓐ Ⓑ Ⓒ Ⓓ	75 Ⓐ Ⓑ Ⓒ Ⓓ	85 Ⓐ Ⓑ Ⓒ Ⓓ	95 Ⓐ Ⓑ Ⓒ Ⓓ	105 Ⓐ Ⓑ Ⓒ Ⓓ	115 Ⓐ Ⓑ Ⓒ Ⓓ
66 Ⓐ Ⓑ Ⓒ Ⓓ	76 Ⓐ Ⓑ Ⓒ Ⓓ	86 Ⓐ Ⓑ Ⓒ Ⓓ	96 Ⓐ Ⓑ Ⓒ Ⓓ	106 Ⓐ Ⓑ Ⓒ Ⓓ	116 Ⓐ Ⓑ Ⓒ Ⓓ
67 Ⓐ Ⓑ Ⓒ Ⓓ	77 Ⓐ Ⓑ Ⓒ Ⓓ	87 Ⓐ Ⓑ Ⓒ Ⓓ	97 Ⓐ Ⓑ Ⓒ Ⓓ	107 Ⓐ Ⓑ Ⓒ Ⓓ	
68 Ⓐ Ⓑ Ⓒ Ⓓ	78 Ⓐ Ⓑ Ⓒ Ⓓ	88 Ⓐ Ⓑ Ⓒ Ⓓ	98 Ⓐ Ⓑ Ⓒ Ⓓ	108 Ⓐ Ⓑ Ⓒ Ⓓ	

Reading Comprehension

117 Ⓐ Ⓑ Ⓒ Ⓓ	127 Ⓐ Ⓑ Ⓒ Ⓓ	137 Ⓐ Ⓑ Ⓒ Ⓓ	147 Ⓐ Ⓑ Ⓒ Ⓓ	157 Ⓐ Ⓑ Ⓒ Ⓓ
118 Ⓐ Ⓑ Ⓒ Ⓓ	128 Ⓐ Ⓑ Ⓒ Ⓓ	138 Ⓐ Ⓑ Ⓒ Ⓓ	148 Ⓐ Ⓑ Ⓒ Ⓓ	158 Ⓐ Ⓑ Ⓒ Ⓓ
119 Ⓐ Ⓑ Ⓒ Ⓓ	129 Ⓐ Ⓑ Ⓒ Ⓓ	139 Ⓐ Ⓑ Ⓒ Ⓓ	149 Ⓐ Ⓑ Ⓒ Ⓓ	159 Ⓐ Ⓑ Ⓒ Ⓓ
120 Ⓐ Ⓑ Ⓒ Ⓓ	130 Ⓐ Ⓑ Ⓒ Ⓓ	140 Ⓐ Ⓑ Ⓒ Ⓓ	150 Ⓐ Ⓑ Ⓒ Ⓓ	160 Ⓐ Ⓑ Ⓒ Ⓓ
121 Ⓐ Ⓑ Ⓒ Ⓓ	131 Ⓐ Ⓑ Ⓒ Ⓓ	141 Ⓐ Ⓑ Ⓒ Ⓓ	151 Ⓐ Ⓑ Ⓒ Ⓓ	161 Ⓐ Ⓑ Ⓒ Ⓓ
122 Ⓐ Ⓑ Ⓒ Ⓓ	132 Ⓐ Ⓑ Ⓒ Ⓓ	142 Ⓐ Ⓑ Ⓒ Ⓓ	152 Ⓐ Ⓑ Ⓒ Ⓓ	162 Ⓐ Ⓑ Ⓒ Ⓓ
123 Ⓐ Ⓑ Ⓒ Ⓓ	133 Ⓐ Ⓑ Ⓒ Ⓓ	143 Ⓐ Ⓑ Ⓒ Ⓓ	153 Ⓐ Ⓑ Ⓒ Ⓓ	163 Ⓐ Ⓑ Ⓒ Ⓓ
124 Ⓐ Ⓑ Ⓒ Ⓓ	134 Ⓐ Ⓑ Ⓒ Ⓓ	144 Ⓐ Ⓑ Ⓒ Ⓓ	154 Ⓐ Ⓑ Ⓒ Ⓓ	164 Ⓐ Ⓑ Ⓒ Ⓓ
125 Ⓐ Ⓑ Ⓒ Ⓓ	135 Ⓐ Ⓑ Ⓒ Ⓓ	145 Ⓐ Ⓑ Ⓒ Ⓓ	155 Ⓐ Ⓑ Ⓒ Ⓓ	165 Ⓐ Ⓑ Ⓒ Ⓓ
126 Ⓐ Ⓑ Ⓒ Ⓓ	136 Ⓐ Ⓑ Ⓒ Ⓓ	146 Ⓐ Ⓑ Ⓒ Ⓓ	156 Ⓐ Ⓑ Ⓒ Ⓓ	

CUT HERE

Quantitative Ability

166 Ⓐ Ⓑ Ⓒ Ⓓ	176 Ⓐ Ⓑ Ⓒ Ⓓ	186 Ⓐ Ⓑ Ⓒ Ⓓ	196 Ⓐ Ⓑ Ⓒ Ⓓ	206 Ⓐ Ⓑ Ⓒ Ⓓ
167 Ⓐ Ⓑ Ⓒ Ⓓ	177 Ⓐ Ⓑ Ⓒ Ⓓ	187 Ⓐ Ⓑ Ⓒ Ⓓ	197 Ⓐ Ⓑ Ⓒ Ⓓ	207 Ⓐ Ⓑ Ⓒ Ⓓ
168 Ⓐ Ⓑ Ⓒ Ⓓ	178 Ⓐ Ⓑ Ⓒ Ⓓ	188 Ⓐ Ⓑ Ⓒ Ⓓ	198 Ⓐ Ⓑ Ⓒ Ⓓ	208 Ⓐ Ⓑ Ⓒ Ⓓ
169 Ⓐ Ⓑ Ⓒ Ⓓ	179 Ⓐ Ⓑ Ⓒ Ⓓ	189 Ⓐ Ⓑ Ⓒ Ⓓ	199 Ⓐ Ⓑ Ⓒ Ⓓ	209 Ⓐ Ⓑ Ⓒ Ⓓ
170 Ⓐ Ⓑ Ⓒ Ⓓ	180 Ⓐ Ⓑ Ⓒ Ⓓ	190 Ⓐ Ⓑ Ⓒ Ⓓ	200 Ⓐ Ⓑ Ⓒ Ⓓ	210 Ⓐ Ⓑ Ⓒ Ⓓ
171 Ⓐ Ⓑ Ⓒ Ⓓ	181 Ⓐ Ⓑ Ⓒ Ⓓ	191 Ⓐ Ⓑ Ⓒ Ⓓ	201 Ⓐ Ⓑ Ⓒ Ⓓ	211 Ⓐ Ⓑ Ⓒ Ⓓ
172 Ⓐ Ⓑ Ⓒ Ⓓ	182 Ⓐ Ⓑ Ⓒ Ⓓ	192 Ⓐ Ⓑ Ⓒ Ⓓ	202 Ⓐ Ⓑ Ⓒ Ⓓ	212 Ⓐ Ⓑ Ⓒ Ⓓ
173 Ⓐ Ⓑ Ⓒ Ⓓ	183 Ⓐ Ⓑ Ⓒ Ⓓ	193 Ⓐ Ⓑ Ⓒ Ⓓ	203 Ⓐ Ⓑ Ⓒ Ⓓ	213 Ⓐ Ⓑ Ⓒ Ⓓ
174 Ⓐ Ⓑ Ⓒ Ⓓ	184 Ⓐ Ⓑ Ⓒ Ⓓ	194 Ⓐ Ⓑ Ⓒ Ⓓ	204 Ⓐ Ⓑ Ⓒ Ⓓ	
175 Ⓐ Ⓑ Ⓒ Ⓓ	185 Ⓐ Ⓑ Ⓒ Ⓓ	195 Ⓐ Ⓑ Ⓒ Ⓓ	205 Ⓐ Ⓑ Ⓒ Ⓓ	

Chemistry

214 Ⓐ Ⓑ Ⓒ Ⓓ	224 Ⓐ Ⓑ Ⓒ Ⓓ	234 Ⓐ Ⓑ Ⓒ Ⓓ	244 Ⓐ Ⓑ Ⓒ Ⓓ	254 Ⓐ Ⓑ Ⓒ Ⓓ	264 Ⓐ Ⓑ Ⓒ Ⓓ
215 Ⓐ Ⓑ Ⓒ Ⓓ	225 Ⓐ Ⓑ Ⓒ Ⓓ	235 Ⓐ Ⓑ Ⓒ Ⓓ	245 Ⓐ Ⓑ Ⓒ Ⓓ	255 Ⓐ Ⓑ Ⓒ Ⓓ	265 Ⓐ Ⓑ Ⓒ Ⓓ
216 Ⓐ Ⓑ Ⓒ Ⓓ	226 Ⓐ Ⓑ Ⓒ Ⓓ	236 Ⓐ Ⓑ Ⓒ Ⓓ	246 Ⓐ Ⓑ Ⓒ Ⓓ	256 Ⓐ Ⓑ Ⓒ Ⓓ	266 Ⓐ Ⓑ Ⓒ Ⓓ
217 Ⓐ Ⓑ Ⓒ Ⓓ	227 Ⓐ Ⓑ Ⓒ Ⓓ	237 Ⓐ Ⓑ Ⓒ Ⓓ	247 Ⓐ Ⓑ Ⓒ Ⓓ	257 Ⓐ Ⓑ Ⓒ Ⓓ	267 Ⓐ Ⓑ Ⓒ Ⓓ
218 Ⓐ Ⓑ Ⓒ Ⓓ	228 Ⓐ Ⓑ Ⓒ Ⓓ	238 Ⓐ Ⓑ Ⓒ Ⓓ	248 Ⓐ Ⓑ Ⓒ Ⓓ	258 Ⓐ Ⓑ Ⓒ Ⓓ	268 Ⓐ Ⓑ Ⓒ Ⓓ
219 Ⓐ Ⓑ Ⓒ Ⓓ	229 Ⓐ Ⓑ Ⓒ Ⓓ	239 Ⓐ Ⓑ Ⓒ Ⓓ	249 Ⓐ Ⓑ Ⓒ Ⓓ	259 Ⓐ Ⓑ Ⓒ Ⓓ	269 Ⓐ Ⓑ Ⓒ Ⓓ
220 Ⓐ Ⓑ Ⓒ Ⓓ	230 Ⓐ Ⓑ Ⓒ Ⓓ	240 Ⓐ Ⓑ Ⓒ Ⓓ	250 Ⓐ Ⓑ Ⓒ Ⓓ	260 Ⓐ Ⓑ Ⓒ Ⓓ	270 Ⓐ Ⓑ Ⓒ Ⓓ
221 Ⓐ Ⓑ Ⓒ Ⓓ	231 Ⓐ Ⓑ Ⓒ Ⓓ	241 Ⓐ Ⓑ Ⓒ Ⓓ	251 Ⓐ Ⓑ Ⓒ Ⓓ	261 Ⓐ Ⓑ Ⓒ Ⓓ	271 Ⓐ Ⓑ Ⓒ Ⓓ
222 Ⓐ Ⓑ Ⓒ Ⓓ	232 Ⓐ Ⓑ Ⓒ Ⓓ	242 Ⓐ Ⓑ Ⓒ Ⓓ	252 Ⓐ Ⓑ Ⓒ Ⓓ	262 Ⓐ Ⓑ Ⓒ Ⓓ	
223 Ⓐ Ⓑ Ⓒ Ⓓ	233 Ⓐ Ⓑ Ⓒ Ⓓ	243 Ⓐ Ⓑ Ⓒ Ⓓ	253 Ⓐ Ⓑ Ⓒ Ⓓ	263 Ⓐ Ⓑ Ⓒ Ⓓ	

Critical Thinking Essay

Write your essay on lined paper.

Verbal Ability: Analogies

Directions: Select the word that best completes the analogy.

1. TALK : SHOUT :: DISLIKE :

   A. scream
   B. detest
   C. frighten
   D. admire

2. CONDUCTOR : ORCHESTRA :: SHEPHERD :

   A. film
   B. canine
   C. control
   D. flock

3. TOOL : DRILL :: POEM :

   A. popular song
   B. sewing machine
   C. nursery rhyme
   D. mystery story

4. TENSION : STRESS :: VIRUS :

   A. living
   B. disease
   C. bacteria
   D. immunity

5. MISER : MONEY :: GLUTTON :

   A. food
   B. envy
   C. literature
   D. nutrients

6. PROUD : HUMBLE :: FUNNY :

   A. intellectual
   B. energetic
   C. serious
   D. confident

7. BOUQUET : VASE :: GARBAGE :

   A. urn
   B. stomach
   C. sewer
   D. carton

8. CANDID : TRUTHFUL :: ANGRY :

   A. harmony
   B. quarrelsome
   C. connected
   D. unpleasant

9. LINK : UNDO :: FORGET :

   A. remember
   B. think
   C. careless
   D. guess

10. BAROMETER : PRESSURE :: RULER :

    A. cutting
    B. length
    C. thickness
    D. pliers

11. SANCTUARY : REFUGE :: IMPRISONMENT :

    A. hand
    B. punishment
    C. country
    D. helium

12. BATHING : CLEANLINESS :: SCHOOLING :

    A. harm
    B. education
    C. kindness
    D. chef

GO ON TO THE NEXT PAGE

13. SMILING : HAPPINESS :: SCOWLING :

    A. running
    B. travel
    C. breakfast
    D. displeasure

14. HANDS : CLOCK :: LEGS :

    A. music
    B. court
    C. body
    D. tiger

15. QUARTER : DOLLAR :: WEEK :

    A. yawn
    B. month
    C. money
    D. lift

16. DANCER : ENSEMBLE :: STUDENT :

    A. milk
    B. class
    C. mountain
    D. flock

17. ANARCHIST : DISORDER :: PACIFIST :

    A. boredom
    B. year
    C. best
    D. peace

18. DOCTOR : HEALING :: AUTHOR :

    A. guard
    B. paleontologist
    C. writing
    D. computer

19. POLICE : LAW :: CLERGY :

    A. den
    B. conductor
    C. library
    D. religion

20. COOL : FRIGID :: DISLIKE :

    A. assembly
    B. cold
    C. water
    D. detest

21. CRUMB : LOAF :: PUDDLE :

    A. canvas
    B. ocean
    C. sound
    D. fall

22. BREEZE : GALE :: SNOWFLAKE :

    A. rain
    B. malevolent
    C. hostile
    D. blizzard

23. CROISSANT : PASTRY :: HAIKU :

    A. fish
    B. peach
    C. poem
    D. knife

24. ROMANCE : NOVEL :: RAP :

    A. blessing
    B. music
    C. immoral
    D. friction

25. TANKER : SHIP :: MINIVAN :

    A. sail
    B. trucker
    C. automobile
    D. horse

26. WHALE : OCEAN :: BEE :

    A. crowd
    B. steeple
    C. court
    D. hive

27. ACTOR : STAGE :: TEACHER :

A. doctor
B. bench
C. garage
D. classroom

28. TYRANT : CRUELTY :: SYCOPHANT :

A. speaker
B. despot
C. award
D. flattery

29. SLOTH : LAZINESS :: INSOMNIAC :

A. genteel
B. sleeplessness
C. vulgar
D. tired

GO ON TO THE NEXT PAGE

Verbal Ability: Sentence Completions

Directions: Select the word or words that best complete the sentence.

30. It was never my intention to _____ her in the show, since I have a lot of respect for her.

    A. supplant

    B. unite

    C. recall

    D. stop

31. She was able to create her best work, living in her _____ cottage by the canal.

    A. old

    B. famous

    C. quaint

    D. rural

32. Not a day goes by that I don't appreciate that he's a major _____ to this company.

    A. investor

    B. visitor

    C. asset

    D. blight

33. He tried to _____ his fear, but the specter of failure continued to _____ him.

    A. integrate . . . . . enjoin

    B. deal with . . . . . please

    C. submit to . . . . . slow

    D. suppress . . . . . haunt

34. It is a well-known fact that the visual acuity of certain dogs is extremely _____, while other dogs are known for their unparalleled hearing.

    A. wide

    B. keen

    C. genuine

    D. woeful

35. It was a strange _____ that frequented the restaurant, from the very wealthy to the down-and-outers.

    A. clientele

    B. jury

    C. club

    D. happenstance

36. They grew tired of their neighbors, who often _____ upon their good graces and forced them to give up some of their privacy.

    A. waited

    B. traveled

    C. cautioned

    D. infringed

37. It was _____ the way the teacher always knew who had done the homework.

    A. immature

    B. uncanny

    C. insincere

    D. welcome

38. I was held spellbound by the mystery, and the _____ between the two main characters.

    A. requests

    B. intrigue

    C. happenings

    D. corruption

39. Cut out that _____, I can barely understand what you're saying!

    A. filibustering

    B. gait

    C. jargon

    D. smiling

40. The cost of war has become _____, especially when you consider the loss of airplanes, tanks, and trucks, not to mention the loss of manpower.

    A. unusual

    B. exorbitant

    C. superior

    D. harmful

41. His father was so incensed, that the poor child _____ in the corner, awaiting the _____ of the anger.

    A. moved . . . . . beginning

    B. fell . . . . . horror

    C. cowered . . . . . abatement

    D. walked . . . . . strength

42. She had never had a peach so _____, she thought, as the juice ran down her chin.

    A. pale
    B. rare
    C. sharp
    D. succulent

43. "Boring," said the art critic, "I've never seen work so _____

    A. pedestrian
    B. childish
    C. old
    D. disturbing

44. As they sat in the hospital, they were _____ about what was happening to their friend in surgery.

    A. reluctant
    B. grieving
    C. bored
    D. apprehensive

45. The professor could not have been more _____ about his insistence with his class about their coming on time.

    A. cautious
    B. emphatic
    C. diplomatic
    D. immediate

46. The new supervisor worked hard to eliminate the workers' _____, and hoped to build productivity.

    A. tedium
    B. insecurity
    C. regret
    D. enjoyment

47. When you've completed your essay, please _____ a list of the resources you've used from the library.

    A. emend
    B. intend
    C. append
    D. explain

48. As a result of the numerous accidents, the construction site was under _____ by the local inspectors.

    A. repair
    B. patrol
    C. attack
    D. scrutiny

49. Whenever there's a new administration, the politicians want to _____ many of the similar assistance programs.

    A. clear
    B. consolidate
    C. change
    D. create

50. The basement leaked, the roof sagged, and the house was cold. Obviously, the architect was _____.

    A. unsteady
    B. uninspired
    C. lazy
    D. inept

51. Although they lost the battle, the defeated general asked for _____ for his captured men.

    A. amnesty
    B. improvement
    C. shame
    D. supplies

52. They weren't sure who had _____ the money, so the manager asked for a full investigation of all the employees.

    A. purchased
    B. arranged
    C. pilfered
    D. drained

53. As soon as the laughter began to _____, he quickly began his next joke.

    A. start
    B. wane
    C. reappear
    D. rise

GO ON TO THE NEXT PAGE

54. The author continued to write, despite his fame and fortune, not for the _____ or financial gain, but because he felt driven.

- **A.** money
- **B.** exercise
- **C.** style
- **D.** kudos

55. It's not so easy to _____ someone who _____ undying support to you.

- **A.** spurn . . . . . pledges
- **B.** meet . . . . . wants
- **C.** scare . . . . . unleashes
- **D.** praise . . . . . pleads

56. A week at the spa left her feeling _____ and she thought she'd go back again, as soon as she had the free time.

- **A.** tired
- **B.** hungry
- **C.** rejuvenated
- **D.** empty

57. I can only say that your decision was _____ and he deserved the punishment.

- **A.** wasteful
- **B.** expedient
- **C.** wicked
- **D.** thoughtful

58. The president was uncomfortable with his position, and therefore his speech sounded _____.

- **A.** loquacious
- **B.** wary
- **C.** unusual
- **D.** stilted

Biology

Directions: Select the choice that best answers the following questions.

59. A scientific "theory," such as the Theory of Evolution, is based on

   A. the results of a single scientific investigation.

   B. the results of numerous, peer-reviewed scientific investigations.

   C. hypotheses put forth by respected scientists.

   D. assumptions.

60. When constructing a graph of scientific data, the _____ should be placed along the x-axis and the _____ should be placed along the y-axis.

   A. experimental variable; control variable

   B. control variable; experimental variable

   C. dependent variable; independent variable

   D. independent variable; dependent variable

61. The plasma membranes of plant and animal cells allow the cells to regulate their interactions with the surrounding environment because the plasma membranes are

   A. differentially permeable.

   B. permeable to all substances.

   C. permeable to water only.

   D. not permeable.

62. Enzymes can be described as

   A. proteins that determine our physical characteristics.

   B. hormones that determine our physical characteristics.

   C. proteins that catalyze biochemical reactions.

   D. hormones that catalyze biochemical reactions.

63. Which of the following organisms is prokaryotic?

   A. yeast

   B. fungus

   C. bacteria

   D. all of the above

64. Protein synthesis involves

   A. transcription of mRNA from DNA at ribosomes in the cytoplasm, followed by translation of mRNA into a polypeptide in the nucleus.

   B. transcription of mRNA from DNA in the nucleus, followed by translation of mRNA into a polypeptide in the nucleus.

   C. transcription of mRNA from DNA at ribosomes in the cytoplasm, followed by translation of mRNA into a polypeptide at ribosomes in the cytoplasm.

   D. transcription of mRNA from DNA in the nucleus, followed by translation of mRNA into a polypeptide at ribosomes in the cytoplasm.

65. Photosynthetic organisms produce their own food by

   A. using chemical energy in glucose molecules to produce ATP.

   B. using chemical energy in glucose to produce oxygen.

   C. using light energy, carbon dioxide, and water to produce glucose.

   D. using light energy, carbon dioxide, and water to produce ATP.

66. Which of the organisms listed below does not have mitochondria in its cells?

   A. *Escherichia coli*

   B. amoeba

   C. sponge

   D. corn plant

67. Cellular respiration produces energy for organisms through

   A. the breakdown of glucose molecules to produce ATP.

   B. the breakdown of ATP to produce glucose molecules.

   C. the breakdown of ATP to produce starch.

   D. the breakdown of carbon dioxide and water to produce glucose.

GO ON TO THE NEXT PAGE

68. Which of the following combinations of gametes would be produced by an individual with 18 chromosomes in each of its somatic cells?

  A. 2 gametes, each with 18 chromosomes

  B. 2 gametes, each with 9 chromosomes

  C. 4 gametes, each with 18 chromosomes

  D. 4 gametes, each with 9 chromosomes

69. The genotype of an individual is established

  A. at fertilization.

  B. in the four-cell stage.

  C. in the eight-cell stage.

  D. just before birth.

70. If long tails are dominant to short tails in mice, what proportion of the offspring from a cross between a heterozygous mother and a homozygous recessive father would have short tails?

  A. 0%

  B. 25%

  C. 50%

  D. 100%

71. Red-green color-blindness is a sex-linked recessive trait. Which of the following offspring could be produced by a man with normal vision and a color-blind woman?

  A. All children would have normal vision.

  B. Daughters would have normal vision; sons would be color-blind.

  C. Sons would have normal vision; daughters would be color-blind.

  D. All children would be color-blind.

72. When a DNA molecule is replicated prior to cell division

  A. the two resulting molecules each consist of two new strands of DNA.

  B. the two resulting molecules each consist of one old strand and one new strand.

  C. one molecule consists of two old strands and the other molecule consists of two new strands.

  D. the two resulting molecules each contain a random mix of old and new strands.

73. Accurate transcription of an mRNA molecule from a DNA template occurs because

  A. of the phenomenon of complementary base-pairing.

  B. both DNA and RNA have the same four nitrogenous bases.

  C. both DNA and mRNA are double-stranded molecules.

  D. DNA polymerase fixes any errors that occur during transcription.

74. Genetic transformation can be used to

  A. produce a DNA fingerprint of an individual.

  B. grow cells in tissue culture.

  C. create cloned cells.

  D. introduce foreign DNA into an organism.

75. DNA fingerprinting has been used to

  A. implicate suspects in a criminal investigation.

  B. suggest paternity in child support cases.

  C. identify missing individuals.

  D. all of the above

76. The process by which an agricultural field is left fallow and allowed to return to its natural state is referred to as

  A. biological magnification.

  B. succession.

  C. ecosystem cycling.

  D. biological cycling.

77. The incidence of skin cancer worldwide is on the rise and likely to continue increasing due to

  A. the destruction of the ozone layer by chlorofluorocarbons.

  B. global warming caused by excessive levels of carbon dioxide in the atmosphere as a result of the burning of fossil fuels.

  C. acid rain caused by an increase in the levels of nitric acid and sulfuric acid in the atmosphere as a result of high industry emissions of nitrous oxide and sulfur dioxide.

  D. the melting of the polar ice caps as a result of increasing global temperatures.

78. In a typical food web, the organisms responsible for the breakdown of organic matter and recycling of nutrients back into the ecosystem are referred to as

A. producers.
B. autotrophs.
C. heterotrophs.
D. decomposers.

79. A change in the relative frequency of alleles or genotypes in a population over time is referred to as

A. genetic drift.
B. natural selection.
C. evolution.
D. relative fitness.

80. Differences in relative reproductive fitness among individuals in a population form the basis for

A. natural selection.
B. gene pools.
C. mutation rates.
D. genetic drift.

81. If two groups within a population become geographically and, therefore, reproductively isolated from each other, over time they are likely to

A. share a gene pool.
B. go extinct.
C. stop evolving.
D. form two separate species.

82. The field of comparative embryology has provided evidence in support of the theory of evolution by showing that

A. all vertebrate organisms start out as embryos.
B. all vertebrate organisms look the same as embryos.
C. related vertebrate organisms go through similar stages during embryonic development.
D. related vertebrate organisms have the same gestation period.

83. The protein coat surrounding the genetic material in viruses is referred to as a

A. capsule.
B. capsid.
C. phage.
D. nucleus.

84. Which of the following organisms requires a host cell, because it cannot make proteins on its own?

A. parasite
B. bacteria
C. protozoa
D. virus

85. The earliest photosynthesizing organisms are thought to be

A. algae.
B. mosses.
C. euglenoids.
D. cyanobacteria.

86. Which method used for sterilizing medical equipment has the highest sporicidal activity?

A. exposure to ultraviolet radiation
B. exposure to ionizing radiation
C. use of pressurized steam
D. pasteurization

87. Amoebas move about through the use of

A. cilia.
B. flagella.
C. cytoplasmic streaming.
D. pseudopodia.

88. Transduction of bacterial cells involves

A. the introduction of foreign DNA into a bacterial cell through the use of a bacteriophage.
B. the introduction of foreign DNA into a bacterial cell through the use of a plasmid.
C. the introduction of foreign DNA into a bacterial cell through formation of a tube connecting the cell with another bacterial cell.
D. the introduction of foreign DNA into a bacterial cell through the use of electroporation.

Practice Test 5

GO ON TO THE NEXT PAGE

89. For which of the following diseases would the taking of antibiotics be helpful?

    A. influenza
    B. measles
    C. pertussis
    D. chicken pox

90. A common disease picked up by backpackers is giardiasis. This disease, which affects the gastrointestinal tract, is caused by a

    A. protozoan.
    B. bacteria.
    C. fungus.
    D. worm.

91. Fleas can transfer Bubonic plague from one individual to another because Bubonic plague is a bacterial disease that affects the

    A. skin.
    B. blood.
    C. gastrointestinal system.
    D. respiratory system.

92. Bacillus thuringiensis (Bt) is an insecticide considered acceptable for use by organic farmers. This natural insecticide is made from

    A. soil particles.
    B. chrysanthemum flowers.
    C. a fungus.
    D. a bacteria.

93. What do botulism, typhoid fever, and leprosy all have in common?

    A. They are all caused by bacteria.
    B. They are all caused by viruses.
    C. They all affect the skin.
    D. They all affect the gastrointestinal tract.

94. The microorganisms used to impart flavor to Roquefort cheese are

    A. bacteria.
    B. fungi.
    C. protozoa.
    D. yeast.

95. Failure to take the entire prescription of antibiotics for a bacterial infection may result in

    A. enhanced immunity if that strain of bacteria is encountered again.
    B. the immune system taking over and producing more antibodies against the invading bacteria.
    C. a faster buildup of the normal, non-pathogenic bacterial strains present in the body.
    D. the development of an antibiotic-resistant strain of bacteria.

96. The coordinated function of the various organ systems in the human body allows the body's internal environment to remain relatively stable despite changes in the external environment. This internal body stability is referred to as

    A. homogeneity.
    B. homeostasis.
    C. homeothermy.
    D. homeopathy.

97. The system responsible for coordinating communication between different regions of the human body and between the body and the external environment is the

    A. circulatory system.
    B. endocrine system.
    C. nervous system.
    D. excretory system.

98. In humans, oxygen is taken in and delivered throughout the body and carbon dioxide is removed from the cells of the body and expelled through the coordination of which of the following two major systems?

    A. circulatory system and respiratory system
    B. circulatory system and endocrine system
    C. respiratory system and endocrine system
    D. respiratory system and digestive system

99. The average life span of a human red blood cell is

    A. 30 days.
    B. 60 days.
    C. 90 days.
    D. 120 days.

100. A patient found to have a higher than normal white blood cell count is most likely

   A. anemic.
   B. at a high risk for contracting an infection.
   C. trying to fight off an infection.
   D. bleeding internally.

101. Blood flows from the heart to the lungs through the _____ and returns from the lungs to the heart through the _____.

   A. pulmonary veins; pulmonary arteries
   B. pulmonary arteries; pulmonary veins
   C. pulmonary veins; carotid artery
   D. pulmonary artery; carotid artery

102. A person's heart rate can be measured by

   A. taking his blood pressure.
   B. monitoring the diastole phase of his blood pressure.
   C. taking his pulse.
   D. monitoring the systole phase of his blood pressure.

103. In humans, pockets of lymphatic tissue in the pharynx, which function to trap and filter microorganisms, are referred to as

   A. lymph nodes.
   B. tonsils.
   C. epiglottis.
   D. alveoli.

104. Which of the following statements regarding dietary fats is incorrect?

   A. Fats help insulate the human body against cold temperatures.
   B. Fats help protect the internal organs from injury.
   C. Fats are not considered an essential nutrient in the human diet.
   D. Fats aid in the metabolism of vitamins A, D, and E.

105. The macromolecules most often used directly as an energy source in humans are

   A. fats.
   B. carbohydrates.
   C. proteins.
   D. vitamins.

106. During digestion, humans absorb nucleotides from plant and animal tissues consumed. These nucleotides are then used by the human body for synthesizing

   A. ATP.
   B. proteins.
   C. DNA and RNA.
   D. lipids.

107. The digestion of starch molecules begins in the mouth with the production of which of the following salivary enzymes?

   A. amylase
   B. protease
   C. lipase
   D. polymerase

108. In the human digestive system, most chemical digestion takes place in the

   A. mouth.
   B. stomach.
   C. small intestine.
   D. large intestine.

109. The majority of metabolic wastes in humans are removed from the body through the

   A. small intestine.
   B. large intestine.
   C. liver.
   D. kidneys.

110. Chemical coordination within the human body takes place through a series of glands that are situated throughout the body. This system of glands is referred to as the

   A. nervous system.
   B. pituitary system.
   C. endocrine system.
   D. lymphatic system.

111. Over-secretion of the hormone thyroxine results in

   A. an unusually high metabolic rate.
   B. cretinism.
   C. myxydema.
   D. diabetes.

GO ON TO THE NEXT PAGE

Practice Test 5

112. Which of the following hormones is responsible for preparing the body for emergencies or other stressful situations (i.e., promoting the fight-or-flight response)?

    A. cortisone

    B. cortisol

    C. androgen

    D. epinephrine

113. In human males, meiosis gives rise to

    A. the seminiferous tubules.

    B. sperm.

    C. semen.

    D. the testes.

114. In humans, the brain and the spinal cord comprise the

    A. sympathetic nervous system.

    B. the parasympathetic nervous system.

    C. the peripheral nervous system.

    D. the central nervous system.

115. In the human brain, the function of the hypothalamus is to

    A. control hunger and thirst.

    B. control body temperature.

    C. synthesize hormones for storage in the pituitary gland.

    D. all of the above

116. In humans, the specific immune system response is controlled by

    A. white blood cells called monocytes.

    B. white blood cells called neutrophils.

    C. white blood cells called lymphocytes.

    D. white blood cells called macrophages.

Reading Comprehension

Directions: Read each of the following passages and answer the questions that follow.

Passage 1

(1)   Hummingbirds are small, often brightly colored birds of the family Trochilidae that live exclusively in the Americas. About 12 species are found in North America, but only the ruby-throated hummingbird breeds in eastern North America and is found from Nova Scotia to Florida. The greatest variety and number of species are found in South America. Another hummingbird species is found from southeastern Alaska to northern California.

(2)   Many hummingbirds are minute. But even the giant hummingbird found in western South America, which is the largest known hummingbird, is only about 8 inches long and weighs about two-thirds of an ounce. The smallest species, the bee hummingbird of Cuba and the Isle of Pines, measures slightly more than 5.5 centimeters and weighs about 2 grams.

(3)   Hummingbirds' bodies are compact, with strong muscles. They have wings shaped like blades. Unlike the wings of other birds, hummingbird wings connect to the body only at the shoulder joint, which allows them to fly not only forward but also straight up and down, sideways, and backward. Because of their unusual wings, hummingbirds can also hover in front of flowers so they can suck nectar and find insects. The hummingbird's bill, adapted for securing nectar from certain types of flowers, is usually rather long and always slender; it is curved slightly downward in many species.

(4)   The hummingbird's body feathers are sparse and more like scales than feathers. The unique character of the feathers produces brilliant and iridescent colors, resulting from the refraction of light by the feathers. Pigmentation of other feathers also contributes to the unique color and look. Male and female hummingbirds look alike in some species but different in most species; males of most species are extremely colorful.

(5)   The rate at which a hummingbird beats its wings does not vary, regardless of whether it is flying forward, flying in another direction, or merely hovering. But the rate does vary with the size of the bird — the larger the bird, the lower the rate, ranging from 80 beats per second for the smallest species to 10 times per second for larger species. Researchers have not yet been able to record the speed of the wings of the bee hummingbird but imagine that they beat even faster.

GO ON TO THE NEXT PAGE

(6)   Most hummingbirds, especially the smaller species, emit scratchy, twittering, or squeaky sounds. The wings, and sometimes the tail feathers, often produce humming, hissing, or popping sounds, which apparently function much as do the songs of other birds.

117. According to the passage, where are hummingbirds found?

    A.   throughout the world

    B.   in South America only

    C.   in North America only

    D.   in North America and South America

118. The author indicates that the ruby-throated hummingbird is found

    A.   throughout North America.

    B.   in California.

    C.   in South America.

    D.   in the eastern part of North America.

119. The word "minute" in the second paragraph is closest in meaning to

    A.   extremely tiny.

    B.   extremely fast.

    C.   unique.

    D.   organized.

120. The word "which" in the second paragraph refers to

    A.   western South America.

    B.   the giant hummingbird.

    C.   all hummingbirds.

    D.   Florida hummingbirds.

121. What does the author imply about the rate hummingbirds' wings beat?

    A.   Although the bee hummingbird is the smallest, its wings don't beat the fastest.

    B.   A hummingbird's wings beat faster when it is sucking nectar than when it is just flying.

    C.   The rate is not much different than that of other birds of its size.

    D.   The speed at which a bee hummingbird's wings beat is not actually known.

122. The author indicates that a hummingbird's wings are different from those of other birds because

    A.   they attach to the body at one point only.

    B.   they attach to the body at more points than other birds.

    C.   they attach and detach from the body.

    D.   they are controlled by a different section of the brain.

123. The author implies that the hummingbird's unique wing structure makes it similar to what type of vehicle?

    A.   a helicopter

    B.   a sea plane

    C.   a jet airplane

    D.   a rocket

124. The word "bill" in the third paragraph is closest in meaning to

    A.   beak.

    B.   body.

    C.   tail.

    D.   wing.

125. The word "sparse" in the fourth paragraph is closest in meaning to

    A.   meager.

    B.   thick.

    C.   fishlike.

    D.   unique.

126. According to the passage, what causes the unique color and look of hummingbirds?

    A.   the color of the feathers

    B.   the structure of the feathers as well as pigmentation

    C.   the rapidity of flight

    D.   the pigmentation of the body

127. The author indicates that hummingbirds emit noise from their

    A.   wing and possibly tail movement.

    B.   unique vocal chords.

    C.   song only.

    D.   wing movement only.

Passage 2

(1)   The term "lichen" refers to any of over 20,000 species of thallophytic plants that consist of a symbiotic association of algae and fungi, plural for alga and fungus. Previously, lichens were classified as single organisms until scientists had the benefit of microscopes, at which time they discovered the association between algae and fungi. Thus, the lichen itself is not an organism, but the morphological and biochemical product of the association. Neither a fungus nor an alga alone can produce a lichen.

(2)   The intimate symbiotic relationship between these two living components of a lichen is said to be mutualistic, meaning that both organisms benefit from the relationship. It is not certain when fungi and algae came together to form lichens for the first time, but it certainly occurred after the mature development of the separate components.

(3)   It appears that the fungus actually gains more benefit from the relationship than does the alga. Algae form simple carbohydrates that, when excreted, are absorbed by fungi cells and transformed into a different carbohydrate. Algae also produce vitamins that the fungi need. Yet, fungi also contribute to the symbiosis by absorbing water vapor from the air and providing shade for the algae, which are more sensitive to light.

(4)   Lichens grow relatively slowly, and it is uncertain how they propagate. Most botanists agree that reproduction is vegetative because portions of an existing lichen break off and fall away to begin a new organism nearby.

(5)   Lichens are hardy organisms, being found in hostile environments where few other organisms can survive. Humans have used lichens as food and as sources of medicine and dye. The presence of lichens is a sign that the atmosphere is pure. Lichens help reduce erosion by stabilizing soil. They also are a major source of food for the caribou and reindeer that live in the extreme north.

128. Which of the following is true about the association of the lichen?

- **A.** The association is more beneficial to the alga.
- **B.** The association is solely of benefit to the fungus.
- **C.** The association is merely a joint living arrangement, with neither organism receiving any benefit from the other.
- **D.** The association is beneficial to each organism, although it provides more benefit to the fungus.

129. The word "previously" in the first paragraph is closest in meaning to

- **A.** currently.
- **B.** formerly.
- **C.** believed.
- **D.** no longer.

GO ON TO THE NEXT PAGE

130. Prior to the invention of microscopes, what did scientists believe about lichens?

    A. The entire plant was an alga.

    B. The entire plant was a fungus.

    C. A lichen constituted a single plant.

    D. The fungus was the catalyst of the association.

131. The word "intimate" in the second paragraph is closest in meaning to

    A. distant.

    B. parasitic.

    C. close.

    D. unusual.

132. The author uses the word "mutualistic" in paragraph two to describe

    A. the fungus's benefits from the association.

    B. the harmful effects of the relationship.

    C. the joint benefit each organism receives from the relationship.

    D. the alga's benefits from the association.

133. The author implies that

    A. neither plant requires carbohydrates to survive.

    B. the fungus manufactures carbohydrates on its own.

    C. the alga receives carbohydrates from the fungus.

    D. the fungus uses the carbohydrates manufactured by the alga.

134. The author states that the relationship between the words "fungus"/"fungi" and "alga"/"algae" is

    A. singular/plural.

    B. compound/complex.

    C. symbiotic/disassociated.

    D. mutual/separate.

135. The author implies that vegetative reproduction means that

    A. vegetables combine with other vegetables.

    B. reproduction occurs using vegetative plant growth.

    C. new organisms are grown from pieces of existing organisms.

    D. propagation occurs slowly.

136. The author states that

    A. fungi are more sensitive to light than algae.

    B. neither plant is sensitive to light.

    C. neither plant individually can thrive in sunlight.

    D. algae are more sensitive to light than fungi.

137. The word "nearby" at the end of paragraph four is closest in meaning to

    A. almost.

    B. completely.

    C. connected.

    D. close.

138. The word "hardy" at the beginning of the last paragraph is closest in meaning to

    A. tender.

    B. ubiquitous.

    C. scarce.

    D. strong.

139. The word "hostile" in the last paragraph is closest in meaning to

    A. unusual.

    B. dry.

    C. harsh.

    D. complex.

140. The author indicates that lichens are beneficial because they

    A. purify the air.

    B. reduce fungi.

    C. destroy algae.

    D. reduce soil erosion.

Passage 3

(1)   Hepatitis C is an illness, unknown until recently, that has been discovered in many individuals. It has been called an epidemic, yet unlike most illnesses with that designation, it is not easily transmitted. It is accurately referred to as epidemic in that so many people have been discovered with the illness, but it is

different in that these people have actually carried the virus for many years. It is only transmitted by direct blood-to-blood contact; casual contact and even sexual contact are not believed to transmit the illness. Hepatitis means an inflammation or infection of the liver. Hepatitis C is generally chronic, as opposed to acute. This means that it continues to affect the patient and is not known to have a sudden onset or recovery.

(2)   The great majority of people infected with the illness either had a blood transfusion before the time that the disease was recognized in donated blood, or experimented with injecting illegal drugs when they were young. Many victims are educated, financially successful males between the ages of 40 and 50 who experimented with intravenous drugs as teenagers. There are frequently no symptoms, so the illness is discovered through routine blood tests. Most commonly, people learn they have the illness when they apply for life insurance or donate blood. The blood test reveals elevated liver enzymes, which could be caused by any form of hepatitis, by abuse of alcohol, or by other causes. Another test is then performed, and the result is learned.

(3)   Because the illness produces no symptoms, it of itself does not affect the victim's life, at least at first. But the constant infection in the liver can eventually lead to cirrhosis of the liver, which is scarring and death of portions of the liver. The cirrhosis in turn can lead to liver cancer and, ultimately, death. Severe cases can be reversed with a liver transplant. Yet, because the virus may exist in the body for more than 20 years before being discovered, after reviewing the condition of the liver, doctors often suggest waiting and periodically checking the condition rather than performing radical treatment procedures. The liver's condition is determined by a biopsy, in which a device is inserted into the liver and its condition is viewed. If there is little or no cirrhosis, it is more likely that treatment will be postponed.

(4)   Treatment frequently causes more discomfort than the illness itself. It consists of some form of chemotherapy. Currently, the most frequent treatment is a combination therapy, with one drug injected three times a week and another taken orally, costing hundreds of dollars a week. The therapy causes the patient to have symptoms similar to influenza, and some patients suffer more than others. Unfortunately, many patients do not respond, or do not respond completely to the therapy. There is no alternative therapy at this time for non-responders, although researchers are continually trying to find a cure.

GO ON TO THE NEXT PAGE

Practice Test 5

141. The author implies that

   A. physicians have been treating patients for
       hepatitis C for over 20 years.
   B. other forms of hepatitis were known before
       the hepatitis C strain was discovered.
   C. hepatitis C is generally seen as an acute
       illness.
   D. hepatitis C is easily transmitted through any
       type of contact.

142. The word "onset" at the end of paragraph one is
closest in meaning to

   A. illness.
   B. termination.
   C. inception.
   D. treatment.

143. The best title for this passage would be

   A. "Treatment Choices for Hepatitis C."
   B. "The History of Different Forms of Hepatitis."
   C. "Hepatitis C — Its Characteristics and
       Treatment."
   D. "The Causes and Symptoms of Hepatitis C."

144. The word "great" at the beginning of paragraph
two is closest in meaning to

   A. vast.
   B. magnificent.
   C. small.
   D. important.

145. The word "routine" in paragraph two is closest in
meaning to

   A. standard.
   B. elevated.
   C. required.
   D. complex.

146. The word "they" in paragraph two refers to

   A. symptoms.
   B. illness.
   C. enzymes.
   D. people.

147. The author implies that

   A. patients usually learn of the illness because
       they have severe symptoms.
   B. liver transplants are a very common form of
       treatment.
   C. many people with hepatitis C were not
       addicts but simply experimented with illegal
       drugs.
   D. people are still in danger of acquiring the
       illness from blood transfusions.

148. The author indicates that a biopsy is performed in
order to

   A. prepare for a liver transplant.
   B. determine whether one has the virus.
   C. learn the degree of damage to the liver.
   D. decide which form of drug to prescribe.

149. The author implies that hepatitis C

   A. attacks rapidly.
   B. does not affect many people.
   C. only rarely results in liver cancer.
   D. attacks the central nervous system.

150. The author states that people sometimes choose
not to take treatment for hepatitis C for all of the
following reasons except

   A. the medicine must be taken intravenously.
   B. the treatment does not work for everybody.
   C. often the level of illness is not severe.
   D. the side effects of the medicine are
       sometimes worse than the symptoms of the
       illness.

151. The word "its" in the third paragraph refers to

   A. device.
   B. liver.
   C. biopsy.
   D. doctor.

Passage 4

(1)   Tube worms live anchored to the sea floor, 1,700

feet below the ocean surface, near natural spring

vents that spew forth water from the earth. They live

off geothermal energy instead of sunlight. There are

two species of the tube worm family, with very different lengths of life and growth rates, but similarities as well.

(2) The slow-growing tube worms are known to live as long as 250 years, making them the longest-living sea invertebrates known. This species lives near cold sea-floor seeps and may not grow at all from one year to the next. Even when they do grow, it is generally from ½ inch to 4 inches per year. In spite of their slow growth, due to their long lives, they can reach 9 feet before they die, although they are thinner than the hot-water worms.

(3) The seeps under the slow-growing tube worms are rich with oily materials. The environment in which they live is slow and peaceful, stable and low-energy. The cold-water seeps and the tube worms that reside there may live hundreds or thousands of years.

(4) In stark contrast, the fast-growing tube worms live a quick and short life, growing rapidly. They attach themselves near hot steaming vents that force water into the sea, growing about 2½ feet a year, and up to 8 feet overall. They live by absorbing sulfur compounds metabolized by bacteria in a symbiotic relationship.

(5) The hot-water vents spew forth scalding water filled with hydrogen sulfide, which the tiny bacteria living in the worms' tissues consume. These

tube worms live a rapid life, with none of the relaxing characteristics of the cold-water tube worms.

152. The word "anchored" in the first sentence is closest in meaning to

A. affixed.
B. contentedly.
C. feeding.
D. above.

153. The expression "spew forth" in the first sentence is closest in meaning to

A. inhale.
B. discharge.
C. control.
D. eliminate.

154. The author implies that a vent and a seep are

A. the same.
B. different in that a vent involves rapid discharge while a seep involves slow discharge.
C. different in that a vent involves discharge while a seep involves intake.
D. different in that a vent involves slow discharge while a seep involves rapid discharge.

155. The passage indicates that the two types of tube worms discussed are

A. from totally different families.
B. different in that one is not a true tube worm at all.
C. from the same family but different species.
D. from the same species and only differ because of habitat.

156. The author states that the cold-water tube worm

A. grows slower than the hot-water tube worm.
B. grows faster than the hot-water tube worm.
C. does not grow as high as the hot-water tube worm.
D. does not live as long as the hot-water tube worm.

GO ON TO THE NEXT PAGE

Practice Test 5

157. The word "stark" in the fourth paragraph is closest in meaning to

    A. complete.

    B. somewhat.

    C. comparative.

    D. interesting.

158. The word "overall" in the fourth paragraph is closest in meaning to

    A. lifetime.

    B. annually.

    C. generally.

    D. rapidly.

159. The word "scalding" in the last paragraph is closest in meaning to

    A. hydrogen-filled.

    B. bacteria-filled.

    C. boiling.

    D. rapidly spewing.

160. The author indicates that the ingredients in the water that comes from the two types of vents are

    A. different only because the heat of the hot vents destroys the oil as it spews forth.

    B. different in that one contains bacteria and the other contains oily materials.

    C. the same.

    D. different in that one contains oily materials and the other contains hydrogen sulfide.

Passage 5

(1)   A new procedure has been developed to treat aneurysms, particularly those that occur near the brain stem, where surgery is dangerous.

(2)   Aneurysms are blood sacs formed by enlargement of the weakened walls of arteries or veins. They are dangerous and, thus, must generally be removed before they cause considerable damage. If one ruptures, it can cause strokes or fatal hemorrhaging, the latter of which occurs in 50 percent of all patients. Before rupturing, an aneurysm frequently shows no sign or symptom that it exists. Brain aneurysms occur in approximately 5 percent of the population. Most patients are between 40 and 65 years old, with hemorrhages most prevalent in those between 50 and 54.

(3)   The new procedure involves inserting a soft, flexible micro-catheter through the femoral artery in the groin area and snaking it up through blood vessels to the brain. Inside the catheter is a small, coiled wire, which can be extruded after it reaches its destination. After the coil is outside the catheter, a low-voltage electrical current is applied, and the coil detaches at a preset solder point. Additional coils are snaked through the catheter and also detached at the site, creating a basket, or metal framework, which causes the blood to clot around it. The micro-catheter is withdrawn, the clot remains, and the healed aneurysm no longer is exposed to the stress that can cause another rupture.

(4)   The procedure lasts two hours, which is half as long as invasive surgery, and recovery time is generally limited to a few days instead of a few weeks. The procedure was discovered in the 1990s, was approved by the U.S. Food and Drug Administration in 1995, and is available in various hospitals where there are advanced neurology departments and specialists trained in the procedure. Many lives have

been saved by use of the procedure, because the alternative would have been to watch and wait rather than risk the hazards of surgery.

161. The author implies that the procedure described is useful for

    A.   all aneurysms.

    B.   aneurysms that occur anywhere in the brain.

    C.   aneurysms that occur near the brain stem only.

    D.   aneurysms that occur near large blood vessels.

162. The word "They" in the first paragraph refers to

    A.   aneurysms.

    B.   brain stems.

    C.   surgeries.

    D.   procedures.

163. The word "considerable" in the first paragraph is closest in meaning to

    A.   slight.

    B.   kind.

    C.   significant.

    D.   recurring.

164. The word "one" in the first paragraph refers to

    A.   brain stem.

    B.   aneurysm.

    C.   procedure.

    D.   surgery.

165. The word "snaking" in the second paragraph is closest in meaning to

    A.   meandering.

    B.   extruding.

    C.   living.

    D.   damaging.

GO ON TO THE NEXT PAGE

Quantitative Ability

Directions: Read each of the questions and select the choice that answers the question.

166. An employee earns $8.25 an hour. In 30 hours, what earnings are made?

    A. $240.00
    B. $247.50
    C. $250.00
    D. $255.75

167. Standing by a pole, a boy $3\frac{1}{2}$ feet tall casts a 6-foot shadow. The pole casts a 24-foot shadow. How tall is the pole?

    A. 14 feet
    B. 18 feet
    C. 28 feet
    D. 41 feet

168. On a map, 1 centimeter represents 4 miles. A distance of 10 miles would be how far apart on the map?

    A. $1\frac{3}{4}$ cm
    B. 2 cm
    C. $2\frac{1}{2}$ cm
    D. 4 cm

169. Roxanne deposited $300 into a savings account earning $5\frac{1}{4}$% annually. What is her balance after one year?

    A. $15.75
    B. $315.00
    C. $315.25
    D. $315.75

170. How much change would you get back from a $20 bill if you purchased 8 CD covers costing $1.59 each?

    A. $7.28
    B. $10.41
    C. $12.00
    D. $18.41

171. If $k(x) = \left(\frac{1}{27}\right)^{-x}$, then $k\left(\frac{1}{3}\right) =$

    A. $\frac{1}{9}$
    B. $\frac{1}{3}$
    C. 3
    D. 9

172. Cards normally sell for $3 each. How much was saved if five cards were purchased on sale for two for $5?

    A. $2.50
    B. $5.00
    C. $12.50
    D. $15.00

173. If $\cos y > 0$ and $\tan y < 0$, then $\angle y$ must lie in which quadrant?

    A. I
    B. II
    C. III
    D. IV

174. Joann ate $\frac{1}{4}$ of a peach pie and divided the remainder of the pie among her four friends. What fraction of the pie did each of her friends receive?

    A. $\frac{1}{3}$
    B. $\frac{7}{12}$
    C. $\frac{3}{16}$
    D. $\frac{1}{8}$

175. If three cans of soup cost $5, how much do ten cans cost?

    A. $15.00
    B. $16.45
    C. $16.67
    D. $17.33

176. In a nut mixture, there are $1\frac{1}{8}$ pounds of almonds, $2\frac{3}{4}$ pounds of cashews, and $3\frac{1}{3}$ pounds of peanuts. The total weight of the mixture is

    A. $6\frac{1}{3}$ pounds

    B. $6\frac{23}{24}$ pounds

    C. $7\frac{5}{24}$ pounds

    D. $7\frac{7}{12}$ pounds

177. What are the x-coordinates of the extreme points of $y = x^3 - 3x + 7$?

    A. $x = 0, 1$

    B. $x = -1, +1$

    C. $x = 1, 3$

    D. $x = -1, 3$

178. If $a + b = 6$, what is the value of $3a + 3b$?

    A.   9

    B.   12

    C.   18

    D.   24

179. What is the value of $8^{\frac{4}{3}}$?

    A.   4

    B.   8

    C.   16

    D.   32

180. If $7p + 5q = -3$, find q when $p = 1$.

    A. -1

    B. -2

    C. $-\frac{8}{7}$

    D. $-\frac{2}{7}$

181. How many minutes are there in one week?

    A.   10,080

    B.   1,440

    C.   420

    D.   168

182. Seven more than 3 times a number is equal to 70. Find the number.

    A.   10

    B.   17

    C.   21

    D.   30

183. If x is a positive integer, solve $x^2 + 6x = 16$.

    A.   2

    B.   4

    C.   8

    D.   10

184. A winter coat is on sale for $150. If the original price was $200, what percent has the coat been discounted?

    A.   50%

    B.   40%

    C.   33%

    D.   25%

185. $\log_{12}1 =$

    A.   0

    B.   2

    C.   6

    D.   12

186. Janice buys a quart of milk and two dozen eggs. If milk costs $1.39 and eggs are $1.28 a dozen, how much change will Janice get back if she pays with a $10 bill?

    A. $3.95

    B. $5.94

    C. $6.05

    D. $7.33

187. What is the amplitude of the function $k(x) = 5 - 3\cos8x$

    A.   2

    B.   3

    C.   5

    D.   8

GO ON TO THE NEXT PAGE

188. A batch of cookies requires 2 cups of milk and 4 eggs. If you have 9 cups of milk and 9 eggs, how many batches of cookies can you make?

    A. 9

    B. 6

    C. 4

    D. 2

189. If $y = 6x^3 - 5x^4$, then $\dfrac{dy}{dx}$

    A. $18x^2 - 20x^3$

    B. $-2x^2$

    C. $-2x$

    D. $3x^2 - 4x^3$

190. Interest earned on an account totals $100. If the interest rate is $7\frac{1}{4}\%$, what is the principal amount?

    A. $725

    B. $1,333

    C. $1,379

    D. $1,428

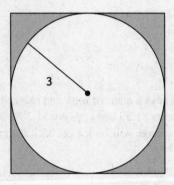

191. The area of the shaded region above is

    A. $9 - 3\pi$

    B. $36 - 3\pi^2$

    C. $36 - 9\pi$

    D. $81 - 9\pi$

192. Which mathematical statement best represents the following?

Six less than a number is four.

    A. $6 = n - 4$

    B. $6 < n + 4$

    C. $6 - n = 4$

    D. $n - 6 = 4$

193. If $b^{-\frac{1}{4}} = 2$, then what is the value of b?

    A. -16

    B. $-\dfrac{1}{16}$

    C. $\dfrac{1}{16}$

    D. 16

194. $\dfrac{5}{16} + \dfrac{9}{24} =$

    A. $\dfrac{11}{16}$

    B. $\dfrac{14}{40}$

    C. $\dfrac{7}{20}$

    D. $\dfrac{14}{48}$

195. Find the area of a triangle whose base is 3 inches less than its height, h.

    A. $\dfrac{1}{2}h^2 - 3h$

    B. $\dfrac{1}{2}h^2 - \dfrac{3}{2}h$

    C. $\dfrac{1}{2}h - \dfrac{3}{2}$

    D. $\dfrac{1}{2}h^2 - 3$

196. If $\log_x 27 = 3$, then what is the value of x?

    A. 1

    B. 3

    C. 9

    D. 18

197. If $2y + 6 = 3y - 2$, then $y =$

    A. -2

    B. 2

    C. 4

    D. 8

198. Round $(2.5)^4$ to the nearest tenth.

    A. 10.0

    B. 25.4

    C. 39.0

    D. 39.1

199. How many blocks with sides 4 inches in length can fit into a crate $3' \times 2' \times 2'$?

A. 3
B. 32
C. 196
D. 324

200. Simplify $(3x^2 + 2x - 5) - (2x^2 - 5) + (4x - 7)$.

A. $x^2 + 6x - 17$
B. $x^2 + 4x - 7$
C. $x^2 + 6x - 2$
D. $x^2 + 6x - 7$

201. If $2^{3x} = 4^{x+1}$, then what is the value of x?

A. 0
B. $\frac{1}{2}$
C. 2
D. 4

202. The expression $1 - \cos^2\theta$ is equivalent to

A. $\tan^2\theta$
B. $\cot^2\theta$
C. $\sin^2\theta$
D. $\csc^2\theta$

203. If $y = \log x$, then $y'(x) =$

A. $\frac{1}{x}$
B. $2\log x$
C. e^x
D. x

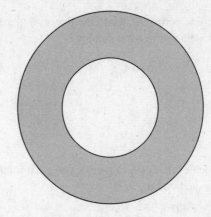

204. The radius of the smaller circle is $\frac{1}{4}$ as long as the larger. What percent of the figure shown above is shaded?

A. $6\frac{1}{4}\%$
B. 25%
C. 75%
D. $93\frac{3}{4}\%$

205. What is the probability of flipping three heads in a row using a fair coin?

A. $\frac{1}{2}$
B. $\frac{2}{3}$
C. $\frac{1}{8}$
D. $\frac{3}{8}$

206. If $\log A = 2$ and $\log B = 3$, then $\log AB =$

A. 5
B. 6
C. 8
D. 9

207. If C represents the constant of integration, then
$$\int \left(4x^3 + 2x\right) dx =$$

A. $12x^4 + 4x^2 + C$
B. $x^4 + x^2 + C$
C. $x^3 + x^2 + x + C$
D. $x^3 + C$

GO ON TO THE NEXT PAGE

208. The line perpendicular to the line $y = -\frac{1}{8}x + 7$ has a slope equal to what number?

A. -8

B. $-\frac{1}{8}$

C. $\frac{1}{8}$

D. 8

209. Which of the following values of x is a solution to the equation $\tan x = 0$?

A. $x = 0°$

B. $x = 30°$

C. $x = 45°$

D. $x = 60°$

210. What is the product of the median and the mode of the following set: $\{1, 2, 2, 5, 7, 7, 7\}$?

A. 4

B. 10

C. 35

D. 49

211. How many different four-digit numbers can be made from the digits 1, 2, 3, and 4 if digits *can* be repeated?

A. 24

B. 64

C. 128

D. 256

212. The expression 5! is equal to what number?

A. 24

B. 120

C. 240

D. 720

213. What is the first derivative of $y = x^2 e^x$?

A. $2xe^x$

B. $x^2 e^x$

C. $2xe^x + 2e^x$

D. $2xe^x + x^2 e^x$

Chemistry

Directions: Select the choice that best answers the following questions. To consult the Periodic Table of the Elements, please go to the Appendix.

$$H - C \equiv N:$$

214. What is the hybridization of the carbon shown in the figure above?

- A. sp^2
- B. sp^3
- C. sp
- D. sp^3d

215. What type of bond is the C–O bond if the electronegativity of carbon is 2.5 and oxygen is 3.5?

- A. ionic
- B. hydrogen
- C. non-polar covalent
- D. polar covalent

216. Dissolution always involves an increase in what?

- A. enthalpy
- B. entropy
- C. free energy
- D. temperature

217. What is shown in the above figure?

- A. isotopes
- B. anomers
- C. isomers
- D. resonance

218. Which combination of acid and conjugate base would be suitable as a buffer?

- A. HCl/NaCl
- B. NaOH/NaCl
- C. HCl/H_3PO_4
- D. $H_2PO_4^-$/HPO_4^{-2}

219. What effect would be greatest for stabilizing a free radical?

- A. presence of a highly electronegative functional group
- B. presence of a good leaving group
- C. a higher order carbon (that is, first degree carbon, second degree, etc.)
- D. resonance through conjugated pi systems

220. What do we call a compound that can act as either an acid or a base?

- A. at equilibrium
- B. amphoteric
- C. anomers
- D. Arrhenius

221. If the C–H bond energy is 414 kJ/mol and H–H is 435 kJ/mol, what is the energy change for the formation of methane in the reaction C (g) + 2 H_2 (g) → CH_4 (g)?

- A. 456 kJ/mol
- B. 21 kJ/mol
- C. 414 kJ/mol
- D. 786 kJ/mol

222. If the molar mass of sodium hydroxide is 40 g/mol, how many grams of sodium hydroxide are found in 10 mL of 0.1 M sodium hydroxide solution?

- A. 0.04 g
- B. 0.4 g
- C. 40 g
- D. 4 g

223. What is the order of the reaction for the rate law Rate = k[Reactants]^2?

- A. 3rd
- B. 2nd
- C. 1st
- D. 0th

GO ON TO THE NEXT PAGE

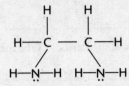

224. In the figure above, what term most accurately describes the ethylenediamine molecule?

A. acceptor
B. lone pair donor
C. chelating agent
D. bidentate ligand

225. In NO_3^-, what is the oxidation number of nitrogen?

A. 0
B. –1
C. +5
D. +2

226. In a given process, the entropy change of the system is calculated to be +23.05 j/mol·K. What is the entropy change of the surroundings?

A. exactly –23.05 j/mol·K
B. This entropy change could be anything, but not less than +23.05 j/mol·k.
C. at most +23.05 j/mol·K
D. It must be negative, but we cannot determine how much.

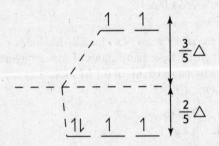

227. Using the above diagram, determine the crystal field splitting energy for a high-spin Co^{+3} complex.

A. –2/5 △
B. 2/5 △
C. 16/5 △
D. –16/5 △

228. What is the percent iron in $FeCl_3$?

A. 50%
B. 34%
C. 64%
D. 25%

229. The most energetic electrons are found where?

A. in the LUMO
B. in the HOMO
C. in the sigma bonds
D. in the pi bonds

230. What concentration unit means moles of solute/liter of solution?

A. molarity
B. molality
C. mole fraction
D. percent

231. If we dilute 100 mL of 0.2 M calcium nitrate to 500 mL, what will the final concentration be?

A. 0.4 M
B. 0.01 M
C. 0.1 M
D. 0.04 M

232. How many flartles are in one kflartle?

A. 100
B. 0.001
C. 1000
D. 0.01

233. Using the half-reaction method to balance $Cr_2O_7^{-2}$ (aq) → Cr^{+3} (aq) in an acidic solution, how many electrons will we have to add and to which side?

A. 6 to the product side
B. 1 to the reactant side
C. 6 to the reactant side
D. 5 to the product side

234. Whose law lead to the concept and first estimation of absolute zero?

A. Boyle
B. Van der Waal
C. Charles
D. Dalton

235. What type of isomers are $[Pt(NH_3)_4Cl_2][PtCl_4]$ and $[Pt(NH_3)_4][PtCl_6]$?

   A. linkage
   B. hydrate
   C. optical
   D. coordination

236. The specific heat of Aluminum is about 0.9 J/g.°C. How much heat is required to raise 100 g of Al 10 °C?

   A. 900 J
   B. 0.9 J
   C. 90 J
   D. 9 J

237. The solubility of some given salt, AB_2, is 10 M. What is the K_{sp} for this salt?

   A. 200
   B. 1000
   C. 2000
   D. 4000

238. The Lewis Dot structure of one resonance form of NO_2^- will have a total of how many lone pair electrons?

   A. 5
   B. 6
   C. 3
   D. 4

239. Which law relates temperature and volume of a gas?

   A. Charles's
   B. Combined
   C. Dalton's
   D. Boyle's

240. Which of the following is not an assumption of an ideal gas?

   A. that there are only weak intermolecular forces between gas particles
   B. that the average kinetic energy is directly proportional to the absolute temperature
   C. that gases are comprised of small particles
   D. that the volume of gas particles is zero

241. What type of spectroscopy is most useful for direct identification of functional groups?

   A. MS
   B. NMR
   C. FT-IR
   D. UV-Vis

242. What is the molar mass of chromium(III) phosphate?

   A. 131 g/mol
   B. 147 g/mol
   C. 253 g/mol
   D. 83 g/mol

243. Which of the following is based on the octet rule?

   A. Molecular Orbital
   B. Lewis Dot
   C. Valence Bond
   D. VSEPR

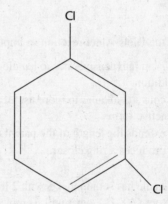

244. What is the name of the compound shown above?

   A. o-dichlorobenzene
   B. p-dichlorobenzene
   C. m-dichlorobenzene
   D. d-dichlorobenzene

245. What is the most stable conformation of cyclohexane?

   A. chair
   B. boat
   C. twist
   D. conformational

GO ON TO THE NEXT PAGE

246. What flows from a region of high temperature to a region of low temperature?

    A. temperature
    B. equilibrium
    C. heat
    D. energy

247. Heptane has how many carbons?

    A. 4
    B. 5
    C. 6
    D. 7

248. In nomenclature of alkenes, what prefix symbol indicates that the two higher-priority groups of four different groups are on the same side of the double bond?

    A. cis
    B. trans
    C. E
    D. Z

249. Why is the Diels-Alder reaction so important?

    A. It is an inexpensive way to handle a halogen addition.
    B. It converts alkanes to more useful and reactive forms.
    C. It extends the length of the parent chain.
    D. It produces a ring closure.

250. If a molecule has set number 5 with 2 lone pair of electrons (AX_3E_2), what will its molecular shape be?

    A. sqare planar
    B. bent
    C. T-shaped
    D. see-saw

251. If it depends on the amount present, what type of property is it?

    A. state function
    B. extensive property
    C. intensive property
    D. physical property

252. Reaction of a tertiary amine with an alkyl halide results in what type of amine?

    A. primary
    B. secondary
    C. tertiary
    D. quaternary

253. In the reaction $Cr(OH)_3 \rightarrow Cr(OH)_2^+ + OH^-$, the species $Cr(OH)_2^+$ is the what?

    A. acid
    B. conjugate base
    C. base
    D. conjugate acid

254. What state is characterized by having a fixed volume, but variable shape?

    A. solid
    B. liquid
    C. gas
    D. glassy

255. What is the principle intermolecular force in alkanes?

    A. dipole-dipole
    B. Van der Waals (or London)
    C. hydrogen bonding
    D. ionic

256. What dissociates to give off a hydroxide anion?

    A. Bronsted-Lowry base
    B. Arrhenius acid
    C. Bronsted-Lowry acid
    D. Arrhenius base

257. In $2\,Fe\,(s) + 2\,NO_3^-\,(aq) + 2\,H^+\,(aq) \rightarrow Fe_2O_3\,(s) + 2\,NO\,(g) + H_2O\,(l)$, what is the reducing agent?

    A. NO_3^-
    B. Fe
    C. H^+
    D. NO

258. Which can differ between two atoms of the same type?

    A. number of protons
    B. number of neutrons
    C. number of electrons
    D. number of nuclei

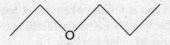

259. The figure above has how many functional groups?

    A. 1
    B. 2
    C. 3
    D. 4

260. What do we call a solution if it has dissolved some solute but could dissolve more?

    A. saturated
    B. supersaturated
    C. unsaturated
    D. dissolved

261. What will be the bond order of a compound with a MO configuration of $\sigma_{1s}^2 \sigma*_{1s}^2 \sigma_{2s}^2 \sigma*_{2s}^2 \pi_{2p}^4$?

    A. 0
    B. 1
    C. 2
    D. 3

262. In sodium carbonate, the oxidation number of carbon is what?

    A. +4
    B. +2
    C. +3
    D. +1

263. What kind of stereoisomer does not have a mirror image?

    A. enantiomer
    B. diastereomer
    C. chiral compound
    D. constitutional isomer

264. A salt that is formed from the reaction of a weak base and a strong acid in neutral water will be what?

    A. basic
    B. neutral
    C. acidic or basic
    D. acidic

265. Of the elements listed, which is the only element that should not be able to utilize the extended octet rule?

    A. calcium
    B. boron
    C. sulfur
    D. bromine

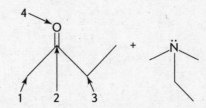

266. In the figure above, the amine will most likely attack which site?

    A. 1
    B. 2
    C. 3
    D. 4

267. In the equilibrium $Ag_2SO_4 \leftarrow \rightarrow 2\, Ag^+ (aq) + SO_4^{-2} (aq)$, adding sodium chloride to the solution will have what influence on the equilibrium?

    A. It will influence equilibrium in an unknown manner.
    B. It will not influence equilibrium.
    C. It will shift the equilibrium to the left.
    D. It will shift the equilibrium to the right.

268. What type of reaction mechanism produces a chiral center if the reactant begins with a chiral center?

    A. S_N1
    B. E2
    C. S_N2
    D. E1

269. What term refers to a reaction or process that gives off heat?

    A. exothermic
    B. endothermic
    C. enthalpy
    D. entropy

GO ON TO THE NEXT PAGE

270. What subshell can hold up to two electrons but no more?

A. s

B. p

C. d

D. f

271. A bond that is formed when one or more electrons is/are completely transferred from one element to another is what kind of bond?

A. ionic bond

B. covalent bond

C. coordinate covalent bond

D. hydrogen bond

Critical Thinking Essay

Directions: You will have 30 minutes in which to write an essay in response to the following statement. This essay will either require you to express an opinion or will present a problem that needs a solution.

"Formal education tends to restrain our thinking because of its formality and rigidity."

Answer Key for Practice Test 5

Verbal Ability: Analogies

1. B	**11.** B	**21.** B
2. D	**12.** B	**22.** D
3. C	**13.** D	**23.** C
4. B	**14.** C	**24.** B
5. A	**15.** B	**25.** C
6. C	**16.** B	**26.** D
7. C	**17.** D	**27.** D
8. B	**18.** C	**28.** D
9. A	**19.** D	**29.** B
10. B	**20.** D	

Verbal Ability: Sentence Completions

30. A	**40.** B	**50.** D
31. C	**41.** C	**51.** A
32. C	**42.** D	**52.** C
33. D	**43.** A	**53.** B
34. B	**44.** D	**54.** D
35. A	**45.** B	**55.** A
36. D	**46.** A	**56.** C
37. B	**47.** C	**57.** B
38. B	**48.** D	**58.** D
39. C	**49.** B	

Biology

59. B	**79.** C	**99.** D
60. D	**80.** A	**100.** C
61. A	**81.** D	**101.** B
62. C	**82.** C	**102.** C
63. C	**83.** B	**103.** B
64. D	**84.** D	**104.** C
65. C	**85.** D	**105.** B
66. A	**86.** C	**106.** C
67. A	**87.** D	**107.** A
68. D	**88.** A	**108.** C
69. A	**89.** C	**109.** D
70. C	**90.** A	**110.** C
71. B	**91.** B	**111.** A
72. B	**92.** D	**112.** D
73. A	**93.** A	**113.** B
74. D	**94.** B	**114.** D
75. D	**95.** D	**115.** D
76. B	**96.** B	**116.** C
77. A	**97.** C	
78. D	**98.** A	

Reading Comprehension

117. D	**134.** A	**151.** B
118. D	**135.** C	**152.** A
119. A	**136.** D	**153.** B
120. B	**137.** D	**154.** B
121. D	**138.** D	**155.** C
122. A	**139.** C	**156.** A
123. A	**140.** D	**157.** A
124. A	**141.** B	**158.** A
125. A	**142.** C	**159.** C
126. B	**143.** C	**160.** D
127. A	**144.** A	**161.** C
128. D	**145.** A	**162.** A
129. B	**146.** D	**163.** C
130. C	**147.** C	**164.** B
131. C	**148.** C	**165.** A
132. C	**149.** C	
133. D	**150.** A	

Quantitative Ability

166. B	**182.** C	**198.** D
167. A	**183.** A	**199.** D
168. C	**184.** D	**200.** D
169. D	**185.** A	**201.** C
170. A	**186.** C	**202.** C
171. C	**187.** B	**203.** A
172. A	**188.** D	**204.** D
173. D	**189.** A	**205.** C
174. C	**190.** C	**206.** A
175. C	**191.** C	**207.** B
176. C	**192.** D	**208.** D
177. B	**193.** C	**209.** A
178. C	**194.** A	**210.** C
179. C	**195.** B	**211.** D
180. B	**196.** B	**212.** B
181. A	**197.** D	**213.** D

Chemistry

214. C	**234.** C	**254.** B
215. D	**235.** D	**255.** B
216. B	**236.** A	**256.** D
217. D	**237.** D	**257.** B
218. D	**238.** B	**258.** B
219. D	**239.** A	**259.** A
220. B	**240.** A	**260.** C
221. D	**241.** C	**261.** C
222. A	**242.** B	**262.** A
223. B	**243.** B	**263.** B
224. D	**244.** C	**264.** D
225. C	**245.** A	**265.** B
226. B	**246.** C	**266.** B
227. A	**247.** D	**267.** D
228. B	**248.** D	**268.** C
229. B	**249.** D	**269.** A
230. A	**250.** C	**270.** A
231. D	**251.** D	**271.** A
232. C	**252.** D	
233. C	**253.** D	

Complete Answers and Explanations for Practice Test 5

Verbal Ability: Analogies

1. **B.** The relationship is of degree. Shouting is an intense form of talking, and detesting is an intense form of disliking.

2. **D.** Function explains the relationship. A conductor leads an orchestra; a shepherd leads a flock.

3. **C.** A drill is part of the category tools, and a nursery rhyme is part of the category poems.

4. **B.** The basis of the analogy is cause. Tension is a cause of stress, and a virus is a cause of disease.

5. **A.** A miser cares excessively about money, and a glutton cares excessively about food.

6. **C.** The relationship is opposites.

7. **C.** A proper location for a bouquet is a vase; garbage should be put into a sewer.

8. **B.** The relationship is synonyms. Enraged means the same as angry.

9. **A.** The relationship is opposites.

10. **B.** The relationship is function. A barometer measures pressure, a ruler measures length.

11. **B.** The purpose of a place of sanctuary is refuge. Likewise, the purpose of a place of imprisonment is punishment.

12. **B.** The function of bathing is to achieve cleanliness, and the function of schooling is to achieve an education.

13. **D.** The function of smiling is to convey happiness. The function of scowling is to convey displeasure.

14. **C.** There are two hands that comprise a whole clock. There are two legs that comprise a whole body.

15. **B.** A quarter is part of a whole month and a week is part of a month. Additionally, one quarter is one-fourth of a dollar, and one week is one-fourth of a month.

16. **B.** A dancer is one member of a whole ensemble. A student is one member of a whole class.

17. **D.** An anarchist promotes disorder while a pacifist promotes peace.

18. **C.** A doctor's primary action is to heal patients. An author's primary action is to write books.

19. **D.** The police characteristically uphold the law in a community. The clergy characteristically uphold religion in a community.

20. **D.** Frigid is an extreme degree of something that is cool. To detest something is to dislike to an extreme degree.

21. **B.** A puddle is a small body of water, and an ocean is an enormous body of water. A crumb is a tiny portion of bread, while a loaf is a huge amount of bread.

22. **D.** A breeze is a soft wind. A gale is a strong and violent wind. A snowflake is one solitary piece of snow, and a blizzard is an abundance of large amounts of snow.

23. **C.** A croissant is a type of pastry while a haiku is a type of poem.

24. **B.** There are many types of novels, including the romance novel. Likewise, there a many types of music, and rap music is one type.

25. **C.** A tanker is a type of ship, and a minivan is a type of automobile.

26. **D.** Whales live in the ocean and bees live in a hive.

27. D. An actor acts on the stage. A teacher teaches in the classroom.

28. D. An attribute of all tyrants is that they practice cruelty to achieve their ends. An attribute of all sycophants is that they practice flattery to achieve their ends.

29. B. To be a sloth is to be lazy and to be an insomniac is to be sleepless.

Verbal Ability: Sentence Completions

30. A. The word "supplant" means to replace, which makes sense in the context of the sentence.

31. C. While all of the choices may seem correct, the word "quaint" really encompasses the concept. Quaint means old-fashioned, but charming.

32. C. An asset is something of value. The word "appreciate" should indicate the positive aspect of the word.

33. D. While Choice **B** might seem correct at first, the second word, "please," makes no sense in the sentence, and therefore, Choice **D** is correct. To suppress is to bury or force down, while the word "haunt" means to continue to bother.

34. B. Keen means sharp, which is the correct choice.

35. A. Clientele means patrons. The other choices are not as logical. Sometimes more than one choice may seem correct, but you must choose the one that is more logical than the other choices.

36. D. To infringe is to intrude, which is what these neighbors did.

37. B. Something uncanny is often strange and unusual, and this teacher seemed to be aware in an almost supernatural way (another meaning of the word uncanny).

38. B. Intrigue is scheming or plotting, which is what goes on between individuals.

39. C. Jargon is nonsensical, incoherent, or meaningless talk, and thus the listener is unable to understand what's being said.

40. B. While Choices **A** and **D** may seem as if they could be correct, only Choice **B** makes sense. Exorbitant mean to go beyond, often used in conjunction with prices or costs.

41. C. To cower means to hide and abatement means to let up. You must take into account *both* words in the choice.

42. D. A piece of fruit would be juicy, which is a synonym for succulent.

43. A. While the artwork might be childish and disturbing, only something that is undistinguished or ordinary would be boring.

44. D. One does not usually know what's going on in surgery, and one would be anxious, or apprehensive.

45. B. The word "insistence" is the context clue in this sentence. When one insists on something, one is usually emphatic—making a point in a forceful way.

46. A. Tedium is boredom, which is a cause of lack of productivity.

47. C. To append means to add on. The word "emend," which could be mistaken for the correct choice means to correct. Look out for words that look or sound similar.

48. D. Inspectors are responsible for examining the cause of an accident, or putting it under scrutiny. Their job is not to repair it; the guards patrol the area, and certainly Choice **C** is incorrect.

49. B. If there are many similar programs, it often makes sense to join them all together (Choice **B**).

50. D. The architect was obviously incapable of designing a well-made house. He was inept.

51. A. An amnesty is a general pardon granted by a government.

52. C. To pilfer is to steal.

53. **B.** To wane is to fade. Choices **A, C,** and **D** don't make sense, since it would be hard to tell a joke when the laughter began, began again, or got louder.

54. **D.** Kudos are praising remarks or awards.

55. **A.** To spurn is to reject and to pledge is to swear to. Only these choices make sense in the sentence.

56. **C.** To be rejuvenated means to feel energized, to feel younger, which is why she would want to go back again. Choices **A, B,** and **D** are not reasons to want to return to the spa.

57. **B.** The word "expedient" means fitting, or something that serves one's purpose.

58. **D.** Stilted means forces and stiff. The other three choices don't fit the sentence.

Biology

59. **B.** A scientific theory, such as the Theory of Evolution, is based on the results of numerous, peer-reviewed scientific investigations.

60. **D.** When constructing a graph of scientific data, the independent variable should be placed along the x-axis and the dependent variable should be placed along the y-axis.

61. **A.** The plasma membranes of plant and animal cells are differentially permeable. Therefore, they regulate what substances can pass through them, as well as the rate at which those substances pass through. Large molecules and highly charged molecules may require the assistance of transport proteins to assist their movement across the cell membrane, affecting the rate at which they pass through. This allows them to regulate the interactions between the cells and their surrounding environment.

62. **C.** Enzymes are proteins that catalyze biochemical reactions.

63. **C.** Only bacteria are classified as prokaryotes.

64. **D.** Protein synthesis is a two-step process involving transcription of mRNA from DNA in the nucleus, followed by translation of mRNA into a polypeptide at the ribosomes in the cytoplasm.

65. **C.** Photosynthetic organisms use light energy to convert carbon dioxide and water into food in the form of glucose.

66. **A.** Bacterial cells are prokaryotic; they lack an organized nucleus and membrane-bound organelles.

67. **A.** Cellular respiration produces energy for organisms through the breakdown of glucose molecules to produce ATP.

68. **D.** Meiosis is a special type of cell division that only takes place in the germ cells that give rise to gametes (e.g., eggs and sperm). Meiosis results in the production of four haploid daughter cells from each diploid parent cell. Thus, an individual with 18 chromosomes in each of its somatic cells would give rise to gametes with 9 chromosomes each through the process of meiosis.

69. **A.** The genotype of an individual is established at fertilization when the egg and sperm unite to form a zygote. As such, an individual receives half of its chromosomes (one copy of each chromosome) from its mother and half of its chromosomes (a second copy of each chromosome) from its father.

70. **C.** If long tails (T) is dominant to short tails (t) in mice, approximately 50% of the offspring from a cross between a heterozygous mother (Tt) and a homozygous recessive father (tt) would have short tails, as they would have a 50-50 chance of receiving a recessive allele from their mother. All offspring would receive a recessive allele from their father.

71. **B.** Red-green color-blindness is a sex-linked recessive trait. Because daughters receive one X chromosome from their mother and one X chromosome from their father, if the father had normal vision X^BY and the mother was color-blind (X^bX^b) all daughters would be heterozygous for the trait, but have normal vision. Because sons receive their X chromosome from their mother and their Y chromosome from their father, all sons would receive the recessive allele from their mother, with no corresponding allele for the trait from their father, and be color-blind.

72. B. DNA replication is a semi-conservative process; therefore, when a DNA molecule is replicated, the two daughter molecules each contain one old (original) strand of DNA and one new strand of DNA.

73. A. Complementary base-pairing, in which adenine always pairs with uracil (in RNA) and cytosine always pairs with guanine, helps ensure accurate copying of a DNA template onto an mRNA molecule. Note: When replicating a molecule of DNA, adenine always pairs with thymine. Thymine is not found in RNA.

74. D. Genetic transformation involves the introduction of foreign DNA into an organism.

75. D. Every individual, except identical twins, has a unique genetic makeup that can be analyzed with DNA fingerprinting techniques. These techniques have numerous applications including the implication of suspects in criminal investigations, the determination of paternity, and the identification of missing individuals.

76. B. Biological succession involves a predictable and gradual change in the vegetation in an area until it reaches a stable climax community. When an area is altered by natural disasters or human-related activities, if subsequently left undisturbed, it will proceed through a succession of vegetation communities until it reaches the climax community stage.

77. A. The ozone layer surrounding the Earth's atmosphere prevents excessive ultraviolet radiation from the sun from reaching the Earth. The widespread use of chlorofluorocarbons, which damages the ozone layer, is leading to an increase in the amount of UV radiation reaching the Earth's surface, which is thought to be leading to an increase in the incidence of skin cancer.

78. D. In a typical food web, the organisms responsible for the breakdown of organic matter and recycling of nutrients back into the ecosystem are referred to as decomposers, and include such organisms as bacteria, fungi, and slime molds.

79. C. Evolution involves a change in the allelic and genotypic frequencies (genetic composition) of a population over time.

80. A. Individuals that have the greatest success at reproducing contribute more favorable genes to the gene pool. Differences in relative reproductive fitness among individuals in a population form the basis of natural selection for the most advantageous genes in the gene pool.

81. D. By definition, a species encompasses groups of related individuals that are able to mate and produce fertile offspring. Thus, if two groups within a population of the same species become geographically and, therefore, reproductively isolated from each other, over time they are likely to form two separate species.

82. C. The field of comparative embryology has provided evidence in support of the theory of evolution by showing that related organisms go through similar stages during embryonic development.

83. B. The protein coat surrounding the genetic material in viruses is referred to as a capsid.

84. D. Viruses are unable to make their own proteins or reproduce on their own and, therefore, must take over the genetic and reproductive functions of a host cell in order to replicate and cause disease.

85. D. Cyanobacteria are prokaryotic organisms that contain chlorophyll and have the ability to make their own food through the process of photosynthesis. They are thought to be the earliest photosynthetic organisms, evolving approximately 3 billion to 3.5 billion years ago.

86. C. The use of pressurized steam (autoclaving) is the only sterilization method with significant sporocidal activity.

87. D. Amoebas use pseudopodia—cytoplasmic projections—to move about and to engulf food particles.

88. A. The introduction of foreign DNA into a bacterial cell through the use of a bacteriophage (bacterial virus) is referred to as transduction. Genetic transformation involves the uptake of foreign DNA by a cell from the surrounding environment, usually in the form of a plasmid (Choice **B**). Transformation can be enhanced through the use of electroporation to make the cell membrane more permeable to foreign DNA (Choice **D**). Conjugation involves the exchange of DNA between bacterial cells through the formation of a conjugation tube temporarily joining the cells (Choice **C**).

89. C. Antibiotics would be helpful in fighting pertussis, a disease of bacterial origin. The other diseases listed (influenza, measles, and chicken pox) are all viral in origin and, thus, antibiotics would be ineffective against them.

90. **A.** A common disease picked up by backpackers is giardiasis. This disease, which affects the gastrointestinal tract, is caused by a protozoan.

91. **B.** Fleas can transfer Bubonic plague from one individual to another because Bubonic plague is a bacterial disease that affects the blood and, thus, can be passed from individual to individual through flea bites.

92. **D.** Bacillus thuringiensis (Bt) is an insecticide considered acceptable for use by organic farmers. This natural insecticide is made from bacteria commonly found in the soil.

93. **A.** Botulism and typhoid fever are bacterial diseases affecting the gastrointestinal tract. Leprosy is a bacterial disease affecting the skin, peripheral nerves, upper respiratory tract, and eyes.

94. **B.** *Penicillium roqueforti,* a fungal organism, is used to impart flavor to Roquefort cheese.

95. **D.** Failure to take the entire prescription of antibiotics for a bacterial infection may result in the development of an antibiotic-resistant strain of bacteria.

96. **B.** The coordinated function of the various organ systems in the human body allows the body's internal environment to remain relatively stable despite changes in the external environment. This internal body stability is referred to as homeostasis.

97. **C.** The nervous system is responsible for coordinating communication between different regions of the human body and between the body and the external environment.

98. **A.** In humans, the respiratory system is responsible for taking in oxygen and expelling carbon dioxide. It works in coordination with the circulatory system, which transports oxygen and carbon dioxide throughout the body.

99. **D.** The average life span of a human red blood cell is 120 days.

100. **C.** A patient found to have a higher-than-normal white blood cell count is most likely trying to fight off an infection and, therefore, their immune system is overactive. A patient with a lower-than-normal white blood cell count is likely to be at risk for infection.

101. **B.** Blood flows from the heart to the lungs in the pulmonary artery and returns from the lungs to the heart in the pulmonary vein.

102. **C.** A person's heart rate can be measured by taking his pulse.

103. **B.** The human tonsils, which are located in the pharynx, consist primarily of pockets of lymphatic tissue and function to trap and filter microorganisms.

104. **C.** Fats are an essential component of the human diet because they help to insulate the body from cold temperatures, protect the internal organs from injury, and aid in the metabolism of vitamins A, D, and E.

105. **B.** Carbohydrates, in the form of glucose, are the most often used direct source of energy in humans.

106. **C.** During digestion, humans absorb nucleotides from plant and animal tissues consumed. These nucleotides, which are the building blocks of nucleic acids, are then used by the human body for synthesizing DNA and RNA.

107. **A.** The digestion of starch molecules begins in the mouth with the production of the salivary enzyme amylase.

108. **C.** In the human digestive system, most chemical digestion takes place in the small intestine.

109. **D.** The majority of metabolic waste is removed from the human body through the kidneys, in the form of urine.

110. **C.** Chemical coordination within the human body takes place through a series of glands that are situated throughout the body. This system of glands is referred to as the endocrine system. The nervous system (Choice A) is responsible for coordinating signals between different parts of the body and between the body and the external environment. The lymphatic system (Choice D) is part of the human immune system, which functions to fight off infections and disease-causing organisms. There is not a pituitary system (Choice B); however, the pituitary gland is a very important part of the human endocrine system.

111. **A.** Over-secretion of the thyroid hormone thyroxine often results in an unusually high metabolic rate. Cretinism (Choice B) and myxydema (Choice C) result from under-secretion of thyroxine. Diabetes (Choice D) results from an imbalance in insulin levels.

112. **D.** Epinephrine, produced by the adrenal glands, is responsible for preparing the body for emergencies or other stressful situations (e.g., promoting the fight-or-flight response). Cortisone (Choice **A**) and cortisol (Choice **B**) are also produced by the adrenal glands; these hormones are responsible for glucose metabolism and protein synthesis. Androgen (Choice **C**) is produced in the testes and is responsible for the production of secondary male characteristics.

113. **B.** In human males, meiosis occurs in the seminiferous tubules and gives rise to sperm.

114. **D.** In humans, the brain and the spinal cord comprise the central nervous system.

115. **D.** The hypothalamus is the region of the human brain responsible for coordinating such activities as hunger, thirst, body temperature, and blood pressure, as well as the production of hormones that will be stored in the pituitary gland.

116. **C.** The specific immune system response in humans is controlled by white blood cells called lymphocytes. The lymphocytes are responsible for the production of specific antibodies to foreign invaders. Monocytes (Choice **A**) and neutrophils (Choice **B**) are types of marcophages (Choice **D**), which engulf and destroy invading microorganisms through phagocytosis. This type of immune response is considered nonspecific.

Reading Comprehension

117. **D.** In North and South America. This is explained in the first paragraph.

118. **D.** In the eastern part of North America. This is explained in the first paragraph.

119. **A.** Extremely tiny.

120. **B.** The giant hummingbird.

121. **D.** The speed at which a bee hummingbird's wings beat is not actually known. The author explains in paragraph five that they have not measured this species yet.

122. **A.** They attach to the body at one point only. This is explained in the third paragraph.

123. **A.** A helicopter. This is the only aircraft listed that can hover and move in different directions.

124. **A.** Beak. The bill or beak is the mouth of the bird.

125. **A.** Meager.

126. **B.** The structure of the feathers as well as pigmentation. This is explained in paragraph four.

127. **A.** Wing and possibly tail movement. This is explained in paragraph four.

128. **D.** The association is beneficial to each organism, although it provides more benefit to the fungus. This is indicated in the third paragraph, in which the author states, "It appears that the fungus actually gains more benefit from the relationship than does the alga."

129. **B.** Formerly.

130. **C.** A lichen constituted a single plant. This is indicated in the first paragraph, in which the author states, "Previously, lichens were classified as single organisms until scientists had the benefit of microscopes. . . ,"

131. **C.** Close.

132. **C.** The joint benefit each organism receives from the relationship.

133. **D.** The fungus uses the carbohydrates manufactured by the alga. This is indicated in the third paragraph, where the author states, "Algae form simple carbohydrates that, when excreted, are absorbed by fungi cells and transformed into a different carbohydrate."

134. **A.** Singular/plural. The author explains in the first paragraph that "fungus" and "alga" are singular and "fungi" and "algae" are plural forms of the words.

135. **C.** New organisms are grown from pieces of existing organisms. This is explained in the fourth paragraph, where the author states, "Most botanists agree that reproduction is vegetative because portions of an existing lichen break off and fall away to begin a new organism nearby."

136. **D.** Algae are more sensitive to light than fungi. This is explained in the third paragraph, in which the author states, "Yet, fungi also contribute to the symbiosis by absorbing water vapor from the air and providing shade for the algae, which are more sensitive to light."

137. **D.** Close.

138. **D.** Strong.

139. **C.** Harsh.

140. **D.** Reduce soil erosion.

141. **B.** Other forms of hepatitis were known before the hepatitis C strain was discovered. The author refers to hepatitis in general, and hepatitis C specifically, implying that there are others.

142. **C.** Inception.

143. **C.** "Hepatitis C—Its Characteristics and Treatment."

144. **A.** Vast. The word in this context is an intensifier, modifying "majority."

145. **A.** Standard.

146. **D.** People.

147. **C.** Many people with hepatitis C were not addicts but simply experimented with illegal drugs.

148. **C.** Learn the degree of damage to the liver.

149. **C.** Only rarely results in liver cancer.

150. **A.** The medicine must be taken intravenously. It is injected, but not in the vein.

151. **B.** Liver.

152. **A.** Affixed.

153. **B.** Discharge.

154. **B.** Different in that a vent involves rapid discharge while a seep involves slow discharge. The author uses the two words in different contexts.

155. **C.** From the same family but different species.

156. **A.** Grows slower than the hot-water tube worm. See paragraphs two and five, which distinguish between the growth rates of the two worms.

157. **A.** Complete.

158. **A.** Lifetime.

159. **C.** Boiling.

160. **D.** Different in that one contains oily materials and the other contains hydrogen sulfide.

161. **C.** Aneurysms that occur near the brain stem only. The first paragraph explains that these aneurysms are dangerous to repair with surgery.

162. **A.** Aneurysms. The noun is found in the previous sentence, and no other noun in the sentence could make sense.

163. **C.** Significant.

164. **B.** Aneurysm. The noun to which one refers actually appears two sentences before the reference.

165. **A.** Meandering. The idea is that it moves slowly and deliberately toward its destination.

Quantitative Ability

166. **B.** The earnings for 30 hours are $8.25 \times 30 = \$247.50$.

167. **A.** Using the ratio $\dfrac{\text{height}}{\text{shadow}}$, the proportion $\dfrac{3\frac{1}{2}}{6} = \dfrac{x}{24}$ models this situation, where x represents the height of the pole. Cross-multiply. $3\frac{1}{2} \times 24 = 6x$ so $84 = 6x$ and $x = \dfrac{84}{6} = 14$ feet.

168. **C.** The proportion $\dfrac{1\,\text{cm}}{4\,\text{miles}} = \dfrac{x\,\text{cm}}{10\,\text{miles}}$ models this situation. Cross-multiply. $1 \times 10 = 4x$ so $10 = 4x$ and $x = \dfrac{10}{4} = 2\frac{1}{2}$ cm.

169. **D.** Interest earned in one year is $300 \times 5\frac{1}{4}\% = \$15.75$. The total amount of the account after one year is $300 + \$15.75 = \$315.75$.

170. **A.** The cost of the eight CD covers is $8 \times \$1.59 = \$12.72$. The change received back is $20.00 - \$12.72 = \$7.28$.

171. **C.** Given that $k(x) = \left(\dfrac{1}{27}\right)^{-x}$, then $k\left(\dfrac{1}{3}\right) = \left(\dfrac{1}{27}\right)^{-\frac{1}{3}} = 27^{\frac{1}{3}} = \sqrt[3]{27} = 3$.

172. **A.** Five cards at $3 each cost $5 \times \$3 = \$15$. If cards are two for $5, the cost per card is $\dfrac{\$5.00}{2} = \$2.50$ so five cards would cost $2.50 \times 5 = \$12.50$. The amount saved is $15.00 - \$12.50 = \$2.50$.

173. **D.** The cosine function is positive in the first and fourth quadrants. The tangent function is negative in the second and fourth quadrants. Thus, $\angle y$ must lie in the fourth quadrant.

174. **C.** After eating $\frac{1}{4}$ of a pie, what remains is $1 - \frac{1}{4} = \frac{3}{4}$. If four friends share the remainder, then each receives $\dfrac{3}{4} \div 4 = \dfrac{3}{4} \times \dfrac{1}{4} = \dfrac{3}{16}$.

175. **C.** The proportion $\dfrac{\$5.00}{3\,\text{cans}} = \dfrac{\$x}{10\,\text{cans}}$ can be used to find the cost of ten cans. Cross-multiply. $5 \times 10 = 3x$ so $50 = 3x$ and $x = \dfrac{50}{3} = \$16.67$.

176. **C.** $1\frac{1}{8} + 2\frac{3}{4} + 3\frac{1}{3} = \dfrac{9}{8} + \dfrac{11}{4} + \dfrac{10}{3} = \dfrac{27}{24} + \dfrac{66}{24} + \dfrac{80}{24} = \dfrac{173}{24} = 7\frac{5}{24}$ pounds.

177. **B.** Begin by finding the first derivative of $y = x^3 - 3x + 7$, which is $y' = 3x^2 - 3$. Now, set the derivative equal to 0, and solve for x. Note that $3x^2 - 3 = 0$ when $x = +1$ or -1. These, then, are the x-coordinates of the extreme points.

178. **C.** $3a + 3b = 3(a + b)$. Since $a + b = 6$, $3a + 3b = 3(6) = 18$.

179. **C.** $8^{\frac{4}{3}} = \left(\sqrt[3]{8}\right)^4 = 2^4 = 16$.

180. **B.** Substitute 1 for p and solve for q. $7(1) + 5q = -3$ and $7 + 5q = -3$. $7 + 5q - 7 = -3 - 7$ and $5q = -10$. Dividing both sides by 5 results in $q = -2$.

181. **A.** There are 60 minutes in an hour, 24 hours in one day, and 7 days in one week. So 1 week = $\dfrac{7\,\text{days}}{1\,\text{week}} \times \dfrac{24\,\text{hours}}{1\,\text{day}} \times \dfrac{60\,\text{minutes}}{1\,\text{hour}} = 7 \times 24 \times 60 = 10,080$ minutes.

182. **C.** Translate to a mathematical expression and solve. $3x + 7 = 70$, so $3x + 7 - 7 = 70 - 7$ and $3x = 63$. Divide both sides by 3. Therefore, $x = 21$.

183. **A.** Set the equation equal to 0 and factor. $x^2 + 6x - 16 = 0$ and $(x + 8)(x - 2) = 0$. Then, either $x + 8 = 0$ or $x - 2 = 0$ so $x = -8$ or $x = 2$. Since x is positive, $x = 2$ only.

184. **D.** The percent discounted is the amount discounted divided by the original price. The amount discounted is $200 - \$150 = \$50$. The percent discounted is $\dfrac{50}{200} \times 0.25 = 25\%$.

185. **A.** If we let $\log_{12} 1 = x$, then, by the definition of logarithms, $1 = 12^x$. This equation is true only if $x = 0$.

186. **C.** The cost for milk and two dozen eggs is $1.39 + (2 \times \$1.28) = \$3.95$. The change is $10.00 - \$3.95 = \$6.05$.

187. B. The amplitude of the function is the absolute value of the coefficient of the cosine term, that is, 3.

188. D. With 9 cups of milk, $\frac{9}{2} = 4\frac{1}{2}$ or 4 full batches can be made. However, with 9 eggs, only $\frac{9}{4} = 2\frac{1}{4}$ or 2 full batches can be made. At most, only 2 batches can be made with the given ingredients.

189. A. By the derivative properties of polynomials, if $y = 6x^3 - 5x^4$, then $\frac{dy}{dx} = 18x^2 - 20x^3$.

190. C. Interest = principal × rate. Let p represent the principal. Then $100 = p \times 7\frac{1}{4}\%$ so
$p = \frac{\$100}{7\frac{1}{4}\%} = \frac{\$100}{0.0725} = \$1,379$.

191. C.

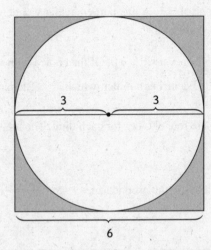

The area of the shaded region equals the area of the square minus the area of the circle. Since the radius of the circle is 3, the square has a side length of 6. The area of the square is 6^2 or 36. The area of the circle is $\pi r^2 = \pi \cdot 3^2 = 9\pi$. The shaded region, therefore, is $36 - 9\pi$.

192. D. Six less a number is shown by $n - 6$. So six less a number is four is represented by $n - 6 = 4$.

193. C. To solve this equation, raise both sides to the power of –4. Thus, $\left(b^{-\frac{1}{4}}\right)^{-4} = 2^{-4}$ or $b = 2^{-4} = \left(\frac{1}{2}\right)^4 = \frac{1}{16}$.

194. A. The least common multiple of the divisors 16 and 24 is 48. $\frac{5}{16} + \frac{9}{24} = \frac{15}{48} + \frac{18}{48} = \frac{33}{48} = \frac{11}{16}$.

195. B. The area of a triangle is $A = \frac{1}{2}bh$. If the base is 3 inches less than the height, then $b = h - 3$. Substituting this value in for b gives $A = \frac{1}{2}(h-3)h = \frac{1}{2}h^2 - \frac{3}{2}h$.

196. B. By the definition of logarithms, if $\log_x 27 = 3$, then $27 = x^3$, so $x = 3$.

197. D. Subtracting $2y$ from both sides leads to the equation $6 = y - 2$. Next, add 2 to both sides to get $y = 8$.

198. D. $(2.5)^4 = 2.5 \times 2.5 \times 2.5 \times 2.5 = 39.0625$. Rounded to the nearest tenth is 39.1.

199. D. The volume of each cube is $4 \times 4 \times 4 = 64$ in³. The volume of the crate, in inches, is $(3 \times 12) \times (2 \times 12) \times (2 \times 12) = 20,736$ in³. The number of blocks that can fit in the crate is $\frac{20736}{64} = 324$.

200. D. $(3x^2 + 2x - 5) - (2x^2 - 5) + (4x - 7) = 3x^2 + 2x - 5 - 2x^2 + 5 + 4x - 7 = 3x^2 - 2x^2 + 2x + 4x - 5 + 5 - 7 = x^2 + 6x - 7$.

201. C. In order to solve the equation, rewrite 4^{x+1} as $2^{2(x+1)}$. Thus, we are given $2^{3x} = 2^{2(x+1)}$, which is only true of $3x = 2(x + 1)$ or when $x = 2$.

202. C. One of the Pythagorean identities is $\sin^2\theta + \cos^2\theta = 1$, so $1 - \cos^2\theta = \sin^2\theta$.

203. A. The first derivative of $\log x$ is $\frac{1}{x}$.

204. D. Let the radius of the smaller circle = 1. Then the radius of the larger circle is 4. The shaded region is found by subtracting the area of the smaller circle from the area of the larger circle. The area of the smaller circle is $\pi(1)^2$ or π. The area of the larger circle is $\pi(4)^2$ or 16π. The shaded region is $16\pi - \pi$ or 15π. The percent of the whole figure that is shaded is $\frac{15\pi}{16\pi} = 0.9375 = 93\frac{3}{4}\%$.

205. C. The probability of flipping one head is $\frac{1}{2}$. The probability of flipping three heads in a row is $\frac{1}{2} \times \frac{1}{2} \times \frac{1}{2}$ or $\frac{1}{8}$.

206. A. By the properties of logarithms, $\log AB = \log A + \log B$, and $\log A + \log B = 2 + 3 = 5$.

207. B. To answer this problem, we need to find a function whose derivative is $4x^3 + 2x$. By trial and error, you can quickly determine that $x^4 + x^2 + C$ has this property.

208. D. The line $y = -\frac{1}{8}x + 7$ has a slope of $-\frac{1}{8}$. A line perpendicular would have a slope equal to the negative reciprocal of $-\frac{1}{8}$, which is 8.

209. A. Since $\tan x = \frac{\sin x}{\cos x}$, $\tan x = 0$ whenever $\sin x = 0$. Of the choices, $\sin x = 0$ only at $0°$.

210. C. The mode is the most frequently occurring number, which is 7. The median is the number in the middle, which is 5. The product is $5 \times 7 = 35$.

211. D. If digits can be repeated, there are four choices for each digit. The total number of possible numbers is $4 \times 4 \times 4 \times 4 = 256$.

212. B. $5! = 5 \times 4 \times 3 \times 2 \times 1 = 120$.

213. D. To find this derivative, we need to use the product rule. $y' = x^2\left(\frac{de^2}{dx}\right) + e^2\left(\frac{dx^2}{dx}\right) = x^2 e^x + 2xe^x$.

Chemistry

214. C. Hybridization is the number of sigma bonds on the central element (in this case, 2) plus the number of lone pairs assigned to the central element (in this case, 0). Pi bonds do not factor into it.

215. D. A difference in electronegativity of less than 0.5 is non-polar covalent, and greater than 1.7 is ionic.

216. B. Mixing is a physical change and is generally associated with entropy increases.

217. D. Resonance does not mean "flipping" of the bond; instead, it's more of an averaging effect. The true structure would be neither of those shown, but instead an average of the two.

218. D. A buffer is a mixture of a weak acid and its conjugate base. HCl and NaOH are too strong, and phosphoric acid is not the conjugate base of HCl.

219. D. Conjugated pi systems are very important in stabilizing carbanions, carbocations, and free radicals.

220. B. Anomers are the same element in two different forms, as in oxygen and ozone.

221. D. We have to break two H-H bonds, and we form four C-H bonds, thus, the bond energy will be $(4)(414) - (2)(435) = 786$ kJ/mol.

222. A. 10 mL is 0.01 L, so we have 0.001 mole of sodium hydroxide, or 0.040 g NaOH.

223. B. The order of reaction is important to determine how the decay will occur. For example, radioactive decay follows first order kinetics. With this information, we can determine how long radioisotopes given to patients will remain in the body. This order of reaction expresses itself as the sum of the superscripts of the concentrations in the rate equation (which is generally determined experimentally).

224. D. While ethylenediamine can be referred to as a chelating agent or lone pair donor, "bidentate ligand" is more descriptive since it tells that there are two lone pair donors on the molecule.

225. C. Oxygen has an oxidation number of –2, and the oxidation numbers must add up to the charge of the species. Thus, $(1)(x) + (3)(-2) = -1$.

226. **B.** If entropy decreases for a system, then the entropy of the surroundings must increase by at least as much as the entropy of the system decreases (second law of thermodynamics). However, if the entropy of the system increases, the entropy of the surrounding can change in any way, as long as it does not decrease more than the entropy of the system increases.

227. **A.** Remember that decreasing energy is always negative, and increasing is positive.

228. **B.** Iron has an atomic mass of about 55.5 g/mol, and chlorine 35.5 g/mol. Thus, the molecular mass is approximately 162 g/mol.

229. **B.** "HOMO" is the "highest occupied molecular orbital," while "LUMO" stands for "lowest unoccupied molecular orbital."

230. **A.** Molality is moles of solute per kilogram of solvent, and mole fraction is moles of solute per total moles in the solution.

231. **D.** Remember that $C_iV_i = C_fV_f$. So, $(100)(0.2) = C_f(500)$.

232. **C.** It doesn't matter what a flartle is; there are 1,000 in a kilo.

233. **C.** First, balance the chromiums, then add 7 waters to the product side to balance the oxygen, and 14 hydronium ions to the reactant side to balance the hydrogens. Finally, add electrons to balance the charge.

234. **C.** Charles's law relates volume to temperature.

235. **D.** Though coordination spheres are differences, both have the same simple formula $[Pt (Ml_3)_2 Cl_3]$.

236. **A.** Remember, $q = mc\Delta T$. Here the mass is 100 g and change in temperature is 10.

237. **D.** Remember, if $[AB_2] = 10$, $[A^{+2}] = 10$, $[B^-] = 20$. So, $K_{sp} = [A^{+2}][B^-]^2 = [10][20]^2$.

238. **B.** Don't forget that the negative charge means you have to add one additional electron. Thus, there are two lone pair on one oxygen, three on the other, and one on nitrogen.

239. **A.** Boyle is pressure and volume; Dalton is for mixtures of gases; and Combined is temperature, volume and pressure.

240. **A.** In an ideal gas, we assume there are no intermolecular forces.

241. **C.** MS identifies compound clustering, UV-Vis is conjugate pi systems, and NMR tells us about the bonding.

242. **B.** You should know some of the more common polyatomic ions. Chromium (III) phosphate will have the formula $CrPO_4$.

243. **B.** You need the Lewis Dot structure for VSEPR and valence bond theory.

244. **C.** The positions are ortho, meta, and para respectively.

245. **A.** In the chair conformation, steric interactions are minimized.

246. **C.** This is the "zeroth law of thermodynamics;" it defines heat in terms of temperature gradient (not in terms of temperature).

247. **D.** You should know at least the first ten parent chain names, and perhaps more.

248. **D.** "Cis" and "trans" only applies if two groups on the two different carbons are the same.

249. **D.** The Diels-Alder reaction is a great synthetic route for producing ring structures in synthesis.

250. **C.** Set number 5 is trigonal bipyramidal. Because the equatorial positions are farthest apart, there is more room for lone pair if we remove two equatorial lone pair rather than in the axial positions.

251. **D.** Extensive properties include things like volume or mass. Intensive properties include, for example, density.

252. **D.** Reactions between amines and alkyl halides are simple addition reactions.

253. **D.** Bases dissociate to form conjugate acids, and acids dissociate to form conjugate bases. This is an important concept, especially for understanding buffer systems, such as the blood buffer system.

254. B. Gases have variable volume and shape, and solids have fixed volume and shape.

255. B. Understanding intermolecular forces is important to understanding the behavior of organic compounds. For example, London forces are the weakest known forces in science, which is why alkanes have very high vapor pressure and low solubility in water.

256. D. A Bronsted-Lowry base acts by accepting protons.

257. B. Iron is going from a 0 to a +3 oxidation state, so it is losing electrons. Loss of electrons is oxidation, so iron is the reducing agent.

258. B. You might think electrons since they are subject to change, but in the elemental state, the number of electrons must be equal to the number of protons, which defines the element.

259. A. This is the ether functional group.

260. C. People often confuse saturated with supersaturated. A supersaturated solution is very unstable and rarely lasts longer than a few minutes.

261. C. We have 4 antibonding electrons, and 8 bonding electrons, so our bond order will be $(8 - 4) \div 2 = 2$.

262. A. You should know the formula and charges of several polyatomic ions. Carbonate is CO_3^{-2}, so since oxygen has an oxidation number of -2, carbon must be $+4$.

263. B. While it is true that a constitutional isomer does not have a mirror image, this is not a stereoisomer in the first place.

264. D. The weaker the base, the stronger the conjugate acid.

265. B. To undergo extended octet, you only need an empty set of "d" subshell orbitals. Calcium has never used the extended octet, but it should be able to if necessary.

266. B. Because they are partially negatively charged and have a lone pair of electrons, amines are nucleophiles. Carbon 2 will be the strongest partial positive charge, and the pi bond between this carbon and oxygen will make this carbon more reactive as well.

267. D. Silver chloride is insoluble, so adding sodium chloride will remove sodium ions from solution. As these ions are removed, more sodium sulfate will dissolve.

268. C. Elimination reactions will produce pi bonds, which cannot be present in chiral compounds. In S_N1 reactions, the chiral center is destroyed in the intermediate.

269. A. Although whether or not heat is released is related to enthalpy, this term can also apply to endothermic reactions.

270. A. Each orbital can hold up to two electrons, and the s subshell has only one orbital regardless of which shell it is in.

271. A. Covalent bonds share electrons; coordinate covalent bonds are electrons shared in which only one of the atoms involved donates both electrons; and the hydrogen bond is actually a non-bonding intermolecular force.